Natural Learning

The Life History of an Environmental Schoolyard

Natural Learning

Creating Environments for Rediscovering Nature's Way of Teaching

ROBIN C. MOORE & HERB H. WONG

MIG Communications
Berkeley, California

Editors: Paul Yee, David Driskell
Cover and Page Design: MIG DesignWorks
Production Assistant: Sheila Wright
Illustrator: Sabine Moore

All photographs by Robin Moore, except: Marty Bovill, 2, 90 top; Andy Stewart, 7; Helen Cox, 32, 151; Herb Wong, 39 bottom, 50, 61; East Bay Municipal Utility District, 66 top, 216; Susan Mullally, 80; PLAE, Inc., 155, 161, 163 bottom, 164 top; and Mimi Anderson, 164 bottom.

Permission to reproduce the following is gratefully acknowledged: University of California Press, maps on page 78, from *Weather of the San Francisco Bay Region* by Harold Gilliam. California State Automobile Association, map on page 126.

Earlier versions of several chapters of *Natural Learning* appeared in *Children's Environments Quarterly:* Chapter 3 in Vol. 12, No. 2 (renamed *Children's Environments*), 1995 (*Children's Gardens and Children in Farming*); Chapter 4 in Vol. 4, No. 2, 1987 (*Children and Water*); Chapter 5 in Vol. 1, No. 3, 1984 (*Children and Animals*); portions of Chapter 2 in Vol. 6, No. 1, 1989 (*Children and Vegetation*); and portions of Chapters 19 and 20 in Vol. 3, No. 3, 1985 (*Schoolyards*).

Moore, Robin C.
    Natural learning : the life history of an environmental schoolyard / Robin C. Moore and Herb H. Wong.
        p.   cm.
    Includes bibliographical references and index.
    ISBN 0-944661-24-6
       1. School grounds—California—Berkeley—Design—Case studies.
    2. School environment—California—Berkeley—Case studies.
    3. Environmental education—California—Berkeley—Case studies.
    4. Outdoor education—California—Berkeley—Case studies.   I. Wong, Herbert H. II. Title.
    LB3251.M56 1997
    371.6′1′0979467—dc21   96-39184 CIP

MIG Communications
800 Hearst Avenue
Berkeley, CA 94710, USA
(510) 845-0953
fax (510) 845-8750

To the children we worked with at Washington School
and their future generations

Acknowledgements

The Environmental Yard project around which this book is woven involved literally hundreds of individuals over many years, especially the children who passed through Washington School during the years of the authors' involvement. We particularly acknowledge the first group of Washington students, who put forth so many imaginative ideas for the design of the Yard, assisted with construction, and enthusiastically participated in the evolving program of learning activities. Through their creative play and enthusiasm for learning, the children from the school and neighborhood were a continuous source of inspiration and enlightenment.

Our further thanks are due to the Washington teaching staff and vice principal, George Yoshida, all of whom participated in the project and helped make it a success in one way or another. Several of the faculty participated over many years in the "core group," which included the authors and many participants from the extended school community. The core group struggled tirelessly to develop curricular concepts and learning activities that would stand up to peer review as viable educational products. Tom Armour, Mel Cox, Maxine Greer, Angela Wong, Lorna Skantze, and Pearline Shannon take major credit for the curriculum that evolved. Many teachers from California and other Western states who participated in the seminars and workshops benefited from this work.

Cecil Garrett, the school custodian, deserves special mention for the dedicated care and attention he bestowed on the Yard, cheerfully adding many extra tasks to his daily round of duties. He loved the place.

Beyond the school faculty, there was a long line of professionals who contributed enormously to the Yard program. We think of Francesca Borgatta, artist and dancer; Aida Brennis, Audubon Nature Trainer; Helen Cox, educator and biologist; Don Hille, ecologist; Jerry Kilker, sociologist; Gina Moreland, educator; John Simon and Sharon Rose Cheadle, poets; "PJ," general Yard worker; Penny Tees, recreation leader; and Chris Raynor, volunteer extraordinaire.

Susan Goltsman and Daniel Iacofano, with Barbara Lubin and many fellow parents contributed a major effort to the Yard with the founding of Project PLAE (Playing and Learning in Adaptable Environments) in 1979. This innovative out-of-school community arts summer initiative, launched by parents to integrate children with disabilities into the community, became a model of creative recreational programming and involved many local artists in contributing their talents to the Yard.

Dozens of parents were involved in the development of the Yard. They turned out for innumerable workdays, organized the annual Yardfest, assisted with special activities, and organized field trips to related sites in the San Francisco Bay Area. Among the many, Rob Browning, Shirley Coleman, Bob Dash, Lenore and Steve Doran, Pat Hom, Eric and Eileen Kopelson,

Steve Lustig, Rina Margolin, Mary Milos, Holly Mines, Glenda and Stuart Pawsey, and Ed and Margot Sheffner dedicated themselves to the Yard to an extraordinary degree.

Many individuals, then students at the University of California, Berkeley, contributed enormously. They included Mike Ashlock, Toni Bava, Marty Bovill, Suzie Boyle, Gil Chan, Randy Davis, Kerry Dawson, Steve Diefenbrock, Joe Donaldson, Barbara Dressler, Jeff Dwelle, Toki Ellengale, Jan Ellis, Patsy Ford, Mark Francis, Claire Greensfelder, Tod Hara, Susan Honeyman, Tom Javits, Wayne Katsumata, Sue King, Donna Kornblutt, Ruth Kreshka, Steve Lang, Michael Lasar, Bruce Levin, Polly Levin, Ron Manley, Michael Mantell, Gary Mason, Mark Maves, Greg Moore, Thom Moran, Michael Morrisay, Cathy Mullowney, Mohammad and Fereshteh Niroomand, Eva Olenmark, Nancy Owens, Sue Pettigrew, Patrick Poulin, Carole Rollins, Bartley Schwartz, Ellen Skotheim, Blue Sloan, Andy Stewart, Larry Wight, Jimmie Wong, Joseph Wong, and dozens of others. Each contributed in their own way to the success of the Yard and simultaneously to their own education, including also Mimi Anderson, then a student from Evergreen State College in Washington. Much of the detailed field research on the Yard was meticulously conducted by research assistants Marie Carmel, Katie Freygang, Joan Kremmer, Stephen Marcus, Jane Robb, and Ellyn Sheprow. Don Young's contribution to the research effort over several years must be especially recognized.

UC Berkeley colleagues and mentors supported the work in various ways: Donald Appleyard, Merle Borrowman, Loren Cole, Clare Cooper Marcus, Garret Eckbo, Joe Hancock, and John Hurst.

One individual stands out for her support and untiring belief in the Yard over many years. Mary Jefferds, manager of the Pacific Coast Office of the National Audubon Society, gave tirelessly of her time as curriculum consultant and political advisor.

In the early, difficult years, the prpoject would not have survived without the unfailing, behind-the-scenes administrative support of Hal Maves, assistant superintendent, Berkeley Unified School District. At the same time, schoolboard member, Lonnie Hancock, gave us essential political support.

Lou Czufin was an extraordinary model of corporate response and responsibility to public education. As community relations officer for Chevron Chemical Company, he took a genuine personal interest and assisted particularly with key media productions: the initial "Green Book" (designed by Craig Siegel as part of his master's program in graphic design), the short film "Help Change This Yard!" (created by volunteer Wayne Leong), and the film strip package called "The Environmental Yard."

In the same vein, Jim Lattie, director of public relations for East Bay Municipal Utility District, contributed his time and talents to the water conservation aspects of the curriculum—and contributed a section of the Mokelumne Aqueduct to the project.

Getting this book together has been a long haul, impossible to achieve without the contributions of many people. We would like to acknowledge the initial interest of Sierra Club Books in the project and the critical assistance of Jon Beckman, Diane Landau, and Daniel Moses in the early days of manuscript development. Above all, Malcolm Margolin gave invaluable advice and helped shape the stylistic treatment of the text.

Special thanks go to Delsey Avery and Kathy Schindler, members of the secretarial staff at the School of Design, North Carolina State University, for their help in keyboarding the manuscript.

The manuscript has benefited greatly from reviews of many colleagues. Louise Chawla's painstaking review of the early draft resulted in many enormously valuable comments. Educators Joe Frost, Eugene Provenzo, and Mary Rivkin made further critical reviews for which we are most grateful. Special thanks are due to Karen Dorion-Coupal for her insightful and detailed editorial suggestions on the later version of the manuscript. Thanks too to Nilda Cosco and Mary Jo Porter for their helpful comments and unfailing encouragement. Special mention must be made of the contributions of Sheila Wright. She not only gave us many excellent insights and comments from her perspective as an educator and former classroom teacher, but also was responsible for the huge task of digital assembly of the book. Her good eye for visual design and placement shows throughout. Her careful nurturing of the project over many months was greatly appreciated.

The gestation of the manuscript extended through two editors at MIG Communications. Many improvements resulted from David Driskell's work on the structure of the book. Paul Yee's editing skills contributed much to the final polishing of the text. He also shepherded the book very effectively and with good humor through the production process—never an easy task. Carie DeRuiter, who designed the book, and her staff at MIG DesignWorks were a pleasure to work with—always willing to discuss design issues until consensus was reached.

To all of the above and the many others who gave of their time, energy, and imagination, we dedicate this work, and hope it is a worthy reflection of their collective contributions.

Table of Contents

PART III: IN THE INTERESTS OF CHILDREN

PART IV: GUIDELINES FOR ACTION

Preface

In 1971 the two of us embarked on an unusual adventure, a ten-year action-research odyssey combining education, design, and community development on a small piece of planet Earth that became known as the Environmental Yard—or simply the "Yard." The idea was to redevelop an asphalted urban schoolyard into an educational resource and community open space. Although there were many facets to the project, our top priorities were to meet the developmental needs of children and to ensure their genuine participation throughout the life history of the project.

The chosen site was Washington Elementary School, a then kindergarten-third-grade university lab school located in a residential neighborhood of Berkeley, California, a city of 100,000 bordering San Francisco Bay. The school was located near downtown, close to the University of California, Berkeley, campus.

At the time, Herb held a joint appointment in the Berkeley Unified School District and the UC Berkeley School of Education—an institution dedicated to national and international curriculum reform. Besides serving as principal of Washington School, Herb was also associate administrative coordinator of several UC Berkeley Laboratory Schools, which were dedicated to training student teachers from UC Berkeley and four other Bay Area universities. The lab schools also served as research sites for developing and demonstrating new curricular ideas, concepts, and methods. Their mission emphasized innovation in both university and primary education. The breadth

of this mandate helped the Yard become one of the most important joint ventures within the university's School of Education. Herb, a field naturalist with a strong background in science education and reform, had already facilitated collaboration between the school and the university on the development of several national elementary school science initiatives. The Yard reflected this earlier work and became the focus of a multifaceted educational partnership between Washington School and UC Berkeley faculty and students. The partnership also strengthened an overlapping coalition of parents and community members committed to the educational principles that Herb had established prior to the Yard.

Robin was a neighborhood resident, Washington parent, and a member of the landscape architecture faculty at UC Berkeley. His background in urban landscape planning and participatory design, combined with a deep research interest in the design of environments for children, made for an ideal interdisciplinary relationship with Herb. Robin began his participatory work with children and youth in the mid-1960s, as an urban planning student at the Massachusetts Institute of Technology. While there, he conducted an action-research, community-built playground project in an inner-city neighborhood of Boston. This initiative revealed the potential of urban schoolyards as educational and recreational resources capable of supporting healthy child development.

Both of us cared passionately about the issue of schoolyard development and saw Washington School as an ideal opportunity to combine our expertise. We envisioned the school as a model of what might be possible when design moves beyond its normal physical and educational limitations.

To produce valid, generalizable results we first had to create an "ecologically valid" space—one with sufficient diversity to accommodate the diversity of users and their recreational and educational needs. We especially wanted to understand how the ecology of children's playing and learning was influenced by natural habitats, as compared to the traditional schoolyard settings of asphalt, game lines, and fixed equipment.

When the project started, the acre and a half (0.6 ha) of school grounds had been biologically sealed for years by an unsightly layer of asphalt. The site was almost devoid of plant and animal life, and children were so bored that they constantly bickered. Serious fights and bullying occurred frequently among the boys. The girls hated the antisocial conditions, as did the teachers. How could children be expected to live and learn in such a degraded and oppressive place?

The antisocial quality of Washington's outdoor environment (so typical of many schoolyards) made it an educational liability. Its painted game lines and few items of traditional equipment provided limited opportunities for healthy, developmentally appropriate activity. Although located in part of the city that lacked public open space, the site was rarely used beyond school hours except for basketball and bike riding.

To justify the scale of change required to dramatically improve the children's quality of life, a policy framework was needed to address the broader realm of children's rights. At the time, the United Nations Declaration on the Rights of the Child was the only official policy that supported our concerns for the developmental rights of children. The expanded Convention on the Rights of the Child (CRC) now recognizes that children have, among others, a right to education (in both skill-based and broad cultural forms), a right to play, a right to developmentally appropriate environments, and a right to participate in making decisions about the things that affect their lives. These were the key themes that supported the child-oriented focus of the Yard.

Our goal was to create an environment incorporating the plant and animal communities of the local region. We followed a community design philosophy—working with students, parents, teachers, neighborhood residents, and school and city officials to upgrade the physical environment and to reestablish the natural habitats that existed prior to the asphalt. For us, remedying the situation became a prerequisite for all other educational reform. We never realized, however, that it would take nearly ten years to achieve this end, and even then not completely.

The chapters that follow describe how we reintroduced life to the erstwhile asphalt desert and how the educational process was impacted by these activities. Using multiple research methods (drawings, questionnaires, interviews, behavior maps, and photography), we gathered extensive data on the educational relationships between the users and the process of naturalizing the Yard.

In 1977, we conducted a formal "post-occupancy evaluation" using questionnaires and drawings returned from the student body of 350 children. The drawings provided a perceptual study of the Yard. We also completed a behavior-mapping study to compare the actual use of the Yard with the children's perception of it. These studies clearly showed that the natural settings were among the most attractive and memorable to the children.

In addition, tape-recorded interviews with the children, compiled over a ten-year period, provided insights into the deeper meaning of the Yard as a natural educational environment. Summarized in Chapter 16, "Speaking of Quality," the interview results reveal how strongly aware children were of the "hidden curriculum" of the school and, in the case of the Yard, show their positive emotional response to the improvement of their physical quality of life.

The evolution of the Yard was integrated into the development of the educational program. Documentation of student growth as a result of curricular connections to the Yard became a critical research goal. In 1976, this effort was advanced substantially by PEET (Project Environmental Education and Training), funded by the federal Office of Environmental Education. Data compiled from interviews with teachers documented numerous Yard-based curricular projects. These studies confirmed the extent of teacher and student growth resulting from the curricular involvement facilitated by the Yard. PEET also produced an array of curricular materials reflecting teachers' experiences.

As a scientific endeavor, the development of the schoolyard included a longitudinal action-research process that was closely linked to several academic units at UC Berkeley: the College of Environmental Design, the Conservation and Natural Resources Program, the School of Education, the School of Forestry, and the Lawrence Hall of Science. Additionally, a number of university research facilities were used as local resource sites: the UC Botanical Garden, the Oxford Tract Experimental Garden, and the UC Biological Control Research Unit. The university staff and students at these facilities helped us enormously throughout the project.

Looking back, we wish that our research could have been more extensive. Still, the results provide a richness not possible in the artificial circumstances of a laboratory separated from daily life. There were other studies we wanted to conduct, including a more quantitative assessment to support our perception that aggression between the children decreased dramatically as the natural environment took hold. Interviews with children and observations of their behavior provided substantial testimony to back up this hypothesis. We highlight this result for all those concerned about today's increasing violence among schoolchildren.

As a community school, Washington had a unique strength contributing to its success: its demographics almost exactly matched the city's overall population profile both socially and economically. For this reason, the school was racially balanced and busing was not necessary (as it was for all other schools in the district). Further, most families viewed the school as a community resource, a perception that helped greatly in implementing the project. Even so, promotion during the early years of the Yard's development was difficult, as nothing existed on the ground to show the potential value of schoolyard naturalization.

As you may imagine, the unprecedented scale of the physical changes brought controversy. Some elected officials thought that removing asphalt from a schoolyard was foolhardy. Conflict was inevitable and reflected the heart of the adventure: taking risks, overcoming barriers, plotting strategies, and helping nature to heal itself. On the other hand, the Yard offered adults a hidden treasure: a magical doorway for the imagination, through which every child could peacefully coexist with nature.

Adults were buoyed by the enthusiasm of the children who loved their school immensely because it was "a special place where you could do special things." Regular subjects like reading, writing, math, science, and social studies became more alive and adventuresome; because of the Yard, students were motivated to excel. The Yard and its users became interwoven into a community of hope—a destiny very different from the overwhelmingly negative atmosphere present in too many U.S. schools today where police officers and metal detectors have replaced trees, sunflowers, and dragonflies. Without a doubt, the Yard illustrated an effective alternative—one based on respect for children and a belief that educational success must be supported by improvements in their quality of life at school.

The pedagogical basis of the Yard was the development of an interdisciplinary, experiential, environmental thrust. This assumed that children learn best through the environment, interacting with peers and teachers in a diverse, changeable, ecologically valid setting. This curricular approach used the environment as a vehicle for teaching all subjects and for motivating children to learn through their play and instinctive curiosity. Through this discovery process, children also learned about the environment: "what lives there, and what you need to do to keep it alive," as one child noted. The experiential focus helped children to understand the environment as a human artifact—an economic, social, scientific, and cultural resource, something we all depend on.

Environmental education at Washington School was an interdisciplinary dimension of regular classroom instruction, an alternative pedagogical strategy for handling the normal range of academic subjects. The Yard supported a web of these interrelationships, which educational reformer John Dewey termed "continuity" and which today we commonly call "integrated studies." The Yard helped Washington teachers understand that sustainable environments must be developed from their cultural, social, scientific, economic, and historical contexts.

One of the most fundamental lessons was the remarkable power of nature to reclaim itself. Many students and teachers identified with this aspect of the Yard and derived great enjoyment from the high adventure of participating in an evolving ecosystem. The first several years saw rapid changes and a dramatic increase in species diversity due to natural invasion and human intervention (see Appendix A). During this period, a core group of teachers tested new educational resources with their students and established indoor-outdoor, interdisciplinary learning stations.

The Yard adventure reached its zenith in the crowning years of 1976 and 1977 when PEET funds enabled core teachers to develop new curricular materials. Funding also supported a full-time outdoor Yard teacher, which made an enormous difference in the number and range of educational possibilities.

In the late 1970s the Yard adventure began to lose momentum as the state and national political landscape started to change—initiated in 1978 with California's Proposition 13 (the first "tax reform" in the country). Over the next several years, school systems across the United States faced financial crises, and the Berkeley Unified School District was no exception. With all district resources suddenly being devoted to keeping the school doors open, it was difficult to get administrative support for the Yard's maintenance.

To fill the void, a nonprofit parent-neighborhood organization called Friends of the Yard was formed and began taking on responsibility for managing the site. For these parents, the Yard reflected their personal values and strong desire to maintain a habitable school for their children. Friends of the Yard carried out general maintenance tasks such as pruning, replacing fences, and caring for the pump that kept water moving through the aquatic system. These necessary volunteer efforts maintained the Yard at a reasonable level of quality even though it was less than what paid, professional staff could have done.

Even though the Yard as described here no longer exists (see Epilogue), we are thankful for the fundamental lesson the Yard taught us—that improvement of the school environment can be a significant

vehicle for educational reform and a positive response to childhood issues that extend beyond school boundaries. Educational systems need to be rebuilt on a broad community foundation to create habitable, high-quality environments that will empower children and develop their environmental values and competence. Environmental yards provide a good place to start these reforms since young people are required by law to spend time at school.

Natural Learning is the story of a reinvented school, with its own backdoor ecosystem populated with hundreds of species of plants and animals. Certainly, the story reflects special circumstances of time and place, as all dramas do; nonetheless, we feel we learned things of immense general value from our successes and failures. It is the story of how teachers and children responded to the expanded classroom of nature and the myriad daily learning opportunities it offered. It illustrates how to create a new type of child-centered educational institution based on community participation, environmental education, and ecosystem health. We are thankful for this experience and offer the results, with warm wishes for success to those working around the world to carry forward the struggle for interdisciplinary environmental education and children's rights to a developmentally appropriate habitat.

Robin Moore
Raleigh, North Carolina

Herb Wong
Menlo Park, California
July 1997

Part I:
Making the Place

CHAPTER I

Transforming the Status Quo

Critical to success was the children's direct participation in the planning, design, construction, and management of the Yard. They had a right to participate, and their involvement improved the quality and meaning of the eventual outcome. It was truly their space.

The surface was macadam. Hard tar, y'know, no grass. There was a lawn facing the street, but the schoolyard was macadam. We had different games back then. We had rings on chains where we swung back and forth. I used to stay after school and play on them. And we played baseball, basketball, tennis, and volleyball. The girls played volleyball too. In the classroom, there were boys and girls. The only time they separated us was outside. I remember the schoolyard had a high, wire fence all around and there was a fence that went down the middle. The girls were on one side and the boys on the other.

I started in kindergarten in 1907. Back then it went to the eighth grade. You graduated at Washington. Each class had thirty to forty children. Outside of regular classes, we had other classes like drawing. We had a regular drawing teacher and a regular music teacher. Classroom teachers only taught us reading, writing, and arithmetic. In those days, teachers couldn't marry. You've heard of old-maid school teachers? I suppose it was to protect the children's morals, but that's only a guess.

When kids were naughty, we were sent to the principal. He'd tell us to hold out our hand and we'd get us a couple of whacks with the ruler. About 1912, they outlawed corporal punishment. After that, when kids were bad, they'd call the truant officer. He'd come down from the city hall, give them a good talking-to, and go to see their parents.

— Malcolm Schmidt, *lifelong Berkeley resident living two blocks from Washington School, reminiscing about his student days.*

W hen Malcolm Schmidt started in kindergarten in 1907, he attended school in a wooden, two-story building covered with redwood shiplap. "Later, they tore down all the wooden schools," he said, "because they were fire hazards and built them out of brick. Then they were afraid the brick schools would fall down in an earthquake, so they tore them all down and rebuilt them out of wood and stucco."

Surviving the two rebuildings was the hard layer of asphalt that covered the schoolyard. In 1971 the problems with this play environment were apparent. There was not a single blade of grass. Nothing relieved the hard tar surface, game lines, and old metal play equipment.

This extreme degree of alienation from nature had not always been the case. In *Suggestions for Garden Work in California Schools,* a fascinating circular published in 1909 by the UC Berkeley College of Agriculture, Agricultural Experiment Station, there are two photographs of Washington School students gardening—in a large bed along the school building and in a nearby vacant lot.[1] In the 1950s, when the school was completely rebuilt, the planting beds were presumably asphalted over.

The garden was not mentioned by Malcolm. Maybe he did not see it as part of the schoolyard, the quality of which did not matter so much in his day because of all the vacant land in the neighborhood.

"There were vacant lots all over Berkeley and people who had cows used to stake them out, one or two to a lot. After it rained everyone got paper bags and we used to go out and pick mushrooms. We took a silver spoon when we cooked the mushrooms, and if the spoon turned black, they were poisonous and we threw them away. But we knew them pretty well. I don't remember ever picking any bad ones."

Over the years, however, the childhood landscape of the neighborhood was sacrificed bit by bit to urban development. Apartment buildings now stood where children once roamed. By the 1970s, the verdant Flatlands had become the city district most lacking in open space. Outside school hours, the schoolyard went virtually unused except for occasional weekend basketball players. There was literally nothing else to do. As Gertrude Stein once said of neighboring Oakland, there was no "there" there.

While educational activity in the schoolyard was out of the question, the classrooms at Washington were rich in hands-on, experiential learning. Students cared for doves, roosters, mice, and gerbils. Potted plants and experiments in botany lined the windows. Dress-up costumes awaited children wanting to enter the world of make-believe. Ethnic art decorated the walls. Cooking stations allowed children to learn about nutrition in a fun way. The measurements of each student, as tabulated by classmates, were displayed at math stations. Open-access bookshelves lined reading corners. Lofts provided a place to escape and study in peace. Child-rendered illustrations of ocean,

forest, prairie, and tundra habitats expressed curricular connections to the global environment.

The school's experiential, child-centered educational setting and the excellence of its hand-picked faculty provided an added impetus to develop what became known as the Environmental Yard, or simply the "Yard." The idea was to upgrade the school's outdoors to match the standard of the indoor learning environment.

A great advantage was the deep roots of the Washington community. "Before busing in the 1960s, all the children went to the school nearest to them," Malcolm noted. Washington had not changed in this regard. Its central location ensured a racial balance of households. The school remained within easy walking distance for most children, a factor that greatly facilitated their ability to maintain friendships outside of school. Washington was a rare case of a socially integrated school community with a level of solidarity that profoundly affected the quality of the participatory process for developing the Yard.

ASPHALT REALITIES

The doors of the two-story, south-facing school building opened abruptly into often glaring sunlight. A featureless expanse of asphalt stretched outward, bounded by tall, chainlink fences. Each day, more than twenty thousand cars traveled along Martin Luther King Jr. (MLK) Way, which ran parallel to the schoolyard's longest boundary. The traffic brought constant visual and acoustic intrusion. In hot weather, children quickly became overheated and often restricted themselves to the confines of two strips of shade provided by adjacent apartment buildings.

Even though the fence separating boys and girls had long since disappeared, children were still *de facto* segregated. The boys' ballgames dominated the asphalt. Girls occupied the bars in one far corner, played hopscotch, or watched the ballgames from narrow, uncomfortable wooden benches against the boundary chainlink fences. The play repertoire was limited to traditional games because the sparse physical environment offered no possibility of the creative playing and learning that

The doors of the two-story, south-facing school building opened abruptly into often glaring sunlight. A featureless expanse of asphalt stretched outward, bounded by tall, chainlink fences (top). Children made drawings of how they saw the schoolyard *before* construction (middle) and how they envisioned it in the *future* (bottom).

had taken place on the vacant neighborhood lots in bygone eras.

Most recess periods saw at least one serious fight among the boys. The physical surroundings were so boring and unresponsive that petty squabbles and relentless teasing were the only diversions. The lifeless physical environment reinforced the antisocial tendencies that some children brought to school—that the strong could dominate the weak, that boys could dominate girls, and that the first move in any argument was a show of fists. Peers stood around goading prospective combatants to strike first as if engaged in war. Too often fights were along racial lines, even though the School Board Committee on Desegregation had confirmed that Washington maintained the lowest frequency of racial conflict in the school district. Teachers hated the dog-eat-dog recesses, where they were constantly pestered to intervene in children's disputes.

More rigorous empirical evidence gathered later from the children supported these pre-Yard observations. In 1977, following the completion of many Yard improvements, we interviewed the graduating fourth graders who had been in kindergarten when the project started. They were therefore uniquely qualified to reflect on their feelings about the old schoolyard prior to redevelopment.

"Boring!" was the most common reply, followed by comments like "all bare," "plain cement," and "too hot."

Some children went into more detail.

"There wasn't enough to play with so there was more fighting. It was scary."

"Kids were always tripping and falling, hitting their heads on the concrete and hurting themselves. It's dangerous to have just concrete. Kids get bored, so they mess around a lot, more than they would if they had something to play with. The worst thing is that kids smash glass all over, not because they're bad but just because they need something to do. They go s-m-a-s-h! People get hurt. There's nothing to do on concrete. You can sit down. You can play jump rope. Maybe you can play ball, or tag, or jacks, but you can't have much fun."

The apparent relationship between poor environmental quality and physical, social, and psychological health was supported by the accident records. According to the school secretary, the day redevelopment of the Yard started, tearful children stopped lining up at her desk with bumps and grazes. We discovered that a sizable proportion of children got hurt simply by running into each other or falling on the blacktop. Many injuries also resulted from physical conflict between children (although vaguely reported to avoid further conflict between the parents of the warring children).

If the schoolchildren had been unionized, they would have surely gone on strike to protest such unsatisfactory working conditions. The fact that these conditions are prevalent in most urban schools in the United States and many other countries is a measure of adults' disregard of children's basic right to grow up in a safe, life-enhancing, and developmentally appropriate environment. Bare, asphalt schoolyards have become such an accepted part of the image of public schools that their negative aspects are no longer recognized. We would not keep domestic pets in these environments. Why then our children?

ENVIRONMENTAL QUALITY, PLAYING, AND LEARNING

We felt that school should be a place where children learn understanding and respect for each other and their environment. Positive child development requires a social, high-quality physical setting where natural learning and motivation through play is woven into the fabric of the formal curriculum. Play is critical to socialization. It is the primary way in which children relate to one another and make sense of their surroundings. In this regard, no matter how progressive Washington's indoor learning environment was, the condition of the outdoor setting was counterproductive. In high-quality surroundings, instruction can be made a lot more engaging. Furthermore, informal play in high-quality environments can be a useful tool for assessment. By observing students at play, teachers can understand their personal styles more clearly and determine the learning activities necessary to reinforce the formal program.

The idea of the Yard was to demonstrate that a higher quality outdoor environment would help improve the quality of children's social relationships and broaden their range of educational opportunities. The basic concept was to create an integrated, child-centered curriculum, based on the value of informal play as the first motivational step in both nonformal education (as one would find, for instance, in an adventure playground or urban farm)[2], and formal classroom instruction.

PARTICIPATORY COMMUNITY DESIGN

The Yard was conceived by the two of us in the spring of 1971. With a grant pending, we organized a planning task force composed of interested teachers, parents, and volunteer professionals. We realized that if we continued looking at the asphalt as an insurmountable problem, we would never realize our goal of bringing the outdoors alive as an educational setting. We had to create a shared vision and get it down on paper.

Our most important strategy was to involve as many as possible of the existing and future users of the site in the planning process. We knew from previous experience that the participatory process would take time— seven months as it turned out—and that to take short cuts would be to risk failure.

As a first step, the task force organized a systematic survey to solicit ideas from children, teachers, parents, and residents living around the school. The magnitude of the response was encouraging—almost fifty percent of the parents returned the "take-home" survey.

We often create programs and projects without involving children, yet they have a right to participate, as anyone else, to help decide changes that directly affect their lives—now supported by Article 12 of the Convention on the Rights of the Child (CRC).[3] Every student completed a written survey (with the kindergarten class receiving help from the teachers) that asked three basic questions:

• What do you like about the yard at Washington School?

• What do you dislike about the yard?

• What would you like to see added or changed to the yard?

The results of the student survey presented some very clear points of view. The children, especially the girls, highly valued the old play equipment. The boys enjoyed the ballgames. Most respondents expressed a desire for natural spaces. The sheer volume, seriousness,

June 9, 1971

WASHINGTON ELEMENTARY
University of California Laboratory School

STUDENT QUESTIONNAIRE

Age __8__

Boy ____ Girl __X__

Grade __3__   Teacher __mr. cox__   Room __210__

1. What do you like most about the school yard?

ladder Bars
Jungle Gym

2. What don't you like about the school yard?

ther are to many Lines and
hopScotchs. to Many People get
hurt on the ground. and it is to
plain. I don't like the asphalt
KicK Ball field

3. What new things would you like to see added or changed?

trees SwingS slides graSS
tires and ropes long tunnel
Bird Bath MaZe pond and
Fish. Flower qavden

Design ideas were shared with residents during the planning phase (top). All possible users were involved in the planning process, including parents, teachers, students, and community members. For example, the student survey asked the children three basic questions: "What do you like?" "What don't you like?" and "What do you want to see added or changed?"

and imagination of the children's responses vindicated our trust in their ability and motivation to represent their own needs.

In addition, several teachers and groups of students conducted studies on the Yard's potential as part of their daily curriculum. They went on field trips around the neighborhood to visit the several vacant lots that still existed at that time, to observe and sample the local flora and fauna. It did not take long for the children to realize that many of the species identified were good candidates for the Yard once the asphalt was removed. One group drafted plans for the entire site. A third-grade class went on a field trip to observe and test existing play areas in the neighborhood. Based on their evaluations, they made design proposals for play settings in the Yard.

Architecture and landscape architecture students from UC Berkeley worked with us on compiling and analyzing all the gathered information. Based on the results, they proposed alternative layouts for the site in response to its particular characteristics: size, shape, flat topography, solar orientation, exposure to cool Pacific breezes, as well as its location on a noisy arterial street that divided the residential neighborhood from downtown.

A community feedback clinic was held to review all the information and preliminary proposals. Different groups discussed their needs and further contributed to the growing pyramid of design ideas.

At this point, a master plan began to take shape and was presented to city commissions, the fire department, the school board, and the city council for endorsement. Given the shortage of open space in the neighborhood and the obvious child development potential of the schoolyard, these agencies could hardly refuse to support the scheme. We were careful, however, not to ask for money or material contributions at this stage. Instead we limited our request to a formal agreement that changing the schoolyard would benefit the entire community.

With community support and official endorsements in hand, we scheduled a meeting with the school superintendent. Although he recognized and accepted our mission and expressed personal support, professionally, he felt we were being too ambitious. He essentially gave us informal permission to move ahead, but at the same time warned us not to come running to him for help if things went awry. Success or failure would rest solely on our own shoulders.

FIRST STEPS IN TRANSFORMATION

Following the end of the seven-month planning process, a bulldozer arrived (complete with an operator donated by the regional parks district) and scraped off an area of asphalt skin covering about one-third of the site. Seemingly permanent and impervious, the asphalt was just a thin veneer over the ground that was easily removed. The pieces of tarry pie crust were transported by dump trucks to the Port of Oakland, so that the material could be recycled as construction fill. In a couple of days, the job was finished, leaving behind a third of an acre of dirt ready to activate its life-giving potential. The core group of teachers began to explore the learning potential of the new outdoor environment and to suggest ways to make it a more effective educational resource.

Reactions were mixed.

"Wow, *real dirt* on our schoolyard," one teacher enthuses. "It's hard to believe. My kids are so excited about everything that's going on . . . How can I use it in my class?"

Some students were upset: "Hey! They took away our kickball field!"

Most people were unsure how to react. A frequent comment was "Well, I guess they know what they're doing."

We hoped so.

As it hardened under the sun, the exposed dirt rapidly became almost as unworkable as asphalt. To overcome this problem, the bulldozer returned and regraded the hard, flat surface into a landscape of small mounds and valleys. Now the sun got to work on the churned-up lumps of soil, providing an instant building material similar to the adobe bricks used by the early California settlers.

"Come and look at my dirt fort," a child builder cries, "it's neat!"

Then the rains came. Magically, a green haze spread across the dirt, comprising thousands of sprouting leaflets, growing into plants with characteristic

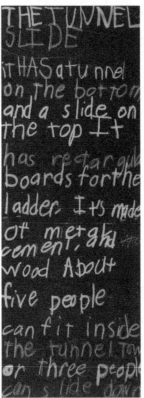

As part of the planning process, children created drawings of activities they most wanted to see in the Yard. The drawing above, along with its description, illustrates one example that was incorporated into the final design.

In parallel with what was essentially a professional assessment of the site, several classes launched their own investigations. Some built design models (top). Others studied neighborhood geography (middle right), conducted traffic counts (bottom right), and observed existing uses of the Yard; others took temperature and wind readings and acclimated themselves in preparation for the changes that were about to take place. From a curricular point of view, everything about the site had learning potential.

circular leaves and clusters of pinkish, violet flowers. What was this urban survivor, this hardy denizen of vacant lots, this bane of Flatland gardeners? It had many names—mallow, wild hollyhock, cheeseweed, *Malva parviflora*. But regardless of what it was called, it became the symbol of rejuvenating Yard life.

How could the mallow have arrived so quickly? Could the seeds really have been sleeping under the asphalt for the twenty years since the last time the school was rebuilt and the yard paved over? No other assumption was plausible. Mallow was part of the front line of pioneer species, along with dandelion, dock, cow's tongue, and other wild plants that had lain dormant or now reinvaded from the neighborhood. Together, they reinhabited the Yard and provided the first, self-sustaining resources for playing and learning.

Something less positive resulted from the rains. Everywhere, adobe turned to mud—enormous quantities of mud. It was no lark for the school custodian, or for parents whose children had a great liking for this primordial play material. The lost-and-found box provided a clothing supply for those who got dirtied.

INDOOR-OUTDOOR CONNECTIONS

For the first time, loose materials were available outdoors, which children used to invent a variety of games: "gold mines," "witches brew," "balancing tag." Children created their own reality, their own primitive tools, their own "appropriate technology." There were "diggers" who found the most conveniently shaped sharpened sticks for conducting exploratory excavations into the dirt mounds. There were sandcastle architects and stream flow engineers who pursued their special interest—and perhaps future careers.

Classrooms were enriched by a flow of souvenirs from children's investigations: a bouquet of wildflowers for the teacher, a headdress of woven grasses, a favorite rock, a boat made of three sticks bound together. This creative activity brought increased motivation to classroom learning, which core group teachers were quick to capitalize on.

The outdoors began to occupy a significant part of their daily curriculum, providing them with far more ideas than they could ever put into practice. Many ideas came directly from the children. A new awareness of the Yard developed as a place of rich surprises and opportunities never before encountered in a schoolyard.

One day, a UC Berkeley maintenance crew delivered a load of campus landscape prunings. Instantly, a settlement of shelters, forts, and camps sprung to life. Camps turned into *ad hoc* theaters as children acted out improvised dramas stimulated by the new things around them. Logs became spaceships and boulders distant planets as children's imaginations interacted with the ever-changing landscape.

"I wish I could take a blanket and some food and camp out there," a girl wrote in her Yard journal as part of a language arts project launched when the first changes were made to the Yard. We observed that Yard activity strongly motivated some children to write.

DREAM WALL

During this period of exploration and discovery, members of the community painted a giant mural that eventually covered the twenty-five-by-twelve-foot former ball wall in the west end of the Main Yard (the larger section of the site where the asphalt had been retained).

The original, messy mural was painted by a group of revelers at the first Yardfest (the annual Yard celebration described in Chapter 15). The unsightly result reflected a confused, disjointed day when people started groping excitedly into a murky future. From this experience, we learned an important lesson: you cannot just let a group of people loose with a hodgepodge of leftover paint and expect a visually satisfying result.

The mural was not without meaning, however. A variety of slogans appeared, such as "Off the asphalt" and "We love Washington." These important sentiments, however, were interspersed with words considered in poor taste. The sloppy layout was a waste of space. Above all, children had not participated in creating the mural.

Everyone agreed that the mural should be repainted with the children fully involved. The second version took a whole term to complete, a process coordinated by two resource teachers (free-floating staff able to work with children from any classroom) and community

The Dream Wall provided an ideal way for the children to explore visually their personal feelings about the Yard. It served as a constant reminder of the spirit of community and the collaboration underlying all aspects of the project's construction.

GETTING IN TOUCH

Urban schoolyards are about the most "taken-for-granted" space one can imagine, except perhaps for city streets. Thus it becomes imperative that a systematic effort be made to assess what really happens there. Such an effort immediately raises problems about the nature of environmental and social values and their measurement.

From the beginning, children should be involved in looking at their site afresh. Site assessment should be treated as a curriculum activity as well as an external "planning factor." One must be careful, however, to keep the distinction clear. Although curriculum activity can make a valid input into planning (as illustrated by the children's designs and questionnaire contributions), it is unlikely to be comprehensive or accurate enough.

The question should always be asked: "Can it be used as valid data?" You will quickly discover that your site embodies several different types of factors. Some will be stable, easily measured fixed features such as mature trees or chainlink fences; others will be harder to assess, such as noise levels; still others will be difficult to assess without a properly conducted systematic study, such as afterschool use.

You will also find that outdoor spaces provide a wonderful opportunity to invite local community participation. Nearly every schoolyard represents potential neighborhood open space for use by local residents. For example, research has shown that most users of neighborhood parks (especially children) live within two blocks and rarely more than four blocks away. Therefore, it can be argued that neighborhood open space should be distributed in small, closely spaced sites throughout residential areas. In this respect, any proposed schoolyard development can be partly justified as meeting neighborhood recreation needs in addition to educational functions. Surveys and studies of your site can help you become sensitive to the various actual and potential user groups and their needs.

volunteers. The wall surface was divided into manageable subsections for each class to develop ideas for their dream of the future Yard. Somebody scrounged enough money to purchase top-quality acrylic paints. With a carefully managed process of group participation, the result was magnificent.

An intricate, colorful assortment of animals, plants, and human figures populated the lower half of the work, with the word "LOVE" hovering over everything. Among the painted clouds, a great, Aztec-style bird flew, perhaps drawn by a child of Mexican origin. It appeared in almost the exact location where, in the first mural, a faculty jazz fan had scrawled "Bird Lives" (Charlie "Yardbird" Parker, the legendary saxophonist, was still in flight).

The mural served as a constant reminder of the Yard's mission. It kept spirits up during the years of struggle to turn our dreams into a reality. Eventually surrounded by the living Yard, it became an historic symbol of the journey taken and the task accomplished. It stood sacrosanct, every year a little more weather-beaten, but never maliciously damaged—until 1985 when it was used as one of the Yard's several "canvasses" by a group of teenage graffiti artists. In a certain way, the youthful vernacular gave symbolic expression to the dramatic downturn of concern for the quality of public education in the 1980s.

MOTIVATING PROGRESS

Beyond the core group of teachers, reactions to the children's discoveries and inventions were mixed. Put yourself in the place of a teacher faced with a line of dripping milk cartons, forever getting knocked over, spilling their muddy contents onto the floor. Some teachers took it in stride and thought of ways to integrate these spontaneous events into the flow of classroom activity; others found it more difficult.

It was hard for any teacher to simply ignore the Yard. The constantly changing environment prompted a dynamic mix of perceptions, opinions, and stimuli. For some, the Yard provided opportunities to implement dormant ideas that the asphalted schoolyard had failed to support. These teachers immediately moved part of

their classroom activity outdoors in the fresh air and sunlight. For others, though, the Yard presented a challenge to their secure, professional boundaries.

To whittle away the reluctance of some faculty members, a childhood memories workshop was held. During the session, teachers recalled favorite childhood play activities. Many remembered playing in the water, digging dirt, collecting things, making places to hide, hunting for wildlife. One teacher recalled riding the tops of apartment elevators in New York City. An intense discussion followed about the need for children to take risks and to meet challenges. Later, in the Yard, the teachers put their memories into practice: turning over rocks, digging, looking for insects, testing their curiosity. By sharing their forgotten childhood instincts, teachers helped each other make personal contact with the child-centered learning possibilities of the new resources. Inevitably, they became more receptive to the notion of integrating classroom and Yard environments.

With renewed enthusiasm, the teachers found that more outdoor resources were required to sustain long-term educational objectives. A few rocks, weed-covered dirt, and insects were not enough to satisfy the requirements of daily classroom involvement. They wanted trees, gardens, ponds, workstations, meeting areas, potting sheds, a fireplace, habitats for birds and larger terrestrial animals—the list went on.

Following the removal of the asphalt and regrading, we tried to establish priorities, but the uncertainty of what might or might not be technically and financially feasible made planning difficult. Classroom motivation was kept alive by organizing activities and events that attracted people and kept them involved, and at the same time provided useful feedback about how to use the space. During this period, the children took many field trips to investigate the broader community and to find items to incorporate into the Yard.

ECODRAMA

Events like the Dream Wall made the Yard's early days seem like a theatrical production. The site itself was a stage, part solid, part ephemeral. Principal characters such as public officials and prospective financial supporters determined the overall fate of the enterprise with their positive or negative responses. A much larger cast of community organizers, auxiliary staff, playleaders, artists, volunteers, and teaching assistants supported the enterprise and wrote much of the script as the drama developed.

An outer circle of characters contained detractors, hecklers, and neutral bystanders. Like the chorus in a Greek drama, they commented with approval, disapproval, or indifference without involving themselves directly in changing the course of events, although they indirectly influenced the atmosphere by conveying messages to those in positions of authority. There were also random individuals, usually strongly voiced critics, whose unexpected appearances brought unpredictable results. For instance, the damage caused by a single call from an irate neighbor to the superintendent's office could be impossible to repair.

As *de facto* directors in this drama, we discovered that dealing with people's prejudices and personalities took more time and energy than planting trees and digging out ponds. Some of the most heated discussions were prompted by the proposal to reintroduce the natural environment into the school site where all the local flora and fauna had been eliminated. On the one hand, as the community surveys had revealed, the majority wanted the natural environment reinstated in the Yard; on the other, a minority of individuals were fearful of children being bitten by bugs, drowning in the water, getting dirty, falling out of trees, and hiding in bushes where teachers could not see them. Police were also concerned that they would not be able to view inside the schoolyard from their patrol cars.

Unfortunately, it was several years before the appearance of research results from other sources demonstrated the health-giving properties of the natural environment. This scientific evidence would have helped defuse the arguments.[4]

Although it would be nice to present the Yard as a smooth evolution—the spontaneous flowering of a worthwhile idea—the truth is we endured considerable struggle and conflict. We could not avoid stepping on toes, sometimes heavily. And our own toes got stepped

A class worked with college students to create a drama about plant growth, about the need for sunlight, water, soil, and nutrition, and about what happens when these elements are lacking (top). UC Berkeley students helped to construct the wetlands (middle), and families participated in tree planting (bottom).

on as well. Some people in power thought we were crazy and destructive, or well-meaning but basically irresponsible. They felt offended when we took the law into our own hands. We felt they were misusing their power, acting vindictively or contemptuously and failing to respond to the needs of the children and community. To sing only praise while hiding an often nasty struggle would be to falsify, and thus diminish, the actual situation. Much of the time, in spite of our attempts to avoid confrontation, the drama became a serious battle of "us" versus "them."

Eventually, the Yard became a reality. Yet scars of the many battles remain—anger, really, for the lost months and years required to convince people to take the Yard seriously and to overcome attempts to block its progress. The only defense against bitterness was the joy of working creatively among an energetic community of people. Often, the liberated imagination of children, the wondrous reclaiming power of nature, and our belief that the outdoors could be a powerful supporter of child development were all that we had to keep us going.

In the early days, it was difficult to demonstrate how the curricular process would work in detail. There was simply too little to work with on the ground. But as the Yard took shape and was filled with "stuff," it became easier to articulate to others, as well as to ourselves, what we were trying to achieve. "Feedback" knowledge and awareness grew and we were able to modify new developments so that they continued to support the original goals. Curriculum and Yard co-evolved, presenting teachers and children with learning opportunities of ever-increasing richness and diversity.

•

The chapters that follow demonstrate how the natural diversity of the Yard functioned as a tripartite vehicle—stimulating healthy child development through informal play, supporting formal curriculum development in interdisciplinary environmental education, and accommodating a variety of nonformal in-school and out-of-school educational and recreational programs. We will see how the Yard stimulated positive changes in the children's social behavior, how it affected their attitudes and knowledge of each other, and how it helped them understand the world around them.

REFERENCES

1. Babcock, E. B. (1909). *Suggestions for Garden Work in California Schools.* Berkeley, Calif.: The University Press (Circular No. 46, UC Agricultural Experiment Station).

2. For a description of adventure playgrounds and related models of creative outdoor play and learning environments, see: Brett, A., R. C. Moore, and E. Provenzo (1993). *The Complete Playground Book.* Syracuse, N.Y.: Syracuse University Press.

3. United Nations (1989). The Convention of the Rights of the Child. New York: UNICEF.

4. Lewis, C. (1996). *Green Nature, Human Nature: The Meaning of Plants in Our Lives.* Chicago: University of Illinois Press.

CHAPTER 2

Greening

"It's my favorite place above all others," says Erik. "It's our special island where we hold meetings. You go through a skinny passageway until you reach the spot where little redwoods are sprouting at the bottom of the trunks. Everything is there—trees, spiders, squirrels, and all kinds of stuff to fiddle with. I like to sit leaning against the trees by the rocks. If I have some homework, I'll look at the stream and watch the fish swimming around in the shallow water. I'll just have a good time and if a friend comes along, he'll sit by me and we'll talk in the shade."

When we use the term "extinct," we usually refer to a species that no longer exists on Earth, to genetic material lost forever. This notion of extinction, however, can also be applied to landscapes, where human intervention—namely, cultivation and urban development—has led to a reduction of species diversity and ecological value. This process of degradation has been evident in the replacement of forest groundcovers with suburban lawns. At the neighborhood level, though, we strongly believed that it was possible to reverse this process. We knew of several examples where degraded urban land had more or less been restored to its native condition—such as the ecological parks in London, which in some cases surpassed the original quality of the site.[1]

The results of the community survey indicated a clear mandate to naturalize the Washington schoolyard with trees, shrubs, and flowers. Many respondents also expressed a preference for a "natural" approach to the design. This view coincided with our desire as educators to recreate the natural communities of the San Francisco Bay region: redwood, chaparral, cool woodland, meadow, riparian, and aquatic.

The recolonization process was fascinating to observe and explore with the children, as the small patch of Earth began to regenerate itself. Equally intriguing was the link between the increasing diversity of life and the increasing diversity of the children's behavior. New games and stories burst forth as the natural materials stimulated and supported an ever-widening repertoire of behavior. The alienation of the old schoolyard was gradually replaced with positive relationships—between children and between children and their environment—which led eventually to a richer childhood culture.

FIRST ARRIVALS

Borne by the wind, piggy-backing on animals, or circulating through the digestive systems of birds, seeds fell into hospitable cracks in the dirt and took root. For a while we were content to let nature's abundance take its own course and to learn from observing the process. Except for known poisonous species, every plant was encouraged to grow.

Aggressive invaders included bindweed, dandelion, dock, chickweed, chicory, clover, field sorrel, fleabane, lamb's quarters, mallow, mugwort, pigweed, plantain, purslane, Queen Anne's lace, sow thistle, St. John's wort, wood sorrel, yarrow, and many handsome grasses. Large Himalayan blackberry vines bearing tender juicy fruit lunged through the chainlink fence from adjacent back-yards, their barbed tentacles spreading along the edge of the area. Scotch broom followed the same route, settling along the peripheral path, showering its surface with bright yellow pea flowers each spring.

Sweet anise, also called common fennel, was another early arrival. Its long stems, supporting lacy, bright green foliage, were surmounted by golden, invert-ed umbrella-shaped flowers. Host to the elegant anise caterpillar and its biological alter ego, the handsome anise swallowtail (*Papilio zelicaon*), anise was a perfect example of a "resource plant" that furnished a wide vari-ety of play and learning opportunities. It grew six to seven feet high and provided excellent camouflage dur-ing games of hide-and-go-seek. Anise was so prolific that it could be harvested year-round as building material for camps and clubhouses. Old anise stems were hollowed out to make musical instruments and "pea shooters" (with seeds as ammunition). Anise was also an accepted part of the indigenous edible landscape. Many children called it "licorice" because of its similarity in taste. In the spring children chewed on the fresh growth; in the fall they crushed the ripe seeds between their teeth for the anise flavor. A couple of girls called the seeds "little brown beans" and wrapped them in large mallow leaves to make pretend enchiladas.

One class took a bucket of soil from the Yard and brought it into the classroom. After sifting out the visible remnants of vegetation, the students placed the soil in a shallow seedling tray and gave it a good soaking. The amorphous, uniform soil soon showed signs of life as the many naturally deposited seeds began to sprout. For each plant that appeared, the children recorded the type, quanti-ty, and rate of growth. They compared these results with the plants growing in the Yard. The project was a great introduction to propagation, germination, seasonal dor-mancy, and population dynamics.

As we began to observe how strongly the children's motivation to learn was stimulated by the nascent ecosys-tem, we intervened deliberately to enhance the Yard's power. A rotting log, for instance, was installed in a shady corner of the site. Fungi soon appeared, signaling the onset of decomposition. The children were fascinated by toad-stools and the many intriguing tales and facts about fungi. As a result, it was easy to teach them about the process of decomposition and the recycling of nutrients through the ecosystem.

DESIGN WITH NATURE

Under the laissez-faire recolonization of the Yard, it was not long before a few hardy, invasive plants like mal-low, anise, and eucalyptus began to dominate the site. Although the process was fascinating and offered many educational benefits, we realized that deliberate design intervention was required to create a true microcosm of the bioregion.

By the end of the two-year fallow period, we had raised sufficient funds to begin developing the Natural Resource Area. It was a small piece of land, occupying about a third of an acre and measuring 100 by 160 feet (30 by 50 m). Once the main pathways had been finely graded and defined, the design was implemented in stages and organized around the natural communities we hoped to establish. Each community supported the design philosophy of the Yard to accentuate diversity of shape, size, color, texture, and seasonal variation.

GOING NATIVE

To facilitate the naturalization process, we realized that we needed to import many species from natural plant communities of the region. Indigenous Bay Area species were emphasized—those that were native (always lived there) or naturalized (got used to living there). These species had withstood the test of time by resisting disease and adapting to local conditions. Even so, while plants at the "hardy" end of the scale could tol-erate a wide range of conditions, others had very specific requirements.

Many indigenous species unavailable at local nurs-eries were discovered on "plant safaris" around the Bay.

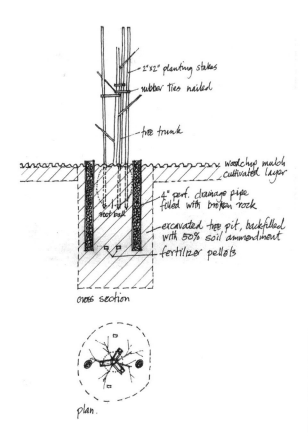

2"x2" planting stakes

rubber ties nailed

tree trunk

woodchip mulch
cultivated layer

4" perf. drainage pipe
filled with broken rock

root ball

excavated tree pit, backfilled
with 50% soil ammendment

fertilizer pellets

cross section

plan.

HOW TO PLANT A TREE

1. Dig a large hole. Make it large enough and deep enough for your tree.

2. Make a small mound in the bottom of the hole. Place your tree in the hole with the roots spread over the mound.

3. Fill the hole around the tree with good soil. Leave a three-inch space below ground level where water can collect.

4. Press the soil down firmly around the tree. Then water well.

Sour grass (oxalis) corms were transferred from nearby vacant land; in the early spring, kids loved to chew on the tender stems and wander around with the bright yellow flowers dangling from their mouths. Species of willow were propagated from creekside clippings gathered from regional parks. Soap plant, a multipurpose staple of the Bay Area Ohlone Indians, was transplanted from surplus highway land a few miles out of town.

Like all plans on paper, our vision of the dynamic and complex natural world was grossly oversimplified. The species, their level of adaptation, and their habitat requirements varied enormously. Our strategy was to include as many representative communities as possible on the site, while also leaving room for the random consequences of nature's built-in abundance. We achieved this objective by creating many small niches, overplanting, scattering seeds by hand, and severely limiting maintenance activities such as pruning and grass cutting in the early years as the young vegetation struggled to survive.

Natural events continued to illustrate the role of chance in nature. For example, the first tree in the Yard sowed itself as a eucalyptus seed from some prunings brought from the university campus for a summer play program. Within eight years the tree was more than fifty feet high—the tallest living thing on the site. It began shading out the garden and would have eventually created an insurmountable problem by reaching a height of two hundred feet or more. This confrontation with nature required human counteraction. Although the towering tree looked magnificent, we had no alternative but to ask the city forestry department to cut it down. This first urban forestry event—and action "against" nature—netted the forestry crew more than half a cord of firewood to heat their homes as compensation for their exacting task.

SHERWOOD FOREST

One November weekend, following fine grading of the Natural Resource Area, a work crew gathered to plant forty saplings donated by the California Redwood Association. Excited children unloaded the eighteen-inch-high trees along with parents, university students, and other community members, many of whom had never planted a tree before. We reflected on the fact that these skinny snuffs of green would not enter their prime of life until our children's children's children were being born. The redwood grove, we felt, could become a powerful symbolic connection in time and space between the Yard and its regional hinterland.

At five feet apart, the saplings were spaced unconventionally close to each other, with the intention of progressively thinning them out over the years. An immediate payoff was that the grove quickly became a miniature forest. Children used the closely spaced trees as a private refuge to "spy" on classmates playing one or two paces away.

"We call it Sherwood Forest," says Anna. "You can look out, but it's so dense no one can see in. Me and my friend like to scuffle in there and eat our lunch where no teachers can nag us. If somebody is coming, we blink our eyes—it's a secret code. When the coast is clear, we climb out. It's our secret hiding place. I escape back there when people tease me. I'm glad I'm wearing green today so I can make myself invisible."

Trips to the Muir Woods National Monument (the famous 550-acre grove of virgin redwoods northwest of San Francisco) thrust the children forty generations into the future. They saw how trees, even under more spacious circumstances, still grew in many shapes, sizes, and spacings. Even among these centuries-old giants, minute offspring were just beginning life in lighter patches of the forest floor, nestled between a multitude of ferns and delicate violet-flowered oxalis, the wood sorrel, a cousin of the Yard's yellow sourgrass.

Within a few years, the Yard's own forest became an evergreen phalanx rising from the rocky promontory overlooking the little sandbank, lapped by the running water of the creek.

CHAPARRAL HILL

Closely spaced shrubs were planted on the low hill in the center of the Natural Resource Area, located between meadowland and redwoods. The idea was to import some of the character of the larger hills—visible from the Yard—that divided the Pacific-cooled East Bay from the hot hinterland. Before long, intense blues of ceanothus rose above a carpet of golden California poppies and red flax. The open feeling of the adjacent

The trees grow good when the sun in up and they get water. They need a lot of water and sun every day. If thay do not get water and sun ever day they will soon die we will not have paper and birds will not have food and thy will die soon.

Vegetation was a source of inspiration for the children as they harvested dried grasses to make dens in the shrubs, created drawings, and practiced their writing skills to demonstrate their understanding of biological processes.

Students take part in a Japanese plum tree planting ceremony.

RULES FOR ESTABLISHING VEGETATION

1. Concentrate on hardy species indigenous to the region.

2. Look around the neighborhood on vacant lots and see what thrives best, including so-called weeds.

3. Develop a topographic and planting plan to reflect as closely as possible the natural ecological associations of the region, paying particular attention to plants that attract, shelter, and nourish local wildlife.

4. Do not try to create a manicured, park-like landscape with large expanses of lawn.

5. Recognize that plants are a major source of play material for children. Children love to pick flowers and harvest seed heads—daisies, flowering shrubs, sunflowers, marigolds —all kinds of wildflowers and grasses work well.

6. Children can help gather seeds in the neighborhood for planting—scatter them on dug-over areas and let nature take over.

Danielle

7. Plant semi-mature trees as early as possible. This will give the site visual form and impact.

8. After an overall pattern of trees is established, introduce smaller scale shrubs and indigenous plants for a natural look.

9. During the establishment period, which may last up to five years for some plants, trees and shrubs need loving care and protection.

10. A system of barriers can be used to define pathways, planted areas and social places for the children—not to exclude use but to deflect environmental impact. Most trees and shrubs should be heavily staked, in some cases for several years.

meadow extended up over the hill, with wildflowers thriving in sunny patches between the shrubs. But this effect was short-lived; by the third year the shrubs shaded out most of the wildflowers. As compensation, selected species were planted around the hill in small microhabitats—here a rock rose, there a clump of Fuller's teasel, wild iris, or Matilija poppy. These plantings were experimental. Inevitably some failed and some succeeded; all the while, various indigenous species continued to invade and adapt to the changing array of limiting factors.

Because of its central location, hill-like form, and woodsy feeling, the Chaparral Hill became a favorite place for clubs and den making.

Two girls and a boy play in a clump of toyon bushes. They bend down the branches, tape them together, and try to spread dry grass across to make a roof.

"Make it like an Indian house," instructs one of the girls, undoubtedly inspired by the Ohlone cultural program being conducted in the Yard at that time.

"We need more hay," yells the other girl. "This stuff is really good for building. I want to be a builder when I grow up. I want to build lots of things so people will come over. I'll get new friends and we'll play in the structures."

"We're training the plants to grow in the right direction," says the boy. "Eventually, e-v-e-n-t-u-a-l-l-y (accentuating each letter to emphasize the time it will take), they'll cover the roof. Then the hay will fall off and segregate from the branches and they'll stay and we won't need the hay."

"How long will it take?" someone asks.

"Oh, a couple of thousand years . . ." he chuckles.

"What's it like in there?" inquires the first girl.

"It's cozy and cool. Yes, cool—cool and dark," jokes the boy. "Quick, get some more anise on the top and tie up the bigger branches 'cause it's caving in. Quick! Get more hay."

The following day, the boy has become "Caveman," and a second boy is "Big Bull." The shelter has been turned into a farm building and the game has taken on an agricultural aspect in addition to its Native American theme.

"Caveman, don't eat the hay," commands the first girl. "Hey, Caveman, don't do that, okay!"

"Big Bull! Big Bull!" shouts the other. "Come and get your dinner before Caveman eats it."

This was a wonderful example of how the hands-on, manipulative quality of the natural environment could stimulate cooperative, child-to-child playing and learning. It helped children develop interpersonal skills as they built their culture, skills that they could transfer to other educational settings.

THE JOY OF PLANTING

Planting was a highly cooperative activity, helped by the fact that it was the least discriminating by age, gender, or ability level. The sense of solidarity that came with working on a project together made the experience more memorable. Children, long after graduating from Washington, dropped by to marvel at the rapid growth of the redwoods they had helped plant. A Swiss family, in town for a year of post-doctoral study, planted a trio of California pepper trees behind the swings, the first trees they had ever planted. Noting that the event made them feel more connected to the neighborhood, they expressed desire to return one day to visit the grown-up trees.

Planting activities touched many aspects of child development, including large-muscle activity, fine-motor coordination, sensory discrimination, and cooperative working. The children gained practical knowledge of plants by experiencing every step of the process: digging the hole, smelling the dirt, filling the hole with water, slicing the sides of the nursery can, pulling the sides apart, observing the constrained roots, pulling the roots apart with a hand hoe ("How would you feel if your legs had been bound up all your life?" asked the teacher. "How far do you think the roots will travel now they're free?"), grasping the smooth gray trunk, lowering the root ball in the hole, mixing in rice-husk soil amendment, back-filling the hole, working the soil around the root ball, wetting the soil to bed the roots, selecting the stakes, hammering the stakes, and tying up the trunk.

The children also learned responsibility. "How shall we care for the tree?" the teacher asked. "What does it need? Who wants to be on the tree-caring team to do the watering, measure the growth, and check the stakes each week?" Consistent with current educational studies, it was easy to observe how strongly the project approach increased interpersonal skills by motivating children to allocate tasks, to take collective responsibility for implementation, and to achieve success by following through.

Classes adopted trees and shrubs, kept records, and held birthday parties to celebrate each new planting. A Japanese fan dance was performed for the planting of an ornamental flowering plum tree. On Arbor Day, greetings adorned new arrivals wishing them long and prosperous lives. At Christmas, young redwoods were decorated with colored paper, tinted autumn leaves, and late-blooming flowers. Children drew sketches showing how they thought the trees would look in ten, twenty-five, fifty, and one hundred years. In cross-sectional views, they showed roots spreading through the soil, sun shining on the leaves, rain and hoses providing water, and animals taking shelter. Leaf displays became increasingly diverse in size and shape, indicating that the mixed woodland was becoming well established.

Opportunities to practice language skills constantly arose. Staff from the Urban Integral House helped one class write an "ecodrama" in which students played the sun, water, air, soil, and earthworms.[2] Another class composed a "tree haiku" on a large sheet of paper:

> Sun up, tree grows
> No water, tree dies
> Birds disappear
> No paper

LIFE IN THE TREES

"We love to play up in the trees," comments George. "Our favorite one is over by the pond where all the frogs go hopping round and make new frogs. It's a good tree because it's so hard to climb that no one else can get up there; or if they can, we're already down and long gone."

George's tree was an alder by the waterfall. Children were always climbing it, sometimes to the top, where they hung from branches and pretended to be monkeys. Some of the more anxious teachers forbade climbing. Others, knowing it would happen anyway once they turned their backs, insisted that children take their time, exercise care, and stay close to the trunk where branches were strongest.

"We call it the 'roller coaster,'" continues George, "because you can climb up inside, then out along one of the branches and slide down the outside."

"Yahoo, yahoo," a boy yells as he swings from one of the pendulous weeping willow fronds across the narrow band of water by the bridge.

"Boy, I went way over there," shouts another. "I'm the Amazing Spiderman."

A succession of boys jump for the fronds. Sometimes they succeed; sometimes they fail. One boy swings in circles and attempts all types of tricks. A bird comes along and lands on the branch. The boys stop swinging and watch the bird for several minutes. They start swinging again as the bird flies away.

"I'm an experienced climber," says Tyrone. "I'm not afraid. I've climbed about three hundred trees in my seven years of life. There's a pine tree that we climb way up to the top where there's lots of room 'cause it's all flattened out (because it was "topped"). Four of us can get up there at one time because there's so many branches under us. We used some boards to make a treehouse there. It's our favorite hideout."

TIME LAYERING

As Yard vegetation became firmly established and increased in physical diversity, the time dimension of the landscape became more diversified and visible. At one end of the temporal scale were the annual cycles of flowers and vegetables. Radishes, for instance, produced edible results in a couple of weeks. At the other extreme was the one-time planting of redwoods for the next several millennia. Who can say which end of the greening spectrum was more significant? Temporal layering was the best way to accentuate a wide range of impacts: the impact of a grove of trees on succeeding generations of children over hundreds of years at one extreme; the cumulative effect of each generation of children daily baptizing their hands in the dirt at the other.

At the other end of the bridge was a large Bailey acacia that had self-seeded itself beside the sitting log. This resilient specimen, with its low-slung, almost horizontal branches, made an ideal climbing tree for younger children. A group always seemed to be playing on it. The tree was so tough and grew so rapidly that within four years it became a living jungle gym, offering more varied, bouncy, shady perches than the rigid, metal monkey bars in the Main Yard.

COMPACT COUNTRYSIDE

Within a few years, the Yard became an engaging polymorphy of trees, bushes, and groundcovers. Settings such as the meadow, Chaparral Hill, and redwood grove offered special play and learning opportunities. Stimulated by the Yard's diverse natural resources and encouraged by imaginative teachers, a conservation ethic began to emerge in the children's classroom work.

"A lot of kids have learned how to respect plants and not pull them out," a child wrote. "They've figured out that animals live in certain areas. Kids enjoy the Yard, so they won't destroy it."

Other children used the plants as resources.

"The cattails are nice and furry, I like to feel them," says Alice. "I picked some after school once and took them home to my mother. She still has them in a vase. The stems are all dried up, but not the other parts (flower heads). I don't usually pick them. I just look at them. Most of the time you can't reach them, anyway. My mom thought it was neat . . . She put them together with flowers that live forever. They're like paper flowers, but they're not. I like it in the spring when all the flowers bloom."

The Yard connected home and school. It was a place where imaginations soared, where children invented their own world, where education nurtured mind, body, and spirit.

"There's a forest in our neighborhood," writes a third grader in a classroom assignment about special places in the neighborhood. "If you're lonely you can go in there and think to yourself. Whenever I feel like thinking I like to go to a dark place to concentrate where no one is. When I'm alone in the trees, I feel I'm in a big, big country all by myself. When I see little bugs, I pretend they're deer and big animals. I pretend I'm on a farm all by myself. Whenever I see a path, I walk down it. I pretend that I'm walking down the road to a whole bunch of apple trees to go apple picking."

"I like to get lost in there," writes another. "It feels like I'm hiking with my Dad."

NURSING THE VEGETATION

To ensure that the delicate microhabitats were able to withstand hundreds of children's feet each day, standard approaches to landscape design and management were modified to protect the plantings during the critical two-year nursing period.[3] Carefully designed procedures made the vegetation as accessible as possible, while protecting it enough to ensure survival.

Installed as environmental protection devices, curving eucalyptus-pole fences defined main pathways and channeled movement through, between, and around plant communities. It was fascinating to observe the rapid growth of plants along the fence lines, especially in the moist, shady spots around each post. The effect was so pronounced that if the fencing had been removed, the layout of the entire area could have been read in the fluorescent green lines of wild plants and grasses. To protect new plantings from getting trampled, secondary fences were installed within main zones such as the redwoods and Chaparral Hill. This treatment of spaces within spaces inhibited rapid movement, though still allowed children to use the areas as hideouts and camps.

Stakes were used extensively as protective measures, especially for the young shrubs that could easily get trampled. Each tree was protected with three two-inch-by-two-inch stakes and rubber loops or bindings of heavy-duty garden tape. In particularly vulnerable locations, stakes were nailed together with one-by-four-inch struts, placing the tree in a wooden "cage." As unattractive as the protection was, it worked.

The combined effect of soil amendment, fencing, staking, and close spacing of trees paid off in the rapid establishment of plant communities. Most trees survived their infant years. Every object that disturbed the smooth flow of movement across the ground surface had a protective effect. Every staked tree became a pedestrian "traffic diverter." At the same time, the amended soil at the base of each tree became a receptive microhabitat where groundcovers took hold before advancing from under their protective tree mantles.

Meadow rocks became cradled in green halos of plants, as nature transformed them from alien objects into ecological niches for increasing numbers of micro-

SOME COMMON BUTTERFLIES AND THEIR FOOD PLANTS

West coast lady	Mallow
Painted lady	Thistle
Red admiral	Nettle
Virginia lady	Everlasting
Common checkerspot	Bee plant
Buckeye	Plantain
Mylitta crescent	Thistle
Satyr angelwings	Nettle
Mourning cloak	Willow, cottonwood
California tortoiseshell	Ceanothus
Lorquin's admiral	Willow, cottonwood
California sister	Canyon oak, coast live oak
Gulf fritillary	Passion vine
Flying pansy	False indigo
Orange tips	Mustards
Cloudless sulfur	Senna
Western tiger swallowtail	Willow, cottonwood
Pale swallowtail	California coffee berry
Blue swallowtail	Dutchman's pipe vine
Anise swallowtail	Anise (fennel)
Monarch	Milkweed

organisms. Children sometimes dislodged and moved the lighter rocks, hoping to find worms for fishing expeditions. Each relocation produced more green halos that overlapped with others, thereby extending the carpet of vegetation. We had selected rocks in the 140- to 160-pound range for this exact purpose; lighter rocks would have been moved around too easily, while heavier ones would not have been moved at all.

MEADOWLAND MANAGEMENT

To achieve the effect of a softly bounded flowing meadow, the invincible adobe-like soil of the Yard was dosed with truckloads of tree leaves donated by the city parks department. The soil was tilled with tractor-drawn equipment operated by the UC Agricultural Extension Service. The California-based Clyde Robin Seed Company prepared wildflower mixes suited to the Yard's particular combination of moisture, temperature, and light conditions. Each fall, the seeds were sown around each new tree and shrub, as well as in the microhabitats along the fence lines and around rocks and logs. The result was a springtime blaze of red flax and golden California poppies intermingled with patches of blue flax and fluffy white Shasta daisies. Thrusting spiky heads of Fuller's teasel and occasional columns of giant yellow evening primrose punctuated the meadow and added color to the native flowering shrubs around its edge. The sensory impact heightened each succeeding spring; it was hard to imagine a more dramatic contrast to the former asphalt desert.

After a few years, however, the meadow became so attractive that it took the brunt of active play. Worn patches appeared, jarring adult aesthetic sensibilities. Instead of accepting the wear as inevitable, we tried to counteract it by planting extremely tough Bermuda and kikuya grasses. Unfortunately, these species rapidly invaded the meadow and eventually crowded out most of the wildflowers, reducing the biodiversity. Nevertheless, the thickly matted, green meadow did look nice. And to bring balance back to the meadow, we planted narcissus, iris, and native bulbs, which flowered above the grass each spring in a showy display of golds, blues, yellows, and whites.

Thus we learned a once-and-for-all lesson, that our laissez-faire, happy-go-lucky approach towards vegeta-

tion establishment was not always the most effective. We realized that a carefully considered managerial approach was necessary to achieve equitable trade-offs between people and plants.

•

At some point during the greening process, we realized that we were indeed creating a new form of recreative-educative urban landscape. Even though achieving this environment had always been our core objective, the Yard was far more complex and dynamic than we had ever imagined. The remarkable variety of vegetation, ranging from stately trees to common weeds, brought a special richness to the site. The children's active, hands-on interaction with the vegetation added to the vitality in the Yard—in stark contrast to the formal, "hands-off" plantings around the perimeter of the school.

While some components in the Yard were designed by children and some by educators, in actuality the two sets of proposals exhibited few differences. Both groups wanted to see the establishment of a natural environment. The diversity of vegetation stimulated a hands-on playing and learning style. Together, they offered tremendous opportunities in all three realms of education: informal, formal, and nonformal. The significance of vegetation for child development was arguably the most important lesson of the whole Yard enterprise.

REFERENCES

1. Johnston, J. (1990). *Nature Areas for City People*. London: London Ecology Unit.

2. Farallones Institute (1979). *The Integral Urban House*. San Francisco: Sierra Club Books.

3. For more details about these techniques, see Moore, R. C., S. M. Goltsman, and D. S. Iacofano, eds. (1992). *Play For All Guidelines: Planning, Design, and Management of Outdoor Play Settings for All Children*. 2nd ed. Berkeley, Calif.: MIG Communications.

Hands in the Dirt

"We planted a garden. First we cleaned away the grass. Then we dug up the soil. We made a big hole. We put in water to make it soft. We made planting beds. We grew plants inside. When they were ready, we put them in the planting bed. We have carrots, peas, radishes and tomatoes."
— Valerie
Washington School Nature News

We knew from the UC Berkeley Agricultural Experimental Station circular that gardening activities took place in or adjacent to the Washington schoolyard around the beginning of the century.[1] Old photographs from the school district archives showed the site still being cultivated in the 1920s. In one picture, girls were thrusting rakes and hoes into the dirt, as boys hammered away constructing the roof of animal hutches. What had happened to these gardens? At some point, educational priorities had shifted. Gardening went out of fashion, and blacktop dominated everything else, perhaps as part of a post-WWII, neat-and-tidy approach. Our goal in the 1970s was to reintroduce the natural environment as an interactive educational resource, with gardening as a leading strategy. If schools had had gardens so long ago, it did not seem especially radical or impractical to reintroduce the idea fifty years later.

Gardening provided an easy way for teachers to initiate interdisciplinary environmental education, making a direct connection between indoor and outdoor learning. From the earliest days, gardening attracted more involvement from teachers and university students than any other Yard activity. For children, it was a direct channel to the planet's biological processes and served as a first step towards acquiring sustainable development values.

THE FIRST PATCH OF DIRT

The idea of gardening in the Yard so excited the public relations director of a major San Francisco corporation that he sent several truckloads of topsoil to the site and personally delivered hand tools and packets of seeds for the children. Space was set aside near classroom windows to sprout seedlings in milk cartons and other dairy containers. These carefully tended horticultural corners produced quick results. Lines of children, gently cradling seedlings, soon emerged from the school building. They planted the seedlings along one edge of the Yard next to a chainlink fence, where a ten-foot-wide (3 m) strip of asphalt had been removed and replaced with topsoil. Patches of marigolds, pansies, snapdragons, and daisies began to bloom, alternating with rows of the classic vegetables of a child's garden: radishes, carrots, squash, and green beans.

ENVIRONMENTAL PROTECTION

The initial dirt-patch gardens were difficult to sustain. Irrigation water had to be carried from a single spigot on the side of the building, a major task for the young children. Furthermore, the best planting spots were also the best places for dirt play, an irresistible activity for children wanting to explore the environment. Unfortunately, this play often came at the expense of the gardens.

Balls from nearby games also got into the gardens and damaged the seedlings. In response, the children and teachers—like intelligent farmers—decided to enclose their land. Ecology Action, a local community organization, delivered a load of used lumber and helped classes build a fence to protect the garden strip from the adjacent kickball area. By planting close to the fence or between the pickets where ballplayers could not tread, children discovered that plants would flourish. They saw that those planted in the middle of the plot, even when protected by well-driven stakes, had fewer chances of survival.

Despite their vulnerability, the early gardens were a crucial first step. They were the source of ample learning, from which permanent gardens evolved as we experimented with different survival techniques. To improve irrigation efficiency, we laid a water line along the strip, with a separate spigot for each classroom plot—a major improvement. Along another chainlink fence, we used sections of discarded sewer pipe to create elevated planting beds, which protected the plants from trampling feet.

COMPOSTING

The next variable to tackle was soil quality. In the early days, soil in the Yard consisted either of adobe-like clay or sandy loam trucked over from San Francisco. Both lacked organic matter and drained either too fast in the case of loam or too slow in the case of clay. And under the sun, both became as hard as furnace lining. The solution to this problem was to start composting.

Ecology Action conducted afterschool workshops for teachers to learn how to make simple jam-jar compost piles. The teachers then taught this activity to children as an initial step in observing and understanding the decomposition process.

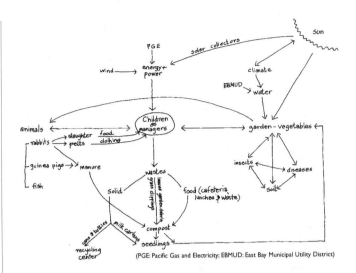

(PGE: Pacific Gas and Electricity; EBMUD: East Bay Municipal Utility District)

GARDEN ECOSYSTEMS

Gardens have two great advantages as educational resources. They can easily be managed by primary-aged children, who will readily assume ownership and responsibility. Second, they can easily be connected to other levels and elements of the ecosystem—ranging from sunlight to cafeteria waste.

"Carrots are really like roots. Beans are vegetables and so are radishes. Worms help grind up the soil. The top isn't all of the plant. It has roots, but we don't eat that part. It's all really simple once you know about it."

— Dana
Washington School Nature News

Turning the compost introduced cooperative learning and was good exercise! "Worms are useful. They make the soil soft, so it's easier for the plants to breathe. When we planted the plant I saw a lot of worms. Some worms aren't helpful. Some are. I like worms. Some people don't like worms. Some people say they are not useful. But they are."

The second step was to construct a simple compost box in the garden strip. Measuring about three feet (90 cm) square and two feet (60 cm) high, the box was constructed from four pieces of recycled plywood and decorated with children's paintings of composting organisms. A special song written by the children with Ecology Action's assistance made the compost-turning a special event. Everyone danced around the box, singing greetings to the worms and bacteria.

The following year, two university students replaced the primitive box with a professional, tri-compartmented upgrade. They worked on the construction closely with the children, who loved the opportunity to work with adults and create a project using real tools. This was an important demonstration of the value of university involvement in the Yard, where adult students provided the kind of early real-life experiences that today are so often inaccessible to urban children. And the university students reaped the educational benefits of working directly with children.

One class conducted a simple experiment to demonstrate the effect of composting on garden productivity. The children planted beans in three pots with different contents: dirt from the Yard, dirt from the landscape strip in front of the school, and compost. The accelerated growth rate of the bean in compost made a dramatic point.

Turning the ripening compost became a popular afterschool activity. Students from the university's experimental urban horticulture facility worked several times a week with the children. The process included layering new batches of compost, soaking them down, taking the temperature of decomposition, turning the compost from one compartment to another, and marveling with the children at the heat and steam. Slowly, the weeds, rabbit droppings, riding stable manure, apple cores, half-eaten sandwiches, and cafeteria waste transformed into a rich brown humus ready for recycling into the ground. Previously, food scraps had gone directly into the school's unpleasant-smelling dumpster. Now, through composting, they helped the healthy rows of lettuce, carrot, beet, and chard. By the end of the summer, a sprawling squash plant had spread its great translucent leaves up and over the boundary fence.

Children conducted their own scientific investigations with the steamy compost box. For instance, they were fascinated by the decomposition of an apple tucked underneath the top layer, peeking at it every few days as it transformed from a hard red object to watery slush.

Other students liked the worms, eagerly fingering them, not with squeals of "ugh," "yuk," and "yeck," but with comments like "Hey, I found a f-a-t one!" One class constructed an earthworm farm from a gallon-sized glass pickle jar covered with black paper to simulate darkness. The paper was removed periodically so the children could observe the worms in their microhabitat churning away at the layers of soil, filling them with the air that is so essential to plant growth. The children learned that the worms were important soil makers, processing dirt and waste material that passed through their bodies.

A group of children, viewing themselves as coworkers in the soil-making process, formed a club called the Composting Agents, advertising themselves with handmade badges. They designed posters that announced, "Recycle Your Waste!" Each noon the Composting Agents brought buckets of lunchtime scraps to add to the compost box.

THE HAPPY GREENHOUSE

Another innovative step was an indoor gardening center set up by a landscape architecture student in a vacant classroom. To create a growing chamber, a section of recycled close-boarded fence was laid across four desks pushed up against classroom windows. Children helped construct side frames of two-by-fours to support shelving. The whole structure was covered with broad sheets of translucent polyethylene to create an enclosed, warm, humid microclimate within the larger space of the classroom. Children painted a colorful paper skirt around the base of the structure, proclaiming it the "Happy Greenhouse."

Indoor plants soon began to flow from the greenhouse to the classrooms, the gardens in the Yard, and the children's homes. University students helped children make pressed-flower Christmas decorations to hang in windows. Children constructed terraria from one-gallon wine bottles, and designed "plate gardens" on old dinner plates (bought for pennies at a local thrift store). The miniature landscapes consisted of soil, sand, rocks,

THE HAPPY GREENHOUSE

"If I look in a garden, what do I see? I see plants, big plants, little plants, and flowers."
— Jennifer
Washington School Nature News

The message board in the main corridor updated the school community about upcoming events.

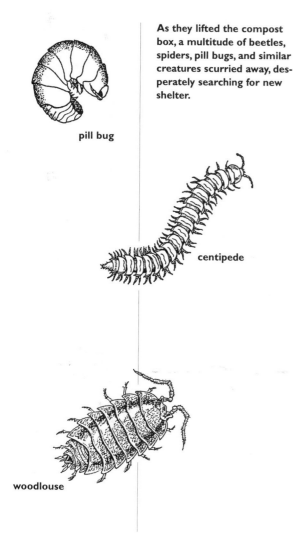

pill bug

As they lifted the compost box, a multitude of beetles, spiders, pill bugs, and similar creatures scurried away, desperately searching for new shelter.

centipede

woodlouse

sticks, dried seed heads, fungi, mosses, pieces of colored glass, aluminum foil, flower heads, petals, and small clusters of leaves. Some children incorporated plastic animals, action figures, and toy cars.

FROM STRIP TO ENCLOSURE

Despite the valiant effort to protect the garden strip, the fencing was still not enough. Classrooms held meetings to discuss the problem. Ballplayers were urged to be more careful. For a while, children and teachers were hopeful that the gardens would flourish. But the plants continued to get trampled, and spirits dropped to a new low. People were reluctant to abandon the investment of compost box, irrigation line, and fencing, but a new site was needed before the gardening efforts died completely.

A fenced compound on the other side of the Yard—originally used for storage and more recently converted into a temporary barnyard (see Chapter 13)—became the most practical alternative. With support from a federal environmental education grant, a team of parents and teachers converted the former pig pen into a potting shed.

To relocate the compost box, a work crew of university students loosened it from its foundations. As they lifted the box, a multitude of beetles, spiders, pill bugs, and salamanders scurried away, desperately searching for new shelter. Such moments were good reminders of the increased diversity and ecological interdependencies that even then were part of the Yard.

BREAKTHROUGH:
AN OUTDOOR RESOURCE TEACHER

The federal grant enabled us to appoint Tom Armour as a full-time *outdoor* resource teacher. For several years, Tom had been the indoor resource teacher. Working out of a basement studio, he had created a place where every student could use tools and materials for hands-on projects. In this special position, with salary support culled from several sources, Tom knew all the children and had developed a good rapport with the entire teaching staff.

Tom's practical experience and schoolwide scope made him ideally qualified for his new job: to connect class groups and community resource people, to acquire printed and audio-visual curriculum material, and to find sources for tools, equipment, plants, and seeds. Using the new garden as his headquarters and the whole Yard as his classroom, Tom coordinated the energies of teachers and community volunteers in a clearly defined indoor-outdoor educational program.

GARDEN LOGS

One of the activities coordinated by Tom were the gardening groups who recorded their daily activities in "garden logs."

"Today we tied up the peas and planted garlic. It's good for wounds. You can use it for toothpaste and to keep mosquitoes away," wrote one student, after conducting library research.

Another noted: "We found a pupa on a cabbage leaf . . . I like to watch the bugs eat the vegetables."

Children were encouraged to view micro-organisms as an important part of the garden eco-system—as creatures that needed to eat. Unfortunately, their appetites made them garden pests, which led to discussions about the merits and disadvantages of vari-ous methods of pest management: "Wash them off . . . pick them off . . . stop them from getting on the plant in the first place . . . poison them . . . get something else to eat them . . . or just leave them alone and not be bothered by a few holes in the lettuce leaves?"

Gardens provided the most direct source of chil-dren's emotional involvement with living systems. They accommodated every stage of the learning cycle, stimu-lated by a diversity of flowers and vegetables, constantly changing, interacting with their surroundings, adapting to new circumstances as children counted, measured, observed, described, interpreted, and recorded different plants' growing habits—sideways, upwards, in all direc-tions, in one direction.

The gardens attracted a variety of seed-eating and insect-eating birds—finches, sparrows, juncos, black-birds, wrens, warblers, vireos, and kinglets. An excep-tionally well-dressed scarecrow was constructed in an attempt to thwart the birds' energetic blitzes on the gardens. The children recorded observations in their

My class and I have been working in our yard. We've been digging so we can plant seeds. We are making a map for the yard.

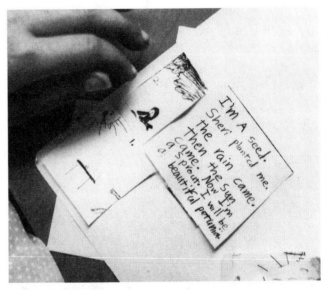

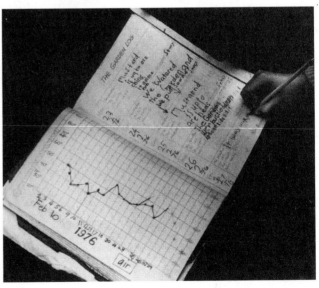

Children wrote stories about life in the garden (top, middle) and kept records of the garden's progress in "garden logs" (bottom).

I took a walk to the vegetable garden. It was hot. My nam is Jenn

FROM KATE GREENAWAY'S *LANGUAGE OF FLOWERS* [2]

Saffron	*Beware of excess.*
Saffron crocus	*Mirth.*
Meadow saffron	*My happiest days are past.*
Sage	*Domestic virtue.*
Garden sage	*Esteem.*
Sainfoin	*Agitation.*
St. John's-wort	*Animosity. Superstition.*
Sardony	*Irony.*
Mossy saxifrage	*Affection.*
Scabious	*Unfortunate love.*
Sweet scabious	*Widowhood.*
Scarlet lychnis	*Sun-beaming eyes.*
Schinus	*Religious enthusiasm.*
Scotch fir	*Elevation.*
Sensitive plant	*Sensibility. Delicate feelings.*
Senvy	*Indifference.*
Shamrock	*Light-heartedness.*
Snakesfoot	*Horror.*

Children used the garden to study math concepts.

journals and drew conclusions about the influence of the scarecrow on the birds' behaviors.

GARDEN EXTENSIONS

Although the enclosed garden became the center of activity, it is important to realize that gardening opportunities continued elsewhere in the Yard and even beyond its boundaries. The original strip garden was converted into a small orchard of fruit and nut trees, later called Orchard Wayside. On one side of the Yard's central play area, a giant planter was constructed out of split wooden utility poles. Other planters were made from upended sewer pipes; painted to depict favorite garden animals, they provided flower beds along the MLK Way boundary fence.

Along one side of the potting shed, a lean-to bean house was built from strips of scrap lumber. After a few weeks it turned into a shady green-veiled room dotted with scarlet runner bean flowers.

A plant propagation greenhouse was developed in an ancillary basement room with direct access to the Yard. Here, buckeye, hollyhock, mint, morning glory, passion vine, and pussy willow were duplicated from seeds and cuttings. Greenhouse seedlings became garden rows of beets, carrots, chard, and lettuce. Flower seeds scattered between the rows spotted the green vegetables with bright colors.

One year, a parent who was a professional gardener worked with classes on each of the hexagonal planting beds at the base of twenty trees planted in the remaining asphalt. Together they prepared the soil, planted annual alyssums and candytuft, sowed wildflower seeds, and made commitments to care for the small plots. The following year, every student planted a daffodil, narcissus, crocus, or grape hyacinth bulb in the beds. As a result, bright colors punctuated the gray asphalt each spring.

Gardening space was always limited. This forced a search for knowledge and ingenuity in improving soil quality; in dealing with irrigation and drainage; in understanding microclimate; in responding to seasonal cycles; and in using that scarcest of all resources, time, to the best advantage. The children demonstrated their newfound knowledge in occasional newsletters that followed the "Adventures of Gardenman." The newsletters went home to parents, accompanied with vegetable and flower seedlings to transplant.

"It means a great deal to children to take something they have created home to their parents," a teacher noted in her evaluation. "It's very educational . . . they're expanding the idea of ecology as something that includes people, the different ways in which we live, and our future well-being on this planet."

OFF-SITE CONNECTIONS

Once they had gained basic gardening experience, classes took field trips to explore other garden opportunities in the neighborhood. A couple who lived down the street had a raised-bed vegetable garden to compare with the Yard gardens. They also had chickens, rabbits, and a beehive producing tasty honey—experiences unavailable in the Yard.

On visits to the University's Oxford Tract experimental garden, children observed innovations that broadened the concept of a garden. Common houseflies were trapped in a fine mesh cage and fed to chickens (instead of corn, thus saving food that could be eaten by humans). Other favorite exhibits included an experimental fish farm, beehives, a rabbit colony, and a multitude of vegetables grown using intensive, high-yield methods— with composting as an essential element.

"I liked how the chicken manure was used for fertilizer," writes one child after visiting the University garden. "It's good for the plants and helps them grow better . . . I liked the artichokes, too (a reference to a tall stand of Jerusalem artichokes being promoted as a food source). They looked so funny."

One group returned from the garden with beautiful comfrey (*Symphytum officinale*) plants. Before long, their classroom garden was punctuated with heads of delicate blue-mauve flowers and large velvety leaves ready to steep in boiling water for a light, refreshing herbal tea. Mint tea competed with comfrey as the favorite brew. Some children experimented with a "Yard blend" of the two. The level of interest was so strong that a project called "Nature's Medicine Chest" was started. A "healing herb garden" of some fifteen species was designed, planted, and labeled by the children in a raised bed under the mulberry trees just outside the enclosed garden.

Children understood the medicinal and health properties of plants. The group of boys are busy preparing a "Yard brew" of herb tea.

THE CULTURE OF MINT

Peppermint and spearmint, are in the mint family, which includes sage, thyme, marjoram, basil, bergamot, pennyroyal, catnip, and yerba buena. All plants in this family are distinguished by their square stems.

Peppermint and spearmint are not native to the Americas but to the Mediterranean. They were brought to the United States by early settlers.

Mint has been important in many cultures for centuries. Early Egyptians, Romans, and Greeks were accustomed to using mint to rub into their dining "boards" and also as a table decoration. The use of mint sauce has also been recorded as early as the third century.*

In the sixth century, mint was important as a tooth cleansing preparation and for medicinal purposes. For example, mint is said to be a diaphoretic (producing or increasing perspiration) and a carminative (expelling gas from the stomach and intestine). In Balkan countries, mint tea is called "nana" and, in Portugal, "char."

In the Middle East, it is a tradition to send out a boy to buy mint tea when a guest or visitor arrives. He returns with tiny china cups of sweetened tea on a large, round, brass tray, which is passed around to all present.

Peppermint and spearmint can be easily grown from a cutting: place the sprig in water until roots appear, then plant in moist soil. Mint plants prefer shade and plenty of moisture and some people grow a plant right under their garden faucet.

*Mint sauce: Mix one cup of vinegar, half a cup of water, and one tablespoon each of sugar and finely chopped fresh mint. Let stand for one hour.

— Helen Cox, classroom notes

GARDENING, COOKING, AND LEARNING

Gardening, cooking, and nature crafts integrated educational objectives into an experiential and skill building setting. All children, regardless of ability level, participated in these activities. Nutrition, energy alternatives, and food self-sufficiency were underlying themes. During weekly sessions, children learned to harvest and use the produce for food or crafts and to prepare the garden for the seasonal cycles ahead. On a typical day, pole beans would be tied up, weeds pulled, and samples pressed into an art project. Vegetables would be chopped and stir-fried in a wok over a campfire built by the children.

All cooking sessions used produce from the garden or wild edibles from the Yard. Measuring, fractions, estimating, and adding were some of the mathematical objectives reinforced.

— Project **PLAE** summer program log

YOU ARE WHAT YOU EAT!

A major educational benefit of gardening was the development of skills in growing, buying, and preparing food. Activities ranged from grocery shopping to growing vegetables, reading and writing recipes, cooking and eating, math and language, and concepts of nutritional science and health.

Classroom investigations delved into different food groups, the seasonal cycle of reproduction, the problem of keeping foods fresh, and transportation costs. Children conducted surveys at local stores to compare the market prices of vegetables with the costs of garden-grown vegetables. Older students researched different countries where food comes from and researched the processes of production. It was a vivid demonstration of the interdependency of foreign markets.

"What can we do with all this food? We can't eat it all at once. How can we keep it from going bad?" Methods of food preservation and processing were explored: canning, bottling, jams and jellies. Nuts and seeds were identified as nature's method of preservation.

An experimental "solar dryer"—a half-dozen slatted shelves supported on runners in a plywood box made by university students—was installed in the garden. The front of the box was covered by a sheet of solar-gain plastic. Circular ventilation holes allowed air to circulate through the trays. The back of the box slid up to allow removal of the trays. The children discovered that the dryer brought quick and tasty results with various fruit. Enough batches were made that even the most skeptical child was convinced that it was a feasible idea. Most children knew how expensive dried fruit was at the store.

Vegetables were harvested to make soups and stews to accompany hot-dog and marshmallow roasts over open fires. Even on uncomfortably hot summer days, children thrilled to the experience of outdoor cooking. As shade trees grew larger and improved the microclimate, cooking became a firmly established Yard activity.

•

Looking back, it is sobering to realize that nearly ten years elapsed between the primitive dirt-patch gardens and the first harvest from the raised beds in the enclosed garden. During that time, three generations of children learned from the gardens. In the early days they discovered how to reclaim an asphalt desert and make it productive. Pioneering parents and university students shared in the discovery; they were the heroes of the gardens, whose voluntary labor made possible the creative programs and abundant harvests of later years. Eventually, a vast array of plants was available for food, for medicinal purposes, and for making the Yard more attractive for all users.

Gardening was at the leading edge of community participation in the development of the Yard. The activity provided evidence of progress when all else seemed to be at a standstill. Garden projects had the unique capacity to generate a collective sense of purpose through the shared experience of getting one's hands in the soil. No other activity duplicated such an intimate combination of freedom of expression and discipline. For teachers, it provided opportunities to connect individual personality, aesthetic expression, culture, and geography more closely than in other areas of the curriculum. In this sense, one may indeed speak of the pedagogy of gardening.

As vehicles for interdisciplinary environmental education, gardens are unsurpassed. They provide a constantly changing, highly attractive, motivational setting—a fertile source of expression and scientific investigation. Gardening is a direct way for people to acquire an awareness of themselves as part of the Earth's life-support system. The time-lapsed scale of the garden is especially attractive to children. A bean tentacle spiraling up a pole, popping flowers that become dangling clusters of delectable green flesh, is the type of small-scale, natural event that will enthrall children and motivate them to seek the answers to "why?" and "how?"

Gardener Alan Chadwick once said, "It is not the gardener that makes the garden but the garden that makes the gardener. For us, it worked both ways.

REFERENCES

1. Babcock, E. B. (1909). *Suggestions for Garden Work in California Schools.* Berkeley, Calif.: The University Press (Circular No. 46, UC Agricultural Experiment Station).

2. Greenaway, K. (1884). *Language of Flowers.* Reprinted by Gramercy Publishing Co., New York, 1978.

Like Diamonds Melting

Thoreau wrote of White Pond and Walden as "great crystals on the surface of the earth, Lakes of Light. If they were permanently congealed, and small enough to be clutched, they would ... be carried off ... like precious stones ... but being liquid and ample, and secured to us and our successors forever, we disregard them, and run after the diamond of Kohinoor. They are too pure to have a market value; they contain no muck. How much more beautiful than our lives, how much more transparent than our characters, are they!"

His reference to the ponds as "precious stones" is similar to one of the children's thoughts that the Yard's waterfall was "like diamonds melting." How wise of Thoreau to have imagined as a child the wonders of nature!

Water provided an extraordinary stimulus for playing and learning in the Yard. Its power to attract children reflected the truth that all life depends on water, a substance that covers three-fourths of the Earth's surface. Water was a popular play material because of its sensory and manipulative qualities and the broader attraction of the plants and animals supported by its life-giving properties. The naturally diverse aquatic habitats had high educational potential for teaching the basic principles of life.

The aquatic settings of the Yard were created with relative ease; or rather, they created themselves with our design assistance. In the end, these settings more than fulfilled their educational promise. Ironically, they were also the most contentious element and several times had to be protected from uninformed, negative actions by the school district's maintenance department.

CONSERVATION

As in most schools, the site planning of Washington had paid little heed to the water cycle. On average, twenty-two inches (56 cm) of rain fell on the site each year, enough to fill the school building from top to bottom. Yet, as on any parking lot, the runoff was dispatched as quickly as possible down the nearest drain, through storm sewers into San Francisco Bay. This traditional engineering solution bypassed several critical stages of the natural hydrological cycle: soil percolation, collection into aquifers (underground reserves), absorption by plant root systems, migration through the leaves as water vapor into the air, and eventual return to the earth as precipitation. Through this natural process, toxic substances could be biologically filtered out at every step along the way, instead of becoming concentrated in the Bay.

Increasing public awareness of this cycle had been a focus of water quality and conservation efforts for many years in California, a state plagued with reoccurring droughts. Water conservation was an obvious early childhood educational priority. Children themselves had voted strongly for water in the Yard.

Teachers also emphasized the value of aquatic settings, noting that they provided rich biological environments that could be used with existing curricular materials.

Even so, they were not exactly sure how to integrate water into their daily lesson plans. Naturally, some teachers were also concerned about the potential problems with students getting wet and muddy, and asked the designers to carefully consider the practical aspects of classroom use. An encouraging number of parents wanted aquatic features, but many assumed they were impractical.

Strong negative reactions to the idea of introducing a water element came from the school district's maintenance department and insurance carriers, as well as the city's public health department (see Health and Safety Tangles sidebar). Their concerns heightened the challenge of designing an aquatic environment of lasting play and learning value.

SOURCES

To increase our knowledge on these issues, we visited a number of aquatic settings in the Bay Area (both indigenous and people-made) and consulted numerous experts, including a biologist who had experimented with ponds at several local schools.

In an earlier schoolyard renovation project at another local school, two small ponds had been constructed by Robin's landscape architecture students. They became a favorite place for children and were well used by teachers for classroom projects. The ponds, however, were too small to withstand the heavy impact of dozens of children. Ponds in the Yard, we realized, had to be a lot larger to achieve a balance between children's play, classroom use, ecological diversity, and aesthetic appearance. There was no point in creating something so fragile that it would need constant protection from its primary users. On the other hand, a diversity of plants and animals was essential and required protection.

Another helpful contact was the regional water utility district, an agency eager to introduce its water conservation efforts into the school system. Their community relations officer conducted workshops with the teachers to educate them about the regional water supply system, the statistics about local consumption, and the need for household conservation. The group brainstormed on how to integrate this information into the curriculum (see Dripping Faucet sidebar).

HEALTH AND SAFETY TANGLES

Although the ponds and creek presented several challenges, they were well worth the time and effort, as witnessed by the many positive reactions following their full installation. Like any project involving many partners and levels of political approval, careful consideration had to be given to such issues as gaining the consent of school authorities, managing state and local policy regulations, and incorporating these elements into the overall vision.

Water was a critical issue in the development of the Yard. Given the natural processes involved in the evolution of handmade ponds and streams, it is easy to see how some officials might have been concerned. For example, standing water over a period of time could cause some public officials to be alarmed—particularly those from the public health department.

Such was the case with the Yard. Water samples had to be taken, insurance issues covered and, in general, positive public perceptions maintained. Somehow, we worked through the potential roadblocks; for instance, by changing the language (referring to the early ponds as "environmental learning puddles").

We also discovered support in unlikely places. For instance, the county mosquito abatement officer (whom we thought would voice strong objections to the project) became one of our advocates. He applauded the idea of children learning about aquatic life first hand. "If everyone grew up with this kind of educational experience," he said, "my job would be a lot easier. Instead, I have to deal with a public who by and large knows nothing about pond life, and certainly can't tell the difference between good and bad aspects."

By keeping an open mind, we were able to turn a politically sensitive (and potentially damaging) situation into a positive one. This was the case with the mosquito abatement official. He presented us with a list of local aquatic sites where we could find aquatic specimens and suggested putting mosquito fish into the ponds to control the larvae that had begun to collect in our "starter" ponds. His overall attitude was an open-minded one. Referring to general concern about the mosquitoes, his advice was "let's wait and see if it becomes a problem."

THE DRIPPING FAUCET

Do you know how many gallons can be wasted in twenty-four hours through a single dripping faucet? It is an excellent problem for children to figure out.

Approx. 13 gallons (50 l)

Water brought special experiences to the Natural Resource Area: the sound and light of cascading water (top); the "what if" testing of boats in the stream (middle right); and the counting and classifying of new wetland vegetation (bottom right).

PRELIMINARY PUDDLES

After several months of preliminary investigation, we were still unsure about the feasibility of constructing ponds in the Yard. As a result, we experimented with a rough-graded, bare-bones scheme that could be later modified or scrapped if it did not work. The regional parks district supplied a bulldozer and an operator, who spent several days contouring two bowl-like depressions in the Natural Resource Area.

On a hot, lazy afternoon in July, we filled the lower pond with water to see what would happen. The result was dramatic; we were not prepared for such a big response. That same afternoon, a mother sat beside the pond and watched benignly as her two young children undressed and frolicked in the water. A group of older children, in cut-offs or underpants, floated around in the water on sheets of plywood and a couple of logs. The following day the children were there again—until a resident in the adjacent apartment building complained that the activity was unhealthy (at least this was the presumption, as the water had not been tested). To be on the safe side, bodily contact with the water was discouraged and the pond was allowed to gradually evaporate away during the rest of the summer. However, when the rain returned in the fall, both ponds filled up and provided us with another opportunity to monitor aquatic activity.

Indigenous aquatic plants began to take hold, creating a green necklace along the edge of each water surface. Teachers were quick to pick up on this "oasis effect" and marshaled their students' interest in conducting population studies of the plants to monitor progress.

Outside class, children made bridges from wooden boards, constructed toy boats, and even tried to build rafts large enough to support themselves in the water. They threw rocks and pieces of wood into the water to observe the splashing and rippling effects. Their fascination and creativity clearly indicated the educational potential of aquatic environments to stimulate problem-solving and thinking skills. Eventually, the aquatic system became the most powerful stimulator of behavior and linchpin of the Natural Resource Area. But the initial form was crude. The two inelegant puddles needed to be developed further and become a more diverse, fine-tuned aquatic ecosystem.

TWO PONDS AND A RIVER

Encouraged by the positive response from children and teachers and by the apparent technical feasibility, we proceeded with the design of a more substantial, self-sustaining aquatic system (even though the maintenance and liability issues had not been laid to rest). The final proposal was to construct two ponds, each thirty to forty feet (9 to 12 m) in diameter, with a fifty-foot (15 m) stream running between them. Running water was necessary to support children's play. The stream also reflected the natural creeks running down to the Bay from the East Bay Hills. Teachers suggested making one of the ponds large enough to locate a wildlife island sanctuary in the center. Hard-edged, cement-lined ponds were rejected as an alternative because they were too expensive; besides, we wanted an aquatic system that functioned as naturally as possible.

Many natural aquatic forms were included in the design: a curving creek; a beach or sand bar; a waterfall; a marsh; soft, muddy edges; hard, rocky edges; treelined banks; open banks; abrupt changes between land and water; bridges and stepping stones; promontories; peninsulas; inlets; islands; gorges; reedy places; springs; and open water. All of these elements had to evolve naturally, though the setting also had to accommodate the vitality of children's play. We did not want to create an overprotected, static "aquatic museum," but rather a system of microhabitats that children could explore without seriously damaging the plants and animals.

CHARLIE AND HIS D6

The final grading of the Natural Resource Area could not have happened without Charlie and his D6 bulldozer. To save money, it had to be done in five days without removing any dirt from the site or importing any new material.

Charlie was an expert, experienced operator. "Just show me the model," he said.

We looked over the simple contour model together and marked with surveyors' stakes the main lines of the design on the ground. Charlie got to work scraping, pushing, pulling the dirt, fingers deftly dancing on the controls, making the great lumbering D6 obey his slightest whim. He

was a master dirt-shaper. Large rocks, donated by the regional parks district, were maneuvered into place at strategic points on the curve of the creek and around a promontory in the lower pond (the future Willow Island). Several of the largest were used to form the waterfall. One, extra long and flat, was ideally shaped for the primary cascade rock. It took Charlie hours to set it at the right height and angle in relation to the rocks on either side. Together, the rocks helped enhance the natural form of the new landscape and were the only way of creating small, clifflike niches in the otherwise smoothly flowing ground surface.

HELPING NATURE ALONG

Late autumn rains filled the reformed ponds, but the slightest disturbance churned up their muddy bottoms and made the water very turbid. To combat this, the water surface of both ponds was covered with a thick layer of leaves donated by the city's street sweeping crew. After a few days the leaves sank and formed an organic bottom layer to boost the naturalization of the ponds by improving water quality and providing a viable habitat for micro-organisms. The water became transparent overnight. The brown, leafy bottom was clearly visible, giving a feeling of connection between the ponds and the surrounding leaf-covered terrain.

To help the naturalization process along, we foraged the regional aquatic sites for plants and animals. Cattails, tule rushes, sedges, and brass buttons were brought from Berkeley's Aquatic Park on the Bay shore. Watercress was lifted from a small creek on the university campus. Hardy marsh pennywort, with its bright green circular leaves, came from a lake in Golden Gate Park. A fine specimen of water plantain was collected from Lake Hennessey in the Napa Valley, and soon became established in the lower pond, its soft spear-shaped leaves and sprays of delicate pink flowers thrusting elegantly above the water.

Willow Island was a small, rocky island-like peninsula jutting into the lower pond. Its lone weeping willow tree, visible from much of the Yard, was the first signal that vegetation was an integral part of the aquatic system. The redwoods followed, giving the impression of a creekside plantation growing above a rocky cliff. Willow cuttings were interspersed among the rocks

Water, with its highly sensory impact and constantly changing movement, provided the children with powerfully remembered play experiences. These experiences took on many dimensions, from the infinite possibilities of stream play (top), to playing "Poohsticks" from the bridge (middle), to exploring life systems (bottom). Regardless of the activity, the children were intrinsically connected to water's wonder, beauty, and calming force.

around the edge of the sand bar beach. They grew rapidly and provided a sense of enclosure to the whole creek area, now spotted with patches of golden brass buttons and white-flowering watercress along the shallow edges. Cattails and tules, which grew as tall as eight feet (2.4 m) high, spread vigorously along one side of the lower pond. On the other side, crimson water lilies punctuated the open water surface and survived for two seasons until they were shaded out by the white alders. These trees were planted on the banks of both ponds to create a pleasant microclimate. They were close enough to the water surface to cast green reflections, counteracting the dirt color when children churned up the water. The ponds started to look like part of the natural landscape.

The meeting of land and water was designed in some places with rocks and sedges, willow cuttings, and Japanese-style wooden pilings. In other places, edges were left to evolve more naturally—eroded by water, scalloped by children's digging operations, and invaded by lines of nut grass.

RUNNING WATER

The day finally arrived when the school district laid an underground electricity line connecting the school building to the pond pump, which had been installed to recirculate the water. An automatic timer was added so that the hours of pump operation could be regulated.

Several dozen children were on hand when the switch was thrown. Water gushed from the pipe in the center of the upper pond, for a few moments very muddy, then crystal clear. Within a few minutes, the upper pond level had risen the half inch (1.2 cm) needed to bring it to the level of the waterfall rock. Water edged its way across the flat surface. A few drops fell into dry sand below; first a trickle, then a flood of water fell, creating a little pool beneath the waterfall—a *real* waterfall, though just twelve inches (30 cm) high.

"It was like diamonds melting," a child wrote later.

The pond and creek were mysterious to some of the younger children. Where did the water come from? How did the stream work? They imagined a strange force, adapted from movies and television programs.

As if to confirm the imagined power of the running water, children used the waterfall as a favorite place for fantasy games using plastic figures of intergalactic travelers and spacecraft. The surface of the pond became interplanetary space, rippling from the top of the waterfall to the infinite shores of the further bank.

A group of children are playing space games there one day, moving space travelers and craft in and out of the water, flying them above the surface. Suddenly, the buoyant spacecraft is taken by the momentum of the water. It careens over the rock, crashing to destruction in the little pool below. But no!

"Gimme full power, we're gonna escape from this black hole of doom." A hand pounces on the craft, lifting it up over the waterfall in a triumphant arc.

There was a great temptation not to explain to the children how the system really worked, and let the illusion of a magical perpetual motion machine persist. On the other hand, older children were fascinated by the mechanics of the real system.

"Ya know," a girl said, as if sharing a closely guarded secret, the "ponds are connected. Yeah, they're put together with the creek, and there's a pump that pushes the water around again under the ground."

DOWN BY THE RIVER

The waterfall and creek attracted most of the water play away from the ponds and thus helped reduce environmental impacts around the pond edges. Considering how small the entire creek section was, it stimulated a remarkable range of activity.

A girl and boy are playing in the creek with a piece of wood. They use it as a raft, sailing it down the stream towards the beach. They take pieces of wood and a plastic spoon, throw them down the waterfall, watch them float downstream, but retrieve them before they reach the cement bridge. The girl calls it a "dragon tunnel" and says that others should not let their boats go in it. Another boy watches the bobbing imaginary crafts, runs off, gets a bigger piece of wood, calls it a "ship," and watches it plunge over the waterfall.

"We call it 'Bermuda Triangle' when we send boats down the waterfall," says Jeremy. "We shake the log in the middle of the pond to make all kinds of waves. The boat gets sucked into the rocks and looks sort of weird as it goes under the rock bridge. It gets trapped underneath and never comes out the other side."

"We have speedboat races with little sticks and woodchips *all* the way from the waterfall to the wooden bridge (a distance of forty feet [12 m])," says Rebecca. "When you have no one to play with, you can put a piece of wood in the creek and watch the water carry

The multiple use and constant interaction with water are wonderfully illustrated in the photographs above: a child sails a handmade boat down the "river," another "dams" up the creek to flood the "beach," and two others go "fishing" in the upper pond. Many adults forget their own play experiences with water (and mud); as a result, it is often difficult to convince themselves of the value of aquatic play to children's development.

it down" (noting how an interactive, natural environment can be a nonhuman playmate).

One of the boys uses a stick to dredge the main channel, scraping out the loose mud and sand and dumping it on one side.

"I'm clearing the creek to make my boat go faster, so it won't get stuck. I wanna win this race."

"What if everyone else's boat goes faster?" someone asks.

"That's a risk I'll have to take."

"Hey, get a leaf to make a sail," somebody shouts.

Anything floatable was used in the races: milk cartons, sticks, empty lunch trays, bits of bark, and "real" plastic boats. The games were very competitive.

"Mine's faster."

"I won."

"I was the champion!"

"No, I was the champ."

"I was!"

"I won everything."

"We tried a whole bunch of other boats but this one still won" says Jeff, holding a five-inch (13 cm) stick. "We call it the 'winner.' Tomorrow we'll get a piece of paper from class and stick it in here as the winning flag."

As much activity happened on the beach beside the creek as in the creek itself. As many as eighty children could be observed at one time building sandcastles and other molded sand forms. Access to sand and running water, combined with waterside debris and vegetation explained the attraction.

"It's fun to dam the river and watch it overflow and see the water run all over the place," says Dana gleefully. "I've made three dams today . . . yeah, out of boards and sticks and twigs."

The dams were positioned at the point where the creek entered the marshy redwood glade. Here, the bed narrowed and made the stream easy to block so the water backed up to the cement bridge, turning the normally rapidly flowing creek into a placid shallows. The stilled water reflected the adjacent redwoods in beautiful symmetry, creating the illusion of inverted trees growing down into the earth, their reflected forms blending with the beach on the further side. Surrounded by the pellmell of water play, a child stood apart, quietly observing the reflected trees, transfixed by the magical optics, trying to understand how it worked.

The children's interactions with the aquatic system took many forms. Each day new water-related activities appeared.

Later that day, Christine energetically pulls the dams apart and watches the water gush past the redwood glade into the lower pond.

"I'm clearing the creek," she explains. "It's flooded sometimes and when it dries out the fish get stuck, they never get through because the creek is too muddy where it goes through the cattails by the bridge (an accurate observation), so I try to clear it to let 'em through."

Her friends arrive on the scene.

"The fish are dying," she shouts. "Look, they're stuck in those little holes." The group responds with concern.

"Hurry, they're dying. Hurry, get some seaweed (parrot's feather), they're dying!"

"They need water!" one of the girls screams. "Leave the seaweed there 'cause they like to hide under it. The sun hurts their eyes."

"Let's get some clean water from the fountain."

"Look, he lives!"

"Look at that one, throw him back."

"I got one."

"No, you dropped him."

"He's dead. Hurry, look, there he is."

"Look, he's alive!"

"You saved his life!"

Meanwhile, the recirculating pump has been automatically turned on. The water starts spilling over the waterfall. The dam breaks. In vain the children try to block the water with more plants, but it doesn't work and the fish are washed downstream to the lower pond, just as they would have been eventually, regardless of the children's intervention. However, because of the dam, the children are able to exercise their moral concern for the fish—a nice parable of play.

FISHING

For a split second, as one approached the ponds, the water around the edges seemed to boil as hundreds of mosquito fish (*Gambusia*) picked up the footstep vibrations from more than ten feet (3 m) away and fled to deeper water. During the summer the fish bred many times faster than needed to fix the mosquito problem. Not only were they sensitive to human movement, they were extremely nimble as well. To stand a reasonable chance of landing a catch, children had to learn to be very patient, focus their attention, use their eyes, remain squatting motionless around the pond edge, poised above the water for many minutes, and move fast enough to match the fish's agility. It was a beautiful child development stimulant, combining observation, hand-eye coordination, patience, and inventiveness.

Every type of fishing device was used, held out over water as far as possible. Milk cartons and scooped hands were the most common methods. Several children invented a more elaborate device, using a milk carton attached to a willow branch with bread as bait. Fishing poles were also constructed, usually from a willow sapling with a piece of string and bent pin on the end. We never observed or heard of a child catching a fish by this means, and maybe, rationally, the fishermen never expected to. Children's play has little to do with rationality; but everything to do with dreaming, with imagining the impossible.

The Rube Goldberg devices invented by the children served a serious developmental purpose: to activate the "potential space" defined by British pediatrician and psychoanalyst Donald Winnicott as the locus of playful experience, where the inner life of the child interacts with the external environment and culture is created.[1] If we want a culture that values water, children must play with it so that it might become part of the individual's inner being.

The ultimate fishing instrument was a plastic trashcan lid, used to assault a larger area of water, supposedly improving the chances of catching something. Even with these "technological aids," catches were rare. As there were literally thousands of fish, there was no chance of seriously depleting the population. The few that were caught were either thrown back or taken home.

Many opinions existed among the children regarding what the fish actually were. Ideas included "tadpoles," "polliwogs that will turn into frogs," "minnows," and "guppies." In contrast to the haphazard guessing about the species, the children developed a substantial body of knowledge about how and where to catch them. Strategies varied. Some children, aware of how easily the fish could be scared, took care not to make any noise or sudden movement; others came yelling, throwing things in the water to herd them in a particular direction. In tireless pursuit, the children used every conceivable plan and catching device. It took two or more children working as a team to have any chance of success. Indeed, fishing was a unique activity that combined an understanding of animal behavior and teamwork. The potential for cooperative learning was enormous.

The "Environmental Protectors," a classroom group, clean up the pond.

MAINTAINING THE SYSTEM

The creek was cleaned out once a year. Like farmers maintaining ditches, we removed the silt to help the flow of water. The children loved to be involved in the maintenance work. It was a good moment to instill a sense of stewardship, to discuss the water cycle and the many uses of water (to drink, to swim in, to play with, to wash with, to cook with, to sit by, for frogs and fish to live in, etc.), and to review the importance of water conservation.

Emptying out the pump filter every three months was another routine task. This again was a great opportunity to demonstrate how the filter had to be cleaned and to illustrate the function of the system as a whole. Back in class, children created their own diagrams and murals and explained in their own words how it worked—a fascinating learning opportunity.

The parrot's feather pond weed presented an interesting maintenance issue. Because it was so invasive, the weed counteracted the muddy, bland appearance of the ponds in the early stages of development by covering them with a soft green mantle. It kept them cool and healthy during the hot summer. The garter snake, turtle, and frogs that resided in the pond relied on the weed for cover. At the same time, it denied access to cliff swallows and other bird species adapted to swooping over open water surfaces. Unchecked, the parrot's feather would have hastened the pond evolution to become a meadow. Although it would have been educationally rewarding to allow this natural process to happen, the end result would have been the educational loss of the ponds. Instead, we hauled the parrot's feather out twice a year and spread it around the pathways and meadows to dry in the sun. Within days it shriveled up into almost nothing. In retrospect, a less invasive species would have still improved appearance and provided wildlife cover.

A child quietly explores the pond, fascinated by the play of light on the water, observing the wildlife—like the water skaters below!

NATURE

Oh nature I do not aspire

To be the highest in thy quire,

To be a meteor in the sky

Or comet that may range on high,

Only a zephyr that may blow

Among the reeds by the river low.

Give me thy most privy place

Where to run my airy race.

In some withdrawn unpublic mead

Let me sigh upon a reed,

Or in the woods with leafy din

Whisper the still evening in,

For I had rather be thy child

And pupil in the forest wild

Than be the king of men elsewhere

And most sovereign slave of care

To have one moment of thy dawn

Than share the city's year forlorn.

Some still work give me to do

Only be it near to you.

— Henry David Thoreau

For some children, usually boys, fishing became an obsession, so much so that they had to be banned from the ponds. Otherwise, they would have never returned to class at the end of recess. Even so, when no one was looking, they invariably sneaked in to try to catch something. Nothing else in the Yard had this unrelenting degree of motivation. It was a powerful demonstration of the attraction of wildlife to children.

Fish were the best known Yard animal, just as their pond habitats were the best known place. This was true also for the many children who never actually fished. The fish still had a powerful presence. They were intently observed, admired for their agility and proclivity, but essentially appreciated from a distance. Other children were more directly involved.

"Scare 'em over here!" Jimmy screams to his friend on the other side of the pond.

"Who wants to catch polliwogs?" Christianna asks, naming them inaccurately. She is trying to lure them with a piece of bread on a stick. "I'm sneaking up on them . . . and they're sneaking up on me."

"Look, there's a bunch of really tiny ones, they must have just hatched."

"Oh God, there's a biggie."

"Where?"

"It's disappeared." Always after the elusive, mythical two-inch (5 cm) "giants," the children made do with smaller fry.

"We got some fish yesterday with a fishing pole and they were pregnant and we were doctors and we got the baby fish out," a boy asserted one day. Fish eggs were in fact rarely found. Thus, the children conducted their own investigations to try to explain the fact that the ponds were teeming with hundreds of babies. Another boy reported catching a fish and wondering if there were any "babies inside," so he cut the fish open with a piece of wood to see. There was none. A little grotesque perhaps, but this kind of child-initiated "scientific" investigation, motivated by unquenchable curiosity, provided an immediate on-the-spot cue for teachers to step in and guide investigation along educationally fruitful paths.

On weekends, when children were not restricted by the recess bell, fishing really came into its own. Some children literally went on "fishing expeditions" to the Yard and spent most of the day there pitting their wits against the myriad minnows.

"Sometimes we make nets, or we bring sticks with hooks on," says Marcos. "We put worms on 'em and pretend we're catching salmon in the river." He takes part in a fast-moving dialogue with several fishing companions.

"I've caught one, I got one."

"They're all mine."

"No they're not."

"The big suckers are . . ."

"Okay, but we're splitting them up, right?"

They move to the creek.

"Scare 'em over here and I'll catch 'em."

"Oh my God, I got the biggest!"

"How long?"

"Count 'em up now."

"God, they're so fast. How can we count 'em."

"Hey, fish stop moving!"

"Know why fish are so smart?"

"Why?"

"'Cause they go in schools!"

"The fish are probably older than you. If they were people, they'd be eighteen 'cause half a year is a year to them."

"I know where frogs hang out on the island. Let's try to catch some. I'm going to get one."

"The fish are getting crowded [in the milk carton]. They need more space to move around."

"You wanna let 'em go?"

"No!"

"Come on, we can't take 'em home. They'll die."

"Oh well, okay."

It is the end of a four-hour fishing expedition. They dump the fish back in the pond. One of the boys hides his willow milk carton fishing pole under the pump box and they leave.

SNAKES, FROGS, AND A TURTLE

The largest pond animals were two garter snakes, several bullfrogs, and a pond turtle. The turtle was found by a pair of children on their way to school, crawling along a neighborhood sidewalk. What a way to start the day! They picked the animal up and took it to class. After consulting library books, they decided it was a pond turtle. No one knew how it came to be on the street. Perhaps it had escaped from a domestic backyard pond near the school.

That afternoon the class went to the lower pond with the turtle in a plastic aquarium; it was carefully lifted out and set down beside the water. In a second it was gone. From then on it could be seen most days basking in the sun on a half-submerged log about fifteen feet (4.6 m) out. It was extremely shy and slid off into the water when someone approached unless great caution was exercised, a skill that children quickly learned. Each winter the turtle disappeared, to hibernate in the mud lining of the pond until the following spring when it faithfully reappeared on the same log once the weather warmed.

Garter snakes were added to the lower pond by a herpetologist friend. From then on, one could sit under the weeping willow with children and expect conversations about snakes. Some children said they were scared of snakes, others said they liked them. Some asked if the ones in the pond could bite. Discussions usually turned to rattlesnakes and the reason for the "rattle." Children were curious to know if snakes were harmful, why they strike at people, what they eat, and their usefulness in controlling pests such as grain-eating rats. Some children said they thought snakes were pretty.

One day, children saw bubbles rising from the bottom of the pond and said it was a snake making them. A teacher told them it was probably gas produced by rotting vegetation and tried to prove the hypothesis by poking the bottom with a stick. Again bubbles rose to the surface. The conversation switched from snakes to decomposition.

Bullfrogs arrived in the ponds originally as a bucket of tadpoles taken from Lake Hennessey in the Napa Valley. Most of them evidently survived, because from the next year on the unmistakable low-pitched "jug-o'-rum" bullfrog croak could be heard in the lower pond year after year, following winter hibernation. The frogs frequently basked in the sun, too, on the same log that the turtle used.

"I love to look at the frogs," Lela says. "They're t-h-a-t big and all green. A long time ago we found a white one that was dead. Last time I saw one it jumped right out of the water. I touched it and it hopped away into the bushes. I almost caught it. If I had, I would have taken it to the frog race in San Francisco."

"I'm trying to get that frog," a boy shouts. "That one! He's not moving . . . I'm trying to see if he's alive. Hey you, frog eyes! Move! Why doesn't he move? This'll do it." He takes a long tule rush and flicks it at the frog.

"I hit him! I hit him! He still hasn't moved! He must be real scared . . . scared half out of his misery!"

The boy concedes defeat, makes intermittent frog noises, and sits gazing at the frog who returns an equally cold stare, before slipping under the security blanket of parrot's feather.

Through direct experience with aquatic wildlife, daily play activities, and library research, the children were able to understand how all life depends on water. Top: a child's drawing of a frog with its tongue about to capture a meal. Middle: setting free the pond turtle. Bottom: a student's intricate rendering of the hydrologic cycle.

Evidence of breeding among the bullfrogs was never observed: no large masses of ten to twenty thousand eggs that frogs reputedly lay, no tadpoles. Our guess was that the eggs, the tadpoles, or both, were snaffled by the mosquito fish or garter snakes before they had a chance to mature. Perhaps they happily bred in safety, invisibly, under the pond weed around the island.

CLASSROOM CONNECTIONS

Window-ledge aquaria were started in several classrooms as indoor, miniature versions of the ponds, suitable for close-up study. Some children nurtured personal desktop aquaria in small plastic troughs. Each was started in the early spring with some of the pond bottom layer, water, and plants. Individual organisms were added as they were collected in the field. One group studied mollusks and crustacea. Others studied the effects of the voracious mosquito fish on larvae by having one aquarium with the fish and another without.

From an educational point of view, the mosquito fish were a problem because they reduced the diversity of nymphs, the larval forms of water insects, and micro-organisms such as daphnia and isopods. The mosquito fish certainly controlled the mosquito larvae effectively—along with nearly every other micro-organism, unfortunately.

The importance of the ponds as a nursery for many species of common water insects was easily understood with the aid of hand lenses. Children scrutinized the adults and larvae of water skaters, water boatmen, backswimmers, diving beetles, whirligig beetles, water scorpions, and giant water bugs. All these species could be housed in classroom aquaria and fed with bits of hamburger on the end of a drinking straw.

Indoor and outdoor learning experiences were readily connected through the ponds. One boy described how he threw a piece of bread in the pond and watched the fish "come up and eat it," and how the next morning he checked to find that it was not there anymore.

"I learn stuff like that from watching," he said, "like how fish live in the pond, what they eat, what eats them: other stuff I learn in class, like what I wrote in my pond-life journal [basic math by another name]."

"Today we counted forty-six daphnia and two dead ones in our aquarium. Yesterday there were forty live ones. They are difficult to count. We looked at hydra, too; they look like little shrimp to me. They have five tentacles. I feel creepy when I look at them because they're strange. We are going to put some in our aquarium . . . Today our group put five daphnia in a thing called a vial so we could look at them more closely. We discovered that the hydra ate the daphnia . . . We have only twelve daphnia left. I think they're all going to be eaten. I feel sorry for them . . . Today our daphnia are all dead. I think they died because they had fights with the hydra."

POND POWER

The remarkable thing about the aquatic system was the rapid pace of its evolution. Within four years it changed from being two murky puddles and a muddy stream—which some adults regarded as hazardous eye-sores—to becoming a self-regulating natural ecosystem (aided by the recirculating pump). Evolution was well advanced even after the first annual cycle. Insurance and attendant administrative issues were settled the following season. By the beginning of the third season, the ponds, creek, and surrounding vegetation looked like a unified riparian landscape.

Reactionary negative remarks disappeared and were replaced by comments like, "Isn't it beautiful."

The aquatic habitats were so self-evidently alive. They riveted the eyes with a constant panorama of inter-action and movement. Ever-changing stimulation of the senses engaged the visitor.

"It's like a cool breath of air blowing in your face, but it's water when you pick it up. I feel like I'm swim-ming and I'm not even in the water," a child remarked.

Just think of the descriptive language unleashed in this multisensory setting: the multiple ripples of a rock thrown in the water; the variable splashes of big and small rocks; the swishing sound of a handful of pebbles or sand; splashing water with sticks of different sizes; floating leaves, twigs, bits of lumber, and logs; the play of wind on the surface, from denting gusts to the mirrored reflections of perfect stillness; the sun's dancing reflec-tion, blinding the eyes with refracted multicolor flashes mingled with reflected foliage; the sun coming up and going down on the water, which was warm, cool, cold, or "f-r-e-e-z-i-n-g," depending on the season. During the coldest part of the winter, children played a game called

I float along the pond. In my pretty canoe, made out of a birch, so brown. As I flute along on my bamboo, and pole along down down the pond. As it gets dark I sing a song on my flute.

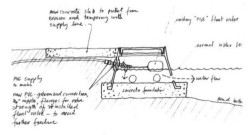

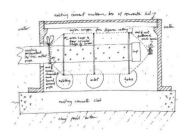

Cross-section drawing of the pond (top). Detail of the float valve (middle) and outlet chamber (right).

"how long can you keep your hand in the [freezing cold] water?"

"It makes me feel speechless, it's so quiet there," Kelli says "It makes me feel warm inside . . . I just feel nice about myself. I just feel good."

What greater expression of empathy could one wish for between a child and her surroundings. Notice too how her self-esteem was boosted by feeling good about her school environment. Too many children today do not have this relationship. They do not feel good about their school or about the neighborhood they live in. As a result, self-esteem and academic achievement suffer.

•

If you ask a group of adults to recall the most powerful memories of their childhood environment, most people will offer memories of outdoor natural places and a large proportion will include water. From a child development perspective, these results are easy to interpret. Water is a marvelously manipulative, multisensory substance. As a play material, it provides light, sound, tacticity, and movement. Water settings are very flexible. They can accommodate solitary and parallel play and groups of any size. Play with water and associated play props provide one of the most attractive, interactive play settings possible

—an irresistible stimulant for dramatic play. Naturalized aquatic settings also bring together plants and animals, a combination that can hold children's attention for hours.

Many of these multidimensional values were captured in a writing assignment by Rohanna, a third-grade student, after her class observed the first time the water was turned on to fill the ponds:

"When the fountain was turned on we waited about four minutes. It scared me a bit. The waterfall started and I was very happy. Water is neat, it has lots of colors. Water is a very pretty substance when the sun shines on it. It makes music. Water is an important part of life. We have to drink water. Animals have to drink water and so do plants. The world would be a total mess without water. Water is a life chain. We all need water. Water can go far. Almost everything needs water for something. But most of all they need it to drink."

Water provides a powerful, experiential bridge between the inner life of the child and the external world—a link that represents the deeper developmental relationship between play and education. Hopefully, the importance of water as a child development setting will be realized more clearly among educators, especially now that the critical role of wetlands for global environmental health has at last been recognized.

REFERENCES

1. Winnicott, D. (1971). *Playing and Reality.* Chapter 4: "The Place Where We Live." New York: Basic Books, 102–3.

Reweaving the Web of Life

While it is true that all spiders use poison to paralyze their prey, very few species are known to be seriously injurious to people. Those that are dangerous, such as the black widow spider and the brown recluse spider, are well known to us and should be treated with respect.

All spiders are predatory in their feeding habits, and the number of insects killed by spiders each year is incalculable. Based on what is known, spiders should be classified as beneficial to man's best interests. Among the tens of thousands of spider species, some live only for one year, while others live up to 25 years or more.

— Helen Cox,
classroom notes

VOCABULARY LIST

Metamorphosis: A change in shape or form. A change into something completely different.

Pupa: A case in which a larva stays until it comes out in a different form (a butterfly comes out of a pupa).

Larva: A caterpillar, grub, or maggot.

Chrysalis: A type of pupa *without* silk on the outside.

Cocoon: A type of pupa *with* silk on the outside.

Recent studies indicate that between 10 and 100 million species of plants, animals, and microorganisms exist on Earth, but only about 1.4 million have been studied well enough to receive scientific names. Many of these species are vanishing or being placed in imminent danger of extinction by the reduction of habitat and other human activities. The loss in tropical rain forest in particular, thought to contain a majority of the species on Earth, may exceed half a percent a year. — Edward O. Wilson, *Naturalist* (61)

Once the first mud puddles formed and the first weeds sprouted, wildlife began inhabiting the Yard. Animal species arrived in all stages of life—as eggs, larvae, and mature adults. They came buzzing, crawling, diving, flapping, flitting, flying, gliding, hopping, riding, sliding, or even freeloading on the fur and feathers of larger animals. Occasionally, people deliberately transported and introduced species. Once arrived, the animals began eating plants, eating each other, procreating, moving nutrients and genetic material through the evolving ecosystem, through cycles of decay and regeneration, each adding more strands to the web of life.

This process of regeneration was fascinating to the children. Through play, they were able to get close to the action, putting their bodies in the habitat and their hands on the animals—or the animals in their hands—their minds intuitively absorbing the miracle of life. Teachers used this first level of exploration and discovery to lead the learning process further along the path of education.

CAGELESS ZOO

The gradual reinhabitation of the site by animals in search of food and shelter, weaving their lives into the untidy patchwork of plants, was a rewarding sight. Each year new species arrived and joined the increasingly intense eruptions of springtime birth.

Hibernating salamanders lay immobile in dark, damp cavities beneath logs and rocks—the warmth of a hand igniting them into wriggling masses. Early flights of birds arrived. Ants, aphids, beetles, butterflies, centipedes, earthworms, houseflies, hover flies, inchworms, ladybugs, millipedes, pill bugs, slugs, snails, spiders, wasps, and a myriad of other species co-inhabited the forest floor. Each spring, teeming populations of mosquito fish colonized the ponds. Water skaters skimmed the surface. Glittering damselflies, mayflies, and dragonflies hovered above, their gossamer dance punctuated by the bass-line greetings of bullfrogs and the sinuous reflections of the gliding garter snake, each species seeming to perform for the silent pond turtle basking in the sun.

Every winter gulls visited, scavenging for lunchtime scraps. Pacific Flyway travelers, en route north or south, dropped by to drink the waters of the ponds. Brown mice were occasionally found under piles of scrap lumber. Squirrels, common in the neighborhood, appeared once the faster growing trees (alder, acacia, and Monterey pine) reached fifteen feet (4.6 m) or so and were tall enough to support their aerial cavorting.

Annual lifecycles were rapidly established by some species. Most insect populations replaced themselves completely each year. Other animals, like the bullfrogs, salamanders, and mosquito fish, lived up to several years in the Yard, hibernating during the winter, gradually replacing themselves with the offspring of their annual matings.

Wildlife was a true animator of Yard events. One day, word spread during recess that there was a "monster spider" in the chaparral. Could it be a stray tarantula? No, a magnificent garden spider, more than two inches (5 cm) across, was putting the finishing touches to a perfectly formed web. A dozen or so children looked on, mesmerized. Noticing the high degree of interest, one teacher later sent her students to the library to conduct a follow-up study on spiders.

"When a bug gets caught, the spider stings it," one student wrote. "The bug is paralyzed but not killed. The spider makes a hole in the bug and lays its eggs in it so the babies have something to eat when they hatch." In an interview held several years later, one student vividly recalled the "big spider in the bushes."

ANIMAL LEARNING STATIONS

Several classrooms had aquaria, terraria, and animal cages to weave wildlife resources into classroom activity. These learning stations also helped children to understand the relationship between organisms and

OVERCOMING (ADULT) BACKYARD PHOBIAS

Something that took us by surprise in teacher training sessions was the degree to which some Yard animals were regarded as pests rather than critical elements of a naturally evolving learning environment. For a majority of the teachers, suburban gardens and backyards provided the first point of reference. This was also a common connection among parents who came to work in the Yard.

We realized that many adults lacked personal experience with wild, unkempt nature. Their perceptions were mostly colored by personal experience of wrestling with home landscape maintenance. Prevailing neat-and-tidy approaches to landscape design—especially artificially fertilized lawns—can also be questioned (especially in relation to children's play needs). This aside, it was interesting to see how, after working in the Yard with children and after much discussion, that adult attitudes gradually shifted towards an appreciation of the Yard as a different type of space, serving very different needs.

As the photographs show, the Yard children were unlikely to grow up with animal phobias. They made good friends with (top to bottom) caterpillars, salamanders, and snails.

habitats, and to develop sensitivity towards animals. In one classroom, small tanks of pond life were distributed among the children at their tabletop workstations. In other rooms, you might have seen children playing with a rabbit, attending to a bevy of mice, feeding hamburger to a praying mantis, or studying a pair of caged doves. Classroom animals also included beetles, caterpillars, crickets, fish, gerbils, hamsters, lizards, parakeets, parrots, roosters, snails, spiders, turtles, and worms.

The growing diversity of life was also evident in the Natural Resource Area. Students conducted a census of animals in the area by making monthly observations of a square yard (or square meter) of the ground. They categorized the animal by general habitat (air, water, land), physical appearance (feathers, scales, fur), and food requirements. The children compared the habitats of spiders and worms. They also investigated whether they could feed plants from the garden to classroom animals.

Studies at classroom animal stations were enhanced with trips to local habitats: the National Livestock Show, the Steinhart Aquarium at the California Academy of Sciences, local pet stores, the San Francisco Exploratorium, the Little Farm in one of the regional parks, and many other places.

In one activity, children learned about the sexual differences between hens and roosters and observed rabbits mating. To call attention to gender differences, one group of students pinned male and female signs on their clothing. They really liked the concept and took the signs home to show their parents.

Observations of live animals were compared to the way animals were portrayed in books, television, and movies. Pet abandonment, animal abuse, vivisection, vegetarianism, and other provocative issues were discussed. The children kept diaries, conducted library research, and wrote stories. Every school subject—reading, math, science, art, social studies, music, and language arts—was integrated into these activities.

"Today we went on the Yard and caught some flies to feed to our chameleon," a child wrote in a journal entry.

Wildlife observation in the Yard was especially valuable for those teachers who were reluctant to keep animals in the classroom (either because it added yet another responsibility to their overloaded agendas, or because they objected to the idea of removing animals from their natural habitats). To extend the limits of outdoor observation, microscopes were set up to probe the ecosystem.

"Once we looked at just the leg of a bug," a child wrote. "You could see the tiny claw it grabbed stuff with."

Although smaller microbiota, such as microbes and bacteria, were invisible even with a microscope, evidence of their existence was present in every piece of decaying matter, especially in the compost pile.

FEATHERED FRIENDS

Forty-three species of birds were sighted in the Yard during the record-keeping years from 1972 to 1982 (see page 54). Every species that frequented the flatland shores of San Francisco Bay was sighted, plus several rare visitors. One summer a red-tailed hawk was spotted circling high above the Yard, far from its regular habitat in the East Bay Hills. An even more uncommon example was a clapper rail with a broken leg found hobbling on the sidewalk outside the Yard. We speculated that this secretive bird had been attracted by the cattail-covered ponds that approximated, in miniature, its natural wetland habitat around the Bay. Unaccustomed to the hazards of the city, the bird perhaps had been attacked by a cat or dog or hit by a car. We took the bird to a local junior museum specializing in injured birds, where it was tended by high school volunteers. After recovering, it was released back in its own habitat. Both stories were good examples of the Yard's ecological pull on the surrounding bioregion.

Injured birds always engendered special sympathy from the children. One day a grounded pigeon was found struggling near the school, injured perhaps by a passing car. The children took it to Mr. Cox's classroom, where caring for animals had become a regular activity. Within three weeks the pigeon's injured leg had healed. The class took the bird to the Natural Resource Area and released it, rejoicing as it lifted itself, strongly now, up, up, and disappeared behind the redwoods.

Approximately one third of the bird species seemed especially well adapted to urban conditions and became Yard kibitzers: scavenging gulls; chattering groups of bush-tits moving en masse from tree to tree; groups of English sparrows giving themselves early morning dust baths; plump western robins pulling worms and grubs year-round from the meadow and garden; the rasping call of a scrub jay cutting through the Natural Resource Area, its rich blue body catapulting through the dark green foliage of Monterey pines; and hummingbirds on zigzag flight paths, sampling the Yard's menu of nectars.

"They fly in real fast," observed one of the children, "and stop in mid-air around the plants."

Getting close to the birds, however, was difficult. Binoculars helped; even so, many birds remained hidden from view, perched high in the trees. One exception was an ancient dove that found the Yard a friendly hangout. Looking for solace as its life faded, it allowed children to approach to within an arm's length.

Every spring, beginning with the mud puddles of 1973, birds could be seen collecting materials from the Yard to construct nearby nests. Cliff swallows would swoop between the school building and the muddy edges of the ponds, retrieving mud to build adobe nests underneath the section of the roof that projected over the school entrance. Inside the building, the cluster of gourd-shaped nests was plainly visible from the window on the second-floor staircase landing—an ideal spot for children to observe the construction. Later, they watched the tireless back-and-forth efforts of the parents trying to satisfy the hungry baby beaks that poked out of the nests. No natural science museum could better this live exhibit. The first bird nest in the Yard itself was built four years later by a bush-tit, in the passion vine on the MLK Way fence.

One of the children wanted to take the nest home.

"How would you like it if someone tore your house down?" asked a classmate.

They left it alone.

Birdhouses and bird feeders were designed and constructed in special workshop sessions that always stimulated curiosity and motivation among the children. Like architects, they investigated different materials and

A student releases the healed pigeon.

BIRDS SIGHTED IN THE YARD 1972–1982

Allen's hummingbird
American goldfinch
American robin
Anna's hummingbird
Barn swallow
Bewick's wren
Black phoebe
Brewer's blackbird
Brown towhee
Bush-tit
California gull
Cedar waxwing
Chestnut-backed chickadee
Clapper rail
Cliff swallow
Dark-eyed junco
Downy woodpecker
English sparrow
Herring gull
House finch
Hutton's vireo
Lesser goldfinch
Mourning dove
Olive-sided flycatcher
Pine siskin
Plain titmouse

Red-breasted nuthatch
Red-shafted flicker
Red-tailed hawk
Red-winged blackbird
Ring-billed gull
Rock dove (domestic pigeon)
Ruby-crowned kinglet
Rufous-sided towhee
Scrub jay
Song sparrow
Starling
Western flycatcher
Western mockingbird
White-crowned sparrow
Wilson's warbler
Wren-tit
Yellow-rumped warbler

JUNGLE LAW

One summer evening near the upper pond we saw one of the cats from the adjacent apartment buildings playing "cat-and-mouse" with something in the long grass at the end of the meadow. As we approached, the cat ran off. We discovered not a mouse but a large bullfrog covered with scratch marks, bleeding from a cut on its side. Too slow on the hop, it had become the deadly cat's plaything.

Mortally wounded, the frog lay on its back barely breathing, or so it seemed. We wondered what we should do— exercise compassion and intervene in the situation? Have you ever thought how you would put a big, fat, injured bullfrog out of its misery? You certainly couldn't stomp on it to deliver a quick dispatch as you would a small animal. Decapitation? Neither of us had the stomach for that and, in any case, we did not have a sharp knife to commit the deed with sufficient swiftness and decorum.

After considering these unpleasant options, we left things exactly as they were. The hunter who comes across a tiger's kill does not attempt to rescue the unfortunate victim. We left the cat to finish its grisly game— without our unnecessary intervention. If the frog had received only minor injuries, our feelings might have been different. It would have

hopped back to the safe confines of the pond, and that would have been that.

Early the next morning we returned to find the frog gone—carried off by the cat or perhaps by some other predator. We never heard reports of the frog's remains being discovered elsewhere. Fortunately, the victim was not the last frog in the Yard. Reassuring "bwarp, bwarps" continued to greet the quiet explorers of the lower pond, where frog sightings were still regularly made.

LADYBUGS

"I found some ladybugs in the bush and I put them in a jar to keep them warm and hid them so no one would take them so when I came back the ladybugs would still be there. But I forgot to come back. So I found three more and I found five on Friday. But some got away, so today I am looking for more again."

— Naomi, 2nd grade

the possible means of joining them together. They calculated quantities and costs. They drafted the layouts and learned how to use hand tools. They surveyed the Yard, studied bird habits, decided on the best locations, and considered security and maintenance.

ALL CREATURES SMALL

Children's everyday wildlife experience revolved around their interactions with members of the large populations of common species of small organisms and insects such as "roly-polys" (pill bugs), spiders, millipedes, ladybugs, and other beetle species.

"I love beetles," Anna confides. "I just keep 'em and look at 'em. The things I hate are slugs and snails . . . slugs and snails and puppy dog tails." She giggles through five verses of "What Are Little Boys and Girls Made Of?"

A boy screams at a bug in a milk carton filled with water.
"Hey you! You have legs, you don't need so much water. Look at him swim around. He looks confused. Maybe he needs to get out. Hey, do you have room to crawl around? Maybe he needs a friend." He dumps out the water; the bug remains sitting in one corner. "He needs more water. He needs to drink . . . I'm going to let him go."
"What do you think he'll do?" someone asks.
"Go in the water and fight with other bugs like him . . . there he goes." The bug crawls towards the water and eventually disappears.

"I've found a ladybug," a girl shouts. "And here's another one on this dandelion . . . Let's make a house for them with these woodchips."

Ladybugs, boosted by frequent classroom investigations, easily won the bug popularity contest. Their attractive shape and brightly colored shell-like wing casings made them highly visible. This, students learned, was to warn potential predators to stay away. Ladybugs taste bad.

"I'm studying ladybugs," a girl says. "I live in an apartment. There's no outdoors. Right now I've got some ladybugs I brought from the Yard and keep 'em in my 'bug house.' You have to feed 'em or let 'em go, y'know, or they'll die really fast. We drop them in the bottom of milk cartons and watch them crawl up the sides, then watch them fly away." She and three friends look for ladybugs in the willows by the beach.
"Look! It's like a tiny lobster. We just had the idea of making ladybug boats. We've got two others already. This one can be the passenger."
"We found a queen ladybug too," one of the others says. "It's bigger and has black spots."

"Here's a longer one, I don't know what kind it is."

"Quick, get it in the boat, get it in. Ahh . . ."

"I'll get some more of this" (the sow-thistle leaves they had found the ladybugs on). They add them to the boat, which is fashioned out of a few sticks bound together. An older, larger leaf is supported vertically to catch the wind. At other times, the children would shape aluminum foil lunch wrappings into simple "barges" to send ladybugs "to sea" or "down the river."

"I can see another of that good species," a loud voice reports, exercising terminology picked up in the classroom.

"We've found another species," her friend replies. "Look here. It has different colored spots. It must have gotten mixed up."

"Let's all go back to the bush where we found our first one."

"I've found a green one with black spots. Let's call it 'greeny bug.' Wow, I thought there was only one kind." (A member of the group has discovered that more than one species can be found within the genera of the ladybird beetle family—a wonderful moment of learning.)

Apart from the wildlife concentration around the ponds, other species were distributed in many other niches that satisfied minimal requirements for food and shelter. Some snails were found almost year-round; populations of butterflies, moths, and caterpillars varied by season and lifecycle stage, which helped dramatize their annual entry into the scene.

"We just caught four caterpillars," say Anne and Linda. "Last year we caught lots of butterflies and caterpillars which turned into butterflies, but our mothers made us let them go. We like to hold them and look at them, then let them go." Best of all, children loved the furry types of caterpillar—almost to death sometimes, if they handled them too keenly.

"I love the dragonflies," says Diego. "I just saw a red one. Earlier we were throwing things at the blue ones. I hit one on the wing, but it still flew great. I don't usually try to hit them 'cause they're real hard to hit they go so fast. The one I hit was feeding, which is a real yucky way to sneak up on them," he says remorsefully.

Diego typified the conflicting motivations of children towards their wildlife playmates. Children's curiosity was so strongly provoked by the aesthetic appearance and behavior of animals that playful interaction was inevitable, with children testing their wits against the wily creatures "to see what happens," even to the extent of causing injury or death. In such an event, children were quite able to feel remorse and to reflect morally on the consequences of their actions.

Classroom studies reflected children's intimate association with the microhabitats of the Yard (top). The children were particularly fascinated by Yard wildlife and often incorporated it into their play activities: gathering ladybugs in an aluminum foil boat to float down the creek (middle) and creating a fantasy city for snails (bottom).

ON SAFARI

Wildlife safaris were good examples of classroom activity that helped foster the moral side of children-animal interaction. They ranged from general "walk-abouts" ("go and see what you can find, make a record, and bring it back to class") to "expeditions" that focused on specific habitats, animal types, or animals with unusual habits.

"I found a salamander under a rock," Dana writes. "I held it for a little bit, then touched its tail and it ran away."

Hula hoops and metal clothes hangers were used to mark off spaces to explore. Hand lenses (essential tools) were used to probe the surroundings, which usually increased motivation. They gave a physical focus to the children's observations, forcing them to really use their eyes, get down on their hands and knees, and investigate the Yard's many niches: rotting logs, crevices in the ground, fissures in the bark of trees, the clefted space of long grass, the undersides of leaves, and cavities under rocks. Children developed their observational skills and at the same time understood that most insects liked to live in cool, damp, protected places.

Ethical considerations with regard to animals were always stressed. Children understood the need to focus attention and to concentrate. They learned about the plants that the different animals lived on before removing live specimens for closer study. As a result, they could return the specimen to the appropriate habitat. These important preliminaries helped safari "hunters" develop the right frame of mind before sallying forth. Over the longer term, these discussions fostered a sense of animal needs and animal rights among the children.

Safari exercises were used to map life along particular ecotones (the junction of two plant communities). Mapping the creek, between the waterfall and the wooden bridge, was a popular safari trip. It gave students the feeling of exploring a river as it flowed over rapids, through gorges and swamps, past sandy beaches, to a point where it disappeared into the dark redwood forest. The Orchard Wayside provided a stimulating trail following the linear separation of asphalt and natural groundcovers.

Walkabouts extended the scope of study into the neighborhood, so children saw the Yard as part of a larger web of life. They discovered that most of the time the same species lived in the same types of niches, and that the numbers of individuals varied greatly, depending on habitat conditions. Few animals (except people) were found living on asphalt. Children grasped the idea that all animals did not live everywhere. Particular species were adapted to particular habitats and were only found when the appropriate conditions existed. As one child wrote:

Salamanders are neat
They run quite fast
Live under logs and
Hide in deep grass

SNAIL TRAILS

Snails were prolific in the Yard and had a certain exotic appeal. The children knew exactly where to find snails and enjoyed interacting with them in creative ways.

"They're all over the place: on the trees, under the garbage cans, under the railings," the children explain. "You find them in damp areas. They make little silvery trails that look like tin foil. We love to play with them. Look, one's laying a turd!" The children giggle.

"How many do we have?"

"Fourteen, fifteen, sixteen . . ."

"Let's get some more. Look in the garden, there's thousands there."

"Watch out, the baby one fell down."

"First, we try to get them to come out of their shells. We put them in the water for a few seconds, then on a rock and watch their heads come out," a boy explains.

"Eck, look at all that yucky stuff."

The children try to organize a race on the big rock, but the snails keep rolling off the steep surface. So they move to the railroad ties. They line the snails up at one end of the tie, and head them towards a stick laying as the "finishing line" about two feet (0.6 m) away, but have difficulty persuading the snails to move in the right direction.

"Mine keeps going round in circles, like she's trying to catch her own shell!" a child complains.

The group collects some milk cartons, bait each one with mallow leaves and put them on the finishing line, hoping the snails will enter. It does not make any difference.

"Look, they've got one foot," a boy observes, picking one up for closer inspection.

"Where's the toes?" his friend responds in a split second. Everyone laughs.

"Now we'll put 'em to bed."

They cover the tops of the milk cartons with plastic lunch bags.

"Put some holes in so they can breathe."

"Sometimes we make little houses for snails out of wood-chips and leaves," one child explains. "Once we found a cardboard box and put grass, dirt, and leaves in it for them. Other times we let 'em fight each other and whichever child wins keeps the snails . . . and whoever has the most by the end of the game is the winner. Then we put them back in the bushes."

"Lots of people don't have respect for snails," a boy comments. "Some people just can't learn to respect them. I don't like snails, but I don't go 'round stomping on them, partly because I think they look gross when they're squished and partly because I don't think it's fair to stomp on 'em. They've a right to live, too."

Snails had enormous educational value.

Look, they're mating," the teacher says, pointing to a pair of snails joined head to toe. To head off any misconceptions, she explains a peculiar thing about snails. Each individual snail is both male and female, so when mating, each snail is both fertilizing and being fertilized. Next time they dig the garden, the teacher suggests that the children look for clusters of white, translucent snail eggs just below the ground surface.

One day Irabe rushes into class with a half-munched paper bag he had found with a couple of snails stuck to it. "Look, they've been eating up the litter!" he exclaims.

The rest of the class goes to see if they can find more examples of half-eaten litter. Within ten minutes there is a pile of partially eaten paper bags, as well as milk cartons with the outer layer eaten off. Everyone is impressed. While they have all seen this kind of evidence around the Yard before, they have never really thought about it or examined it closely. They begin to speculate about the total number of snails in the Yard and how much litter they could dispose of each month.

"It's like the Yard has its own garbage men," jokes Irabe.

Garden slugs and big banana slugs also inhabited the Yard. Like snails, they were obsessive chewers. With increased understanding, children became less willing to dismiss slugs and snails as "yucky." They discussed why they were slimy and the protective function of the snail's shell. They discovered that the Yard species was the European brown snail, deliberately introduced into the United States as a possible food source more than a hundred years ago. But the snails had found the California climate so ideal that they proliferated much faster than in their native habitat, becoming a well-known pest in Bay Area gardens.

Even more than paper bags, snails adored fresh garden vegetables. Children learned that these particular snails could be fattened up, purged, and eaten (even though not the same culinary species as the famous French snail). That line of discussion, however, did not

METAMORPHOSIS

The largest butterfly in the Yard was the anise swallowtail, a most handsome creature. It was often seen flying in the open with soaring and gliding motions typical of light-loaded butterflies (having large wings compared to their bodies). At each stage of metamorphosis, its body was beautifully camouflaged by the bright green, lacy leaves and the golden umbrella flower heads of its host plant (the prolific sweet anise, widespread in the Yard).

One class decided to try to replicate the swallowtail's lifecycle: from egg to larva, to caterpillar, to chrysalis, to adult butterfly, and back to egg again. They found some black, spiny larvae on an anise leaf and put them in a jar of water to keep them fresh. The experiment was displayed in an exhibition case in the school's main corridor, with a book about butterflies open at the relevant page. The larvae munched away at the anise for another ten days, shedding two or three more coats as they got bigger.

After a final shedding, they became smooth-skinned, green and black caterpillars with orange spots. They continued to eat and get bigger and bigger. A pair of horns or "ejectors" appeared on their heads, ready to fire an unpleasant odor at unwelcome intruders, such as human hands.

At this point, all but one of the caterpillars were removed and put back in the Yard. The next day the remaining caterpillar attached itself to an anise stem by a small silky pad at its lower end and spun a cradle of silk that looped around its entire body. Its skin split for the last time, down the back from top to bottom, without breaking the silk cradle. A chrysalis emerged housing the pupa, hanging precariously for a few moments in its silk cradle while shedding the skin from the tip of its abdomen, unanchoring itself momentarily from the silk pad.

"Is it dead?" children asked during the next three weeks, as the pupa hung motionless from the anise stem. The teacher told them to look for an occasional wiggle indicating without doubt that the pupa was alive.

One day the trap-door top of the pupal case opened and a butterfly's head emerged, its antennae waving around haphazardly. Six legs followed and provided enough leverage for the butterfly to drag itself free from its pupal prison. After a moment's rest, the creature feebly opened its crumpled wings and flexed its coiled-up tongue. Within a couple of hours a pair of perfect adult wings were fully extended and tongue coiled in place.

For a few days children hand-fed the butterfly from a dropper with a mixture of honey and water as other children stopped to look, noses pressed against the showcase glass.

One morning they found the butterfly perched on the butterfly book right next to its own picture! When it was time for the creature to return to its natural habitat, the children captured it in a cardboard box, took it outside, and let it join the rest of its family and eventually mate. It would then lay pinhead-sized, yellow-green eggs to start the whole process over again.

The anise swallowtail experiment was so rewarding that other classrooms set up their own butterfly-hatching projects to explore other butterfly-plant connections. The passion vine was checked for the gulf fritillary, the plantain for the buckeye butterfly, willows for

mourning cloaks and western tiger swallowtails. Numerous small "skippers" darted from flower to flower at ground level. A couple of west coast ladies were found around the mallow.

Several classes conducted mealworm metamorphosis studies, starting with eggs of the adult darkling beetle (mealworms being the larval stage of the pest found in stored grains).

Silkworm projects illustrated the human influence on evolution (silkworm breeding having been rigidly controlled for so long that silkworm larvae need an exclusive diet of mulberry leaves. Larvae and moths that escaped over time were "lost" to this highly controlled residual population ecologically chained to its mulberry leaf habitat). Silkworms provided an easily understood connection between mulberry trees, natural processes, historical events, and human artifacts: journeys across the plains of Asia with Marco Polo, silk banners from the Middle Ages, Japanese kimonos handed down from generation to generation, and the fashion salons of present-day Paris. The young minds were fired by these multiple educational ties to geography, history, social studies, science, and the world of fashion.

progress far. On the other hand, snails made a delicious meal for a classroom rooster, demonstrating life as a circular process: the animals circulating through the environment, the environment—even milk cartons—circulating through the animals. Everything had a use, and could be conserved and converted.

DAMSELS AND DRAGONS

During spring and early summer, populations of slender, fluorescent-blue damselflies, powered by invisible, translucent wings, appeared around the ponds, engaged in their characteristic "hover . . . dart, dart" dance. They shared their aerial stage with swooping, red-bodied dragonflies in performances that always attracted the children's attention.

A teacher explains that people used to believe that dragonflies were the spirits of the deceased and should be left alone. "Sometimes they were called 'devil's darning needles,'" she says. "People thought they would sew up your eyes if you were indiscreet."

"Who knows what 'indiscreet' means?" she asks, exploiting the children's fascination to build vocabulary skills.

Outdoors, the teacher directs her students to notice how damselflies and dragonflies groom themselves by sweeping their front legs over their eyes after eating. She encourages them to watch for mating pairs stuck together in mid-flight or perched on a twig. "If you look carefully," she advises, "you may see a female repeatedly dipping her body in the water to deposit eggs."

The children also kept their eyes open for the pale green mayfly, a cousin of the other two species, and distinguished the three insects by color and wing position. Damselflies closed their wings, so they pointed backwards. Dragonflies held theirs horizontally. Mayflies closed theirs also but pointed them upwards, and had three long, threadlike strands projecting from their tails. The children practiced the resting positions.

In class, students used a microscope to look at the dragonfly's bulbous, compound eyes, which can detect moving objects up to eighteen feet (5.5 m) away. They also studied the insect's long, slender, spiny legs—not good for walking, but useful for forming a basket to carry prey caught in mid-flight.

The children learned about the dragonfly's lifecycle, starting with eggs, which took anywhere from a few days to nine months to hatch. Then came the nymphs, which "jet propelled" themselves through their aquatic habitat by expelling water from their rears. Nymphs used protruding bottom lips to scoop up tiny fish and small tadpoles. They lived that way for one to three years, shedding their skins as many as twelve times. When fully grown, dragonflies climbed a convenient plant, split their skins for the last time, and emerged as an adult, ready to mate and start the cycle over again.

A few days later, a couple of children rushed up during lunchtime recess to report that they had just seen a dragonfly "come out of its case" on a cattail in the lower pond. Everyone hurried over and found the glistening, red-bodied beauty drying off in the sun—a memorable moment of learning that once again validated the educational impact of the ponds.

ANT CITY

The small brown Argentine ant (most likely introduced to the United States at the end of the last century in coffee shipments from Brazil) outnumbered every other species in the Yard, as do the twenty thousand or so species of ants that inhabit the rest of the planet, from the Arctic Circle to Tierra del Fuego.[1] Fortunately, these ants did not bite, although most children required a lot of convincing because of the sensation caused by the ants' legs gripping their skin.

The ants lived underground in colonies housed in the hot, dry crevices around planters, along the edge of the asphalt, between cement blocks along the Orchard Wayside, along the edge of the stack-sack wall (described in Chapter 6), and in the fissures of adobe clay. Foraging lines of hundreds and thousands of individuals could be seen moving between the various niches carrying a wide variety of scavenged material. After heavy rains, or when flooded by irrigation, the orderly columns broke into chaotic, scurrying hoards carrying little white egg cases to safety.

"Do ants come in your house?" asks a teacher. "Do they cause problems? How does your family deal with them?" Ants are a good educational connection to children's homes since they are such a common domestic problem. The class suggest solutions, such as not leaving food around and blocking up holes in the floor. They discuss the danger of using "ant stakes" laced with arsenic, especially when young children are around.

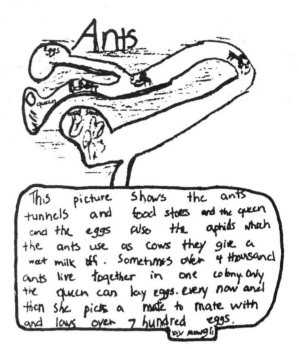

This picture shows the ants tunnels and food stores and the queen and the eggs also the aphids which the ants use as cows they give a wet milk off. Sometimes over 4 thousand ants live together in one colony. Only the queen can lay eggs. every now and then she picks a mate to mate with and lays over 7 hundred eggs.
by mowgli

VOCABULARY LIST

Microscope: An instrument for making very small things look bigger, so they can be studied.

Microscopic: So small that you cannot see it well except with a microscope.

Insect: An animal with six legs (three pairs) and usually wings.

Census: A count.

Colony: A group of similar plants or animals growing together or living together (ants, bees, etc.).

Abacus: A frame with heads on wires used for doing arithmetic. Used a lot in Asian countries.

Estimate: To make a good guess at something.

— Helen Cox,
classroom notes

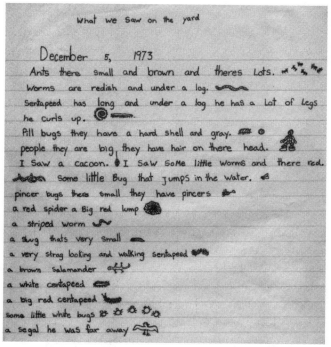

Once they grasped the notion of food webs (top), children were able to express food chain connections between themselves and the broader environment. Further observations of Yard species (middle) extended their perceptions of the web of life and understanding of lifecycles like that of the anise swallowtail (bottom).

FOOD WEBS

Children observed lines of ants marching up and down deciduous tree trunks. With a little prompting from the teacher, they noticed the ants working on the underside of leaves around clusters of tiny green, yellow, sometimes black, sometimes almost translucent aphids. They were being "milked" by the ants for the sweet, secreted honeydew. Ant colonies were found on some of the pine trees feeding off clusters of limpet-like grayish "scales" on the underside of some of the branches. The pine needles on these trees had turned brown, and a black sooty substance coated sections of the tree. The scales produced a secretion that ants again liked to feed on. The scales also killed part of the tree by removing the vital juices rising under the bark. Ladybugs were also found in the vicinity because they ate the scales.

Further evidence of the ant-aphid symbiosis was found in the telltale curled-up leaves of willow and purple plum trees, showing the cumulative effect of thousands of aphid leaf suckers. Ladybugs were also found near the aphids.

"Look with your hand lenses," says the teacher. "See how the ladybugs are eating only the top parts of the aphids, not the whole body. See all those dead bodies left over; maybe they don't taste so good."

"Yeah," says one of the students in a flash, "ladybugs like aphid heads 'cause there's lots of blood in 'em!" Everyone laughs.

Examples like this enabled children to understand the interlocking food web of Yard plants and animals. They saw that ladybugs and ants both lived off scales in one food chain; that ladybugs were predators and aphids were prey in another; that ants were herders and aphids were herded in yet another; and that scales and aphids both lived off plant juices.

Leaf eaters provided another good starting point for investigating cycles. Because evidence in the form of jagged leaf edges was obvious, it was always fun to try to track down the culprit—perhaps a colorful leaf-eating beetle, or tent caterpillars that enveloped the unfortunate twig with their distinctive silken shelter. Rotten logs were also a good place to look. Children gently peeled off sections of bark to reveal the symmetrical corridor patterns made by bark beetles that had eaten the dead cambium layer.

Motivated by these miniature ecodramas, students read more about living systems in the many ecology books that contained illustrations of intersecting food chains up the "dining pyramid" of eaters and eaten. Children gained a sense of the increasingly complex webs of eating habits that demonstrated connections in cycles of energy and nutrient flow through the ecosystem. Without a live environment to observe first hand, these concepts would have been impossible for young children to grasp. The real world was not neatly laid out like a textbook diagram. Many connections in the web, even in the Yard, were impossible to observe—like a Jerusalem cricket chewing off a tasty young vegetable root six inches (15 cm) underground, or a tachinid fly laying eggs on a beetle larva, or a guppy gulping down a caddis fly larva, twig casing and all.

For children to understand these hidden relationships and many other useful facts, the school library was a critical resource. There, for example, the students learned that aphids reproduce prolifically without mating, making them agricultural pests able to swarm to heights of more than two thousand feet (610 m). They learned how ants protect their aphid herds from predators and thereby accentuate the pest problem by raising the numbers way beyond what they would normally be. They learned how spraying aphids with insecticide also kills the ants, which are normally good decomposers and aerators of the soil, besides being predators of housefly and termite larvae.

SCAVENGERS

A daily winter sight were the sentinel California and ring-billed gulls perched along the south edge of the school's flat roof at lunchtime recess, surveying the Yard for scraps left by children. When the Yard was empty, the gulls would lift off at regular intervals. The scavengers would circle around, wheeling and swooping, cries piercing the air, their eyes scanning for food. We wondered what signal they saw from thirty feet (9.1 m) high. Colorful lunch boxes? Reflections of their tinned insides? Whatever the answer, the birds certainly received the message.

Observing the gulls' daily ritual, one teacher hit on the idea of including the birds in the Yard scavenging

AUDUBON NATURE TRAINING

A popular Audubon Nature Training activity focused on the relationship of birds' beaks and claws. First, the trainer hung up cards with illustrations of different claws. One by one, children identified the use of each foot: webbed for paddling in water; partially webbed for walking in mud; large and clawed for grabbing smaller animals; small and curled for clinging to trees; and naturally vertical for clinging to trunks (woodpecker). Five "beak cards" were matched with the feet. One beak was hooked (hawk), one was spoon-shaped (duck), one was long and needle-like for digging in mud for insects, one was short and needle-like for digging bugs out of trees, and the last was short and "ordinary" for pecking at seeds under trees. The children played a relay game. Five of them held the feet cards and each of the remaining children held a beak card. Children in two teams ran to a child with the correct foot to match the beak card they were holding. If the card was wrong, it was rejected. The team to finish first was the winner.

program. Each day a small group of children gathered leftovers from the cafeteria, placed them in the middle of the asphalt, and took cover in the trees and shrubs along the MLK Way fence. As the gulls took the bait, the children observed them at close quarters with binoculars. The plan worked beautifully. One day more than thirty gulls were counted scrambling for food.

While watching the gulls, the group talked about other scavengers, organisms that feed on refuse and decaying organic matter: cockroaches, earthworms, hyenas, rats, sharks, slugs, snails, sow bugs, vultures, and the bacteria that decomposed compost. And then, of course, there were people: beachcombers, for instance, and people who recycled clothes, cans, paper bags, bottles, and even bath water (the majority of children said they reused one or more of these items in their households). They realized that everything in nature was either a scavenger or was scavenged at one time or another in its lifecycle.

A search continued for other scavengers, such as ants, beetles, pill bugs, and worms. Children noted that, with the exception of ants, these organisms were usually found in shady areas where the ground was damp and where environmental conditions seemed to favor the recirculation of organic matter back into the soil.

ECO-ETHICS

What did all this wildlife experience add up to educationally? What difference did it make? Clearly it stimulated children's play and learning. What comes across most strongly is the broad humanizing effect of these close encounters with other forms of life.

Five boys dig for bugs in the large pile of woodchips waiting to be spread on the pathway surfaces of the Natural Resource Area. One boy finds a bug; another boy tells him to put it back. He grabs the bug and puts it back in the ground. The other boy gets upset and starts looking for the bug. The boy who put it back sweeps chips over the area so the first boy cannot find it. They are clearly friends, but this incident nearly provokes a fight. The first boy is close to tears. A discussion follows about killing bugs. The first boy says he was not going to kill it. They start talking generally about small organisms. Worms are our friends. Worms help plants grow. The second boy adds that caterpillars become butterflies, that butterflies pollinate fruit and help all kinds of food to grow.

Without the natural resources of the Yard and the possibility of interacting with them, such a conversation about respect for life would never have happened.

•

Animals are quite different from other natural phenomena in relation to children. First, animals move from one place to another, show up at different times of year, and often change form through time. They eat each other. They visibly reproduce. This dynamic quality means that animals have immense "pull" for children to fully engage their curiosity. Second, partly for these reasons, and partly because animals are biologically closer to humans, children have a stronger emotional relationship to animals than to plants. Perceptually, plants provide a kind of powerful "ground" to the "figures" of animals that readily absorb children's attention. These characteristics give animals tremendous educational value; again, as with all living things, animals provide a strong bridge between the informal, formal, and nonformal realms of education.

The primary issue in activating this potential in our schools is to convince educational leaders of the value of small animals as a learning resource and to provide healthy habitats on school sites. Biologically, it is not that difficult. By far, the hardest barrier to overcome is institutional—the lack of attention to these topics in teacher training and the difficulty of convincing administrators to take them seriously.

REFERENCES

1. Wilson, E. O. (1992). *The Diversity of Life*. Cambridge: Harvard University Press.

CHAPTER 6

Creating a Sense of Place

A "shelf" for sand play.

Creating a place where children could feel at once connected to their environment was a design challenge. The Yard focused not only on the diversity of play but also on the learning potential inherent in the activities children typically engage in when adults "are not around." Included in our approach was an underlying respect for the children's need for privacy. Aside from "common" spaces where large group activities could take place, there were areas where the children could have a sense of both "belonging" and "separateness." The complexity of the design encouraged learning and playful exploration among the children and supported their need to personalize spaces and make the Yard their own. More importantly, the faculty and staff gave the children "room" for simple but substantial discovery learning within the spaces provided.

"Sense of place" describes the feeling of belonging that exists between people and the environments in which they live. In environments with a strong sense of place, users know exactly where they are because the place looks and feels different from every other space. They feel it is *their* place; they belong *there*. Environments with the highest level of this quality are unforgettable.

The sense of place in the old schoolyard was woefully limited. The space looked like any other urban school site: a large area of asphalt with painted race lines, ball courts, and a collection of old metal play equipment. Vertical features were limited to three steel poles supporting basketball hoops, a flag pole in one corner, the play equipment, and a chainlink boundary fence. The visual impact of these items was negligible.

The design objective was to create such a powerful sense of place in the Yard that children would remember it for the rest of their lives. Our strategy for achieving this was to fully involve the children in the design process. We sought their ideas for diversifying the environment, for broadening its play and learning opportunities, and for making it visually attractive.

All user groups offered suggestions throughout the planning process. The majority of children and adults wanted to replace the asphalt with a natural environment of ponds, woodland, meadows, and gardens. Children wanted additional items: tunnels, bridges, and balance beams, as well as places for climbing, swinging, sliding, and hiding. Teachers desired places for group learning and a performance area. Residents wanted comfortable gathering places to socialize and to hold community meetings. Everyone agreed that part of the asphalt should be conserved for ballplay.

FOUND OBJECTS

One of the first objects to arrive on the site was a five-foot (1.5 m) section of the five-foot-diameter Mokelumne Aqueduct, which brought water to the East Bay from the Sierra Nevada. The item had been donated by the regional water utility district.

Imagine a five-foot-long steel pipe weighing several hundred pounds perched on a truck—ready to be positioned wherever we wanted, a tiny object in the middle of a vast asphalt "canvas." It was like holding a loaded paint brush; the challenge was deciding where to place the first stroke. After we selected a spot in relation to the design of the central part of the site, the pipe was carefully lowered by crane onto a pair of wooden blocks shaped to support its curved shape. It became an instant tunnel, which had been one of the children's original requests.

The pipe was the first new place in the Yard the children could call their own. They clustered around the pipe, hanging out, talking, reading, observing others, their bodies curved up against the sides. The children danced in it, climbed on it, sat on it, slid off it. A ladder was built against one side (following a student's design for a "tunnel slide" proposed during the planning phase) allowing children to climb on the top and slide down the other side.

Months later, a group of older children turned the pipe on its end, which initiated a flurry of new uses. It was a wonderful invention. Suddenly—in the middle of the asphalt where everybody was visible—the pipe provided a hideaway, the only such place available in the Yard at that time. More then ten children could hide there at once, whether as part of a game or as an escape from the pell-mell of play. The pipe offered a relaxed, secure sense of enclosure. This arrangement was so successful that it was left undisturbed for more than a year. As other hiding places were phased in, however, its attractiveness faded. The pipe was righted and became a tunnel once again, serving also as a special child-scaled entrance to the central play area where a climbing net was now suspended from the climbing structure.

"It's where we walk in," says Dana, "or we climb on top, lay on our stomachs, hang our heads down and look through at the upside-down children on the net. It's neat. We sit on the top and have lunch, or spy on our friends. Sometimes we spin a ball around on the inside. The most I've gotten is four times round. Or we try to run up on the insides. That's difficult."

Older children frequently lay inside the pipe, facing each other, gossiping, their backs supported by the curved sides: an inanimate object wordlessly commanding their body language.

The search for other "found objects" intensified as a group of university students looked for attractive ready-

The arrival of the pipe in the Yard (top) meant students had a new a place to have lunch (middle) and a tunnel entrance into the sand play area (bottom). These activities helped the students make connections between the tunnel as a water supply pipe to the city and as a play object.

COMMEMORATING THE AQUEDUCT

Along with the section of the Mokelumne Aqueduct, an accompanying plaque was donated. It displayed the date and name of the aqueduct and was riveted on a steel stake. With great difficulty, the utility crew hammered it into the asphalt beside the pipe, which now looked like the sole exhibit in a vast asphalt gallery. Once in place, the men stood back to admire their work. The photographer took final publicity shots for the organization's in-house magazine. They packed up their gear, said good-bye, and slowly edged their truck out onto MLK Way. As they drove out of sight, two young children emerged from the group of onlookers, walked over to the plaque, effortlessly pulled it out of the ground, and, hardly stopping, continued on their way with the plaque tucked under their arms. It was a perfect piece of silent theater, an intuitive gesture such as only children could offer, perfectly pointing out the absurdity of the plaque and its inadequate installation.

TREE MARKERS

Trees were integrated with the many found and designed objects added to the Yard. Examples include the grove of silk trees (*Albizia julibrissin*) and the elegant, carved "Environmental Yard" sign marking the entrance to the Main Yard (top); and the Aleppo pine (*Pinus helepenis*) arching over the magic circle of rocks in the Natural Resource Area (bottom).

made items. Their finds included a pair of ancient wooden carriage wheels mounted on the ends of a solid-steel axle. The students installed the wheels vertically, with the lower wheel held down firmly by a pile of heavy rocks. The upper wheel turned freely, about four and a half feet (1.4 m) off the ground, inviting children to grab the rim and swing around. First one, then two, then as many bodies as possible hung on and zoomed around, swinging out with the centrifugal force.

The wheels were moved to the Natural Resource Area months later, lodged among the chaparral shrubs, which grew up around them (see top of page 69). Children sat and chatted on the now horizontal axle or used the wheels as "base" in games of tag. The antique appearance of the wheels made them one of the most evocative, "time-layered" spots in the Yard, offering extra play value by stimulating imagination in a special way.

The most amazing part of these two found objects—the pipe and the wheels—was that they were originally designed for entirely different purposes. Fortunately someone recognized that the items could be recycled to serve as catalysts for creative learning.

ROCKY SPOTS

Twenty small boulders, like those found in the grasslands north of the Bay, were positioned throughout the meadow to enhance its visual character and to provide habitats for small organisms. Most lay directly on the ground. They were heavy enough to require the coordinated efforts of two or three children to turn them over to see what lay beneath. Six smoothly domed, gray boulders, each about a foot (30 cm) in diameter, were partly buried in the ground, their crowns poking through the grass like a magic circle of giant mushrooms.

"It's where we play 'monster catch,'" says Jenny. "The rocks are 'base.' When you're on them you can't be caught. You have to keep going 'round. If you stop, you can be 'it.' And if you go on the grass you can be 'it.' The monster lives in the bushes [the thicket behind the rock circle]. When the monster catches you, you have to be 'it.'"

"It's sort of popping out of the earth, orange and sugary-looking," says Amy, referring to a rock beside the meadow. "I like to step on it because it feels hard and it's sort of funny to be standing on it. It's fixed to the ground. Sometimes we sit on it and make 'potions.' One time I saw some mushrooms growing beside it . . . it was neat. I sure like that rock."

One rock, much larger than the others, became known as the "big rock." We had sited it at the confluence of two main pathways by the beach, hoping it would become an enduring landmark. For a while, surrounded only by dirt, it served as the visual linchpin of the whole area; as the plant communities grew up around it, however, its visual prominence declined. Still, it remained a special place of mystery and surprise.

Rocks and water made an especially powerful combination. The waterfall and vernal pool, created from large boulders, reinforced the contemplative feeling of falling water. Children noted how peaceful the place felt.

"I go there first thing every morning," says one of the boys. "I just like to watch the water go over the rocks and splash down and fill up the little round pool. I like the sound it makes. You can step on the rocks, too, and jump over the pool. Once my sister dared me to sit in the waterfall. It sure felt funny!"

At each water setting, the rocks presented a visual contrast that enhanced the sense of place (they also provided a practical defense against soil erosion). A curving miniature cliff of rocks was used to separate the redwood grove from the creek. From a child's perspective, it really looked like a forest-topped cliff. Another curving line of rocks, interspersed with willows and bay laurel, enclosed the beach on the other side of the creek. More rocks were positioned in the creek bed itself to diversify the pattern of eddying currents.

Part of the bank of the lower pond was enclosed by a semicircle of boulders to form Willow Island, making it look like a true island.

"It's my best campground," says Amy. "See how the tree hangs down and lets the sunlight through. It makes me feel so good. It's so pretty. Its leaves are so soft and shady. If I were a bird, I would make my nest there. I like to come here with my little radio and sit around in the shade and listen to it when I'm camping. I pretend to take a shower in the early morning. I pretend to wash my clothes in the river. I cook in the campsite. Do you know how good it smells in the early morning in a campsite? Well, once we went out there really early to do a class project. It smelled exactly like that, and I did my work there."

LOGS, SPOOLS, AND TIRES

In the search for other multiple ready-mades, design students discovered that a couple of huge eucalyptus trees had been felled on the grounds of a local

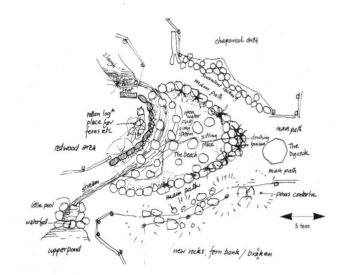

Rocks designed as a part of the Yard landscape (top) became visual markers for the passage of time. The "big rock" standing alone in the dirt during the early phases of construction (middle) was gradually integrated into the whole as it became surrounded by shrubs and other vegetation (bottom).

THE FIXED/LOOSE MATRIX

Found and ready-made objects worked beautifully as elements that could be freely moved around and integrated into the natural landscape. The site sometimes felt like a huge constructivist artwork with hundreds of people involved in its planning, building, and use. To satisfy both ecological and social criteria, artifacts like the old carriage wheels (top) were moved from one position to another in the biological matrix.

The dynamic aspects of these objects were increased by the children who used "loose parts" to make their own designs. A wonderful example was an old, heavy-duty machine belt about as big and heavy as some of the children. Looking like an oversized rubber band transported from a giant's kingdom, children used it as a portable "launching pad" for a variety of jumping and bouncing games.

The moveable ready-made objects and loose parts, such as cable spools (above), were intertwined with the matrix of natural systems. They stimulated an increased diversity of children's activities and helped generate a feeling of a child-centered cultural landscape with its own identity.

college and cut into foot-long segments. A neighborhood resident in the hauling business trucked dozens of the logs to the Yard. Each log measured up to three feet (0.9 m) in diameter and often required three or four people to lift. A crowbar or block and tackle was needed to shift them into position. For this reason, the logs were ideal for creating semipermanent spaces.

A large circle of logs enclosed the geographic center of the Yard. The logs seemed to beckon, "Come sit on us." And people came, helping to define the spot as a community gathering place. Children hopped from one log to another, danced around them, used them as "base" in tag, and invented a game based on being "outside" or "inside" the circle.

When permanent development of the central community area began, the logs were distributed to other locations and served as seats and work surfaces. They also harbored wildlife on their undersides.

To support hopping and jumping games, a string of recycled, painted truck tires were loosely chained together and laid on the asphalt. An extra large one, painted bright yellow, usually served as "home base." In "hot lava," anyone who slipped off and touched the asphalt became the "hot lava monster." Lines of children could be seen hopping, jumping, and bouncing around the rims, trying hard not to fall off.

Recycled trees provided another valuable resource. The city forestry crew cut down three dying trees from city streets and relocated them in the Natural Resource Area. One trunk overlooked the upper pond, providing a place to sit, balance on, or jump over. Another was left on the ground, just as if it had fallen at that spot. It served often as "base" for children's games ranging from "house" to "space wars." The third trunk was positioned on one side of Chaparral Hill, under the large acacia tree. With a view across the wooden bridge, it quickly became a favorite lunchtime spot.

"I like looking at the fungus on the log," says Sabine. "I sit there and count the rings to see how old the tree was."

Even though it was no longer alive, the tree still supported life and, to an observant child, conveyed evidence of its former state.

Cable spools were another classic ready-made item for constructing play spaces. A pyramid was constructed from a dozen spools of different heights, assembled in three diminishing layers. The hollow interior of each spool was exposed by removing some of the slats from the sides, thereby creating small lookouts and hideaway spaces.

"When we play 'girls-chase-the-boys,' we can climb right up into our 'cubby' where no boys can get us because it's so cramped," says one of the girls. "It's our little house. We stay right there, and they can't get us. And when we want to get them, we suddenly pop out of our secret trap door and scare 'em away."

A second cable-spool structure was built from a curved line of same-size spools abutting one another, laid alternately flat and on end. Core spaces were again used as places to hide. They offered shelter from the wind, sun, or rain. The spools also provided places to sit, eat lunch, play house, and observe the activities in adjacent areas.

"It's our lookout," a boy reports. "There's a hole in it, where the spindle went. You can spy on people and say 'hi' as they walk past and they'll be fooled 'cause they don't know where the voice is coming from."

Not all children liked the spools. Some complained that they were "boring," "full of splinters," "too crowded," and "covered in ants." In this respect, the spools were no different from any other part of the Yard; practically every element in the environment received mixed reactions. But the Yard was designed to meet the needs of individuals, and thus the needs of children as a whole. Inevitably, the favorite places of some were disliked by others. By using ready-made objects, we instilled a strong sense of place in the various play settings, which collectively satisfied many individual needs.

GATHERING PLACES

It was also important for the Yard to accommodate group activities.

The five-sided structure known as the "Gazebo" or "Clubhouse," for example, served as a popular gathering place in the Yard. Originally built to support a play net of old inner tubes, it was later converted by adding a pitched roof and second-level "loft." It accommodated groups of up to fifteen people.

The Yard provided many types of gathering and resting places. The railroad ties served as a place for class meetings (top); the fences supported social interaction and friendship among small groups of children (middle); and, for some, the logs provided for a peaceful nap (bottom).

CREATING PLACES

The creation of a variety of places to fill social and educational functions is the backbone of the Environmental Yard concept. The physical potential of these places is as infinite as the materials that can be used to create them. Initial attention should focus on some important basics:

1. Large, permanent play structures should be provided to attract high energy away from fragile resources. There are many source books available, full of play-structure ideas. Several manufactured systems are on the market.

2. Traditional equipment (all-time favorites such as swings, slides, monkey bars, etc.) is still as popular as ever.

3. Place for ballplay will always be important to many children.

4. Appropriate meeting and working places are important in outdoor settings—places for individuals, for small groups, for an entire class, and for mixed groups from the community.

5. Natural systems—dirt, water, and especially vegetation—are extremely important components of the play/learning environment. They can be designed in a broad variety of ways.

6. Weather is an important consideration when establishing places—the path of the sun across the site each day, wind patterns, precipitation, and seasonal change.

7. Working and storage areas should be located centrally on the site, protected, and secure.

8. Major circulation routes should be direct and connect major settings.

9. Pathways should be considered places in their own right—for people to meet, stroll, and ride their bikes.

Careful attention to user needs, feedback on past construction, and suggestions about future additions will result in an environment that truly belongs to the users.

"It's like a big house with a slanted roof," says Sabine. "There's stairs [a ladder] up the back to a platform—a sort of second floor next to the roof. There's benches around the downstairs part. It's cool on a hot day under the roof, but the second floor is a good place to get the sun."

Because the Gazebo could not accommodate an entire class, a small amphitheater was constructed. Three layers of railroad ties were laid one upon another. This all-purpose meeting space enabled good eye contact for groups of up to twenty-five people. Some called it the "circle" (although its basic shape was hexagonal); most often children called it the "railroad ties." Nestled in a blanket of kikuya grass within the fast-growing grove of Monterey pines, it supported many classroom activities as well as informal social interactions. It was a "spaceship" for space travel players. To other children, it was "a good place for lunch," a place to talk, play with toys, and have fun.

"We use it as 'home base' when our class has treasure hunts," says one of the teachers.

"It's where you can do your own sort of thing," says Kara, "sing a song, do a dance, do any show you want. It's a good place to sit and watch each other."

A group of girls are eating lunch. One of them puts a carrot up her sleeve, conjures it out of the air, and says it is a "goldfish." She then eats it with appropriate expressions of disgust, amid giggles all around.

One day a group of girls pretend to be rock-and-roll stars. Using sticks as microphones, they silently shout into them, swaying up and down and side to side. They turn into "strippers" until a noontime supervisor comes by and tells them in jest to get back to class before they lose all their clothes.

Ready-made picnic tables provided essential workstations for outdoor classroom activity. Though more costly, they provided comfortable places to eat lunch or socialize. Children being children, they would just as likely sit on the table with feet on the benches, as sit on the benches with feet on the ground. The tables made excellent game "bases" and were sometimes turned upside down to become "space ships." The most esoteric of these unintended uses occurred when heavy winter frosts turned tabletops into elevated rinks of frosty rime. For children living in a temperate climate like Berkeley, even a ten-minute slide on a six-foot-high tabletop was a significant winter event (it sounds hazardous, but no one got hurt).

The largest gathering place in the Yard was the wooden stage overlooking the asphalt ballgame area. Geometrically shaped and elevated eighteen inches (46 cm) above the ground, it was a good example of how a newly built facility could stimulate new activities. Classroom performances, community events, afterschool workshops, and recreation programs were held there. The backside of the stage was defined by a set of symmetrically positioned, six-foot (1.8 m) vertical poles that could be used as supports for scenery and theatrical props during performances. Gatherings of up to several hundred people were easily accommodated, with the audience sitting in chairs on the asphalt. A large parachute was temporarily suspended above the audience (from utility poles installed for the purpose) to provide shade.

NOOKS AND CRANNIES

As spaces were formed and shaped, we kept in mind the small-scale character of the child's world. We constantly looked for opportunities to create little corners, alcoves, shelves, ledges, hooks, nooks, cubbies, and crannies. We wanted to provide places where children could perch themselves, play with small objects, or stash personal belongings. Many elevated, comfortable spots were provided by logs, tree trunks, elevated cable spool tops, rocks, railings, raised spots in the sand area, and tables and benches throughout the Yard. Sometimes nooks were built into larger spaces like the play structure, Gazebo, and railroad ties. It was a design strategy that greatly helped children gain a sense of ownership of the Yard.

"My little lunchbox place is between two rocks," Amy explains, pointing to Willow Island. Her repertoire of personal spots includes other things "just my size: a pole where I hang my coat, a little tree I sit under that's just as tall as I am."

Plants also supplied special nooks and crannies. One child said he liked the century plant because it looked so "strange," especially the spiky leaves on which he sometimes hung his jacket. He remarked how the leaves caught the water when it rained so you could get "juice" at their base.

Plants offered an attractive, ever-changing array of hideouts.

The "stack-sack wall"—a vegetated resting place overlooking the Main Yard.

GREEN EMBELLISHMENT

At the midpoint of the Yard's evolution, we completed a behavior mapping study. This investigation showed that the asphalt was the most underused surface in the Yard (ironically, it was designed to endure the greatest impact). For this reason, as well as to soften the sharp contrast between the "biotic" Natural Resource Area and the "abiotic" Main Yard, we installed several groups of trees in various locations in the asphalt, including many flowering species. The city provided a back hoe to dig tree wells four feet (1.2 m) in diameter and six feet (1.8 m) deep.

Flowering plum trees were installed in a circle around the enclosure of the blue climbing net, to soften the harsh outline of the climbing structure. The glossy green and red foliage of Bradford pear trees shaded the central community area benches and accentuated the "green tunnel" effect of the path between the giant planter and the Natural Resource Area boundary fence. The path continued under a canopy of fruitless mulberry trees to a small MLK Way gate, which was flanked by Chinese wisteria winding in and out of the chainlink fencing, arching over the entrance.

A circle of six silk trees (*Albizia Julibrissin,* known as mimosa trees in the eastern United States) offered fluffy pink flowers and bright, green, fernlike foliage, lightly shading the gathering space beside the community bulletin board overlooking the ballplay area. In late spring, deep blue jacaranda trees punctuated another side of the same space, giving identity to the traditional play equipment and basketball court.

Along the far side, we planted a line of *Eucalyptus ficifolia,* with brilliant red clusters of hairy flowers and dark evergreen leathery leaves. They gave the area identity, increased the sense of enclosure, and offered protection from the ever-present, cold Pacific winds.

The mulberries, mimosas, eucalypti, and jacarandas surrounding the ballgame area, together with the Orchard Wayside olive and pepper trees, transformed a bland, anonymous space into an attractive "place" with form and identity.

Children appreciated the opportunity to be with their friends and explore their own private world. Each social niche had its own special character: a circle of bamboo (top), a recycled drainage pipe (middle), and a handmade bench designed to encourage conversation (bottom).

"The bushes are really good to hide in," Julie explains, "but right now everyone knows about them and you always get found there when we play tag. Now we hide in the weeds that fall over the path around the pond—you can scoot over to one side and the weeds will cover you and the chasers will go right on by. The bamboo is good for hiding in, too." (There were two areas of clumping bamboo in the Natural Resource Area.)

Nooks and crannies provided children with a complex *terra incognita* of hideaways across the whole site, to be discovered, used, outgrown, and re-inhabited by the next generation of children. Private places, where children could hang out alone or with a friend, were particularly valued. Children liked to perch above their surroundings in such a way that they could survey the whole scene yet at the same time remain separate—having the ability to see while not being seen.

Jay Appleton, the British landscape geographer, suggests that this prospect and refuge is a primordial, instinctive need of all people.[1] We explored different ways to accommodate this need. The cable spools, the upper level of the Gazebo, the roofs of the potting shed, the H.Q. fieldhouse (described in Chapter 14 as the base for recreational programs), and the storage space behind the ball wall provided private spaces in the Yard.

"You can use any kind of shoes to climb up there," a girl says, pointing to the roof of the H.Q. fieldhouse. "You just stick your foot in the gate hinge, grab the top with your hands, pull yourself up, and throw yourself on the roof. I learned it by watching other children. We have lunch up there, play tag up there, spy on other children in the Yard, or just lay back and get the sun."

"It's one of the best places for lunch on the Yard," a boy says, talking about the fieldhouse roof. "I feel like I'm floating when I'm up there, like I'm in a boat or taking a swim in the fresh air. It makes you feel good. There's two million ways of getting up and down. Sometimes we climb the fence, sometimes the trees, sometimes straight up the wall. It's sort of dangerous because you have to take a big step to get over. We pretend it's our very own planet up there. We don't go up on the other side 'cause you can get caught by the teachers."

Several small, hexagonal enclosures were designed by returning wooden-railing fences back on themselves. Called "corrals," three structures were located along the low mound between the meadow and the main fence along MLK Way. The fences primarily served as protection for the newly installed trees and bushes along the fence. As the vegetation matured, each corral acquired the distinctive identity of the species around it. Children used them as hideaways.

"It looks like a cave," Jennifer says, referring to one of the corrals. "We use it as a clubhouse. There's a front entrance up one step from the meadow and a back entrance under one of the rails. We like to play 'house' there and sweep it out. We pretend there's a doorbell on one of the poles. It's under the tree and smells of eucalyptus. A lot of people like how it smells . . . That's why I go there. It's a sort of a private spot."

Some children called the corrals "tepees" because of their pointed, open-frame roofs. They were designed that way so that children could make temporary roofs themselves with scraps of lumber or dried weeds to personalize the space.

In front of the school's administrative offices, sacks of wet concrete were laid to create a freeform "stack-sack wall" to support a south-facing planting bed along the full length of the main building. Undulating walls created tunnels, caves, and platforms for children's play, interwoven with a showy display of permanent and annual plantings, such as a thicket of sunflowers (see photograph, page 72).

CREATING A CENTER

Early in the planning process, we decided to concentrate community activity in the highly visible and accessible central portion of the site. A multipurpose area was needed to accommodate children's play as well as to provide a place for neighborhood residents to relax, socialize, and watch their children.

Development began with the construction of a timber play structure, which was designed by landscape architecture students and built by a local contractor. Most children simply called it "the structure." Its multilevel platforms offered several ways to climb up, slide down, and move through the varied spaces. An elevated bridge ended in one direction with a fireman's pole and a steep flight of steps. In the other direction, platforms descended to a low, wide slide and a second staircase. A ramped, tunnel-like space penetrated the structure at its midpoint, providing a connection between the surrounding asphalt and a large interior sand area. On the upper level, a favorite spot was the "balcony" that projected above the tunnel entrance, where children would play quietly, sometimes using it as a lookout.

Different spaces encouraged privacy and group interaction in which children shared personal possessions (top), played in their own secret hideaways (middle), or enjoyed each other's company (bottom).

"I peek out and spy on my friends and enemies," a girl confides, "where the boards have little spaces between them."

Each year the central area slowly expanded. With help from the local utilities company, we constructed a line of swings from utility poles, which served as an extension of "the structure." A second, smaller play structure was installed in the sand at the request of neighborhood families with very young children who used the Yard outside of school hours. Composed of wooden poles, metal pipes, open-ended steel barrels, and bright green, plastic panels, it was the only piece of manufactured equipment on the site (besides the climbing net and picnic tables). We called it by its brand name, "Big Toy." Most often, children pretended the structure was some sort of vehicle because of the cast-metal "steering wheel" mounted at one end. They twirled it madly around, at the same time uttering "driving" noises.

The central area was defined on one side by a waist-high solid timber wall capped with a continuous ledge (where children constructed small sand gardens). A raised concrete walkway bordered the other three sides. The pathway, built for wheelchair and stroller access, also let people walk through without getting their shoes full of sand. Park benches lined the path, shaded by Bradford pear trees in a giant planter fronting the walkway. Children called the planter the "giant dragon" because of its elongated, angular shape, and played in the shady patches of dirt beneath the pear trees.

Sand was the fourth major ground surface in the Yard (after asphalt, dirt, and vegetated ground covers). Apart from providing a safety surface, the sand served as play material, especially in the more secluded corners where there was less chance of sandcastles getting jumped on. Protected spots against fences, under the slide, below the bridge, and within the rocks encouraged the most elaborate sand play.

The central sand area continued under the play structure bridge into a bulbous, timber-walled polygon. Above it, suspended between one side of the bridge and poles on each side of the Mokelumne Aqueduct entrance, was a bright blue polypropylene climbing net. This erstwhile hammock attracted a constantly shifting mix of girls and boys playing games, shinnying down the chains that suspended the net from the bridge, lounging, faces to the sky, eyeing the drifting clouds, chatting, and watching the adjacent ballgames. It was a place of pure delight.

"About five people get on the net and five people shake it," says one of the children. "If someone falls off, all the people on the net get off and switch with the people pushing. I never fall off. I stay in the middle and roll 'round and 'round, but I never fall."

In response to changing user needs, the central community area evolved over the years, according to the availability of materials, money, labor, and equipment. As a finishing touch, we erected an eighteen-foot (5.5 m) entrance sign proclaiming "THE ENVIRONMENTAL YARD" (see photograph, page 67). Supported on four high poles, it hung over a community bulletin board that invited people to relax, socialize, play with their children, or just lay back in the sun.

•

About six years after the groundbreaking, we felt we had successfully developed a sense of place in the Yard. By then, it bore little resemblance to the original asphalt site. The community's many positive comments about the Yard's natural character supported a feeling of success. But the primary evidence came from the children. The results of systematically conducted research clearly indicated the Yard's positive influence on the children's attitudes towards their school experience (see Chapter 16).

REFERENCES

1. Appleton, J. (1975). *The Experience of Landscape.* New York: Wiley.

Exploring the Biosphere

We could not love the earth
half so well if we had not
had childhood in it.

— George Eliot,
Mill on the Floss

SPRING

In the spring the rainbows
go to work. The plants and
trees sing their own songs.
At night towards morning,
sleeping outside, I noticed
the beat of the earth.

— Riley

Wind, sunlight, the glowing moon, the cloud-patterned sky, the various forms of precipitation, streams, rivers, lakes, forest, and savanna —these were some of the universal attributes of the Earth's biosphere that we wanted to bring into the children's daily experience.

Our task was to create a place where the great range of the Earth's expression could be appreciated, from mild tranquillity to moments of tempestuous fury. Living in the temperate climate of the Bay Area, far from the countryside, people were inclined to discount the occasional unleashing of nature that washed away homes, uprooted trees, and turned placid urban creeks into raging torrents (charged by the rapid runoff from roofs, asphalt streets, and parking lots). The Yard was designed to respond to the local actions of weather and climate at a single point on the Earth's surface. The idea was to help children and teachers feel as if they were part of the biosphere and to encourage them to explore this relationship further.

GOING SOLAR

Children's drawings of the Yard invariably included the sun, smiling down from a corner of the sheet of paper. Was this an intuitive expression of the sun's gift of life—or was it the result of the teacher's common request to include the sun? Whatever the reason, how could this solar expression be extended towards a more explicit understanding of solar phenomena on Earth as it orbits the sun?

With the help of an architecture student, the children designed and painted a giant directional compass in an existing twenty-five-foot-diameter (7.6 m) game circle on the asphalt. Visible from the upper floor of the school, a single bright orange zigzag line joined the cardinal points, labeled with a large "N," "S," "E," and "W." The children called it the "Super Compass."

Early in the morning, when the sun was low, classroom groups anchored a sundial post in the center of the Super Compass. Each hour, a group of students lined a cord along the shadow, chalking in the location and noting the time. By the end of the day, everyone could admire the solar clock, noting how the shadow shortened before lunch and lengthened throughout the afternoon. Some of the children were so intrigued that they stayed after school to continue marking the shadows; some even stayed until sunset and returned early the next morning as the sun rose to complete the full cycle.

"What makes the shadow change? Why does it change direction? What makes it get shorter and longer?" asked one teacher. In pursuit of the answer, children drew each other's silhouettes on the asphalt at periodic intervals. They also recorded the changing shadow patterns of various objects in the Yard, such as play structures, swings, trees, fence posts, and rocks.

One year, inspired by Japanese shadow plays, children made puppets and wrote playlets. A shadow theater was constructed by stretching an old sheet across one end of the Mokelumne tunnel during the late afternoon. It worked beautifully. Everyone gathered around to applaud the child-authored tales and cast of silhouette characters dancing on the backlit canvas.

To celebrate Bay Area "Sun Day," Helen Cox asked her students to create sun pictures—sunrises, sunsets, stormy skies, sunny skies—with dyes made from natural materials such as beets, marigolds, dandelions, and onions. They discussed biological clocks, jet lag, the effects of working the graveyard shift, people living in the Arctic region experiencing the *aurora borealis* and the midnight sun, the significance of shadows and darkness in different cultures, the differences between natural and artificial light, and the importance of sunlight for living things and their adaptation to changes in light.

Miniature sundials, constructed of dirt-filled milk cartons with chopsticks in the middle, were placed on a sheet of paper in a sunlit window. Children recorded the shadows at the same time each day to get a sense of the annual and daily cycles of the Earth turning on itself and orbiting the sun—rather than the sun traversing the heavens. As Buckminster Fuller once noted, "It's the Earth that rises and sets not the sun . . . we should really talk about 'earthrise' and 'earthset.'"

With exquisite timing, a partial eclipse of the sun occurred at a point when Helen Cox's students were midway through studying the life of Galileo. The sky was cornflower clear that day. Fascinated children made pin-

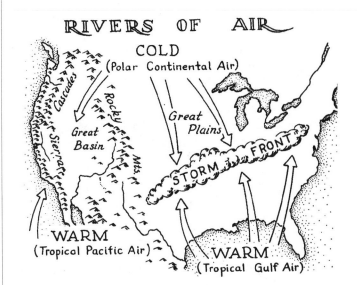

The climate of the Yard reflected its location in northern California, opposite the Golden Gate Bridge—a climate and weather system dominated by air movements and contrasting wet and dry seasons.[1]

CLOUD COUNTS

"Sometimes I try to count the clouds or count how they move—well, to see how long it takes to get from there to there. I count one . . . two . . . three. The last one I counted took sixty seconds. Some move fast and some move slower."

— Maibo

NATURAL LEARNING

Children drew their silhouettes with chalk and carefully observed the movement of their shadows and sensed the dynamic relationship between the Earth and the sun. These perceptions were readily expressed in their classroom work.

GALILEO MATH

How many years is it since the birth of Galileo in 1564?

answer: 1978 - 1564 = 414

How old was Galileo when he died in 1642?

answer: 1642 - 1564 = 78

How old was Galileo when he was imprisoned by the Inquisition in 1633?

answer: 1633 - 1564 = 69

How many years did Galileo live as a prisoner in his own house before he died in 1643?

answer: 1642 - 1633 = 9

— Helen Cox,
classroom notes

hole projections of the heavenly alignment on bits of paper (emphatically not looking directly at the sun). They first saw the silhouette of the moon biting into the bright disc of the projected sun. It then slowly receded as the moon continued its orbit and Earth continued turning. Later, this dramatic demonstration of Galileo's doctrine was recorded in wonderful drawings of the sun and Earth, as well as Galileo looking through his telescope at the solar system. Young imaginations had no problem capturing the universe on paper. It was a wonderful example of how children could be drawn into an experience of visual representation when the teacher provided sufficient motivation.

SKYWARDS

It was intriguing to think of the Yard as a column of air, beginning in underground cracks, crevices, and mud layers; rising through the minuscule sheltering gaps between woodchips on the ground; up through layers of niches in grasses, indigenous plants, shrubs, trees, and play structures; continuing upward to the roof of the school building; and beyond, until the last few air molecules gave way to the infinite vacuum of space.

A tradition developed of exploring the Yard's air space with many types of airborne objects: hot-air balloons, kites, paper airplanes, parachutes, sails, wind chimes, windmills, and windsocks. One of the most successful examples was a sky sculpture constructed out of twelve-foot-long (3.7 m) strips of silver Mylar, suspended from a nylon chord stretched diagonally across the Yard, between a corner of the school building and a high point on the boundary fence. Incredibly sensitive to the wind and sun, the structure was never still. It became a glittering pulse of bobbing columns of light suspended in an ocean of air, marking the faintest breezes with languid reflections, at other times dancing before the setting sun. The Mylar strips became shimmers of light and emitted hard, crinkling sounds when blown horizontal by strong Pacific winds.

A PLACE FOR ALL SEASONS

One of the most alienating aspects about the Yard prior to redevelopment was that it offered little visual indication of the passage of seasons. During most of the winter season, thick, gray clouds matched the uniformly gray asphalt. The foggy skies during other times of the year produced a similar effect, especially in the mornings before the fog burned off. The sole indicator of wind speed and direction was an occasional dead leaf or piece of litter rolling across the asphalt. About the only time the asphalt looked attractive was when springtime showers transformed it into a giant glittering mirror reflecting the blue skies that had cleared before the surface water dried off—but this was a rare occurrence.

In the old schoolyard, the children shared a nearly identical microclimate, whether they raced around in a ballgame or sat in quiet conversation. When temperatures were high, the schoolyard was uniformly hot, except for two thin areas of shade along the southern edge. Little relief was provided on cold, windy days, except for the windbreak effect of the apartment buildings to the west. When it rained, no shelter was available. The children needed shady spots where they could be active yet cool in hot weather, as well as sheltered sunny spots where they could feel warm and relaxed during cold spells. The redeveloped Yard modified the microclimate and made the space more comfortable for all users, year round.

As vegetation matured, the Yard worked like a gigantic weather instrument that responded to the seasonal climatic cycles as well as to every nuance of daily weather. Trees gauged the seasons and indicated the merest puff of wind. They marked the angle of the sun and the time of year. Complex patterns of seasonal shadows were formed by opaque leaves and light transmitted through bare branches. The aftermath of a storm was read not as a sheet of cleanly washed asphalt but by clots of blown leaves and twigs swept around obstructions, conforming to the unmistakable patterns of waterborne debris. The biggest storms of the year were marked by cracked and broken branches. Great storms, when houses in the region were washed away in torrents of mud and water, were marked by fallen trees—as happened in 1982, when the weeping willow by the pump box was blown down and had to be cut up for firewood.

The original Washington schoolyard offered minimal educational value. An exception was the beautiful drainage pattern created by the shimmering hailstones of a cold spring shower (top).

Following construction, students easily noticed the seasonal changes in their surroundings. The winter landscape (middle) invited the children to use the sticks, leaves, and other found materials for making everything from "dolls" to "swords for great battles." Teachers, aware of the hidden potential in these activities, used the children's imagination as motivation for reading and writing.

The summer landscape (bottom) provided a multitude of possibilities for school and community.

SUPER BANNERS

"Super banners" were created as a way to express the naturalization of the Yard through art. As a first step, the children created full-size paper mock-ups of the banners and suspended them in position to see what they would look like. The final versions were made of appliqué canvas. Over a period of several days, the students assembled banners in every available corner of the school; everyone could see what was going on and participate. An infectious spirit gripped the banner-making group. It was a rare and rewarding event, quite different from the standard community gathering aimed at solving administrative crises. Some children were so intensively motivated that they worked non-stop for three days, eating their lunches as they went along.

A few days before the 1975 Yardfest, the banners were brought to the roof of the school buildings, unfurled, and hung symbolically in the Yard's column of atmosphere. Six colorful proclamations were made to passers-by, informing them that something was going on and inviting them to take part:

The Sky (blue background): community in the foreground, hills behind, birds, weather, clouds, kites flying.

The Neighborhood (orange background): people helping people, trees, streets, buildings, traffic.

The Pond (green background): pond life, fish, birds, cattails.

Children at Play (yellow background): games in the Yard.

Barnyard and Garden (red background): pigs, goats, chickens, pumpkins, beans, sunflowers.

The Yard (green, yellow, black background): "WEY" written large, standing for Washington Environmental Yard (top left).

RAINWALK

After much forethought, discussion, and carefully worded permission slips to parents, Ms. Cox organized a dozen interested children to bring their swimwear to school and prepare for the next heavy spring rain. When the expected downpour arrived a few days later, the children took off their clothes, donned swimwear, danced around barefoot in the meadow, turned their faces to the sky, and let the cool water stream over their bodies. Several minutes later they were back in the warmth of the classroom to dry off and dress amidst lots of giggling. Like mountain climbing, the activity was done for the sake of pure experience. No ill effects were recorded.

The great freeze of 1973 was a rare climatic event that brought more than two weeks of continuous frost. The ponds froze over. Children lifted up sheets of ice, looked at one another through them, and skimmed pieces of broken ice across the frozen pond surface. Several teachers realized the educational possibilities. Children took the temperature of the water, compared it with the temperatures of other parts of the Yard, and recorded further evidence of the weather's impact: the hard ground, wilted plants, and hungry birds.

WINTER'S TALE

As the annual winter solstice (around December 21) approached, teachers explained how current holidays (holy days) were originally pre-Christian celebrations of the most important times in Earth's annual cycle, drawing attention to the natural order of the universe and the interdependence of all living things. Winter solstice marked the Northern Hemisphere's longest night, the midpoint in Earth's journey around the sun between autumnal equinox (around September 22) and vernal equinox (around March 21). Winter solstice was a time for introspection, for looking at the direction of one's life, and for spending more time at home.

Nature rested during the darker part of the year, children observed. Animals hibernated or became less active. Salamanders, discovered in their winter habitats under logs and rocks, were an example of an animal that was well adapted to the winter season.

Vegetation decayed and decomposed, renewing the soil with humus for next year's rebirth. There was much beauty to observe: yellowing stands of cattails on a misty morning illuminated by pale winter light; the still waters of the dormant lower pond reflecting the naked, drooping branches of the weeping willow; an orange carpet of maple leaves resting on the surface of the upper pond, moving softly with the wind, gliding slowly towards the waterfall, then, one at a time, rushing over, floating downstream to add nutrients to the lower pond. Observations such as these helped children to view life and death in nature as continuous cycles of transformation of energy from one form to another.

Helen Cox and the children arranged a special display entitled "Winter on the Yard" in the main corridor exhibit case. The display included a variety of decomposing organic materials such as dead leaves, dried branches and seed pods, and rotting logs covered with shelf fungi. "Is death bad?" the display asked. "Is death ugly? Is death sad? Do we need death? What would happen if nothing ever died?"

FUNGI FUN

Fungi, a herald of spring, appeared with the first warm spell. They included the short-lived, moist, bell-shaped fungi poking through the carpet of dead leaves in the redwood grove; the permanent shelf fungi growing on one end of the log by the wooden bridge; and the large white domes thrusting through the forest litter in the chaparral.

Reactions were mixed.

"The mushrooms on the log are gross," one child wrote.

To counteract such attitudes, Ms. Cox organized mushroom hunts for children to record where mushrooms were growing, what they were growing on, their habitat characteristics, spacing patterns, sizes, colors, and smells.

Children collected ripe samples with open gills. They removed the stems and laid the heads, gill side down, onto paper to make spore prints. From each head, up to sixteen billion spores replicated the fine radial pattern of the gills.

The students learned that the puffball fungus contains a central sack that, when ripe, bursts to release the spores into the atmosphere. Another day, a mycologist brought water-gathering earth star fungi to class. When placed in cold water, the specimens absorbed water before silently exploding, leaving a layer of spores floating on the surface.

Children observed Yard mushrooms being nibbled away by ants, beetles, flies, and slugs. They learned that mushrooms also served as food for cattle, deer, mice, rabbits, squirrels—and people. In addition, the students discovered that fungi do not have flowers, roots, or leaves. They learned that fungi do not produce their own

ABOUT THE MUSHROOMS IN THE YARD

There are many types of mushrooms. Those in the Yard are mostly agarics. Agarics are mushrooms with gills.

A mushroom is a fungus. Molds and yeasts are also fungi. Fungi are plants without flowers, seeds, roots, or leaves. They cannot make their own food like other green plants. Fungi have two ways of getting food:

1. from living plants and animals (this type of fungi is called a parasite);

2. from dead plants and animals, like rotting wood and leaves (this type of fungi is called a saprophyte).

There are no general rules to tell an edible mushroom from a poisonous one. Some people say "it's a toadstool" if they think it is poisonous, but this is only a nickname and not scientific. Only an expert can tell poisonous mushrooms from the edible ones, and often people will call an edible mushroom "a toadstool" because it looks ugly or poisonous to them. Some brightly colored and some ugly mushrooms are very delicious, and some that look pretty and white are deadly poisonous. One of the most poisonous mushrooms is an agaric like the ones in the Yard. Its scientific name is *Amanita bisoprigera*. Never experiment by tasting a bit— it could be deadly!

The main part of the fungus is called the mycelium. The mycelium is under the ground. It is a feathery, white, network of filaments. The mushrooms (or "fruiting bodies") develop on the mycelium. The mycelium goes on growing for years, but many mushrooms only last a day or so.

Mushrooms grow on the mycelium when there is enough moisture and the temperature is right. Then they seem to pop up overnight. Once a mushroom begins to swell and grow and push up, almost nothing can stop it! A mushroom can actually break through a concrete floor!

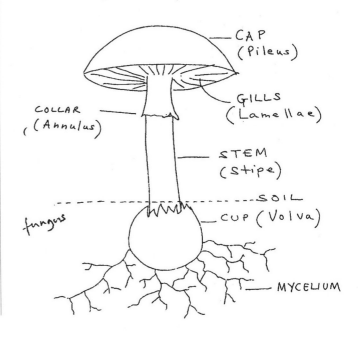

morel

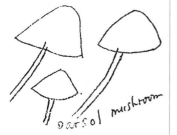

parsol mushroom

The mushroom is called the fruiting body because it contains the spores for making new plants. The spores of agarics are on the gills under the cap. They are microscopic (can only be seen with a microscope), but if you make a spore print by placing the cap gill-side down on white paper, then you can see the spores. Some mushrooms have 16 billion spores in one cap! The spores fall on the ground or are blown away. The ones that fall in a good place grow into mycelium.

Although fungi "steal" their food they give it back (with interest!) to the soil when they decay. The mushrooms that feed on decaying wood break it down into soil—otherwise our forests would be full of dead wood! Fungi are food for flies, beetles, ants, slugs, tortoises, mice, rabbits, red squirrels, sheep, cattle, deer—and people!

— Helen Cox,
classroom notes

STUDYING MUSHROOMS IN THE YARD

We will go in small groups to look at the mushrooms today. We will observe and record the following information:

Where are most of the mushrooms?

What do they seem to be growing on (wood, leaves, etc.)?

Are they in open places or darker places?

Do they grow singly or in groups?

Do they grow in any particular pattern (a circle, for example)?

What color are the mushrooms, top of the cap, and gills?

What different characteristics can we note?

How do they smell?

Make a sketch of one or more mushrooms.

What does the mycelium look like?

food like green plants, but instead derive nourishment from other organisms—either living ones (parasitic fungus) or dead ones (saprophytic fungus). Fungi's vital role in breaking down and returning organic matter to the soil was well demonstrated. "Otherwise," a student reflected, "forests would turn into stacks of dead tree trunks and piles of leaves."

The teacher stressed the fact that there was no easy way to distinguish edible and poisonous mushrooms. "Toadstool," she explained, was a name used for a mushroom that looked ugly and poisonous, but it was a worthless notion, since some ugly mushrooms were good to eat and some pretty ones were deadly poisonous. Only an expert could tell, so children were told not to experiment, not even with a little piece!

When digging around a mushroom, children discovered the feathery white filaments of mycelium weaving intricate lines of tracery among the dead leaves, twigs, and woodchips from which the short-lived fruiting mushrooms sprouted. The mycelium, however, lived for years. In some places, a "magic ring" of mushrooms emerged, caused by the spreading of the mycelium out from the point where the original spore had fallen.

Some classrooms experimented with bread mold and discussed the fact that bread itself was made with a fungus: yeast. The students grew black bread mold (*Rhizopus*, the common mold of starchy food) by scraping dust from the floor and wiping it on damp slices of bread. After storing the bread in a warm place for two to three days, the children used hand lenses to inspect the gray, tangled mass of mycelium threads, which later bore the black heads of spore-bearing sporangia. By placing two additional saucers of bread—one covered, one uncovered—next to the moldy bread, the children discovered that the spores can travel through the air. Mold showed up on the exposed slice long before appearing on the covered slice.

As a "fungus finale," children and their families visited the San Francisco Mycological Society's annual Fungus Fair at the Oakland Museum where more than 250 species were displayed with portions of their natural habitats.

HERALDS OF SPRING

As a prelude to spring, small branches from alder, birch, flowering plum, hazelnut, maple, and pussy willow trees were pruned and displayed in water-filled vases throughout the school. As the days passed, the buds began to open: first the pussy willow catkins, covered with rich, yellow powdery pollen; then the delicate pink flowers of the plum; followed by the tight oval catkins of the alder and birch and the drooping elongated hazelnut catkins. Each bursting bud and bright green, leafy branch reinforced the themes of rebirth and regeneration, stimulating closer investigation of the means of reproduction for each species.

Each year the springtime chain of events in the Yard became increasingly exuberant and uplifting. Moving outdoors became irresistible. Teachers encouraged students to study the complex orchestration of birds, their territorial squabbles, and their home-building flight patterns as they carried twigs, fabric, and paper in their beaks.

Brilliant clusters of daffodils, crocuses, and irises competed for attention with the lowly, but equally splendid, sour grass and dandelions. Anise and teasel seedlings carpeted the ground beneath the tall, dried remains of the previous year's growth. Early flowering trees indicated the spring surge, a time of renewed hope: the white "candles" of the buckeye, with bees constantly hovering about; the bright yellow, pompom blossoms and heady scent of acacia; the silvered cliff of pussy willow at the far end of the meadow; the growing tips of redwood branches, outlining each tree in vivid yellow-green. Spring never failed to boost energy. It displayed the fruits of the past year's labors and urged redevelopment to continue.

Spring was also a time to read Rachel Carson's *Silent Spring*, to remind ourselves of her deep concern for children and their planetary inheritance. Children read about the use of insecticide against beetles that spread Dutch elm disease, and how the poison stayed on leaves, fell to the ground, and was eaten by worms and birds—causing damage to the entire ecosystem.

THE HERALDS OF SPRING

Herald: **A person or thing who makes an announcement of what is to come.**

Who or what are the heralds of spring? Examples are:

Return of the birds: **Some birds migrate during the colder weather to warmer climates. In early spring they begin to return. Have you seen a robin yet?**

Male birds sing to let other birds know where their territory is. In the spring you can see squabbling between male birds. Usually, male birds are more brightly colored than the females. Have you noticed single birds singing or groups of birds twittering?

Sometimes you see a bird flying with something in its beak —a piece of string, a twig, a scrap of fabric, a piece of paper to build its nest. Some nests rest on a tree limb, some hang and swing from a branch, some are woven, some are glued together. Have you seen a bird carrying something?

Spring flowers and leaves: **The acacias are in bloom. So are the sour grass, dandelions, and fruit trees. The pussy willow catkins are out too. Bulbs (daffodils, crocus, hyacinth, tulips) are among the first plants to bloom, followed by the California poppies. How many different flowers have you seen? Which trees have new leaves? What shade of green are they? How do they feel? Will they get bigger? Which trees look the same as they did in the winter?**

The seedlings from the fall are really beginning to grow. Look in the Natural Resource Area. What do you see? Do you see masses of anise and teasel seedlings? Where are they located?

Fungi: **Fungi prefer to live in climate that is mild and moist. They like shady locations and take their nutrition from other vegetation such as rotting wood and leaf mulch. Fungi are not green because they do not make their own food like other plants. They help to recycle organic matter. Study the big log; it is covered with shelf fungi, so named because of its growth habit.**

— Helen Cox, classroom notes

FRUITS OF THE FALL

The return to school in September was an especially intriguing time. Many children did not use the Yard during the summer because they lived too far away or chose to participate in other activities. On the first day of school, the children excitedly walked around the Yard, checking up on things.

"Hey, look at the pumpkins! Remember how small the plants were?"

"We'll carve them for Halloween."

"Look, they put some benches in."

"D'ya see they fixed the swings?"

"Wow, look how much the bamboo has grown!"

Classes were assigned to record the changes and new additions to the Yard: the hard, bright green olives nestled amongst the dense foliage of the olive trees; the large nuts of the buckeye, their casings just beginning to crack open to expose shiny brown nuts; the drying seed heads of teasel, anise, and dock beginning to shed their abundant crops to produce next year's plants; and the fall-colored leaves of liquidambar, gingko, willow, and maple.

While many of the small increments of change could not be pinpointed, together they created an overall impression of substantial growth due to the time-lapse effect: new growth on the ends of thousands of small branches, sections of chainlink fence taken over by vines, enlarged patches of shade provided by trees around the play structures, increasing insect and bird populations supported by improved habitat conditions.

Comments such as "Oh, the Yard is looking really nice," though sounding like platitudes, expressed delight in the gradual changes that continued to provide shape and coherence to the whole—a fragment of the planet renewing itself bit by bit each year.

In Part Two, the focus will shift from the naturalization process, the associated changes in human behavior, and the teachers' responses described in these opening chapters. The new emphasis will be how the Yard functioned day to day as a curricular resource and space for child development and education.

REFERENCES

1. Maps reprinted, by permission, from Gilliam, H. (1962). *Weather of the San Francisco Bay Region.* Berkeley, Calif.: University of California Press.

Part II:
Developing the Whole Child

CHAPTER 8

Moving

Moving stimulates the kinesthetic, proprioceptive, and vestibular senses. It is a critical part of normal child development. Given access, opportunity, and adult encouragement, children will naturally explore their surroundings. The need for movement provides a rationale for creating quality environments capable of sustaining positive learning and physical and mental growth. This is particularly important in highly industrialized societies where children's opportunities for movement are becoming restricted by television viewing and issues of safety and liability.

oo many children today have stopped moving. In industrialized countries and in affluent, middle-class communities across the world, children are spending too much of their time indoors with television, computers, and video games, rather than exercising their bodies in outdoor, free-play activity. In the United States, where these trends are the most advanced, childhood obesity has become a major health issue.[1]

The increase in sedentary, indoor activities has been driven in part by a decrease in opportunities for outdoor play. The growth of public violence has made parents fearful about letting their children out to play on their own. In the majority of families with children, the parents work and are not at home when children return from school. Apprehension about social risks in the outdoor environment has encouraged many parents to enroll their children in afterschool programs, such as music, gymnastics, ecology, cooking, and art. The best programs offer an array of creative, nonformal activities to serve children's varied interests; many programs, however, do not provide this level of quality. For the millions of children whose parents cannot afford afterschool care, watching television has become their primary leisure activity.

Indoor programs have begun to replace outdoor informal play in the leisure time of many middle-class children. Many programs, of course, incorporate physical education (though rarely outdoors). But few programs focus on free play as a main activity, largely because it is hard to "sell," at least in the United States. In other countries, such as the United Kingdom, the Netherlands, and Germany, an impressive range of leisure programs are offered by nonprofit organizations, labor unions, and housing associations, often with government partnership. Such programs have existed for at least three decades. In a handful of countries, public policy in the nonformal education sector addressed the need for community-based leisure programs much earlier; in Sweden and Denmark, for example, efforts began in the 1940s with the development of urban playpark and adventure playground programs.

In much of the world, in marginal communities lacking the luxuries of industrial development, children lead lives deprived of material comfort. However, as long as there is enough to eat, they are constantly on the move in outdoor play. Their level of physical grace and agility are striking to the visitor from the developed world, where children's movement outdoors has fallen below the threshold required for good health—even though geographic movement has increased via cars and school buses.

The negative consequences for children's health are dramatic.[2] The projected impact in added health-care costs over the lifetimes of these children is an entirely avoidable burden. Physical education should be part of the answer, but it disappeared long ago from the curriculum in many school districts in the United States—a shocking fact to educators visiting from abroad. The most extreme signal of this trend has been the abandonment of recess in some school districts, which deprive children of their only opportunity to let off steam during the school day.[3]

Washington School definitely still had recess! By the time the Yard was fully developed, it provided such a range of attractive three-dimensional spaces and physical supports for creative body movement that it was impossible for children not to move. This is how an effectively designed movement space should work—not set apart from other settings but designed as a catalyst in the entire environment, irresistibly motivating children to move and exercise their bodies in myriad ways.

BODY LANGUAGE

With each increment of development, an increasing number of children, regardless of ability, would practice moving their bodies through space. With grace and agility, they exercised their muscles, ligaments, and limbs—balancing, chasing, climbing, crawling, dodging, hanging, hopping, jumping, leaping, rocking, rolling, running, sliding, spinning, squirming, swinging, tumbling, twirling, twisting—without a single instruction from a physical education teacher.

This was a far cry from the old schoolyard, where girls hung around admiring the boys' prowess at playing ball or felt excluded because they were not attracted by the crowded play equipment; and where nonathletic

The diversity of challenging environments stimulated a diversity of movement. Especially for children with disabilities, the Yard provided a sense of freedom unavailable in less diverse play spaces.

NATURAL LEARNING

TRADITIONAL GAMES

Each recess, patches of asphalt rang with the ancient chants and game cries heard around the world.

"Green light!" a girl yells, her back turned towards a line of children a few yards away. The line advances, each player moving as fast as possible while retaining an ability to freeze suddenly.

"Red light!" She whips around, facing the group, and sends anyone who is still moving back to the baseline. She repeats the calls until she is tagged by a player, who then becomes the new "light."

"Simon says" was played on any handy spot of asphalt with much giggling as the children contorted themselves into the most impossible positions. There were also the raucous back-and-forth dashing of "red rover" and the circular "duck, duck, goose" played around the giant compass circle.

Children enjoyed many variations of traditional catching and jump rope games. Chinese jump rope was particularly popular. To play, children tied a large number of rubber bands together to make a string long enough to loop around the legs of two children standing six to eight feet (1.8 to 2.4 m) apart. Three or four then jumped back and forth, inside and outside the loop, as it was slowly raised inch by inch. Players dropped out when they tripped on the "rope." The last player remaining was the winner.

Mostly girls played hopscotch on the three or four hopscotch designs painted along the edges of the asphalt. Sometimes they chalked their own designs. In the old Forum in Rome, there are still hopscotch diagrams scratched in the pavement. The Romans supposedly learned it from the ancient Greeks and then introduced it to the British, who took it to America. Different designs and versions of the game are found in many countries, including Burma, India, Japan, China, Russia, and Scotland.

children were ridiculed and ostracized for not participating in the unchanging routines of ball courts, game lines, and metal bars.

The Yard celebrated the exuberant fun and excitement of creative movement and expanded beyond the opportunities provided by standard play equipment.

As new elements were added, children invented games with more flexible sets of rules. These games sometimes served as an extension of existing traditions, sometimes reflected the impact of mainstream mass culture of television and film, and sometimes resulted in intriguing, imaginative action games that defied categorization.

Physical diversity stimulated a broader variety of activity. Traditional games that were the base of the children's culture in the Yard became increasingly varied and interwoven with new activities that flourished in response to the expanding choices in the landscape. As the range of physical challenges broadened, more children were able to participate and feel better about themselves regardless of their ability. Movement helped children acquire physical competence and self-confidence through interaction with their surroundings.

"YOU'RE IT!"

Chase games were excellent examples of how the diversified landscape expanded the play repertoire.

"Last one in the dirt area is 'it,'" shouts Rachel. "We play a lot of tag back there because it has lots of things to run around and it's soft when you fall down," she notes, reflecting the children's preference for playing chase games in the Natural Resource Area. The children found the space more interesting and challenging.

"You have to know the bases," Joel explains. "Usually we take time out to decide on them. They could be the logs, parts of the railings, certain rocks, the picnic tables, the bridge, the Gazebo, railroad ties—there's lots of possibilities."

"When we play tag in the meadow, you have to talk to a rock," says Devin. "If you don't, you're out of the game. They're 'talking rocks.' You can say things like, 'How are you doing? Want some tea?'"

"We play 'Marco Polo' around the weeping willow tree," says Harriet. "One person's 'it' and the others have their eyes closed and they say 'Marco' and you have to say 'Polo' so they can hear where you are. The tree [Willow Island] is base, except you have to be careful not to fall in the water."

The children who put the highest premium on running complained that there was not enough room in the Natural Resource Area. The unencumbered expanses of the Main Yard, though, easily allowed them to play tag in groups of six or seven. There were still many places to hide: in the far corners, behind the structures, in the weeds and bushes around the edges. These children enjoyed the spread-out feeling.

"We use the [Big Toy] barrels as base," explains Devin. "You can only stay there for five counts, then you have to get off. Sometimes when the chasers are about to get you . . . when they're about to kill you, you're scared. The fun part is the running. I run like crazy. I just like running. I like the air to get at me and when I don't get tagged I feel proud. I run every day. My dad's a runner. We go up in the park and run first thing in the morning."

"In 'TV tag' you squat down and say the name of a TV show," says one girl, "but you can't say it again in the same game and if you don't say a name, you'll be 'it.' In 'freeze tag' you have to stay still when you're tagged, and you can only get untagged if one of the players touches you. 'Tunnel tag' is where you make your legs like a tunnel and the only way you can get free is if someone goes through them."

"'Freeze tag,' 'mashed potatoes,' and 'bottle of poison' are what we usually play," says George. "Hey Jeffrey, you be 'it'; we're playing poison. Ha, ha, you've got the poison. Do anything you like except with a 'p,' like 'popcorn' or 'potatoes.'"

The bars were the scene of many tag and chasing games.

"For monkey tag," Muffin explains, "we have 'time boxes' [formed by the monkey bars], where the person who's 'it' can't catch you. If a person touches you, you're 'it.' My friend and I trick each other. Every time I go into a box, she goes out; then, when I go out, she goes in."

Jenny and Amy run over from the rings and climb the monkey bars. Larry is there and says, "Let's play 'hot lava.'"

Both girls watch him dangle, threatening to drop. They both dangle and drop.

"Hot lava!" they yell in unison.

Larry moves over to the rings and hangs upside down.

"Mommy, oh Mommy!" he yells. "I just turned into the hot lava monster!"

He tries to catch Jenny. She runs away.

He catches Amy. Jenny tries to save her.

They try not to touch the ground ("hot lava") and get back on the bars. Larry catches Jenny.

"I'm going to take you to my hot lava house," he says.

She runs away and starts chasing him, hits him playfully, scolds him, and tells him to go under the ladder bar. Another boy joins in. The game turns into "boys against girls." The girls grab another boy, get him down on the ground, count to twenty, and dance around yelling.

Settings were designed to stimulate hopping, balancing, running, jumping, and walking. They offered children a variety of ways to experience the Yard environment through movement. A "magic circle" of rocks motivated a special form of tag (top) while the railroad ties encouraged balancing games (bottom).

I like the big wooden sculpture
Out side. Some times I play tag
on it.

BALL TAG

"Ball tag," a free-form chasing game with many variations, was played all over the Yard.

Lamonte explains the counting-out routine to avoid being "it." "I'll say, 'Put your foot in the middle.' Then I'll say 'eeny, meeny, miny, mo' or 'eeny, meeny, gitchalini, ba ba lini, and out goes you!' Then we'll start playing, but I won't go on base—I'll say, 'Na, na, na!' And they'll throw the ball at me, but I'll dodge out of the way and it'll hit the guy behind."

He runs across the asphalt, gets hit with the ball, laughs, picks it up, and starts to chase the thrower, who runs behind the spools. Lamonte gets tired, sits on the ball, and bounces up and down. His friend clambers across the spools behind him and gives him a raspberry.

Lamonte leaps into action. Both race off across the asphalt around one of the basketball poles. Lamonte hurls the ball and hits his friend in the back. A boy and girl who had been sitting on the bench join in. The girl grabs the ball. The boys dance around her, smiling and having fun. She throws the ball at one of the boys, who catches it, tucks it under his arm, and pulls out a set of Star Wars cards! They huddle around the boy, admiring the cards and passing them from hand to hand.

Peter explains how they play ball tag on the play structure, making use of the structure's third dimension.

"The guy who's 'it' has the ball down below in the sand," he explains. "The rest of us climb around on the structure and try to keep from being hit. Sometimes we'll jump off into the sand if we think we can dodge the ball."

"He's a girl—you're on our team now."

Jenny teases Larry, calling him a baby. He chases her, teases her; she keeps teasing in return. They all laugh. The recess bell signals the end of their otherwise endless chasing "fugue" that plays its final bars as they continue running around each other on the way back to class.

SPYING, HIDING, SEEKING

"There's a boy we spy on," says Christine, "to see what he's doing, in case he's making up a plan. I spy on him, then he chases me to get all the news he can about the girls."

"I spy all over the place," says Kent. "I just follow people without them knowing. Sometimes I creep up on them, jump out of the bushes, and surprise them. Me and my friends just go in the passageway between the bushes, with all our army stuff, or we make stuff out of what's around—like a stick with a knob for a trigger can be a gun."

"We camouflage ourselves by sticking leaves in our hair when we play 'army,'" says Mark. "We hold branches in our hands and stick leaves in our shoes."

"We play 'secret agents,'" says Kevin. "I bring badges from the air force and police sets I have at home. I get the chief's badge and then we spy around looking for crooks, around the ponds mostly, 'cause there's no good places to hide out on the Main Yard."

"The pond section is the hardest place to find people," says Edith. "There's a space between two trees where my friends can't find me; or I hide in the bushes in the corner, and when my friend comes up I go to another place. I know all my friends' hiding places and always catch them."

"Where are you?" somebody yells.

"Over here in our hangout," shouts Alice.

Without the complex, interconnected landscape of the Yard, none of this creative peek-a-boo movement and social interaction would have been possible. Time and time again, when asked what they liked about the Yard, the children mentioned "lots of places to hide," "spying on people," and "playing hide-and-go-seek," as well as favorite hiding spots such as "behind the weeping willow," "in the redwoods," "in the bamboo," "under the eucalyptus," "around the ponds" and, most frequently, "in the bushes."

One version of hide-and-go-seek was beautifully adapted to the meadow. All the "hiders" lay in the long grass. The "seeker" stood on one spot trying to identify the children lying around her.

"I feel excited when I'm hiding from other people, because I don't want them to find me," says Anna. "It's scary, like a bank robber's coming to the door."

JUMPING

Jumping was mostly an integral part of chasing, hiding, seeking, and spying activities, except for the occasional child who loved jumping for its own sake.

"I jump from the bridge, the slide, and the fire pole into the sand," says Michael. "I feel excited when I jump. It's kind of scary until you're in the air. It makes me think of astronauts. I want to be an astronaut or a parachutist when I grow up."

A group of boys are jumping over one of the railings by the meadow. They take a running start and monitor each other's performance. They try going over sideways holding on with both hands and return by sliding under, and try various other ways of going over and under. One of them starts leapfrogging over a nearby freestanding post.

Girls played climbing and balancing games on the three layers of railroad ties enclosing the meeting area. On the top layer of ties, they walked around and hopped down into the enclosed space. They held contests, jumping out into the space surrounding the ties, beginning at the lowest level and then going higher and higher, making a mark on the ground for each advance in distance.

Children also saw how far they could travel by taking running leaps off a sheet of plywood supported on one end by a log. The homemade springboard offered a most satisfying jump.

TWIRLING

What ballgames were to boys, the bars—especially the twirling bars—were to girls. Despite the vast array of additional opportunities available in the Yard, the bars remained the girls' haven, a place where they could escape into their own subculture, as in every schoolyard in the land.

"It's our whole life," explain Julie and Jenny. "We play on other things, too, but we like the bars best. We learn all sorts of things." One of them carefully balances the small of her back across the waist-high horizontal bar. She grips it on either side with both elbows and slowly tilts her body backwards until it is almost vertical. Suddenly she drops frontwards, breaking her fall by bending her knees up against her chest just before her feet hit the rubber mat.

"That's a backwards jump," she says. "It's one of the first things you learn."

"There's a frontwards jump too," chimes in her friend. "It's harder than backwards. You have to balance on your stomach and it can really hurt." They both cup one leg over the bar and begin twirling fast. First one way, then the other, with remarkable agility. It is a virtuoso performance.

"It's scary when you first start; your legs have to get used to it," Julie comments. "It feels like you're on a Ferris wheel, spinning through the air. It feels like you're falling, but you're not really."

Clearly, the bars were a great stimulant for kinesthetic and vestibular perception, so important for child development.[4]

"I get excited when I learn new things," says her friend. "I like to get dizzy; it's part of the fun."

She hangs upside down, hair brushing the mat, and watches Jackie and Beth as they each cup a leg over the other bar and rock back and forth.

"You have to do that before you can twirl," comments Alice. "It gets your legs used to it."

"When you can twirl with only one hand, it's called 'one hand,'" says Bosmi, "and when you can do it with no hands, it's called 'criss-cross.' You can put your fingers through your belt loops, or if you have an elastic top, you stick your fingers in there, to keep your hands out of the way. We don't know how to do that yet, but we're going to learn from our cousin."

"Seesaw, seesaw . . . teeter totter, teeter totter . . ." the girls chant. They are now interlaced and balanced on the bar in such a way that they can rock back and forth as one. They call it "seesaw" and mention a version where you can twirl all the way around together—but they can't do it yet.

Two girls challenge each other to a "chicken fight." They hang from the bars, twist their legs together, and try to pull each other down. "Whoever lets go first loses," they explain.

A boy joins in. "I like to see everything upside down," he explains. "You see people walking on the sky and you see people walking sideways—it's fun. It makes you laugh and fall off and hit the mat." The three start counting to see who can stay up the longest.

Alice goes to one of the vertical poles of the high bars, hangs on with one hand, and spins around with her other arm extended.

"I feel dizzy," she shouts. "I feel like someone is pushing me round and round." Now she swings around both poles, alternately, using one hand and then the other in a figure eight.

One of the girls puts her legs through the rings, hangs upside down, confidently flips over, and drops to the ground. "The rings are good," she says, "'cause you can get a good grip. I never have to worry about falling down when I hang upside down . . . I get more blood in my head so I can concentrate on things," she giggles.

SWINGING

"I close my eyes and feel I'm going faster and faster and higher and higher. When I throw my head back it feels like I'm not on anything, I'm falling from the sky and then you swing back and your stomach feels nervous like you're on a roller coaster. It's sort of a neat feeling. It's weird, like you're going to fall but you don't. I can't get that feeling any other way."

The girl's description was a wonderfully articulate reference to kinesthetic perception and the related

vestibular sensation, recorded by the mechanisms of the inner ear as the body moves through space.

The sensation of flying and falling, the feeling of weightlessness, and the imagery of overcoming gravity make swings the most popular item on most playgrounds. In the Yard they provided yet another opportunity for mastering a skill, for acquiring a sense of competence and self-esteem through motor activity.

"It's scary when you're little and you've been swinging on the little swings," says Jeanine. "And all of a sudden you try to swing on the big ones and then you fall, but you say I'm gonna try again 'cause I wanna keep on trying 'til I get it right! Then when you try it again and you can do it, then you feel really good inside."

"Bail-outs" or "parachutes" were the most active challenges presented by the swings. Children pumped themselves as high as they could and launched themselves at the zenith of the forward stroke. The most skillful held contests to see who could bail out the farthest. Some would "bail out backwards," twisting their bodies in midair so they faced downwards and were therefore traveling backwards. Bail-outs were the closest that any child could come to flying.

"We play 'Superman.' We really fly."

Fortunately, by design, the area was large enough to accommodate the sandy landings of these fantasy flights.

Some children went to the swings when they had no one to play with or when they just wanted to be by themselves to enjoy the feeling of freedom and vestibular stimulation.

"It's like flying in a spaceship, without anyone bossing you . . . soaring in the sky, finding where you want to go and landing there. You fly so high the whole world is just a dot in the universe."

SLIDING

Sliding, like swinging, is attractive to children because it also offers vestibular stimulation and interaction with gravity.

Laree and Jason run up the slide, sit at the top, shoving each other while trying to stay in place. Eventually, Laree slides down, stands at the bottom and catches Jason. They both run-climb to the top again.

"I like the slide," says Jason, "because I'm sort of scared to go down the fire pole. We pretend we're being chased and have to

PLAYING BALL

Traditional games like kickball remained a favorite pastime for many children and illustrated societal influences and values related to ballplay and sports. Children adapted the games to fit their more immediate need for movement rather than for competition.

Most kick-about games were called "soccer" even though they bore little resemblance to the formal sport. According to the players, an advantage of soccer was that "you can play it anytime you've got a ball."

Kickball was by far the most popular team game in the Yard because it had a simple format, was easy to organize on short notice, and only required modest levels of skill. Because of high demand, two kickball squares were provided: a smaller one next to the McKinley Avenue fence and a larger one in the main ballplaying zone next to the ball wall.

"I love to run the bases . . . I imagine I am running 'round the whole block," a player confides. "I feel like a winner."

Basketball was a different scene, much less formal than kickball because a team was not needed to play. With all ballplay, different boundaries were established daily. For example, the games would sometimes reflect the formal nature of a particular "sport" and, at other times, the children would pursue the simple enjoyment of movement.

"We practice for real games that we play on weekends," a boy comments. "I won a trophy and it's on top of our TV at home." He admits later that he likes the "feeling of getting tackled and then escaping."

go down the slide real fast. It's really fun, especially now I can run right up to the top. Not everyone can do that."

Laree runs up the slide and shows off by sliding down while standing. He then grabs Jason's feet and pulls him down to the bottom.

"Some people slide down head first," says Jason. "Some people go rolling down, some people go down regular. Some people hit their heads on the slide; sometimes it hurts, sometimes they just laugh."

Kim comes by, starts to run up, hesitates, and tries to crawl up. She eventually uses the ladder and slides down hand in hand with Laree. A circular flow of movement is apparent: down the slide, up the ladder, then down again. Seven or eight children go down at once, and pile up on top of one another at the bottom, laughing.

Two boys start playing with their Stretch Monsters on the slide, propping them up along the edge, sitting them on the top, letting them slide down, catching them at the bottom. They pick up handfuls of sand, throw it at the slide, and watch it trickle down.

"Help! Help! An avalanche!" one of them shouts, as they hold their toys in the stream of sand, let them go, and watch them tumble to the ground and become buried in the pretend snow.

BALANCING

Balancing activity was much more common in the Yard than jumping. While jumping was done in the thrill of the moment, balancing was a more social activity, demanding more skill (again involving the vestibular sense), stimulating more drama, and conserving the potential energy of an elevated position.

"Hot lava!" screams Laree, a participant in the most popular balancing game. "The sand is hot lava," he explains. "You can travel all around the structure and if you touch the ground you're the new hot lava monster. Other children call it 'sand monster' or 'quicksand.'"

"We try to get on the tips of the rocks in the stream," says Joel, "without falling in the water. You have to be careful because you don't know if they're slippery. We get our feet a bit wet but our teacher doesn't really mind 'cause we dry off real fast."

"I like to run across the stepping stones in the corner," says Sabine. "You're on the rocks and there's water all around you. It's like you're on an island."

"Oo, oo, oo." A line of children straddle the concrete-block edging of the Orchard Wayside, pretending they are on a train trip.

Children use the Natural Resource Area railings to walk along, trying to keep their balance. They "fight" on them to see who can stay on the longest.

A girl and boy play follow-the-leader, trying to keep their balance by grabbing on to the branches of trees next to the railing. They stop at one of the weeping willows, swing on the branches, and demonstrate different tricks. A teacher remarks that tightrope

WEEKEND PLAY

On weekends, the Yard was used for family activity. The top photo shows siblings playing in the community area. A father and son use the "ball wall" (bottom), a twelve-foot-high (3.7 m), twenty-four-foot-wide (7.3 m) structure located south of the larger kickball square.

Batterball, strike-out, work-up, kick-back, and dodgeball were all played against the wall.

The children reported that it was easy to play dodgeball against the wall because no one had to chase after the ball—after each throw, the

ball came bouncing back. Another version of dodgeball was played around the giant compass.

After school, the Yard was a place to have fun. Children practiced balancing skills (top) and roamed through the landscape (bottom).

walkers usually have a balancing pole. A moment later the pair returns with a long tree stake from the potting shed. They turn the game into a performance, with the boy acting as the impresario. They both proudly show how they can walk the full length of the railing without falling.

The most agile children could navigate the Yard entirely above ground—along the MLK Way planting strip, from the school building to the garden compound. They supported themselves on the post and rail fence and the edges of the sewer pipes. If necessary, they clung to the chainlink fence or even climbed the Monterey pines, swinging between them and the acacia trees.

Amy says she goes "tightrope walking" on the fence "all over the land." Phoebe performs cartwheels on the grass, calling herself a "cartwheelist." Jenny joins the two girls. They get on the railing and start walking along it, hanging on to each other and the pine branches above.

The tightrope tricks are repeated on the railing. Jenny tells Amy, "Look how I practiced today, Mommy."

ROAMING

Not all movement in the Yard was so active.

Alice and her friend go to the eucalyptus tree in the northwest corner of the Yard. They bounce on the lowest branch, picking and smelling leaves. They walk to the chaparral and sit on the fence, and after talking for a while, slowly climb over it. They walk to the top of the hill and down the other side to the beach, where they jump the creek.

One child runs away, followed by the other, back to the chaparral. One picks a flower and says, "Ow, that's my tooth!" She puts her hands to her mouth and pretends to have a toothache. They sit on the log by the wooden bridge and talk with their arms around each other's shoulders. One points to a flower and says, "An ant just crawled out . . . it's an ant house!"

They talk about how they wish there were a big island in the middle of the pond. They return to the eucalyptus and look at a set of cards for a few moments. They then walk to the pine trees, return, and sit on the eucalyptus branch once more. They stand up and try to clear the ground of leaves with their feet. Finally, they climb through the fence into one of the corrals, pick plants, and shred the leaves as they walk through the meadow, past the Gazebo to the corral in the far corner.

"Roaming around" was Alice's phrase for this relaxed strolling through the landscape, which she said was like "being in your own place." Other children called it "walking around and talking," "looking at things," and "noticing things that are different." As children wandered, the surroundings stimulated their imaginations.

Alice quietly looked around as she roamed, concentrating, intermittently saying something under her breath in a private dialogue with her environment.

One girl carries a bouquet of grasses. She and her friend go around the corral, behind the pussy willows and silver birches, picking plants along the way. They walk past the railroad ties through the pine trees and down to the beach, constantly adding to the bouquet. She says they are going to give it to their teacher. They continue to add more grasses and flowers, retracing their steps up and around the railroad ties and returning to the big rock. They lean on the rock as they arrange the bouquet. The bell rings; the children return to class, quintessential best friends quietly sharing their world.

"HORSES"

Between second and third grade, some girls became very interested in horses. We are unaware of a psychological explanation for this, but it was certainly true for a group of Washington students whose lives for a while centered around horse toys, books, and games.

"I'm Little Black," explains Laree, "and Lela is Brownie. Christine is the rider. We play everywhere. We put ropes around ourselves and Christine holds on to them and goes, 'Yah! Yah! Yah!' She says, 'Full speed.' I feel tired, but we have to do it. Horses are slaves. When we get tired, we rest in the bamboo by the pond—it's our stable."

"It's kinda like a house except you have horses in there. Christine is the owner. She takes care of us by putting horseshoes on and feeding us. We crumple up dry redwood leaves and pretend they're oats. She gives us lots of exercise by leading us around; then she rides us into the city across the asphalt and we go 'round looking for people we know."

"When I play horse I feel really big," says Lela. "I feel free like a wild Appaloosa. I always have to be the boy, ugh! Sometimes I get to be a girl. We have fights with a stallion against a mare, or a mare against a mare, or a stallion against a stallion. We act like we're tearing things up, but not really. When we put jump ropes around our bellies and pretend to ride each other, it's really weird. Your tummy doesn't feel too good afterwards."

Like all play activity, horses was not universally popular.

"I like to play horses sometimes," Sabine confesses, "but I'm not usually in the mood for running around and going 'neigh.'"

THE PEDAGOGY OF MOVEMENT

Movement invites social interaction and fosters exploration, mutual understanding, and compassion among children. Elements can be designed to support the pleasure of bodily movement through space, offering variations in heat, light, sound, color, texture, smell, and temporal pattern.

Swing ropes can be long, suspended far above the ground, giving a long, incredible "whoosh"—moving through a big space with each swing. They can also be short, affording a fast-moving, back-and-forth, round-and-round ride, always connecting the rider to gravity.

Slides can be high, low, fast, slow, narrow, wide, bumpy, smooth, straight, or curvy. Children can slide on, over, under, through, between, beside, above, alongside, and around. These are basic concepts describing the child's relationship to physical space. Each can be practiced, discussed, written about, compared, evaluated, and explored. Why do your pants get warm when you slide? What is "friction"? What is "energy"? How many calories is your slide worth?

As children climb, swing, jump, slide, run, move up and down, around and around, and to and fro, teachers can extend the learning process. What are "muscles"? How do they work? What muscles do you use for what? Do all creatures have muscles? Do plants have muscles? How about fish? Why is it important to exercise our muscles? Why do they hurt when we exercise hard? What is good health? Can you balance on that plank? What does "balance" mean? How do you spell it? What other things around you are "in" or "out" of balance?

Movement can prompt questions of perception of time and space—fast and slow, near and far! How far do you live from school? How long does it take you to get there? Who prefers to walk, to ride, why? Do you know how far some birds can fly? How fast some animals can run? What is the slowest animal you've ever seen? What's the farthest you've ever been? Rhythm is the beat of life: the heaving ocean, 24 hours to a day, 60 seconds to a minute, 3.7 people to a family, 6 beats to a bar, 2,000 cars per hour, 22 inches of rain a year, the Earth orbiting the sun each year. The possibilities are endless.

•

In recent years, the private sector has responded to the movement deprivation of urban children and consequential parental concern by developing fran-chised, indoor play spaces. These enterprises offer children a variety of motor activity in three-dimensional structures in restricted interior spaces. To some degree, these activities develop kinesthetic perception and are certainly better than nothing. But the frenetic, noisy ambiance and stuffy air take children far from the freedom and diversity of similar activities outdoors.

It is understandable that parents are drawn to these services when they live in urban settings and are afraid to let their children out to play by them-selves. Children, however, deserve—and have a right to—more than the narrow scope of these offerings.

Since the needs of children are not commercially viable, adequate play provisions must continue to be a public responsibility. Development of healthy chil-dren is clearly an issue in the public interest. Educational institutions must once again assume the responsibility of providing environments that will pull children away from television and video games and engage them in developing their own bodies. An ally in this effort is the outdoor play equipment industry, whose products have improved substantially in quality over the last few years.

But let us not forget that the whole child needs development, not only her or his gross motor capaci-ties. Accomplishing this goal requires many other types of play settings and caring institutions committed to providing them.

REFERENCES

1. Jambor, T. and M. Guddemi (1993). Can our children play? In Jambor, T. and M. Guddemi, eds. *A Right to Play.* Proceedings of the American Association for the Child's Right to Play. September 17–20, 1992. Denton, Tex. Little Rock, Ark.: Southern Early Childhood Association.

2. Ibid.

3. Ibid.

4. Ellneby, Y. (1991). *Children's Rights to Develop: A Handbook on Children's Motor, Perceptual, and Language Development.* Stockholm: Swedish Educational Broadcasting Company.

CHAPTER 9

Imagining

"Today we played 'house.' I found some sticks and some sand and grass and Gabriel, Marcos, Vincent, and Naomi helped. We worked hard on it and then somebody wrecked it. So, we put it back together again and made dinner. We liked it a lot, and it was at school!"

— Matt

As far as we know, humans are the only species able to conceive of a multitude of realities other than the one presently surrounding them. Perhaps Canadian geese are able to imagine the warm coastlines of South America, prompting them to head south at the appropriate time of the year. But this bears no comparison to George Stephenson imagining how to capture the power of steam; Gregor Mendel, the processes of genetic inheritance; Albert Einstein, the relationship between matter and energy; Thomas Jefferson, the Declaration of Independence; Paul Cezanne, the structure of light and space; or A. A. Milne, the imaginative life of a child in nature. The many innovators in the sciences, the arts, and politics represent a measure of progress beyond the bounds of traditional cultures.

We may cite examples of evil applications of human creativity and the effects of cruel inventions in the continuing histories of one group trying to dominate another. But it is not possible to curb the quest of the human spirit. Besides, in the post-industrial era we are now entering, imagination and creativity will be in greater demand than ever before and will increase in economic value. The best we can do is to ensure that the creative quest is for human benefit. One way to achieve this, we believe, is by providing healthy, natural environments to stimulate children's imaginations through dramatic play.

In *The Ecology of Imagination in Childhood*, Edith Cobb wrote that a key to the creative achievements of visionary thinkers was their childhood play experiences.[1] No author has so eloquently described the interrelationship between the quality of childhood experience, nature, imagination, and creative work.

The results of our systematic documentation of children's behavior in the Yard support Cobb's conclusions.[2] Interaction with the natural environment, particularly in the Natural Resource Area, was infinite in its possibilities. As one child said, "There's something new to do every day." We were able to verify this child's assertion with the results of our own observations. Even in the tenth year we were still able to observe *new* activities, thoughts, and comments by the children in the Yard's ever-changing natural environment.

In contrast, the nonbiotic elements and spaces of the Yard (play equipment, asphalt areas, etc.) supported a repeating pattern of behavior, which became predictable after just a few days of observation. We grew bored watching the activity because there were no surprises, though the children still found it engaging because they loved to practice and perfect physical skills.

Despite these differences, children still converted every part of the Yard's material substance, both fixed and loose, into metaphoric, magical worlds—the kind found in children's classic literature.

MUTANT STRUCTURES

For one boy, the play structure was a fire truck.

"I'm usually the chief," he explains, "but I don't boss anyone around. We pretend a house or apartment is on fire somewhere in the sand area, and decide where it is. Someone makes the siren noise. We slide down the pole and drive to the fire. After we've put it out, we go back to the station and up the ladder. I put my coat over my head, pretend to go to sleep, and wait for the next call."

For other children, the structure's metal railings, jutting balcony, bridge, flights of steps, and tunnel conjured a ship at sea or a spaceship. For a group of girls it was "police headquarters."

"Right now we're doing an investigation," they report. "Monday, we found a broken wine glass in the teachers' parking lot and we're trying to find out who was drinking down there."

"I've read lots of adventure books," one of them comments. "We play superheroes trying to catch bad people and rescue good people. We pretend the bad people are in a boat on the lake. We go on expeditions and catch them with a piece of rope and take them to jail; but the trouble is, it's really easy to escape when the guards aren't looking."

At nearly every recess, one or another group of children re-enacted scenes from current television programs around the play structure.

"I wish I could turn into Wonder Woman," one of them says. "I turn around and around with my eyes closed and think I am going to, but nothing ever happens!"

On the spools, a boy ducks down to hide. He sits on the circular core, holding the side, pumping his feet up and down like he's driving a car. He lies down across the spool, facing up. He gets under it and inside it. I'm playing "submarine," he yells out of the spindle hole. A girl goes up and talks to him. He comes out, climbs up again, and starts staggering around from spool to spool clutching his stomach, pretending he is seasick.

Plants provided endless stimuli to children's imaginations. Water collecting in the cup of a teasel plant became a "fairy swimming pool" (top); sunflowers provided "food" for children marooned on a desert island (middle); and the young redwoods became an enchanted forest, the scene of many adventures (bottom).

"Abandon ship!" he shouts. He climbs over the side of the spool, hangs on to the edge, dangles his feet, and drops to the ground.

On the blue climbing net, children are playing "Jaws," pretending the net is a boat. Players who are pushed off the net by a "shark" become sharks themselves. They play until everyone is a shark.

ENCHANTED LAND

Although imaginative games and dramatic play were common on the structures of the Main Yard, they did not compare to the range and subtlety of play opportunities in the Natural Resource Area, where there were no limits on mental transformations.

"It's a lost island," says Kia, referring to Chaparral Hill. "There's monsters living there and a creepy crawly thing that lives in the 'evil wheels' [the old carriage wheels] and a century plant that only blooms once every seven years."

In the meadow's sunny niches where fragile wildflowers grew, the children discovered an enchanted land. Here, children saw "fairy swimming pools" in the thimblefuls of sparkling rainwater trapped in the cusps of teasel leaves, below the plants' bewitching, spiky seed heads.

"The flowers are magic," a girl says matter-of-factly, "especially these." She bends down and picks some red linum. "They'll make your hands magic, then everything you touch'll be magic. Pens will write magic . . . glasses will see magic. Everything'll be magic."

The shadowy redwoods cast another kind of spell.

"We pretend we're lost in the mysterious forest," says Kelli. "It's a great hiding place. We pretend there's only one door. Once you go in, it's impossible to get out. We look for treasure there and hide special things among the rocks."

"We just moved in the forest section one day with our Barbie dolls and made a house," Alice says. "We pretend one part is the bathroom, one's the kitchen, and one's the bedroom . . . things like that. It feels good in the redwoods. It's neat the way the trees make a roof and you can see through a little bit. We use the woodchips for knives, forks, and spoons and use the leaves as food and fix things in the kitchen. We decorate the house with flowers and just talk with each other and go places."

Two boys say they're "hunting in the jungle." They have a stick shaped like a gun and are quietly stalking a small gray bird.

"It's just a baby," one of them whispers.

They motion to each other and creep forward, tracking the bird as far as the Monterey pine grove, where they "shoot" it by simultaneously pointing the gun and throwing a rock. This scares the bird, and it flies away. They watch it disappear behind the apartment building and talk about "going hunting" and "living in the country."

"We pretend to eat animals for dinner," one of them says. "The trees around us are a smokehouse, and we smoke the meat to preserve it."

"This is our favorite spot," says the other boy. "We make-believe Grizzly is waiting for us in the woods. The hunters are after him. Sometimes we come here on weekends and bring Grizzly or our little pretend deer Luciana something to eat."

"We're playing a snake game," says a group of four children at work on a thick clump of anise. One stands inside, and the others weave the stems together from the outside.

"We're making a snake den," they explain. "We've been working on it for three days. We're 'working cobras.' We jump out on people and eat them."

"We mean we eat other snakes and bugs," interjects one group member, laughing. "I read a lot of books about snakes an' stuff, which I s'pose is how I learned about them. This is the only snake house on the Yard—we hope. We don't want anyone copying us." More laughter.

"What's good about the den, actually, is that it doesn't have to be a snake house," another continues. "It's just a good place to come when you're boiling hot, 'cause anise keeps you cool and shady" (a revealing perception of the microclimate).

"FIDDLING AROUND"

Children often called their playful blending of natural loose parts and imagination "messing about" or "nothing" (the ultimate description of pure play). One boy was more informative.

"I just pick up stuff from the ground, like bits of glass and paper, fiddle around, and put 'em down again." he says. "Sometimes I play 'telephone man.' You take some rocks and put 'em in your pocket and walk up to some trees and pretend you're fixin' the telephone. If a friend comes, we fiddle around some more . . . just sit and talk and fiddle around."

A pair of girls mix up some mud in two milk cartons and "plaster" the top of the pump housing as a mason would do, using small sticks as trowels. One girl says she likes the Natural Resource Area "because of all the scraps" that can be "turned into something else, like airplanes and boats for racing down the creek."

"Whatever's there, you can make something out of it—that's what's neat," says the other girl. "If I see a branch that broke off a tree and it has a few leaves on it, I use it as a broom. When I find plants that already fell from trees, I pretend to eat them in my campsite. If I find a plant that has a shape like a mushroom, then I pretend it's a mushroom. I use one of the rocks on the island as a camping stove. Sometimes we make the ground moist and dig it over with a big stick. We collect seeds and plant them like a garden and pretend they're going to grow. They don't really. But they might. I wish they did."

Synthetic play props were as important as natural ones for stimulating dramatic play. Milk cartons, for example, were versatile enough to become boats for ladybug races, nets for catching fish, "lava" holders for sand volcanoes, receptacles for mixing "potions," or saucepans for making "stews" stirred with plastic spoons discarded from lunch. Throughout the Yard, children created concoctions of sticks and stones, insects (dead and alive), candy wrappers, bits of colored glass, bottle tops and pull tabs, toys from home, and anything else that fertilized their flights of fancy. Aluminum lunch trays filled with sand were used to trace hieroglyphic portraits and abstract designs. Flowers, leaves, and grass were added to make what the children called "little pieces of heaven."

In the Yard's treasure chest of play props, the most beautiful and inspiring jewels were plant parts. No one had to "requisition" for supplies of these prolific, regenerative play materials. They automatically reappeared each year, free of charge!

"I make 'flowers' from flowers," Jeanine says. "I take little petals and pretty leaves like the red ones [linum] and I use the green pine needles from stems and I take two green leaves and I stick them on and I take some of the yellow stuff [dandelion] and put it in the middle and make a flower, just like that. Sometimes we make other things with the dried leaves and stuff, like a doll, or a picture of a cat, or a bird."

A girl rolls her upper lip and puts a bay leaf under her nose. "I made a bay leaf mustache so I can smell it," she says.

A group of girls shake "foxtails" (grass seed heads) over some boys during a game of "prisoner" to "paralyze" them. The boys throw them back, exploiting their streamlined, arrowlike shape so that they stick in the girls' hair.

Children made "peashooters" from the hollow stems of dried anise, and used anise seeds as ammunition. Others used plastic spoons as "slingshots to flick berries" and "shoot at targets."

"We play factories," says Erik. "Fr'instance we pretend we're going through the process of making paper. We take some dried leaves and stuff like that. The first guy lays them on one of the rocks and smashes 'em with a little rock—'bam, bam'—and then he passes 'em to the next guy who does something like put them in water, and the next guy lays 'em out to dry on a sheet of real paper, so we pretend we've done the whole thing."

A girl describes how she went "hunting for buds" in the spring. The best place she said was the line of pussy willows at the

Children loved working with different parts of plants and used them for an infinite number of imaginative projects—creating "little pieces of heaven" (top), mixing "poison potions" (middle), making "dolls" (bottom left), and inserting foxtail grass into a drinking straw to create a brush (bottom right).

far end of the meadow. "We call them 'cottontails,'" she declares. "Ya know, those fuzzy things, we pretend they're rabbits' eggs. We get some grass and make a circle like a nest, and the rabbit just sits on the eggs to keep 'em warm and waits 'til they hatch. The father rabbit goes to look for food. We get bitty branches and make 'em into carrots. We know rabbits don't really lay eggs 'cause they're mammals. When they hatch, we make boats out of leaves and sail the cottontails on the pond. If it's sunny, we make them go swimming and pretend they get a tan." (Her friend's rabbit puppet served as the original inspiration for the game. The two girls loved playing with it.)

POTIONS

"We're making a potion to kill our enemies," disclose a trio of girls, as they move along the Orchard Wayside among the trees, collecting ingredients for a very particular form of plant play. On the spool table they assemble piles of anise flower heads; dock leaves; dock seeds (dried and undried); grass seeds; broken-up, dry, rotten wood; dirt and sand; Australian plum leaves; crushed leaves from wild raspberry; and pigweed seeds. After a while, they stop collecting and gather around the table. Using plastic spoons saved from lunch, they carefully count out portions of the ingredients for making each potion and then mix them with water from the drinking fountain. As the girls discuss how they will use the potions, the recess bell rings. They run inside, leaving their concoctions on the table.

DIRT THEATERS

"The dirt's good here," a boy explains, "'cause you can pretend it's exploding. There's no other place like this with lots of hills and 'smoky' dirt."

Five boys play in the giant planter with toy cars brought from home. Half kneeling, half laying on the mounds, they utter motor noises as they play.

"Hmm, hmm . . ."

"Brrum, brrum . . . brrum, brrum . . ."

"Rrr, rrr, rrr, rrr, rrr . . ."

One boy has a plastic sandwich bag. They fill it with pulverized dirt and empty it out around the cars to make "dust storms." Finally, they pile all the cars together to create a "monster dust storm."

A group of girls are "digging for gold."

"We have to be careful," one of them says, "because the gold mine gets invaded by ants." They wrap the dirt in alder leaves, pinning them together with little splinters of wood, to "take to the bank."

A boy plays in the sand with two small Star Wars figures representing Luke Skywalker and Obi Ben Kenobi. The figures have articulated joints and are "dressed in snowsuits." The boy says he's working "on a snow hut with three hatches and a chimney with enough room inside for Luke and Ben to stand up." He moves the two figures in and out and around the model, as if it were a stage set, making up the story as he goes along.

"Ben Kenobi lost his sword. See where it used to be?" he says, pointing to the socket in the figure's plastic arm. "But Luke found a new one—a stick I found laying around. Oh no, I look like Luke Skywalker. Hey, I'm not me, that's the dark side of me. That's it, that's the dark side of me. That was Darth Vader. Eek, he bonked my head off!"

He carefully forms a narrow hole in the sand next to the hut. "That's my hole . . . my time hole . . . that's my time hole . . . my escape from this black desolation of outer space. Take me home, time hole."

Scott and his friends play with a collection of toy soldiers in the enclosure of giant bamboo behind the Monterey pines. He says they're playing the Battle of Waterloo because he's been doing a project on British history in class.

"You know those transfers you can stick on? I got some for the Russians, the British, and the French and read about the Battle of Waterloo in the transfer book." He notes that the bamboo is good for camouflage.

The boys use the ground surface and vegetation to simulate the battlefield. They make gunfire noises as they move the soldiers around on the ground or perch them in little hideouts among the clusters of twigs jutting from the main stems of the bamboo. They begin piling up woodchips, using them as "sandbags to make barricades to stop the French infantry bullets." The French in the bamboo start shooting at the British behind the woodchip barricades. Finally, the children hold the soldiers in their hands and shoot directly at one another.

Partway through the battle, Scott talks about one of the soldiers. "We just made him go swimming in the pond, but he drowned because he forgot to take his armor off [laughs]. It was too heavy. Stupid soldier, I told him not to go swimming with his armor on."

Scott mentions working on a "feeling chart" in his class. "It's where you draw a symbol of your feeling—like a star or a smile, anything like that. I drew a captain with a sword as my feeling."

Two boys arrive with plastic boats from home. One of them floats his craft towards the north end of the beach. "Look at that motorboat speed!" he yells. They float their boats down the stream, pretending to bomb them by throwing mud at them. An older boy comes by and turns the game into a mud-throwing fight. The two boys do not like it and move to "another river" four feet (1.2 m) downstream.

Another day, four boys perch on the rocks in the creek and play with a small plastic alligator. A piece of nylon fishing line is tied around its body. Every so often, they place the alligator in the water, pull it out again, and put it on a rock. They play quietly, making barely audible comments to one another. One boy says they are pretending the alligator is a mile long and eats people.

A couple of small plastic horses are the source of Naomi and Vincent's inspiration for playing around the rocks of Chaparral Hill. One horse is a "she," the other a "he."

"We're making a barn," says Naomi.

"There's two little places for the horses to drink," adds Vincent, pointing to two minute containers fashioned from aluminum foil. They begin trotting the horses around the rocks.

"He jumped . . . look . . . oh man, he fell."

"Okay, I got it. Neighhh . . . neighhh . . . he's running."

They put the horses in a cavity, which they pretend is a stable, to "let them rest." They then begin digging in the soft dirt between the rocks with the horses' feet. The loosened dirt is scraped out to "flatten the stable floor and make it better."

"Oh, the dirt is getting the horses' feet dirty," says Naomi. She trots the horse out to the dish of water. "You need a drink . . . come and wash your feet."

"Let's use these bits of wood for the stable doors," says Vincent. He erects a line of woodchips in the ground in front of one of the crevices. The recess bell sounds.

"Let's wreck it up," says Vincent. The two children hide the horses between the rocks, where they will be ready to play with tomorrow.

"No one will have a clue where they are now," laughs Naomi, after covering the horses with the loose dirt they had scraped out.

The following day, Naomi and Vincent retrieve the horses and begin "riding" from place to place, now "dramatizing" the entire Natural Resource Area.

"Let's go to the woods," they say. They stop at the big rock, where they place the horses on top.

"Oh, what a good view," Naomi says on behalf of the horses. They go to the picnic table, where they put flowers in the horses' mouths, pressing their jaws together in a chewing motion. Beside the upper pond, they point out the "little plants that look like feathers."

"We named them 'plantus,'" says Vincent. "Once we had a little plastic boy. We pretended we were on a mission. We made a little puddle and picked a whole lot of 'plantus,' and the boy had to ride through it like it was a thick jungle."

KINGDOMS AND CASTLES

Sandcastles were constantly under construction in the sand area. The designers, whether working alone, in pairs, or in large groups, created an impressive array of structures.

A boy scrapes sand up into a hill, flattens the top, and carefully inserts a stick as a "radar tower." He builds seven more mounds, ending up with two lines of four. Using his foot, he forms two broad rings around the mounds. With his fingers spread out, he sticks them into the rings, making a pattern of small cavities around each one. "It's an asteroid fort," he declares.

Two girls build a small mound. They pound it down, smooth it out, pat it, blow on it, lie on the sand, and inspect it closely. They run their fingers lightly over it and watch it intently as if inspecting each individual grain. They start working on a large, pyramid-shaped mound with a smaller mound on top and create a ramp up each side. They then start tunneling into the center of the pyramid towards each other, giggling as their hands meet in the middle. They pat down the sides, refine the shape, and scoop out a moat around the mound. As a final touch, they use milk cartons to bring water from the drinking fountain and fill the moat.

Children constantly manipulated dirt and sand as basic play materials. They were often seen in groups or alone digging, playing with toys, enjoying the opportunity to explore their imaginations! In the bottom photograph, the sand pit has become a planet with plastic figures engaged in space adventures.

NATURAL LEARNING

"Oooh, that was f-u-n," one of them says. "Let's work on it some more after school." They sit on the fence, dump the sand out of their shoes, and keep an eye on their castle while waiting for the recess bell. A boy approaches and looks like he is going to sit on their castle.

"Don't you dare!" the girls scream.

Another day, two other girls demonstrate how they sometimes play with toy horses around the sandcastles. "Sometimes we dig for treasure . . . it's not far . . . if you dig for a while you get to it," says one.

"Look, I found it," the other shouts. She uncovers a small area of blacktop about six inches (15 cm) down. "It's where you find gold." Occasionally, real coins were found, dropped from the pockets of swinging kids. But more likely "pretend treasure" was unearthed, like small stones and woodchips.

Larry and Kevin say they make "volcanoes" nearly everyday in the sand area. "We build mountains and make a hole in the top for the volcano. We put water in a milk carton and pretend it's hot lava. We put the water in and wait for 'em to erupt. We watch the sides crack. We keep putting the water in; the sides break open and the lava comes pouring out. We patch 'em up and start all over again. They're just like volcanoes except they don't shoot high." For the two boys, the illusion was nearly complete.

Another pair of boys lie down between the mounds of sand and say they're "making kingdoms." One points to a little hollow in the sand, which is decorated with fragments of a plastic cup sticking up on either side of a "pathway."

"That's the 'feast place,'" he says. He then points to a "forest" of small pieces of anise covering a mound beside another depression, which they call a "reservoir."

"We've been pretending the place is a thousand years old, like the olden days . . . we'll destroy it before we go in, so other kids can play here tomorrow."

SPACE WARS

"We pretend it's the moon," a boy recounts, referring to the big rock. "We wear space helmets and have little ray guns. We pretend we're being attacked by monsters. They can be up on the rock or down on the ground. Sometimes I'm a monster attacking my friends. Sometimes they attack me." He breaks off a piece of willow and pretends "it's a magic wand to turn the whole world into a space fortress."

"The Gazebo is a space fortress," another adds. "The tepee [corral] is a shuttlecraft. I'm the engineer. We've been to all sorts of places in our shuttle. I have to act real fast to fix the engines in an emergency when we break down."

"Tphew, tphew, tphew."

Pretend gunfire noises come from a posse of boys inside the farthest corral. With their arms outstretched and their hands serving as pistols, they "shoot" across the meadow towards a group of screaming "space invaders." A space war ensues.

The adjacent, recycled tree trunk lying on its side has an exposed stump of tangled roots, which the boys use as a spaceship. A half-dozen boys straddle the trunk, face the stump end where the "captain" sits to navigate the ship. Each assumes the role of a character from Star Trek. Periodically, one jumps down and fiddles with the root entrails, adding extra bits of wood and small rocks to modify the "ship's computer."

Another group of boys crouches in the railroad ties. "We're a bunch of space-walking Martians," one of them shouts. "We're in a space cave . . . on planet X."

"Ew-ew-ew-ew-ew." More gunfire, but with a different sound.

"Missed," another shouts, shooting at an unseen enemy. He leaps out of the railroad ties and runs into the chaparral.

"We use sticks for 'phasers' and pieces of rock for 'communicators,'" one of them explains. "Look what I just made from the bush over there." He brandishes a willow stick with two stubby side branches as triggers.

The boys start assigning roles to one another. The group structure is very fluid. Children constantly switch groups. Some leave, while others join in. The captain orders the men on the railroad ties into position.

"Captain, the engines won't work," one boy screams. He and the captain go over to the pine trees next to the railroad ties to fix them (the imaginary spaceship extends beyond the ties, which represent only the navigating bridge). Some girls approach.

"We don't want any girls playing here," complain the boys. The girls walk away.

"Who wants to be Captain Kirk?" the current captain asks. Nobody volunteers, so the boy continues as leader. The boys still argue about roles. The leader assigns them, telling one boy to be Sulu because he looks Chinese.

The captain goes over to one side of the ship's "bridge" and says it is the "beamer." "Let's beam a party down," he orders. He directs two men to accompany him to Mars. The party stands in the beamer, then climb out of the ship, pretending to be beamed. They wander around, exploring Mars, but chaos soon erupts back on the ship. The captain is called back to sort the situation out. After the party beams back again, the captain orders the crew to their battle stations. They sit on the lower ties directing their attention outward, navigating the ship, and imitating emergency signals. The captain orders them to fire.

"We've been hit!" he shouts. Everybody rocks back and forth, pretending the ship is pitching and yawing. Men fall to the floor and are knocked out. One climbs out and then climbs back in again, pretending he is an alien. He points his gun to protect himself. A fight erupts between "aliens" and "Earthmen." The action subsides. Laughing together, they return to Earth as the game ends.

THE DOLL AND THE DONKEY

One of the Yard's most heavily used places for dirt play was the small circle of dirt around the base of a scrawny flowering plum tree. The tree was planted along the MLK Way fence in the sewer pipe closest to the school building. Its height of four and a half feet (1.4 m) gave it a more commanding elevation. Inside the pipe, the level of the dirt was about ten inches (25 cm) below the rim. As a result, children could sit on the edge of the pipe with their feet in the dirt. The higher elevation and sense of enclosure explained its popularity as a place for dirt play.

A girl plays there with a Barbie doll and a plastic toy donkey. There are two holes in the dirt. She puts the doll in one of the holes, sprinkles splinters of wood in a pile, sits the doll on the edge of the hole, and gallops the donkey around it. She lays the donkey in the weeds around the edge of the dirt and makes the doll bury the sticks, which she pretends are a fire. She lays the doll down in the weeds and then places it on the donkey, which gallops away, hopping on both feet in a squatting position. She wants the doll to take a nap on the donkey's back but gets mad and makes the donkey buck.

The donkey is "keeping guard against the buffalo," the girl explains. The crack in the dirt is going to be an earthquake. She gallops the donkey away with the doll to escape from the buffalo. She then lays the doll down and puts a leaf in its lap—"a book to read." The girl pretends her fingers are a baby horse, and puts the baby up against the donkey to suckle. She calls the edge of the planter the "mountains."

"The buffalo are coming back," she shouts, as the donkey gallops and hops to the mountains (twelve inches [30 cm] away) and leads it to a patch of grass to eat. "Let's go out for a ride," she thinks aloud. She puts the donkey and doll on top of the concrete edge. "Yeah, we found water. *Agua! Agua!*" She pretends to give the doll a bath. "This is a famous donkey. He can cook pancakes," she jokes as she continues to gallop it around the edge.

"Let's make a house," she says, as her imagination leaps to the next idea. She fashions a clump of foxtail grass into a shelter and carefully puts the doll inside.

She picks some passion vine leaves and puts them by the tree as beds, and puts the donkey under the covers. She dusts some pollen from pussy willow buds on the doll's face, calling it "make-up." She covers the doll with the grass and picks a piece of dry anise to prop up the canopy. Laying the doll on top, she says "it can be a bed, a shade, or a hammock."

•

The stories in this chapter are examples of imaginative and dramatic play considered essential for healthy child development. It is important to realize the small scale of the spaces and materials used for these activities. Most of the last story, for example, took place within a three-foot (0.9 m) circle of weedy dirt around the foot of a small tree—a completely inconsequential space to adult eyes. Similar imagina-

A group of children visit "planet X" on the railroad ties (top). The "doll and the donkey" (middle) was a drama created around the roots of a flowering plum tree. The doll's "house" was fashioned out of a clump of grass to the left of the tree. The donkey itself seems life-size (left) in relation to the twig.

tive play took place on the tops of fence posts; on benches, tables, and ledges; on the raised walkway around the sand area; and in the crotches of trees and bushes. Many finely grained materials were used (even pollen), which helped children develop visual discrimination and very fine eye-hand dexterity in order to manipulate them.

The highly malleable qualities of these settings provided for genuinely interactive play. The term "interactive" is so broadly used these days that it has lost much of its meaning—all too often applying to anything that can be touched! Perhaps in the context of museums, such "touchable" interactions are appropriate, although the outcomes are limited. In the free-play settings of the Yard, on the other hand, the possibilities were infinite.

The problem for adults is that such settings are untidy, indefinite, unpredictable, and hard to control. Above all, they are very small and difficult to justify to people with an overly rational frame of reference. And yet the Yard demonstrated that these types of settings can impact all aspects of child development: cognitive, emotional, perceptual, and physical. More educators and play professionals need to promote the microsettings of children's play and learning; the first step is to understand the educational value that can be embodied in a few dry leaves, a popsicle stick, and a patch of dirt.

REFERENCES

1. Cobb, E. (1977). *The Ecology of Imagination in Childhood.* New York: Columbia University Press. Republished, 1993. Dallas: Spring Publications.

2. Moore, R. (1986). "The Power of Nature: Orientations of Girls and Boys Toward Biotic and Abiotic Environments." *Children's Environments Quarterly* 3(3), 52–69.

Learning to Live Together

The children's enthusiasm and passion for life were an inspiration to us all. The Yard brought together people of all ages, backgrounds, races, abilities, and economic levels for collaboration and celebration of life. The positive social benefits were many: a greater sense of unity, stronger support systems for children, and a deeper understanding of politics as helping people to coexist. These elements provided the foundation for sound curriculum development and made learning more enjoyable and worthwhile.

The fate of Earth rests with us, its human inhabitants. We need to start caring for the biosphere as much as it cares for us. Achieving this goal requires huge changes in our behavior as a species. We must first learn to cooperate, to place the common good before personal greed, to settle differences peaceably. Even before this can happen, we must start to perceive ourselves as a species interdependent with all other species, with a common interest extending beyond differences in race, religion, and geography. This perception requires skill in the development of positive interpersonal relations, the seeds of tolerance that are best sown on the fertile ground of early childhood. And what better way to grow them than through play and nonformal education.

Initiation of prosocial behavior is typically thought to be an adult role in children's families and classrooms. Our observations of play behavior in the Yard showed that children will carry the process of socialization forward themselves when provided with settings that they can appropriate and respect as a microcosm of their inherited world.

The Yard was a highly appropriated place that could be continuously modified by children to support the development of their own culture with its own values, rules, and mythologies.

BEST FRIENDS

Central to the development of this culture was the encouragement of positive, cooperative attitudes among the children. Dramatic play was a common vehicle for accomplishing this task, as it allowed children to interact creatively with each other beyond the bounds of normal behavior. The great diversity of the Yard landscape enabled children to match their common interests with the opportunities offered by the physical environment. In their invented worlds, children could experiment with social interactions.

Two boys play in the hollow cores of a cable spool. Pretending the spool is a rocket observation post, they peer out of the spindle hole. Moments later they stagger out, one of them walking like a robot, arms held straight out in front. He guides the other around by the shoulders and they both start behaving like robots.

"You-are-programmed-to-play-with-me," one of them says in a R2-D2 monotone.

"No!" the other shouts, shaking his head. The command is repeated as they fool around, making up robot-talk.

With her eyes closed, a girl slowly walks with her hands out in front. She walks around the ladder bars and approaches a group of girls sitting on the bench. When they see her, they run and scream, pretending she is a monster. The girl bumps into her friend, who starts to lead her around the equipment. The friend spins her around and releases her. The girl opens her eyes and staggers around feigning dizziness. Both laugh and change places, with the other girl now leading the way.

One of the most intriguing forms of social-dramatic play between best friends was the testing and elaborating of each other's reactions in mock violence—in this case, using small props plucked from the surroundings.

"Pow, pow! I shot you!" shouts Erik, pointing a piece of dry anise stem at Corin. A third boy joins in with another stem.

"We're Munchkins having a sword fight," they yell. When they are "wounded," they fall down in the grass and roll around laughing.

"We just pretend to hit each other and beat each other up," Erik says, "but we never cry or anything. It's fun. We love to roll around in the long grass."

They move to one of the corrals. Corin holds Erik by his shoulders and shoves him against the railings.

"You're under arrest!" He holds a woodchip "knife" to the boy's back. "Stop, or I'm going to stab you!" He drops his knife on purpose. Erik picks it up.

"Do you think it's easy to get a knife through a person?" he jokes.

Alternately they bend each other back over the fence, threatening one another and laughing.

Erik sits on the fence while Corin collects a handful of woodchip knives off the ground. He throws them at Erik who uses one as a screwdriver, pretending to remove some screws above Corin's eyes. Corin laughs, moves mechanically like a robot, is stabbed by Erik, pretends to short-circuit, falls over, and grabs a long stick, which he pretends to use as a sword. Both boys jokingly threaten each other with stabbing gestures.

"Pretend I'm a police officer," Erik tells Corin. He shortens his stick into a billy club and threatens Corin. "I'm arresting you for invading the Earth. Get back to Mars!"

"No you don't," cries Corin, as he whips out part of a charm bracelet from his pocket and shakes it at Erik. "It's my 'silver thing,'" he explains. "I bring it to school and hypnotize my friends. I'll say, 'Start fighting,' and then I'll say, 'You are friends,' and they'll shake hands." He does this with Erik, and they wander off.

What was the significance of this mock violence between such good friends? The boys maintained a close physical proximity throughout the game, pushing

each other though in an amiable manner, confirming the trust in their friendship. As soon as one boy was threatened, the other backed down and gave a chance for the tables to be turned. The mock violence of their behavior, the vicious threats and pretend stabbings, suggested that something violent had inspired it—the most likely source being television. Be that as it may, the play episode appeared to be a vehicle for the boys to test and develop their friendship using physical interaction and humor, like young lions romping in the savanna. It was interesting to observe how the specific character of the setting defined the game: woodchips became knives, the enclosure forced the boys into close proximity and prevented them from playing a simple game of chase. Corin's "silver thing" was a great example of the role of personal possessions in reinforcing friendship.

CHILD-TO-CHILD

Children have a natural tendency to learn from one another, especially best friends and siblings.

"Most stuff I know, I've learned off other people," one boy explains. "My little brother copies off me when I do stuff. Most brothers learn like that. Children copy other children to know what is right."

This hand-me-down learning process was particularly obvious in relation to skill-based traditional games and ballplay.

"At first I didn't know how to kick that good," recalls Erik, "so Ryan taught me. He's really good. We go up to the park almost every day with my brother and play football and now I'm on the soccer and baseball teams."

Ballgames provided a delicate balance of tension between competition and cooperation. They offered children opportunities to excel in the mainstream culture of competitive sports. The exhilaration of winning boosted self-esteem. Boys called the ballgames "fun," saying that they made "you feel good" and were "good exercise." Many had fathers or older brothers who played sports with them. It may seem difficult to view a game like kickball as socially intimate, but for the boys most deeply involved, ballgames instilled a strong sense of camaraderie and teamwork. Children who could not reach a competitive level eventually shifted to other

The Natural Resource Area stimulated social relations between children. The freedom and diversity of play opportunities ensured that the children were never bored and were more likely to engage in spontaneous social play.

activities. The game, however, was always open to new-comers—new boys, that is—and the group trained them to maintain a certain level of competition.

The equivalent setting for girls was the twirling bars. There, activity was also extremely skill-oriented and even more social than the ballgames. Girls gathered on the bars, practicing and showing off different moves. Learning to use the bars was a challenge for newcomers, a laborious and sometimes painful process mixed with feelings of success and failure.

"I have sort of a good and bad feeling," Amy says. "Bad because I don't know many tricks and I feel jealous of the girls who know tons; but good, because every time I learn a new trick I feel proud. For a long time I was afraid, because all the girls could do flips and fancy stuff. The first time I tried, I hit my head and it really hurt."

Periodically, the girls stopped to chat, legs cupped under the bars, ready to flip around at any moment in a ballet of words and twirls. Social interaction was facilitated by the side-by-side position of the bars; if the bars had been spread throughout the Yard, there would not have been a clearly defined territory for the girls to readily appropriate.

GENDER EQUITY

The Yard demonstrated conclusively that a diversified landscape stimulated integration between different types of children. Some types of activity, however, were so strongly embedded in the children's culture that they remained unchanged.

Two boys approach the bars, start to tease the girls, and try to join in, but without success. The girls laugh and joke about the boys' hopeless efforts.

"The girls always play here because it's more fun and we don't even have to think about the boys," says Hillary. "We just go about our business. We can do anything we want here without the boys interfering."

"Boys like to play basketball and kickball—stuff like that," quips Jenny. "They don't even eat lunch, but play soccer and keep bragging about how they got knocked down and hurt. We sometimes play kickball, maybe once a week. The boys are always playing . . . it's all they think about . . . all they talk about . . . they never share it. We played 'em the other day and scored one point . . . ha, ha! They scored fifty!"

"No, we don't let 'em play, not unless they really want to," Erik admits. "We let 'em play ball tag, but not basketball or kickball. It's too hard for girls to throw baskets that high, and they don't kick good enough for kickball."

Even though many parents and teachers made substantial efforts to reverse such sexist attitudes, the ball-games were particularly resistant to change. Throughout the Yard's development, the games remained the most constant and visibly gender-segregated activity.

Interestingly, pressure to equalize the sexes was not put on the bars, which remained a bastion of female independence. The girls' domination of the bars made boys who played there feel awkward.

"I feel nutty on the bars," says George. "I feel like a monkey. I just don't feel right because it's only girls that do it, and all they talk about is school and home. It just feels nutty. But I still like to play there almost every day. For one thing, I like to jump from high places. The bars are good for that."

A striking thing about the Yard in later years was the extent to which this traditional pattern—found in every elementary school across the country—survived, despite the great variety of choices in the Main Yard. Such was the sustaining power and resiliency of culture.

There was some gender mixing on the play structure, though in aggregate it was used more by boys—perhaps demonstrating their greater proclivity for tower-like places. The structure encouraged use by both boys and girls because it combined elements that supported activities like sliding, jumping, and climbing. This physical diversity increased the permutations of activity and intermixing by gender above the level that would have been provided by dispersed pieces of equipment. Patterns of activity occurred simultaneously side by side, offering the possibility of interaction between the sexes, though it did not happen often. In a typical observation, two gangs of boys chased one another all over the structure, while a quartet of girls played "horses" in the wooden tunnel.

Even the attraction of the Natural Resource Area was not powerful enough to make the bars and asphalt obsolete. We felt it was perfectly appropriate that the girls and boys each had their own territory where they could congregate and do their own thing.

However, for those not interested in traditional activities, the Yard's natural settings offered alternatives. Increased interaction between the girls and boys was the most valuable—or at least the most visible—conse-

quence. Children of different ethnic backgrounds, ages, abilities, and personalities also played together more. The most impressive measure of this broader equity, which the children themselves often noted, was the reduction in bickering, squabbles, and "serious fighting."

"INDIAN" PLAYS

Most cooperative play occurred in the Natural Resource Area, where, as this example illustrates, cultural patterns were adapted freely to the new landscape.

"We pretend the rocks are a stove," says Amy. "There's a sort of niche there between them; that's the oven. We make a 'fire' there and pretend we're playing Indian."

"Me and Alice saw them and we started playing together. We started making a tunnel, maybe for ants—we didn't know. Then we decided to do an Indian project."

The children cook a stew of leaves and seed heads, mixing them with sticks and placing small portions in the oven between the rocks. Alice sweeps the floor with a pine branch.

"Once we found some dead bees, put them on the rock, and pretended to cook them. We pretend to go to the bathroom in the bushes, then wash our hands in the river and catch fish for the stew. We get milk cartons full of river water to make acorn mush from eucalyptus pods."

She buries some pods near the stove "so wild animals won't get them." The girls stir the stew and mush and say "it's full of yucky stuff."

Although the girls cook as they think the Native Americans do, the layout of their house is modeled after their own homes, with the kitchen inside rather than outside and an imaginary bathroom with a toilet. They keep the kitchen clean by sweeping it and putting the "brooms" away in the proper place. They combine what they learned about Native American life at school with things they learned at home (e.g., keeping things clean)—as well as everyday activities such as going to the bathroom.

Chaparral Hill was a perfect place for this type of dramatic play, providing privacy and separation from other games. The clearing with the rocks provided an imaginary room, with a path down to the beach serving as a stairway out of the house. Although other children constantly ran through, they did not stop to play games if another group was using the area.

The next day the girls travel down to the river to play on the beach, forming the wet sand into shapes. Amy builds a mound with a dent on top and fills it with water, calling it a "swimming pool." Alice builds a similar mound and calls it a "bathtub." It springs a leak, which she dams with a piece of wood.

The children were skilled at developing inventive solutions to meet their needs. A group of boys constructed a "clubhouse" out of dried weeds and stems spread on a corral roof (top). In the Chaparral Hill club in the shrubs (bottom), children held more "formal" meetings. Both settings illustrate positive social experiences in leadership development and communication skills—a connection several teachers used in their lesson plans.

During this "Indian" episode by the two girls, Brian, one of their friends, engages in parallel play. Imitating their actions, he makes a pool with an island in it. Together, the children call it "Indian Island."

CLUBS

Several days later, Chaparral Hill was occupied by another group, this time a "club." It provided a fascinating study of nascent democratic politics.

A dozen children sit on the old wheels or stand among the ten-foot-high (3 m) trunks of chaparral, which form a canopy that lightly filters the sunlight.

"This is our 'nature place.'"

"No it's not, it's a girls' club. No, it's everybody's club," Ben, leader of the pack, jokes.

"How long has it been a club?" we ask.

"About a minute . . . ha, ha, ha."

"No talking . . . a meeting is in progress!" Two or three children try to conduct the meeting amid much argument.

"Everyone in the group should . . ." The voice trails off.

"We need a recordkeeper . . . we need a list."

"You know, those boys in Mr. Cox's class have been trying to steal our 'hay.' We should all watch the 'hay.'"

"Let's vote on it . . ."

"There's too many arguments at this meeting. If someone is doing something you don't like, then just say, 'Stop that, you're bugging me' . . . and if they don't stop, you can complain to one of the other members."

"There's too many people," gripes Laura. "We're having meetings every five minutes—that's what I can't stand."

"You know what, I'll pretend I'm in Tito's club and see what his plans are, where his hideout is," says Dana. "The only thing is . . ."

"One at a time!" screams Laura, trying to moderate the pecking order.

"We need assistance," interjects Dana, who has been sweeping the ground with a ceanothus branch. "I don't care what assistance I get. You're all ninnies. Caveman, get someone to dust these spider webs, please. Yuk, look at all those snails everywhere. Let's get the place cleaned up.

"We're putting up some nice pine cones here. They're the only thing we can decorate with." She has an armful, collected from the other side of the meadow, and sticks them in the crotches of the chaparral. "We're going to make this a nice little place for our club. Sometimes we use the pine cones for ammunition against rival clubs. Last year we put peanut butter and birdseed on 'em and hung 'em up for the birds. The peanut butter makes the birdseed stick to the cones, and birds can climb on them to feed."

Chaparral Hill was a more popular spot for clubs that were more freewheeling and larger than groups that met in other parts of the Yard. The reasons, perhaps, were the hill's central location, pleasant shade, spaciousness, easy access, and secluded atmosphere.

Clubs went in phases. They would form, remain active for a few days or even weeks, and then disintegrate and later reassemble with new leaders. Dana explained what eventually happened to their club.

"It fell apart because one of my friends felt that she was being bossed around. She declared war against us and we went to spy on each other. It was sort of like a game. We'd always have to have a secret thing like a rock or a pine cone. And if someone stole it, then we'd win; and then if we declared war, they'd have to have something. Then we had something very special—a piece of licorice—that we could hide. We still have it in our clubhouse. It's really called fennel. We'd fight against each other and we'd have different children on each side and spy on each other, or pretend to be on the other side and get their rules and plans. Ben was in our club and he pretended to be on the other side and told us they were going to attack before first bell, so we went to attack first.

"Then it sort of faded, because my friend quit because she didn't like the idea. Then I quit and everybody quit except Pria. She was sort of sulking. Then there were only three children left in the club and all the others went into Ben's new club for nature, called the Environmental Protectors. So after awhile everything just went kerput. It can fall apart in a day or so."

KISSING/GIRLS-CHASE-THE-BOYS

The most intriguing gender interaction took place in a chasing game, which the boys called "kissing" and girls called "girls-chase-the-boys." According to Peter, the game could happen anywhere in the Yard.

"Sometimes the boys do the chasing and sometimes the girls," he says, adding that the "kissing girls" usually chase him around the ponds and that if he falls down, they prepare to kiss him. But they never succeed, because he gets up and escapes by going under the fence and then behind the bushes, where he hides as the girls run by. He likes the running part of the game, he admits, but not the kissing part. "They grab you by the arms and try to pull you apart. Once I fell down off the bridge because it was blocked by kissing girls trying to stop the boys getting through."

Kissing was very much a seasonal game, most frequently appearing, appropriately, during the spring (also the time of year when children knew each other better).

"We like to spank them, torture them, and tickle them," says Alice. "Sometimes we even put them in the girls' bathroom. It's funny 'cause they don't want to go in there, but we just drag them in. Sometimes we try to wash their mouths out with soap when they use foul language."

The girls were closer to puberty and therefore slightly bigger and more mature than the boys. As a result, the girls maintained a physical dominance. For the most part, the boys seemed willing to take on submissive roles. Both sides appeared more comfortable rehearsing their sexual interaction in chasing games in the Natural Resource Area than at the bars or on the ball courts.

"When we play around the ponds we use the redwood trees as jail," adds Kia. "The guards let 'em out after ten seconds. They run all over the Yard, trying to get away from the guards and people who are helping the guards. We have other prisons in the bushes by the eucalyptus tree, in the Gazebo, and on top of the play structure."

"Then we call it 'prisoner,'" explains Rachel. "First there are two or three children sitting and two or three running around, they can be all girls or all boys, or a mixture. One group is the 'prisoners' and the other group is the 'masters' and it sort of goes off and on so that every kid has a chance to be a prisoner and a master. Sometimes we pick pieces of fennel or the grass that looks like wheat and climb up in the wooden fort [Gazebo] and pretend that we're grinding grain or milking cows, on a farm. But we're prisoners so we try to run away and the masters try to catch us."

The play structure provided a social shelter for girl-boy play because of all the other activities going on, as well as the semi-enclosed spaces that hid such activities from view. One day the children turned the play structure tunnel into a "jail."

"We have to catch the boys, tag them, and put them in the tunnel, then we let them go free and catch them all over again," one of the girls explains. "Hey! Get that boy and tie him up so he can't escape."

The girls sometimes devised ingenious solutions for catching the boys.

"One time we made a 'boy trap' by digging a hole with sticks and covering it with twigs and leaves," recounts Jennifer. "You stepped on it and . . . ahh!"

The "boy trap" was actually only about three inches (8 cm) deep. It was located on the pathway around the back of the upper pond, where the ground was usually damp and easier to dig.

ROLE PLAYING

For some children, playing became an important way to re-enact significant events in their lives, a means of reliving happy times or coping with stressful situations. Play provided a natural form of therapy in which

The Yard environment stimulated many different kinds of relationships among the children. These ranged from care and maintenance (top) to using natural materials in imaginative ways (middle) to playing together for the sheer enjoyment of friendship (bottom).

the subject matter was sometimes expressed in a transformed or bizarre manner.

Christine, Liz, and Sarah play with Christine's pullover, which is neatly folded up and cradled in her arms like a baby.

"This'll be the child . . . takes after her mother, I'll say . . . ha, ha, ha. Hi, honey," says Christine. "It's a headless person. The head's in here, you see . . . it fell off." (The pullover has no "head.")

"Yes, yes, yes . . . I gotta get the head out." They all laugh.

"This is his wife, and this is his girlfriend," says Liz, pointing to Christine and Sarah in turn. "These two had a child and these two had a child too," she says, perhaps commenting on real events in her family.

"Come on, child, let's go to the park," says Christine. "Her husband has to go to the park. We gotta play with our children . . . let's play ball."

Jenny sings, "Oh, Mommy, can we go today? We've got the reservation. We can stay a year."

"We like playing here," comments Sarah. "No one bothers us. Other children just run right past here [the corral] and don't come stomping through."

The "magic circle" of meadow rocks was another favorite meeting place, where the most mundane of role-playing games was played—"school"!

"One rock is the teacher's desk and we use the others as chairs," says Amy. "I like being a student 'cause we always do easy stuff. If we have a piece of chalk, we play 'one plus one.' It's not real chalk; we just pretend." Amy says she also played "campsite" there and liked it because it reminded her of when she camped in Europe for six months with her family in a Volkswagen bus.

"I play with my two friends. One plays the baby, like my brother when he was little and so cute. The other plays the big sister, and I play the mother."

Rocks on Chaparral Hill provided an equally stimulating site (still with a domestic theme):

"We go up there with our dolls," says Jennifer, "and play 'house.' Or we pretend we're a family, and there's a mother with two daughters or two sons, or something, and there's a pretend heater, pretend beds, a pretend stove, pretend food, and we pretend we're eating. Sometimes things happen, like one of the daughters can run away with her boyfriend, or sometimes for a laugh we throw the seeds that look like little pine cones [redwood seed heads] on people when they're not looking. Once we built a little house of stones, with a little garage and little people. I pretended I was a wife with a husband and children. I made a little car by breaking up a piece of wood and adding little rocks for wheels."

Another favorite nook was the underside of the play structure slide, used by groups of girls to play "house." Because the space was articulated so intimately, they had no difficulty designating different parts like the "porch," "doorway," "roof," "fireplace," and "bed." With the aid of props such as plastic spoons, milk cartons, pieces of vegetation, and small dolls brought from home, scenes from their home life were dramatized.

"I'm the mother, and these are my two charming daughters making soup and cookies. Hey! Keep working, you two, or no allowance this week."

Plant parts and other loose scraps provided the props for girls (more or less exclusively) to engage in a year-round culinary program of their own devising, as they concocted "witches' potions," "soups," "mixtures," and "stews."

"I'm cooking, I'm cooking a nice dinner," says Wanda, the leader of three girls working around one of the larger rocks lying in the grass. The other two girls collect meadow "ingredients" and bring them back to the rock: buckeye, ceanothus flowers, dandelions, gingko leaves, honeysuckle, mallow, oxalis, red and blue linum petals, Shasta daisies, and wild mustard, along with the seed heads of carex, chaparral, and nutgrass.

"They're my 'picking girls,'" continues Wanda. "Oh, help, the stove's getting hot. Wow . . . this stuff's too prickly. Oh God, it's prickly. Don't get it so prickly—it'll hurt our mouths. Hmm, the mint smells good . . . get more mint. Get more cherries [Oregon grape]. Hey girl, get to work, we've got to be ready by twelve o'clock." The girls scurry around obediently.

"These are ice cream dinners," Wanda continues, as she pulls the white petals off the Shasta daisies, "but it's not real ice cream. Girls, that's plenty of lettuce [acanthus leaves]. Oh, oh, this is going to be a good salad dinner. We need more lemon [dandelion petals], lots of salt [sand]. Hey, don't spread it out so much; keep it in little piles. We have to cook the licorice [anise leaves]. Mix it up. Mmm, tastes good, like real licorice . . . it grows in our secret hideout where we have our licorice factory. We grind it up to get the juice out." The girls add "oranges" (California poppy petals) as a final ingredient and turn the mixture over with their hands, breaking it up, feeling it, carefully observing, and pretending to taste it.

"We're making tacos and hot tamales," say a couple of girls playing with a mixture of sand and scraps of vegetation on one of the flat rocks. "We're using white cheese, yellow cheese, milk, tomatoes, and hot sauce. It's a good place here 'cause we can find all the foods. The tamale sauce is almost ready; it's brand new."

"I know how to make it," one of them says. "You just buy the tomatoes [toyon berries]. Don't forget to peel them."

WAR GAMES

Children's play always reflects local culture and prevailing social values. Are there any countries where war games do not exist? Berkeley, scene of antiwar demonstra-

Yard vegetation provided many props for social play. Two girls play "tie up" (top) using cattails. Boys pretend to have a sword fight using dried anise stems (bottom).

tions in the 1960s and early '70s and progenitor of many humanistic causes, certainly could not adequately protect its children from the violence of the broader culture. And the Yard, with its emphasis on peaceful play and non-exploitative use of natural resources, could not fully deter the children from war games either. War games in the Yard, however, did not exist to a dominant degree. Like other types of play, they took on several forms, some of which would hardly justify censure.

Two boys sit in the niche below the play structure slide.

"It's bombs falling," one boy says, referring to the grains of sand falling between the planks of the platform above, dislodged by children running back and forth. "They're having target practice from a B-52." The sand falls onto a sheet of paper on which the boys are drawing with crayons.

"I like drawing the missiles and the battles," replies the other. "I like to think about defense and how smart different sides are. But I don't like the blowing up, the killing part. My dad was in Vietnam and almost got killed by a grenade. That turned me off forever."

In contrast to interest in the military, there were also the more basic, all-out war games in the Yard. They usually took place in the Natural Resource Area, which had excellent cover and small structures that could be instantly converted into military installations.

Ten boys gather at their "headquarters" in the Gazebo, playing "Americans versus Nazis." The "captain" of the Americans tells the Nazis to lay their guns on the table (the large log in the center) and commands his own soldiers to stand next to him. They must shoot the Nazis, who must fall down dead.

"Take aim!"

They raise their pieces of stick and point them at the other five boys.

"Shoot!"

The enemies fall dead. The Americans stay in the Gazebo and the Nazis take off to set up their headquarters in the railroad ties.

"When we're playing army, we go up in the loft [of the Gazebo] and pretend we're shooting at the enemy," says Larry. "Or sometimes the Gazebo is a boat and when children get shot, they fall into the water. We have to put bullets in our guns and get ready for another attack. We'll hide behind the logs, shoot at the other side and try to kill them so we can win. We make our guns out of sticks. I don't like to be the captain though. You have to tell everybody what to do. My brother does that to me all the time and I hate it."

The Americans now use the log by the Gazebo as an airplane. They sit, facing the roots. The boy in front is the pilot. He steers with his hands on the roots. The Nazis attack. Everyone scatters and shoots. The Americans keep returning to the plane and shooting from it. Fighting continues around the log, in scattered groups. No one knows for sure who is who.

"Are you a Nazi?" they ask each other. If the answer is "yes" and the interrogator is an American, he shouts excitedly, "He's a Nazi!" and shoots him. Others volunteer the information, yelling "I'm a Nazi (or American)!" They are promptly shot by the enemies; after counting to ten, they come alive again and resume playing.

There is much physical contact, grabbing, and pretend-punching. In one capture, one boy grabs another around the neck, holds a gun to him, and leads him away.

"I like playing army," says Diego, a serious player who uses war toys rather than scraps from the environment. "I have lots of army stuff: an army rifle and an army hat and a camouflage suit and a belt with play bullets. And I have a Colt 45 cap gun. They're the kind of caps that look like real bullets. The other children don't have that. They're the majors. I'm the general because I wear a suit."

Diego calls a war meeting at the railroad ties. The boys sit around facing him. He orders the guns to be put in the middle of the circle. Enemies start fighting each other, pushing and shoving. Some pick up guns and shoot.

A boy comes up and says he wants to play. One member of the group says, "You can't, it's too dangerous." Diego reprimands the soldiers for "acting like babies." There is more fighting.

One boy asks another, "Can you keep track of what's happening?" Several boys call for silence, others start chanting, "Noise, noise, noise!" The game dissolves into a pantomime of fighting, laughing, teasing, and sitting around.

An obvious aspect of war games was that there was never a girl in sight. To that extent, these games accurately reflected social values. At the same time, they were set in the land of make-believe, but almost always with a historical dimension that distanced them from the present day. The last example was a clear game of good versus evil (Nazis already defined by society as such). More political games like "Americans against Russians" were never observed.

Some games reflected issues or concerns that children picked up culturally. While not strictly a war game, this example is a bizarre movie-inspired fantasy combined with a poignant projection of nuclear threat.

"We're playing a 'car game,'" says Reilly, riding the Big Toy with his friends. "Well, we're not now, but it started out that way; then it turned into a 'mutant' kind of game. But we're still in this car . . . but we've all become 'mutants'—except him, he's still 'half-and-half.' We're not considered things, we're not considered anything, we're 'mutants.' You can't call us things or persons or anything. You turn into a mutant if you get exposed to radiation, gamma radiation, stuff like that . . . A hundred gallons of radiation got into him . . . It comes from power plants. There's lots of mutants now, because of power plants and atom bombs. They give you mutant diseases."

War games, especially those with a nuclear aspect, raise the issue of adult values and attitudes towards children's play. Play is an integral part of education; the essence of education is to transmit values. Thus play and values are inextricably connected. As transmitting agents of values, teachers, parents, and playleaders hold the responsibility to intervene and use play episodes as vehicles for discussing values—and facts. What would be the consequences if a nuclear bomb fell on San Francisco? What would happen to people in the East Bay, to life in the Yard? Would such a thing ever be justified here or in some other country? What does "mutation" mean? What are some examples? Is conventional war ever justified? How about the children's war games and war toys? Some countries, such as Malta and Sweden, ban or strictly control the sale of war toys. Is that a good idea?

WHEN SHOULD ADULTS INTERVENE?

Adult intervention in children's free play often brought negative reactions because it frequently resulted in the insensitive control of behavior, which is an anathema to the spirit of play. Intervention should reinforce positive relationships between individuals to help the development of peaceful lives. Following is an example of where intervention would have been justified:

Isabelle and her friend are playing on the large log between the Italian stone pines.

"We're making a bee house," they say. "We found him in the creek; he was drowning." They have constructed a "house" in a cavity of the log using wood chips and a few heads of Shasta daisy. The bee crawls slowly around and does not look too well.

"He can't fly right now, 'cause he's too wet. He'll just rest at home 'til he gets better." After a while, they pick up the bee and carry it, along with parts of its house, over to a more secluded spot behind the pussy willows. They construct a more elaborate house out of woodchips and pieces of bark for walls, roofing it with bay leaves and decorating it with daisy petals. A third girl joins them. They take turns peeking under the bay leaves to see how the bee is doing.

Their peaceful involvement is rudely interrupted by three boys who had been playing war games. One boy starts adding pieces of anise to the roof, calling it "poison." The weight of the anise starts to cause the bee house to collapse. One girl hits the boy and tells him to leave them alone. The boys whoop around, tease the girls, crack jokes, and talk about playing "black hole." The girls think the house should be turned into a grave, "'cause the bee must

have died by now." The boys overhear their comment, pounce on the little sanctuary, and pull it apart, saying they are "grave robbers." They look among the debris of the house for the bee, grow bored, run off laughing, and continue their war game. The girls talk with sad resignation about the boys' aggressive behavior.

In this parable of male domination and attitudes towards living things, there was a justifiable case for adult intervention—to protect the weak and to guide aggression towards more humanistic behavior. If this intervention does not occur at school or at home, where will it happen? Tolerant teachers and parents are necessary to help nurture children's cultural development and to reinforce positive values and beliefs.

•

As far as we could observe, the diverse natural environment of the Yard—designed with children's participation to meet their developmental needs—fostered peaceful coexistence. The most obvious indication was the lack of boredom among the children, who rarely found themselves in negative, antisocial situations where teasing was used to add interest to their lives.

There was also a more profound consequence. Because the Yard environment was a daily part of the children's school experience, they participated in a deeper process of cultural development. The Yard engaged them as a community, with influence from teachers and parents, in orienting their values in a prosocial direction deeply enough to resist the negative influences of the broader culture.

The key to success in developing resilient, peaceful children is the community nature of the process. Peace is a collective phenomenon and a profoundly important characteristic of the human condition. It can only be conserved collectively. We say "conserved" because children are not born violent; they learn it from society. Because the Yard provided a creative, nonformal educational environment, it tested the children's peaceful abilities and helped to reinforce and conserve them each day.

CHAPTER 11

Boosting the Basics

NATURE AND LANGUAGE

A single word—"diversity"—explained the power of the natural environment to stimulate language. Synthetic settings could not compete with the linguistic range of living entities such as the ponds. Here is a list of thirty "water words" that one class came up with in a short brainstorm session:

bed	falling	ripples
blue	fish	river
calm	frozen	ruffled
clear	green	running
cool	lake	slough
creek	muddy	still
dirty	plop	stream
down	pond	swim
drop	pool	trickle
erosion	reflection	waves

How do children learn the three Rs? Two critical aspects of the learning process are motivation and retention. Children must desire to learn as well as remember what they have learned. Furthermore, the process must have continuity, with episodes of learning that reinforce, reexpose, and reapply prior learning.

A key assumption behind the development of the Yard was that indoor-outdoor activity and interaction with diverse, living settings would reinforce and improve the learning process, especially for children with more physical, less abstract learning styles—children who all too often carry the label "learning disabled."

TUNING THE SENSES

Providing visual orientation was the first step in transforming the Yard into a place for interdisciplinary instruction. Pedagogical strategies were developed to help students become so visually immersed in their surroundings that the entire learning process would be affected. Students were instructed to wander slowly around the Yard for fifteen minutes and list everything they saw. The first time around, they typically listed general descriptions, such as "weeds," "trees," "birds," "play structures," "flowers," "leaves," and "clouds." Following a class discussion and prompting from the teacher to focus on one spot, the descriptions increased in detail, with vegetation often the focus of attention—a powerful stimulator of language.

"I saw a flower. It was bright orange. I counted six petals. There was a whole bunch of them under a mulberry tree. The leaves were green and sort of crinkly. I think they're California poppies."

The more students looked, the more they saw. The more they saw, the more they looked. Groups focused their observations on small areas—the lower pond, for example, or even an area enclosed by a hula hoop. Sometimes a time limit was imposed to increase the intensity of attention. One group went to the pond and listed twenty-three objects in one minute.

One teacher explained, "My job is to build upon the children's intrinsic interest and motivation. Students need to exploit the shapes, textures, colors, smells, and tastes of the Yard and become aware of the great vastness and variety of things in the environment which can be learned by the integrated use of our senses." Her group worked on "object properties," using sets of leaves, pieces of wood, seeds, and rocks, re-sorting them into sensory-based sets. They later created a guessing game describing objects in the Yard through the five senses. For example:

> My touch is wet, cold, freezing, gushy;
> My sight is dirty, greasy, gluey, green, messy, muddy;
> My smell is dirty, stinky, fresh;
> My sound is popping, bubbly, sizzling;
> My taste is not healthy for people. What am I?

This was one student's attempt to describe the varied characteristics of the fountain, waterfall, and ponds.

To investigate color, students created color wheels with crayons and paper. Beginning indoors, the children arranged the colors according to how prevalent they thought each color was in the Yard. They then went outside to check their predictions. As most students thought, green and brown were the most common colors. But as the children excitedly searched the Yard, they discovered many other colors: red, purple, blue, white, and yellow, which they matched with the corresponding slots on their color wheels.

Other groups played a camouflage game to help learn visual discrimination. Moving around the Yard, children could see how much they blended in, depending on the colors and shapes of their clothes in relation to the environment.

Investigating temperature was an effective way of learning how to use one's body as a measuring device. Initially, students were instructed to use their hands and spend five minutes going around the Yard listing the hottest, coldest, and "in-between" places. This approach encouraged the children to think of themselves as "walking laboratories" that collected and processed information. As they passed through the environment, it passed through them, reinforcing the idea that the environment dwells within each person as much as each person dwells within the environment. Later, items on the list were checked with a thermometer to "calibrate" the body's response.

Children often began tactile investigations atop the play structure, looking at the sharp contrasts in color and

Children's documentations of natural processes were a great way to integrate language, math, and science. One class charted changes in the Yard during cold weather (top) and measured the temperature for verification (middle). Another class gathered plant parts to construct color wheels to assess the Yard "spectrum" in different seasons (bottom).

texture between the asphalt, the sand, and the banked-up trees of the Natural Resource Area. Back on the ground, they used their hands to compare the smooth, hard asphalt with the soft, granular sand. Moving to the Natural Resource Area, the leaves of the trees not only felt different from the asphalt and sand but also felt different from one another, as evidenced in the children's descriptions of the "scratchy" live oak, "soft, feathery" acacia, "ticklely" weeping willow, "prickly" pine, and "slippery" fig.

The children also discussed how texture affected their feelings. "I feel hard on the cement and I feel soft in nature," one student wrote in his journal.

Investigations of smell had much to offer. There were general differences in smell between the Main Yard and the Natural Resource Area. There were further differences within the Natural Resource Area itself— between aromatic plants like eucalyptus, bay laurel, pine, ceanothus, pepper, walnut, anise, mint, thyme, rosemary, sage, and onion; and between the many species of fragrant flowers. Smells provided interesting descriptive language topics; in describing a plant, one child wrote, "It smells like pizza."

Taste was more difficult to address because of the safety issues surrounding toxic plants. Of course, the best guides were the children themselves, many of whom were experts on which plants in the Yard could be eaten or tasted. Anise, sourgrass, Australian plum, miner's lettuce, blackberries, bay laurel, pepper, and almonds were common examples of plants that could be eaten raw, along with vegetables like radishes, beans, carrots, lettuce, and tomatoes. These plants offered a range of tastes for experimentation and discussion. After discovering that Native Americans had used cattail roots for salads, one teacher harvested some with her class. The students were so intrigued that they continued harvesting cattails themselves and showed other children how to do it. As a result, eating cattail roots quickly became a Yard tradition.

To explore Yard acoustics, groups of children closed their eyes and noted the sounds they could hear at two contrasting locations. At the pond, they heard human voices, wind blowing through the trees, and birds singing. In the Main Yard, they heard the sounds of bouncing balls, children screaming, traffic noise, and a clanging gate. Afterwards, the children discussed Yard "music," including preferred spots, different sources of sound, and why some sounds were more pleasant than others. Their investigation extended to sounds in the everyday environment: a fire engine, a police car, an ambulance, a high school marching band, waves breaking on the beach, parents arguing. The children discussed the different meanings of sounds and their emotional reactions to them.

Guided by sighted partners, blindfolded children went on "trust walks" in the Yard. Using senses other than sight, the children tried to guess the locations of objects or what objects had been placed in their hands. The game was repeated in the classroom, followed by a discussion on the sensory cues people used indoors to get their bearings, compared with those used outdoors. Sounds were classified as "loud," "soft," "pleasant," "ugly," "close," or "far."

Children went outside with tape recorders to find their most and least favorite sounds. Back in class, they tried to guess the subject of each other's' recordings and discussed why they liked or disliked them. The natural sound of the waterfall and the hum of the pump box were cited as favorite "point sources." While falling water was a universally pleasant sound, it was surprising that an alien, mechanical hum in an otherwise natural setting was attractive. Outside, children closed their eyes to see how far from the pump box they could get and still feel the vibrations, which traveled along the fences and through the ground.

These activities also helped students to get along with one another, to build feelings of trust, and to learn that more could be accomplished through cooperation.

WORD POWER

Outdoors, language was everywhere.

"It's like hiking through a dictionary," enthuses one teacher. "You can walk through the Yard and see the words all around you, feel them coming at you, and watch the children use them every moment in their play."

The Yard was an effective tool to expand language skills, build vocabulary, and increase sensitivity to the power of language.

Language was evident even in the use of common play equipment like the swings.

"It feels like I'm in the sky riding on a bird that's going 'swish, swish, swish,'" says Jeanine.

"I imagine the talking children are birds chirping and their screaming is wild horses," says Lela. "It's like being free in nature . . . I love it."

As the girls rode the swings with their eyes closed, they entered their own dream worlds. Through language, they were able to communicate these powerful images to others.

The purest examples of language in the Yard were the children's own voice games:

"Chugga, chugga . . ."
"Psht, psht . . ."
"Ch, ch, ch . . ."
"We're playing cars and planes," says Shelley, one of four girls on the spools. "Yesterday we were sitting an' getting bored, so we just started going 'pp, pp, pp, pp.' Then someone went 'ch, ch.' Then we all started making up stuff, like 'char, char.' Then Lisa went 'schpewch fffwww', so I went 'fww, fww, fww, schpew, schpew, schpew,' and we all went 'chean, chean,' then changed it to 'chugga, chugga, psht, psht.'"

Anything associated with the Yard could be linked to language. Even before redevelopment began, children applied their language skills when expressing what they wanted to include in the master plan. One group designed the "tunnel slide."

"It has a tunnel on the bottom and a slide on the top," one child writes. "There's a ladder you can climb. It's made of metal and cement and wood. About five people can fit inside and about three people can slide down the slide." (This design eventually became the pipe tunnel in the Main Yard.)

Yard language stimulated teachers as much as children. A teacher who enjoyed crossword puzzles created "word mazes" with the names of Yard trees embedded in them. Another puzzle featured the names of Yard animals.

"We did Indian coding," reports one of the students. "My teacher made up a code for each of the letters in the alphabet. Then we had to figure out the things that were written using our coding sheet. One time she used the code to spell, 'Meet you in the Gazebo.'"

Classrooms discovered that many Yard phenomena could provide the subject of verbal exercises: air words, asphalt words, ballgame words, dirt words, flower words, garden words, people words, play words, sharp

Using the Yard as inspiration, teachers invented a number of ways to tap the linguistic potential of the students. Activities ranged from listing words related to water (top) to word puzzles containing names of items found in the Yard (bottom).

words, space words, time words, vegetation words, water words, weather words, wildlife words, winter words, and so on.

ENVIRONMENT AND LANGUAGE

Over the years, we made an important observation. The richness of the natural surroundings stimulated the richness of the children's language during play. This correlation was evident in the differences between what children talked about in the Main Yard and what they talked about in the Natural Resource Area.

In the Main Yard, activities and conversations were predictable. There, movement was fast, usually as part of conventional games. Students occasionally took short strolls in the Main Yard, though the choice of pathways was far more limited than in the Natural Resource Area. Conversations in the Main Yard, with its fixed, unchangeable structures, were less diverse and less imaginative, focusing on conventional topics of everyday life: yesterday's baseball game, a weekend trip, family gossip. Conversations were short and topics changed frequently, as different children constantly entered and left the discussion.

In contrast, play groups in the Natural Resource Area were more stable; consequently, the children's conversations lasted longer, went into greater detail, and covered a wider range of less immediate topics (plans for the summer vacation, recollections of past events, sharing favorite possessions, etc.).

JOURNALS

Journals were the main method employed by the children for recording observations, investigations, and discoveries. The journal is a powerful pedagogical technique. It reinforces self-actualization (viewing oneself as part of the local community and culture) and encourages reflection (developing higher-order critical thinking skills).

"I'm looking at a scarecrow with an old jacket and a hat on. Its head is full of straw. Oh heck, a yellow and black butterfly just flew out of its ear."

This entry later inspired a short story, *The Bug and the Scarecrow:*

"Once a bug sat on a scarecrow and the scarecrow began to shout, 'Get out of here you ugly bug or I will tickle you with my snout.' But the bug did not hear him. He just sat there all day. So the scarecrow tickled him and threw him in the hay."

Through these exercises, children learned that creative writing was not something that had to come directly from their imagination. Instead, personal experience could serve as a source of inspiration.

Everyday observations and special events (e.g., new construction and events such as the barnyard, camp-out, and Yardfest, described in later chapters) presented endless opportunities for journal reporting, along with obvious educational benefits. The children developed language arts and reading skills and learned that records were important for reporting experiences. For teachers, the journals indicated which episodes and objects in the children's experience had the greatest educational impact.

Captioned drawings were a simple yet effective journal task that taught the art of succinct description:

"The willow is wide and shady."
"Acacia is like a feather."
"The pond has a turtle, snakes, and frogs in it."
"Trumpet vine flowers give honey."
"Agave catches water with its leaves."

ENVIRONMENTAL ALPHABET

The most elaborate language exercise involved five classes that created an "Environmental Alphabet" for the Yard. Each of the eighty-four children created their own list of "object" words, "feeling" words, and "action" words, which were then compiled into master lists. Individual "feeling" words totaled two hundred sixty-four! The most popular "feeling" words were, in order of frequency:

quiet	incredible	bored
nice	kind	great
happy	mad	interesting
fun	large	beautiful
dirty	queer	good
dumb	bad	like

"Quietness" was the children's most common emotion, followed by "nice," "happy," and "fun." How different this picture was to the stereotypical schoolyard with children rushing about in constant conflict with one another.

Each class selected one or more words from the complete lists and matched them with each letter of the alphabet. They displayed the words on square boards and attached them to the chainlink fences and other spots, as a way to introduce visitors to the Yard's "land-scape of language."

POETIC LICENSE

John Oliver Simon was a California Poet-in-the-Schools (and neighborhood resident) who came to Washington as part of a program sponsored by the California Arts Council. John had a remarkable ability to excite children about poetry writing. In one of his pro-grams, he "licensed" the children to go "hunting for words" in the Yard.

"After several classroom sessions doing writing exercises to give the children some notion of what a poem is," John reported, "we began using the outdoors in small groups. I would ask them to find their own poem anywhere in the Yard, and later as they became more adept, I'd suggest poetic procedures to sharpen their perception and sense of craft."

Similes: What is the wind like? ("An invisible stream," writes Dana.)

Haiku: Narrow your focus and actively select for intense value of the present moment as it passes. ("When John said see that bird, he flew away," writes Jerquette.)

"Wallace Stevens had 'Thirteen Ways of Looking at a Blackbird.' I asked the children, 'How many ways can you see?' We began in the classroom to play with language, fantasy, and feeling, but I also wanted the children to understand that there could be poetry 'in the moment.' It was in the environment, just so.

"'Explore! A poem can be anywhere in the Yard. Find your poem.' And the students would run in every direction and come back and write—or the younger ones, the first-graders, dictated to me and then would copy over and draw a picture with it, just as the haiku masters often did."

One of John's techniques was to sit on the ground, set his typewriter on a log, and invite the children to

march 28, 1974
I like to be
living in
life.

GARDEN JOURNAL

"Today we made beds out of dirt and we made paths so we can walk in the garden and not step on the plants. I got hot and sweaty. We made a map of the garden and put it on a piece of paper. We planted cabbage, carrots, peas, beets, lettuce, spinach, radishes. It was fun getting dirty. All we have to do is measure a little more and we're finished. We're going to plant some alfalfa soon because the rabbits are run-ning out of food. Today we put up more stakes and strings . . . the weather is very nice, our plants are coming up . . . plants are growing well, the ground was 62°F (17°C). We found a snail trail and put sawdust down to stop them attacking our plants. The air was very cold today, 50°F (10°C) . . . we planted onions and Jerusalem artichokes next to the fence where they will be protected. We saw some mosquito larva in the water in the old bucket. We layered the compost with leaves, kitchen waste, and rabbit droppings. We filled a whole bin! Today we trans-planted lettuce, cabbage, and peas and watered . . . we weeded, it was hard work. Yesterday Milly and I turned the compost by ourselves . . . it was 135°F (57°C), you could see the steam like crazy. Milly flipped the compost and some bugs came out. It was hard work. Today we harvest-ed some lettuce and peas and made a salad in the class-room and talked about differ-ent kinds of foods and made vegetable prints . . . I tried with a green pepper."

SENSORY SOIL TEST

"Sand is tan and smooth and feels teeny-weeny. It's very light compared to clay and soft. Boy, is it soft! It doesn't hold water too well.

Clay is bumpy and dark brown, and is heavy com-pared to sand.

Silt looks sort of loamy but feels like sand.

Loam is rough and looks like little rocks stuck together.

Compost looks like dried leaves and little sticks; it feels moist and smells like manure."

— Gretchen's journal

LOOK BOOKS

Speech therapists emphasize the importance of stimulating children to manipulate their physical environment to promote language development.

One class began its language arts period each week by meeting at the railroad ties, then dispersing with "look books" to observe, draw, and write about something of interest. The teacher moved around, helping students translate their experiences into words. The children then brought their writing back to class and posted them on the "share board" for discussion.

In one session, a child wrote about how he had discovered that parrot's feather—the prolific wetland plant growing in the ponds—closed its leaves when first submerged under water and then opened them again as the air, trapped by surface tension, escaped. The student's discovery was an excellent example of "happenstance science." This observation led to a discussion of the presence of parrot's feather in the ponds. Some children said it was "choking the ponds"; others said they liked the appearance of a "green blanket." The teacher asked, "Is there such a thing as living litter?" The class discussed how one group of plants (or people) can dominate an area and keep others out, and the consequences of these actions.

help him write a poem. Using a Socratic style, he would throw out an idea for the group to run with, as they spontaneously tossed out words or lines to add. It was like a jazz improvisation with Yard themes, as the children played the verbal instruments of their imagination and free association.

Me and the Tree
I am sitting in-between three
green pine trees and a rock,
with grass surrounding me and
my friends the trees. When I
listen to the cars zoom by I feel
in my body a faint cry.
— Brendan

"A typical involvement found me working with five or six children at a time, in rotation from the class, a mix of so-called 'high-potential' and so-called 'educationally handicapped.' In poetry, these types of groupings don't seem to matter."

Wind
When the wind blows
the jails are getting
bigger and bigger.
— Sarah

"Poems sometimes expressed a sophisticated level of environmental awareness the children had gained from participating in the process of the Yard, putting their hands and minds into the earth and living things."

Soil
Underneath the dark black sky
with roots coming into it worms and
slugs asleep in the thick black sky of
dirt surrounding everything underneath.
— Brendan

"Or with the total accuracy of a master of haiku."

The flowers are growing babies.
— Krishna

"Unlike most school environments, where the massive structure of box and clock and desk indicates a degree of alienation, where the child-poet's most promising strategy is fantasy, the Yard is a system that people feel part of. To me, the children are as much a part of the ecosystem as the trees and tadpoles."

I hear tadpoles
rumbling and splashing
in the water.
— Nalini

John's contribution beautifully exemplified the value of using outside professionals to deepen and reinforce the material and concepts taught in the regular curriculum.

ENVIRONMENTAL MATH

Although we were not able to find a "mathematician-in-the-schools," several teachers creatively used hands-on learning opportunities in the Yard to reinforce math concepts.

The first thing to learn was the usefulness of numbers. Numbers were tools for solving problems and making life easier. In a way, math was more immediately accessible than language because the act of measuring was so concrete and applicable to even the smallest situations. Some teachers saw the Yard brimming with things to count and measure—it was a landscape of numbers.

License plate math. The license plates of cars in the staff parking area were a good place to initiate outdoor math activities. A discussion of number plates expanded into the broader topic of identification numbers: social security numbers, student identification numbers, the U.S. census.

Animal population math. To introduce the study of animal populations, a teacher invented a game called "The Shepherd and Her Flock." The game was played outdoors, with one child playing the shepherd and the rest the sheep. Each of the sheep found a small rock to represent themselves and gave it to the shepherd. The Gazebo served as the fold. As the sheep went out to graze in the meadow, the shepherd moved one rock from the "in" pile to the "out" pile (a method still used in some parts of the world). The sheep ran around baaing. The teacher instructed four or five of them to disappear by hiding in the bushes. As the sheep returned to the fold, the shepherd transferred rocks back to the "in" pile. The rocks in the "out" pile thus represented the lost sheep, whereupon everyone went looking for them. The game was a great success.

VOCABULARY LIST

Surveyor: A person who goes to an unmapped area and takes measurements and makes observations.

Cartographer: A person who puts together the surveyor's information and makes a map. A mapper.

Draftsman: A person who draws out all the details and makes a finished map.

Environment: Our physical and social surroundings.

Physical: Our physical surroundings includes all the real things around us, and our relationships with them.

Social: Our social surroundings includes all the other human beings in our environment, and our relationships with them.

Community: A group of animals or plants living together in the same environment. A group of people who share the same interests or work.

Lifestyle: The way a person lives.

Person: A child, woman, or man.

Some people: A group of men, women, or children.

Place: An area or space where something is.

Sensory: Sensory qualities are qualities about something that we learn about by using our senses.

Compass: An instrument that always points to the north.

— Helen Cox,
classroom notes

CONSTRUCTION MATH

Construction of the Yard offered math opportunities with every new event—like the arrival of four tons of rocks one day. The children had calculated ahead of time the individual weight of twenty-five rocks as each had been bought "by the pound."

When the rocks arrived, the children measured their circumferences and tried to guess their weight. By the time we reached the last rock, the children understood the difference between estimating and guessing.

The project continued with the placement of the rocks, using a two-wheeled trolley.

First, we had to measure the locations according to the master plan and then plot them on the ground. This was difficult for the young children to understand because they had to grasp the notion of scale conversion—going from one inch equal to twenty feet to the full-scale meadow. Laying out the rocks also provided useful practice in triangulation as a technique for plotting the locations of objects in space.

The children quickly realized that we could not have completed the job without tape measures and a numbering system. Tasks often required the use of numbers: counting trees and animals, calculating necessary amounts of fencing, estimating gallons of paint. The opportunities were endless.

Pumpkin math. Once again, gardening demonstrated its educational potential, this time for numerical work. In mid-October, close to Halloween, a class harvested two pumpkins, a large and small one. They weighed the orange globes (which were intriguing in themselves) with a portable scale, measured their circumferences, and then measured the circumference of their own heads. The pumpkins were much bigger, the students discovered.

The children then scooped out the seeds. After everyone guessed how many seeds there were, children counted them using egg-carton "counting machines," which had ten sockets, each holding ten seeds. One pumpkin had 550 seeds; the other, 416. The students discussed the similarity in the number of seeds in each pumpkin, despite the great difference in size. They also discovered that the seeds were so light that a single seed could not be weighed. After considering the vast amount of vegetation that grew from just one seed, the children realized that the pumpkins were the largest vegetables in the Yard, both in terms of size and the amount of space occupied. They measured the area and calculated how much space other vegetables occupied in the garden. They concluded that beans were the most economical because they grew vertically.

Time, they realized, also had to enter the calculations. They learned that some vegetables, like tomatoes and chard, kept producing over a long period of time. These vegetables therefore made better use of garden space than root vegetables like carrots, which required replanting after a single harvest.

The group returned to the classroom to wash off the pumpkin seeds and bake them in the oven, to serve as a snack for the entire class.

The pumpkin discussion continued. Who has Halloween pumpkins at home? Where did they come from—a home garden, a pumpkin patch, a store? How much did they cost? How much did they cost to grow at school? The discussion turned to the "costs" of time, effort, and care in running the garden. The teacher helped the students estimate the hours; they calculated that it would cost at least three dollars an hour. The class began to realize that obtaining pumpkins in this way was expensive and that the local pumpkin patch (which they had visited earlier that week) provided a more cost-effective alternative (provided that the transportation costs were not included!).

Here was an example of a math learning cycle that covered all stages, from hands-on experience to the transfer of skills to everyday life.

Transpiration math. Scientific experiments often required math calculations. In one, a dramatic demonstration of transpiration, a plastic bag was used to enclose the end of an alder tree branch bearing about twenty-five mature leaves. The open end of the bag was tightly bound around the branch with a rubber band. After twenty-four hours, the children found that nearly fifty grams of water had collected in one corner of the bag. "How many grams per leaf per hour is that?" the teacher asked.

ENVIRONMENTAL GEOMETRY

The great variety of geometric shapes in the Yard served as another math-related opportunity. A popular exercise was to send the children outside to hunt for examples of squares, rectangles, circles, triangles, diamonds, hexagons, octagons, polygons, and solid figures like cubes and pyramids. The activity also involved language, since the students had to record the location and composition of the figure. It was a more challenging exercise, but once one or two students got the idea, everyone else caught on and began to see diamonds in the chainlink fencing; squares in the hopscotch surface; triangles in the play structures; circles in pipes, tunnels, and faucets; rectangles in railings, windows, doors, and pieces of wood; hexagons in railroad ties and corrals; and cubes in the monkey bars.

When students went up on the roof, they could appreciate the Yard's larger geometry: the shape of the site itself, the huge, circular compass, the rectilinear layout of the bars in contrast with the polymorphous layout of the Natural Resource Area. The children compared these observations with the paper plan of the Yard, an exercise that introduced them to the concepts of scale and proportion.

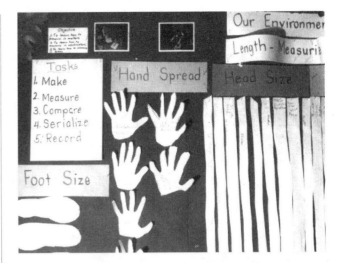

Teachers found that they could introduce mathematical principles by simply using whatever was in the children's immediate world as motivation. Students charted body measurements (top), conducted sidewalk surveys (middle), and analyzed the "Yard geometry" from the school roof (bottom).

CREATING THE IMPETUS TO LEARN

Outdoor educational settings offer a unique sense of exploration and discovery, and a powerful impetus for young children to learn. Outdoor play helps them acquire intuitive knowledge. Skillful teachers can build upon this foundation and guide further cycles of learning. The educational process can be helped immeasurably by resident resource professionals and community artists, as the poet John Simon so clearly demonstrated.

Our view of the learning process accepts developmental stages derived from Piaget, Kohlberg, Hodgkin, and others (see Chapter 17). Each describes the developmental process differently, but common to them all are the notions of a hierarchical, progressive structure and the importance of facilitating continuous sequences of learning. We place special emphasis on the importance of students interacting playfully with living materials and phenomena, especially in early and middle childhood. However, the cognitive benefits of playful exploration of the natural world are not limited by age, as the biographies of many scientists and creative thinkers testify.

Fundamental to effective basic education is that children feel good both about themselves and their school—one reinforces the other, a truth too often overlooked by educators. When children are provided with opportunities to work directly with the living environment, to creatively manipulate it, to interpret it through the imagination, and to invest it with positive feelings of enjoyment and trust, they feel good about themselves individually and collectively, and feel that their school is a great place to be.

•

Our theory of learning required a diverse environment that stimulated each child to move continuously through sequences of exploration and discovery—recording, communicating, and expressing; applying new knowledge to other contexts, issues, and problems; and eventually transferring the results to everyday life and culture. Retention, as in all learning processes, relied on the skill and charisma of teachers, the support of peers, and the enthusiasm of parents. The social reinforcement and facilitation of learning among the children at Washington were further aided by the sensory power of the natural environment. This experience embedded powerful, lasting images in the child. This is what the Yard offered that many other educational environments could not.

CHAPTER 12

Science Inside Out

CHILDREN AS RESEARCHERS

Treasure hunts were one of the many activities facilitated by the Yard that encouraged scientific investigation. Basic scientific principles such as classification could be explored with simple materials, such as sticks of different lengths. The "whole environment" of the Yard offered children unique avenues for developing scientific awareness and research skills.

O ur conclusion from experiences in the Yard was that the learning process of science could be greatly strengthened by studying live events in authentic natural settings. This conclusion seems obvious enough, since the art of scientific investigation lies in the ability to make deductions based on detailed observations and records of events.

When acquiring information experientially, children have greater motivation to extend the learning process through higher orders of thinking. These principles provided a strong foundation on which to build instructional strategies—an approach that has been put into practice in the United Kingdom to redevelop school sites as educational resources (see Learning Through Landscapes Trust, Appendix B).

A hands-on approach means that teachers serve as "instigators of learning." Rather than adopt a rigid, didactic style, teachers need to demonstrate the abilities to intervene at the right time, to prompt the right questions, and to steer the learning process into deeper waters of experience and advanced thinking. This requires a reliance on intuitive ways of knowing which, according to Schubert, teachers often readily admit to in their approaches to curriculum development and methods of teaching. He states further that overlooking this quality can result in "critical inconsistencies . . . and an unruly array of assumptions" in the learning process.[1]

HAPPENSTANCE SCIENCE

The Yard's diversity and constantly changing panorama of natural learning opportunities made this open-ended, intuitive educational process more feasible, more productive—and less predictable. Teachers had to anticipate life's fortuitous events by following a flexible instructional program. During on-site, in-service training sessions, teachers were urged to leave space in their lesson plans for unintended spin-off activities, especially when attempting something new. When an activity did not work out as planned, teachers were encouraged not to view it as failure but rather as "unintended results."

Activities in natural settings provided more sensitive lessons in science, offering children a greater appreciation and understanding of ecological processes.

"The redwoods were planted four years ago," writes Anna in her journal. "Some of them are getting pretty fat. Four years is no age for a redwood tree when they can live for hundreds of years. But four years is pretty old for a person."

Teachers had to be on the lookout for such insightful observations, brimming with nascent scientific awareness.

A girl commented that she liked to "pick up leaves," and wanted to know if they were examples of "organisms." She explained that she was an organism herself and that she picked herself up when playing on the bars. She now saw herself as an organism interacting with the environment—an excellent example of higher-order thinking.

Another child, in making observations about the pond life, noted:

> "I like to watch the fish to see how their tails steer them and see how they turn pale in the winter. Some have kind of brownish spots on them, and they're really tiny. I like to write about them in my journal."

Each winter a large pile of woodchips was delivered to the Yard for student crews to spread around muddy spots in the Natural Resource Area. Clouds of steam rose from the woodchip heap as its decomposing interior was exposed. Children stuck their hands in the pile "to touch the heat," as one of them said. An elaborate discussion about the mechanism of decomposition blossomed to the point where it became the main activity and spreading the woodchips was sidelined, which was fine with the students!

Unusual weather events like storms or frosts provided good examples of the many serendipitous learning opportunities unique to the Yard.

One winter the ponds froze, guaranteeing hijinks and happenstance learning. Children teemed around the edges of the upper pond, shouting as they tried to pry loose pieces of ice. One child said the embedded leaves looked like fossils. Another held the pieces up to the sun and noted that they looked like Christmas decorations. The teacher asked what kinds of leaves were frozen. The students discussed how the fish were able to escape from being frozen because water freezes from the surface down.

The children tried to determine why all the ice was located on the south side of the pond (under the shadow of adjacent buildings). Someone ran to fetch a thermometer to measure the temperature of the water. They took some ice back to their classrooms to see how long it took to melt.

In hot weather, children sometimes poured water on the railroad ties by the upper pond to create steam. It was a ready-made opportunity for teachers to intervene and ask, "What's happening to the water? Look at it closely. How does it turn to steam?"

TRANSECTS

Teachers laid lines of bright yellow yarn across the site, over fences, through vegetated edges, across soft sand and hot asphalt, across rivers, through cool forests and warm meadows. The transects (lines traversing different zones) sliced through the Yard's various ecotones (junctions of zones): the gentle interfaces between land and water, the sharp contrasts across pathways, in-between plant communities in the Natural Resource Area, the precise junctions of asphalt and dirt, and the abrupt vertical breaks of planters. Groups of children followed the yellow lines. At different stations, they read the temperatures from suspended thermometers. They felt the ground-surface moisture with their hands and recorded the characteristics of the wide range of habitat conditions. Differences of twenty to thirty degrees Fahrenheit (10 to 15°C) were common between the hottest, driest habitats and the coldest, wettest habitats—a dramatic illustration of microclimatic variation.

Hula hoops were used to stake out claims for more detailed study along transect lines.

> "Wherever the hoop lands," a student explains, "we're going to see what lives inside the circle, what kinds of insects live there, the temperature of the soil, and stuff."

Back in class, the children plotted the results on a composite chart with small sketches illustrating the observations. They entered "types of species" on the horizontal axis and "number of species" on the vertical axis. Results for the meadow, for example, showed 97 plants, 88 sticks, 28 rocks, 25 clumps of grass, 9 ants, 1 beetle, and 1 worm. This activity provided a powerful stimulus

for students to practice basic scientific procedures: observation, counting, classification, and compilation.

MAPPING

The Yard offered many opportunities for children to develop mapping skills. Maps represented an important recording device. In addition to classroom applications, maps were used throughout the planning process for expressing ideas about how the Yard ought to be developed.

One teacher, a supporter of the metric system, had the children measure themselves: head circumference, height, foot length, hand spread, waist, arm length, and so on. The students then measured objects in the room, distances in the Yard, and spaces around the neighborhood.

Every student kept a metric record book. A metric learning station was set up in the classroom. It offered a variety of metric instruments, measurable artifacts, and displays of the students' investigations. Teachers and students worked together to invent additional exercises; for instance, they held a metric jumping competition, with the distances recorded on the classroom floor.

Using one's body as a unit of measurement was a great introduction to the concepts of measurement and mapping, especially for the youngest children. To gauge the width of McKinley Avenue, a line of kindergarten students lay head-to-toe across the closed portion of the street, and found it was "seven children wide." For comparison, they measured the sidewalk, a kickball square, and the distance from the school building to the Natural Resource Area. This activity helped the children understand comparative distances by developing a sense of the human scale of their bodies in relation to their world.

Older students, armed with tape measures and yardsticks, conducted more systematic mapping activities. Student teams selected square-yard sections of the Natural Resource Area and plotted observations onto graph paper with half-inch squares. The result was a quarter-scale drawing of pebbles, sticks, grass, plants, small animals, and other signs of life—intermingled with the marks of human presence, such as soda can tabs, candy wrappers, plastic cups, and footprints with

Children strengthened their mapping skills by exploring subtle changes occurring in their surroundings (top). Many of their findings were then catalogued in journals known as "metric record books" (bottom).

detailed sole patterns. In contrast, maps of the asphalt were sparse, limited to the surface texture and an occasional crack with a plant sprouting from it.

Back in class, comparison of the two sets of maps focused attention on the differences in diversity and rate of change between dirt and asphalt. For instance, what would the sample areas look like in ten years? It was clear the asphalt would not change much unless it "cracked up a lot," as one boy said. The dirt area, on the other hand, was less predictable. "It'll look like a field," one student predicted, while another suggested that "it'll be a forest."

The square-yard "journeys to the surface of the Earth" allowed students to grasp the concept of scale and realize that they were making smaller-than-real-life records. The maps helped children understand the principle of coordinates. Everything, including moving animals, could be mapped and, if required, counted and charted.

Another mapping activity involved students in surveying the organisms living just below the surface of the ground. Students created digging tools by alternately burning and rubbing sticks on a rock to shape them into good, hard points. The tools were excellent for exposing underground life and demonstrated the transfer of appropriate technology using an abundant Yard resource.

Coding and classification were important scientific skills. Color codes were devised for ground-surface materials such as water, asphalt, sand, dirt, vegetation, concrete, woodchips, and sand. Classification focused on what items should be mapped, appropriate symbols to be used, and methods of representation on paper. Children learned to draw legends and north points. Up on the school roof, maps could be compared with the full-size space spread out below.

A terrific mapping game was developed to familiarize pairs of students with the Yard environment. One student put an X on a copy of the base map of the Yard and the other tried to lead the first child to the indicated spot. The physical conditions of the spot were then mapped.

I'M A SCAVENGER, TOO!

It was encouraging to see how quickly children deduced scientific principles from their own experience. Once understood, principles led to further spin-offs. After a scavenging project, one of the teachers reported a conversation with a student, Leona, as they walked back to class together:

"Suddenly Leona bent down and picked up a hazelnut from amongst the leaves by one of the picnic tables. She asked what it was and I told her it might have been dropped by someone from their lunch. Instead of thinking it was yucky and trash, she remained fascinated with her nut and wanted to know more about it.

"What did it taste like? I suggested that she eat it. Then, of course, we had to figure out how to open it. We stopped at the greenhouse where there were some rocks. Leona chose a suitable one, put the nut on one of the flat planks around the planting beds, and banged the nut gently to crack it without smashing the kernel—which she ate, savoring it with obvious enjoyment.

"Later, when the students shared their experiences, Leona told the class that she too was a scavenger!"

•

The photographs to the right demonstrate the process of finding, observing, sensing, understanding, probing, and sampling the environment. Simple tools were required: sticks, collecting jars, nets, and basters (to collect water samples).

NATURAL LEARNING

Children used behavior-mapping techniques to document where they played during recess (a simplified version of the behavior maps used by the adult researchers). This process allowed students to advance their skills in reading the base map of the Yard and understanding the pattern of human use. After all, they were the major users.

After plotting the lunchtime recess activity, the children counted the number of Xs in different locations and noticed an uneven distribution of use. This discovery led to a discussion of why some parts of the Yard were more attractive than others. Why did girls use the bars so much? Why did so many boys play ball on the asphalt? Why did some children like playing with specific pieces of equipment such as swings more than playing with natural elements such as water? How did characteristics like shade or soft ground affect the children's play?

The significance of microclimate came across strongly.

"The trees are best where we have lunch under the alders or in the bamboo," Sabine says. "It's good because it's warm but the sun doesn't get in your eyes. If you go where there's no trees, it's too hot and 'glary'—like the picnic tables. It's more pretty by the ponds . . . the plants are nice and cool on a hot day. We just sit there, talk, share interesting things, and have a good time. It's like our own little park."

Teachers learned as much from these exercises as did the students, especially about the meaning and value of different parts of the Yard.

To understand the Yard more clearly as an educational resource, teachers mapped the places they most frequently used for classroom work. Results showed that the Natural Resource Area was used much more heavily than other areas of the Yard, with the enclosed garden used most of all (see Chapter 18 for map). This result strongly supported our initial assumption about the value of natural resources as an educational medium.

LAND USE STUDIES

As an example of alternative land use, the Yard provided strong motivation for studying land use in the broader community.

Classes visited the city planning and parks and recreation departments to learn about the land use decision-making processes. They traveled to other city neighborhoods to study specific features. Special devices were used to measure the levels of smog, noise, and solid waste. They conducted traffic counts and compared different transit systems—automobile, bus, and regional rapid transit.

Neighborhood maps made by the students showed the locations of homes, routes to school, bus stops, highly congested streets, favorite hangouts, well-known landmarks, and the best places to play.

One class produced the *Children's Guide to the Flatlands*, with descriptions and a map of children's favorite places like corner stores, parks and playgrounds, the swimming pool, the public library, and hobby shops.

Some groups studied small-scale maps of the city or the whole East Bay, plotting field trip locations, principal features, and circulation systems. Some groups went even further, looking at maps of California, North America, and the world.

Other students conducted "city-building" exercises modeled on the program developed by Doreen Nelson, which engages children in constructing urban utopias using three-dimensional modeling techniques.[2] These activities helped children understand that choice and diversity were important aspects of land use planning—for example, by preserving agricultural land when developing cities.

TREASURE HUNTS

Hunting games (a natural extension of children's play) provided an effective curricular approach to developing observational skills—essential for conducting any type of scientific work. In a simple form of a treasure hunt, pairs of students went outside with labels to tag examples of "something soft," "something smooth," "a plant in the shade," "a nice smell," and so on.

The exercises sometimes consisted of an actual hunt, focusing on different senses, classification (the basic scientific process of establishing categories), or properties of objects. Each student had a paper bag and a list of "treasures" to gather in the shortest possible time.

As a creative, problem-solving extension of the technique, children created their own treasure maps.

First they checked their handheld compasses against the large permanent compass painted on the asphalt (verification of base data). Then they oriented the Yard base map correctly (orientation with respect to a baseline) and verified the orientation of various visible objects (skill application and practice). Returning to the classroom, they worked in pairs (cooperation), oriented the map again (more skill practice), designed a treasure hunt route (review of content to be explored), and devised clues (language skills). They went outside again to pace off the distances on the ground (math and spatial orientation skills) and finally wrote out the directions for the hunt (instructional language). For example:

"At the stack-sack wall, start by the little cubbyhole. Take 38 paces south to the ramp. Take 20 paces east, then 3 paces south. Step on the brick. Take 16 paces towards the apartments and 8 paces north. You should be by an oak tree. The clue is on its lowest branch."

Pedagogically, the "hunting" strategy encompassed a variety of scientific skills and related subject areas. A high level of retention was expressed nicely a few days after one of the treasure hunts. A group of boys asked for copies of the base map so they could "invent ways to trap girls." An hour later, the girls asked for maps to devise "escape routes"—a wonderful example of a child-initiated playful extension of the learning activity.

LESSONS IN LITTER

Another hunting activity focused on litter. Groups of students went to designated sections of the Yard and estimated the amount of litter there. They collected the trash, sorting and piling it into categories: aluminum, plastic, paper, food remnants, wood, and other metals. The number of pieces in each pile was counted and the total amount was weighed—the average daily total was seven pounds (3.2 kg)!

To understand that litter does not simply disappear, a class collected remnants from lunch—tin foil, plastic wrappers, plastic utensils, straws, milk cartons, paper napkins, and orange peels—and divided them into two piles. The children buried one pile in the ground and left the other on top. The majority predicted that the litter would go away or disintegrate; after two weeks, however, they discovered that it had not. Still, the students were convinced that the litter would disappear by the next observation. Their prediction was only partly true: except for the buried biodegradable items, the litter remained unchanged for many weeks. At that point, the children deduced that the nonbiodegradable items were not going to change in the near future.

Teachers initiated a discussion on the aesthetic impact of litter by asking students if they thought it was always ugly. Was litter in the Natural Resource Area— where it contrasted more with the surroundings—uglier than litter in the Main Yard? Were the children equally likely to drop litter in both areas? What was the aesthetic value of the litter when it was removed from the Yard? By creating and exhibiting works of art made from the litter, students began to see how the aesthetic value of an object reflects its context (natural area versus exhibition gallery) and how these values can be artistically transformed according to location.

Classes kept records of the daily litter collection, including the reasons why certain items were thrown away. Students compared lists and discussed the idea of people becoming scavengers. In one classroom session, they brainstormed ideas for reusing solid waste from the school:

"Use scrap paper for airplanes."
"Use milk cartons to catch fish."
"Decorate cans for pencil holders."
"Make bottles into vases."
"Dye old sheets for flags."
"Make new paper out of old."

The last suggestion was a popular activity. The children mashed up old newsprint and laid it out on a drying screen to make new, thick sheets of paper, sometimes layering in dried flowers and small leaves. The handmade paper was used for special messages or poems.

In "litter parades," students paraded through the Yard, line abreast, foraging for litter. These events worked well because they began with each child's individual task (collecting litter as a function of maintenance) and built up to schoolwide involvement in caring for the environment.

Once Upon a Yard...

The healthy development of children was the central focus of the Yard. Their participation offered wonderfully diverse ideas and a strong desire for nature. Groups worked with drawings and models to communicate their vision of the future.

before

after

We took a fragment of the Earth's surface, where nonhuman life was extinct, and through design demonstrated the power of nature to restore itself. This super-rich playing and learning environment brought nature back into the daily lives of city children.

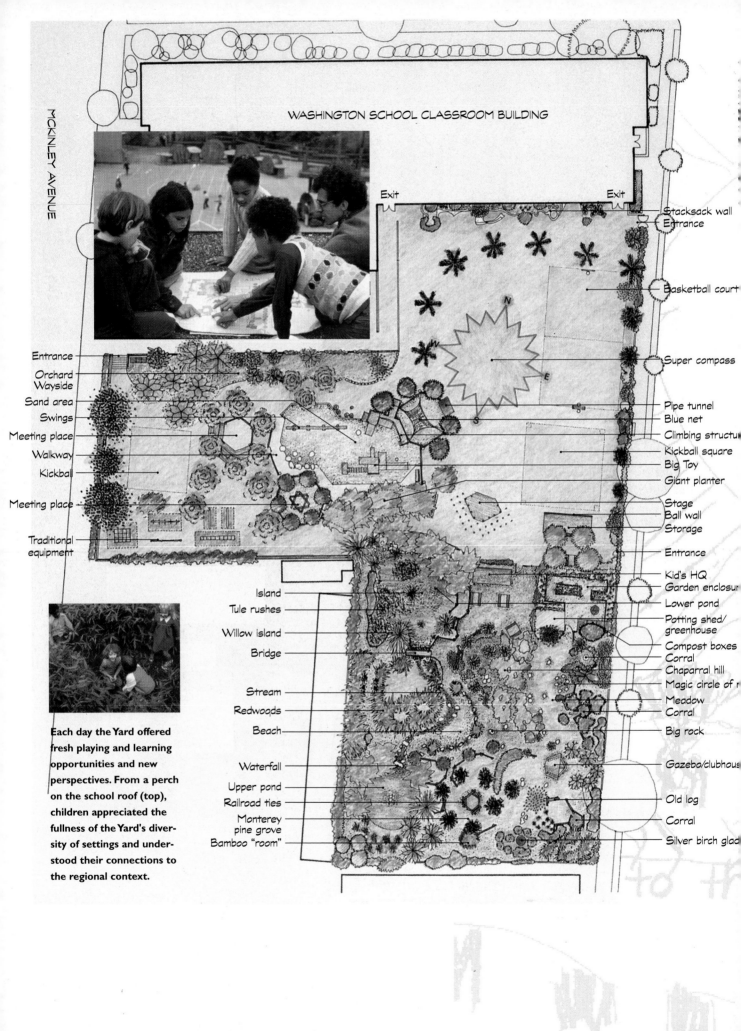

WASHINGTON SCHOOL CLASSROOM BUILDING

MCKINLEY AVENUE

Exit

Exit

Stacksack wall
Entrance

Basketball court

Super compass

Pipe tunnel
Blue net
Climbing structu
Kickball square
Big Toy
Giant planter

Stage
Ball wall
Storage

Entrance

Kid's HQ
Garden enclosur
Lower pond
Potting shed/
greenhouse
Compost boxes
Corral
Chaparral hill
Magic circle of r
Meadow
Corral

Big rock

Gazebo/clubhous

Old log

Corral

Silver birch glad

Entrance
Orchard
Wayside
Sand area
Swings
Meeting place
Walkway
Kickball

Meeting place

Traditional
equipment

Island
Tule rushes
Willow island
Bridge

Stream
Redwoods
Beach

Waterfall
Upper pond
Railroad ties
Monterey
pine grove
Bamboo "room"

Each day the Yard offered fresh playing and learning opportunities and new perspectives. From a perch on the school roof (top), children appreciated the fullness of the Yard's diversity of settings and understood their connections to the regional context.

Construction of the Yard was a community process with many groups working together to improve the quality of life in the neighborhood. College students were essential collaborators. Children measured, mused upon, classified, and wrote about the magical changes happening around them.

The aquatic life of the Yard was especially fascinating to the children, and was the most strongly remembered of all the natural settings. Here, the ecology of childhood and planet Earth were fused in an ethic of caring.

Play and curiosity were the motivating forces that inspired children to learn. Diversity and choice were the open arms that embraced their many learning styles and abilities. Sensory stimulation opened a natural gateway to success. Freedom of expression in mind and body offered students limitless aspirations.

The materials and processes of nature provided a uniquely interactive environment for hands-on learning. The complexity of natural spaces stimulated a greater range of activities. Change, a constant in nature, presented new experiences each moment: poetic revelations, mathematical challenges, scientific engagements, and bonds of friendship. We call it dynamic quality—experience that banishes boredom because it is never repeated.

The children recycled aluminum and glass at the community recycling center located two blocks away. Recycling efforts were described at home. Classroom discussion included a comparison of the personal costs of recycling (e.g., time) and the benefits of recycling to the community. The concept of renewable and nonrenewable resources was introduced; for instance, how would we manage if there were no more metals?

WEATHER STATION

The study of climate was used to link the Yard to the local region and other parts of the planet. The school roof was the uppermost layer of the atmosphere accessible to the students and offered a panoramic view of the entire Yard. It was the obvious location for a weather station. While on the roof, one felt lifted out of the immediate Yard environment into the broader climate of the region.

To the west, the orange towers and graceful cables of the Golden Gate Bridge marked the major "fog gap" that affected the weather of the East Bay. To the east, the nearly two-thousand-foot-high (610 m) East Bay Hills stretched north and south, marking the major climatic break between the narrow coastal zone and the interior valleys of the state. Wind off the Pacific Ocean was usually present on the roof, even if it was calm at ground level.

In an afterschool woodworking class, children constructed simple wind vanes. They taped the vanes to the end of vertical ventilation pipes on the roof. Soon, a line of weather vanes was visible from the ground. "What's going on up there?" passers-by asked, providing a good opportunity to explain the school's environmental education program.

A rain gauge was taped to a ventilation pipe. Classes took turns each month to record the daily readings during the wet season.

"I like the top of the school because there's a rain gauge up there," says one of the excited students. "Once I read it after a storm and it was more than an inch."

The exercise provided an excellent introduction to the study of water conservation.

For a more precise picture of the variations in microclimate—and the reasons behind them—the

WEATHER STATION

The school site (including the roof) served as a weather station. This gave students an opportunity to use measuring instruments (thermometers, rain gauges, anemometers, and hydrometers) to document daily weather changes. Wind vanes were made as an afterschool project and mounted on the roof (two lower photographs). As the seasons changed, students began to understand the difference between the variety of local weather and the predictable cycles of the regional climate.

children took measurements on the roof and on the ground, using handheld wind-velocity gauges and thermometers. The students measured the temperature in a sunny, sheltered area and in the windiest spot they could find. They reported readings of eighty and seventy degrees Fahrenheit (27 and 21°C), respectively, which led to a discussion of the wind-chill factor. To determine the differences between the regional climate and the Yard's particular microclimates, the children watched television weather forecasts at home and compared the official readings with their own observations at school.

Classes designed and displayed Yard weather charts. They studied weather terminology used on television and radio and reviewed literature and films about weather. One class produced an illustrated book entitled *Raindrop Storie*s:

"If I were a raindrop, I would make a puddle for everyone to step in."

Weather provided a marvelous vehicle for indoor-outdoor learning activities. Outdoors, children developed basic observational and data-collection skills using weather measurement instruments and their own senses. Back in the classrooms, they practiced graphing techniques and recorded their observations.

"After it rained we went out to the Yard and tried to find out what the rain did. It gave off a fresh smell. Plants were knocked over. Wet leaves were all over the place. Wood was darkened and soft. The pond was higher. It was real muddy! The plants liked it but I didn't."

As the Yard ecosystems developed, substantial and predictable learning opportunities arose for children to investigate the natural consequences of seasonal cycles—winter decay, the emergence of mushrooms, the discovery of salamanders under damp logs, the bloom of wildflowers, and animal lifecycles. Journals were the main medium for recording observations.

Each time the East Bay experienced winter storms and high winds, groups of children made reconnaissance trips to observe storm-related phenomena—rippling patterns on the pond surfaces, rhythmic movement of the trees, broken pieces of trees lying on the ground, litter blown up against the fences, and swirling piles of dried leaves. Classes discussed wind terminology like "blow,"

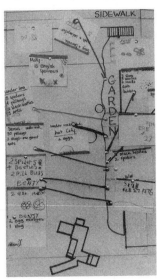

The classroom served as a laboratory where children brought back samples and records collected from their outdoor discoveries to examine and document their findings. Children prepared slides of pond water for further study under a microscope (top). The Schoolyard Ecosystem Project (middle left and right) was facilitated by university students. The project comprised a whole semester of scientific work exploring and mapping the natural systems of the Yard, including recording the weather (bottom).

"breeze, "gale," "gusty," "hurricane," "light," "tornado," and "velocity."

The famous Bay Area fog (caused by differences in pressure that force the meeting of cold Pacific air and hot inland air) and the variable pattern caused by local quirks of geography provided frequent topics of discussion.

"Who knows what 'visibility' means?" asks the teacher.

"When you can't see too good in the fog," a student answers.

"That's close," she says, "but visibility—the distance you can see—can be good, fair, poor, or bad, not only because of fog but from any kind of precipitation."

One student reminds the class about a field trip they had taken to the East Bay Hills, where the temperature increased as they climbed up out of the cold fog belt. This was an interesting phenomenon, because normally, as most of the class knew, the temperature drops with a rise in elevation.

Building on this line of discussion, the teacher asks, "Who thinks you can have snow in the middle of Africa?" The class gathers around the world map on the wall to look at snow-capped Mount Kilimanjaro. They begin discussing the different climates in the world and the impacts of climate on people's lives. Only one student, whose family came from Chile, knows that in the southern hemisphere, the Christmas season takes place during the summer.

•

With motivation to move outdoors, children benefited from an enriched, hands-on learning environment unavailable indoors. The expanded range of indoor-outdoor learning settings accommodated a wider range of learning styles. To demonstrate unequivocally the long-term educational benefits of the expanded learning environment, more longitudinal research would have been required. Although we did not have the financial resources necessary to conduct a costly quantitative analysis, the qualitative data gathered over the years provide convincing support for affective learning processes, especially in the study of science.

REFERENCES

1. Schubert, W. H. (1986). *Curriculum: Perspectives, Paradigm, and Possibility*. New York: MacMillan, 123.

2. Nelson, D. (1975). *City Building Education Program*. Santa Monica, Calif.: Center for City Building Education Programs.

CHAPTER 13

Whole-Life Learning

The Yard offered an open door to the community to contribute special educational resources and programs. One year, university students organized an unforgettable barnyard with 4-H Club animals. Another year, a community artist worked with students to build a bulrush canoe as a part of a social studies unit on Native American culture.

Culture. History. Health. Mortality. How can the broader themes of human society and our place on the planet be tackled experientially in primary education? We found that the resources of the Yard opened up many possibilities for broadening the scope of learning more easily than in most schools, where teachers who want to apply an experiential approach lack the necessary environmental diversity to support a wide range of hands-on experiences. If such resources are available, as in the Yard and related neighborhood and community sites, broader issues can be raised that will be understood by children because they are local and touch their own lives.

Several years passed before we fully grasped why the Yard worked well as a vehicle for providing this broader scope. Its stimulating diversity of materials and living organisms had two effects: it motivated children to learn and it attracted professionals from the extended school community who were interested in developing their own programs and events. For these outside professionals, the Yard provided an inviting and unusual setting that could accommodate a wide range of activities. Some worked extensively as outdoor teachers with support from a variety of state and national programs. Stationed in the Yard, they were able also to pick up on happenstance learning opportunities more readily than the classroom teachers. Through their involvement, community professionals were able to provide an educational program that ranged beyond the scope presented in earlier chapters.

ANCIENT ECHOES

One year, a member of the Karok-Yurok tribe visited the Yard and introduced the children to the Native American natural-resource philosophy. Her plan was to introduce the students to the possible uses of the Yard's natural objects and materials. The students made rope woven from cattails, mats from pine needles, headbands and bracelets from reeds, and baskets from thin willow sticks stripped of their bark and soaked in water.

"Indians used trees for transportation," a child writes later. "They made all sorts of canoes. They used bamboo sticks for fishing poles and peace pipes. And they made tepees to live in."

Building upon the introductory lesson on Native American culture, the community artist who had invited the Karok-Yurok teacher worked with the students on more substantial projects. For example, they designed and built a tepee decorated with multicolored hiero-glyphic designs.

Using the tule reeds (*Scirpus acutus*) surrounding the pond, the children fashioned a magnificent raft, similar to the ones used by the Ohlone tribes that once lived around the San Francisco Bay. Students examined longitudinal sections of tule rush to study its fine cellular structure, which provided the plant's strength and buoyancy. The raft was an excellent example of the practical use of plants—a concept readily understood by the children, who frequently used plants in the Yard as play material (in much the same way as artisans still do in nonindustrial cultures).[1]

Stimulated by their new-found knowledge, the students explored further possibilities during recess.

Kelli ties a long tule reed around the horizontal branch of an alder tree.

"I'm making a chair swing. I wonder if it'll be strong enough." She pulls on it and it breaks. "Oh well, it wasn't ready yet. It was too young."

She starts cutting the end of the reed with the sharp edge of another reed. "Hey, I found a new knife," she exclaims.

She returns to the pond and gets another darker, older reed. "You need to peel it back, see, and get the soft stuff out. It ties better then." She takes out some of the pulp, bends the reed over, and ties it with a piece of grass.

"I never know what I am making," she admits. "I think I'm going to take this home and let it dry." She takes some grass and ties two twigs together into a cross. She holds it up and it falls apart. She picks up the first thing she made, which collapses as well.

"Oh well, everything seems to be falling apart today," she says, "never mind." One can imagine Kelli returning the following day to try further experiments. She will continue to stretch her imagination, while honing her problem-solving skills and refining her manual dexterity.

"We're getting a whole lot of pine needles to try to weave them into a rug for our house," says one ambitious girl. The imagined product lies far beyond any possibility of actual achievement. But in the realm of children's play, "failure" does not exist, as fleeting interim steps of success are accomplished to reinforce a sense of ambition. Adults who understand this process can help it along.

One day a couple of children were trying to break off a piece of anise, but did not succeed (it was very fibrous and impossible to sever by hand). Because no clippers or other cutting tools were available, the teacher asked them to consider using other items—a sharp stone perhaps? They found one and the teacher showed them how to hold the stem taut and saw in one direction. The group continued on their own; some found new stone knives, others borrowed stones that had already been used. The teacher said she felt like a "prehistoric person," but this comment did not impress the children. For them, this "prehistoric" knife was a normal childhood artifact. A fancy, manufactured knife in the context of Native American studies would have been more worthy of comment.

NATURE'S MEDICINE CHEST

The children were fascinated by the fact that many wild plants were edible or could be used for medicinal purposes.[2] Introducing the topic required specialized knowledge that few classroom teachers possessed. We therefore relied on a number of community teachers who worked in the Yard over the years. We did our best to keep an updated list of the Yard plants used in these sessions, including anise, alder, blackberry, California bay laurel, cattail root (which could be eaten like a salad), ceanothus, clover, dandelion, dock, eucalyptus, filaree, mallow, manzanita, miner's lettuce, mint, mustard, plantain, wild currant, willow, and more.[3] Interested children experimented with making meal from acorns and buckeye seeds, Native American–style with mortar and pestle. They tended herb gardens, and made up and tested recipes for herbal salves, teas, and skin tonic.

One day, a neighborhood visitor who had originated from Hawaii commented that the yellow fruits of the passion vine (*Passiflora alatocaerulea*, growing on the MLK Way fence) were edible. He broke one open to show the seeds, coated with a tasty orange gelatinous substance. He said it was used for flavoring island drinks and left with a handful of fruit to try out at home!

GROUND-LEVEL LEARNING

Unlike asphalt, the ground was responsive to the children's touch—for example, simply walking on the

The folk arts tradition became a daily part of the children's lives. Students worked with teachers to make aromatic vinegars using herbs collected in the Yard (top) and explored the edible and medicinal properties of plants such as blackberries (middle and bottom). This favorite snack grew through the chainlink fence from an adjacent backyard.

dirt or grass left footprints. This basic yet profound difference signaled to the children that they could leave their mark on the environment. One of the most poignant examples involved an Israeli boy who had just started at Washington and only had a limited command of English. When two playmates asked him his name, he scratched "I-R-M-O" in the dirt, spelled right to left as if he were writing Hebrew.

What lay underneath the ground prompted great curiosity among the children. They would dig into the soil with whatever tool they could find to facilitate their geological explorations.

Around the ponds, a group of children make small excavations, looking for rocks. They wash them off and try to identify them. Kana has a tiny "black rock" less than a tenth of an inch (0.25 cm) in diameter. She says she likes to look for "interesting rocks" and play with pebbles and dirt.

"We found a fossil once," she explains. "It was like a rock but had a shell on it. Me and my friend share it, 'cause we both saw it at the same time" (a nice illustration of cooperation through play).

Every spring, after the winter rains had ceased, children started "mining" in undisturbed areas of the central sand area where the compacted sand caked together to form a surface of soft "sandstone," as if in an initial geological stage of rock formation.

A group of children carefully push loose sand from above each section of "rock." They make narrow "cuts" around each piece by scraping it with a stick until it can be broken free. The pieces of "mined" rock are then shaped and punctured with pieces of sharp stick or the house keys hanging around the children's necks (a useful tool). Small, abstractly shaped objects and masklike faces or figurines are produced, representing animal and human forms. The activity demands great care, fine muscle coordination, and aesthetic sensibility.

A young sculptor refers to the activity as "making Indian stuff" and contributes a "dog" and a "heart" to the informal exhibition organized by the group during the lunchtime recess.

Exploration of the ground surface was exploited educationally when Josh Barkin, an East Bay Parks naturalist, led children on a "hundred-inch hike" across "prehistoric lakes" (asphalt) and through gallons of "milk" (grass). Children "hiked" on their bellies, with their faces at ground level, pulling themselves through microworlds between blades of grass—a trip that never failed to capture their full attention.

BARNYARD

After visiting several children's farms in Europe, we knew it was possible to introduce larger domesticated animals into outdoor play and learning environments. Prompted by one student who brought his pet goat to school, we set up a temporary barnyard in cooperation with the local 4-H Club. The site selected was the former storage compound. The previous year, it had been used as an adventure playground, so scrap lumber was readily available for constructing shelters for the animals.

Two huge packing crates, donated by a local moving company, were converted into sleeping quarters in one corner of the compound. A metal worker who lived in the neighborhood helped fashion pieces of chainlink fencing into a secure, gated enclosure around and above the animals' new home. Although the design was not elegant by conventional standards, it had the beauty of economy—a minimal design response to a short-term need.

Old nails were picked up so that animals would not swallow them. A recycled, enameled sink was set in the ground and filled with water for the pigs to wallow in. The sides of the compound were lined with sheets of plywood to provide a sense of enclosure and protection. A fresh carpet of straw was spread over the hard, bumpy ground, immediately giving the barnyard an inviting feeling and aroma.

On a Monday morning, a 4-H truck arrived with the animals: four pygmy goats, two pigs, a half-dozen hens, and a rooster. A guard of honor formed to guide the goats and pigs from the truck to the pen. Students gingerly carried the birds in their arms. The children's response to the animals was incredibly powerful. In these first few moments, we realized it was a very special event.

Every recess, long lines of children waited to enter the barnyard, where they could pet the animals and feed the baby goats. There was no shortage of volunteers to assist with barnyard chores: mucking out sleeping quarters, feeding and watering the animals, laying down fresh straw, and mixing the old straw and manure in the compost box.

RABBIT CYCLE
First the carrot grows. A rabbit eats the carrot. The rabbit makes rabbit droppings. The droppings fertilize the soil to make the garden grow. Rabbits are good to eat, there's no fat. And then it starts all over again.

— Sidney

Rabbits offered an incredibly rich source for learning. Children observed rabbits mating (top), learned to care for them outdoors (middle left), practiced drawing them (middle right), and solved rabbit arithmetic problems (bottom).

The students were highly motivated towards these tasks, including several so-called "problem children" who usually showed little interest in schoolwork and presented a constant challenge to their teachers. These children responded dramatically to the practical, hands-on barnyard work. Some children had cats and dogs at home, but the barnyard was different. It offered a shared experience of participation with classmates and an opportunity to help dependent living things. A strong sense of solidarity developed among the students who spent every spare moment working together in the barnyard with the crew of volunteer university students.

Children spent hours observing the animals, writing stories about them, measuring them, researching their history, and considering the roles of domesticated animals in society—as pets and as animals farmed for food. The classroom connections were boundless. Wilbur the pig and Charlotte the spider of *Charlotte's Web* actually lived in the Yard! It was an added incentive to read the book and create animal stories.

Memories of the barnyard persisted long after the sad day at the end of the term when the animals returned to the 4-H Club. Years later, when we interviewed former Washington students (then in their early teens), most mentioned the animals as one of their strongest memories of the Yard.

The barnyard clearly indicated the feasibility and importance of farmyard animals as a learning resource. Although we did not succeed in repeating such an ambitious animal program, the original barnyard inspired many other "animal events" over the years.

RABBIT CYCLES

Tom Javits, a university student working in the Yard, was at the time experimenting with rabbits as a viable meat source that could be raised domestically in the city. He brought some of his rabbits to school and constructed a portable hutch for them in a classroom. The rabbits were frequently brought out to the Yard, where they were let out on the grass and observed in a natural setting.

The children cultivated a patch of alfalfa (a rabbit staple) to feed them. Everyday they removed the rabbit droppings and added them to the compost box, another of Tom's projects.

For a period of time, the children recorded how much of each type of food and liquid was ingested by the rabbits. They also calculated how much was absorbed in increased weight and how much came out as waste. This sequence of measurement and recording, plus other rabbit activities, became known as "rabbit arithmetic," a highly motivational form of environmental math.

One afternoon, following a discussion on how mammals "make babies," everyone gathered around the hutch to watch two rabbits mate. The litter was born six weeks later, an unforgettable experience for the students.

Because Tom wanted to pass on basic information about raising rabbits for food, he could not avoid the topic of butchering. After notification of parents, the children went out to the Yard and gathered around one of the rabbits. Tom gently stroked the rabbit to calm it down and then, with a quick jerk, dislocated its neck.

Tom hung the limp body by the rear legs and cut the jugular vein to drain the blood. As he peeled off the skin, some children turned away, but most stood their ground, curiosity overpowering fear. The skin was later cured and exhibited in class. Meanwhile, the rabbit carcass was butchered, marinated, and barbecued at a school-community festival and cook-out held two days later.

The class discussed the ethics of killing and eating animals. A couple of children from vegetarian families shared their points of view. Teachers gave examples of people who never eat meat, such as Hindus. The nutritional advantages of rabbit meat, which had little fat, were discussed.

"I feel sorry for the rabbits," Jill wrote, "but boy, they're good to eat!"

During the final days of the school year, the complete cycle of rabbit events was depicted in a mural added to the concrete retaining wall below the Orchard Wayside. Painted by the children with the help of a student teacher, the mural displayed Tom's composting project, a field trip to the UC Berkeley Oxford Tract experimental garden to see another rabbit project, mating and babies, and, of course, the slaughter and cook-out.

BEEP-BEEP THE DUCK

Beep-Beep the duck was acquired by the school when it was three weeks old. Interestingly, Beep-Beep was not too fond of water. We never knew exactly why—perhaps he had been born in a waterless, mass-production battery house and had not been introduced to water early enough in life. The children would push him into the pond from time to time, but he would always quickly swim back to shore where he would happily waddle around in the grass.

"Why doesn't Beep-Beep sink?" is a question prompted by the duck's swimming lessons on the pond. It leads to a discussion about the duck's oil gland. The students learn that a duck uses its bill when preening to spread oil over its feathers. To fully understand this point, the children coat the center of a dark-colored sheet of construction paper with vegetable oil. They then use a spray bottle to lightly layer the sheet with water. The children notice how the water collects in droplets, runs off the oily portion, and is quickly absorbed by the rest of the paper.

"If birds are so oily, why do they get into difficulty with oil spilled on the ocean surface?" asks the teacher. It does not take long for the children to note the vast difference between the fine lightweight oil produced by the birds and the sticky black gunk that can engulf the seashore.

Beep-Beep adored snails and could gobble up dozens of them at one sitting. There was certainly no shortage of snails in the Yard; in the vegetable garden, they were considered pests. As a result, the duck became the Yard's chief snail and slug catcher. He also loved the duckweed that grew profusely on the lower pond—it became the main reward for his swimming lessons.

Although Beep-Beep stayed in a mobile cage overnight, he spent most of the day outside with small groups of children. The students were encouraged to make detailed observations of his behavior and to follow up these studies with research in the library.

Every time the students talked to Beep-Beep in "duck language" he stopped beeping and seemed to listen; when the children stopped, he began beeping incessantly in reply. It was quite easy to carry on this form of conversation, which constantly intrigued the students.

A Beep-Beep mailbox was set up in the school office. Here, children could mail questions, comments, and observations, which were subsequently displayed on the "Beep-Beep Board" in the main corridor:

serrivos Duck

Caring for Beep-Beep (middle) was a major source of enjoyment for students. The animal's extraordinary impact on the learning and emotional process is illustrated by the student's drawing of Beep-Beep (top) as a "serious duck"! This level of interaction was often extended throughout the Yard, as shown by a young boy welcoming a hen to the barnyard (bottom).

Events such as the cat burial were incorporated into the curriculum in unique ways, encouraging students' emotional growth and understanding of life's biological processes. The Yard supported this type of awareness by providing an environment where the affective dimensions of learning could be supported.

Ducks can fly between 50 and 70 miles per hour. In winter they fly south, as it is too cold in Canada and Alaska and the ponds and lakes are frozen over. If Beep-Beep flew 2,000 miles down the Pacific Flyway from Canada to California at 50 miles per hour, how long would the journey take?

As a finale to the duck's stay at the school, a Beep-Beep portrait competition was held. The results were displayed on the Beep-Beep Board, representing the most imaginative, realistic, fun, beautiful, colorful, and detailed pictures of the Yard's beloved duck. At the end of the school year, Beep-Beep went to live in the country with the grandparents of one of the students.

BURIAL GROUND

Because the Yard was a living environment, death was a common occurrence. It provided many opportunities for the children to get close to a part of the lifecycle that so often remains hidden in urban cultures.

If a dead animal was found in the Yard, it did not have to be dumped in the nearest trash can. In fact, a tradition of funerals was started by a teacher who dealt with the death of a classroom animal by allowing the students to hold a burial in the Yard. Before long, children were conducting their own animal funerals.

A group of five girls buries a dead mosquito fish in a grave by the pond. They fashion a cross by binding together two sticks. They decorate the grave with flowers, dandelions, a pine cone, redwood leaves, pine needles, woodchips, and a circle of small stones.

One day, a teacher found a dead cat among the bushes on Chaparral Hill. *Rigor mortis* had set in. There was no blood, so it was not clear how the cat had died. The teacher brought together a group of children to discuss what might have happened. The teacher later reported:

"I discussed the fact that animals seek private places to die. The children agreed that the spot among the chaparral felt private. I asked if humans were different? They agreed that most humans liked company when they were dying. All four had known people who had died. We discussed the notion of 'natural causes' and figured it might have been the reason for the cat's demise.

"While I dug a hole, the children picked a bunch of flowers. We discussed the importance of not handling dead animals because of disease. I placed the cat in the grave and the children took turns to shovel in dirt. Before this, we had discussed what we might say as a funeral prayer. One boy said he wished he had his Jewish prayer book. We discussed the meaning of 'R.I.P.' As each placed a flower on the grave, they said something and passed the flowers to the next child.

"'I'm sorry.' 'I wish you were still alive.' 'Good-bye, Kitty.' 'I'm going to beat up whoever killed you, if I'm bigger than they are.' 'Rest in peace.' 'I wish you weren't dead.' I heard one of them say as they left, 'It was a real grown-up funeral!'"

DAYS OUT

To test the viability of the Yard as a teaching resource, the school administration decided that for one day the teachers had to imagine that the school building had been damaged in an earthquake and was no longer usable. Without prior notice, the teachers had to plan how to conduct their regular lesson plans outside, using whatever materials were at hand. More than any other event, this exercise brought home the value of the Yard as a rich and challenging educational environment. Before redevelopment, this idea would have been completely impractical because there simply would not have been enough to work with. Now it was full of the possibilities described in this book.

A cook-out was the highlight of "earthquake" day. Each student contributed to it in some way—constructing the fireplace, gathering the fuel, making the fire, preparing for cooking the meal. The children had organized committees to plan the menu, check prices at the store, estimate the quantities required, compare projected costs against the budget, purchase the food or harvest it from the garden, and plan the cooking schedule.

These activities provided yet another educational opportunity: "How many hot dogs do we need if everyone gets one, two, or three? If there are ten hot dogs per pack, how many packs need to be bought?"

Apart from the "earthquake" exercise, it became the tradition in several classes to spend additional school days in the Yard. For some, it was a special event at the middle or end of the term. One class chose April Fool's Day for its day out.

A fire pit by the picnic tables was re-excavated each time. Children enjoyed digging out the pit and old ashes from previous cook-outs, and lined the spot with small rocks before laying the fire. There was never a shortage of Yard firewood.

Depending on the time of year, food for the cook-out was harvested from the garden, thereby conserving precious classroom funds. The Yard provided a remark-

Cooking out on "earthquake day" was a great deal of fun. Teachers were challenged to develop a host of creative curricular ideas using the Yard as a resource for a full day of educational activity.

able level of educational self-sufficiency considering the large number of people using the site.

For each day out, anyone connected to the class was invited to the feast: children, parents, grandparents, student teachers, and all the people who had volunteered during the school year. Cook-outs were not an end in themselves, but rather an opportunity for children to relate to each other in ways that were not possible in regular classroom settings. They were especially social experiences, invariably facilitated by someone with a guitar or banjo to lead a sing-along.

"It felt like camp," a student reported. "There's nothing that could have made it better."

THE EXTENDED CLASSROOM

The Yard provided an enormous range of possibilities for extending learning activities, far more than could be accommodated within classroom walls, which did not suit all learning styles equally well. Some of the most striking examples were the "classroom misfits" who exasperated teachers and peers alike with their inability to work quietly at their desks. Their active, more boisterous learning styles were better suited to more hands-on activity outdoors, where their willingness to cooperate increased dramatically. In the Yard, where they could freely manipulate the environment and define their own tasks, some of these "problem children" became effective leaders.

Teachers discussed the differences between the children's behavior and learning styles exhibited outdoors with those exhibited indoors. They reviewed the characteristics of the Yard, such as its openness, diversity, manipulability, and sensory range, that seemed to influence children's behavior most strongly and then tried to integrate them into their classroom activities.

Year after year, the connection between the children's informal use of the Yard and the classroom grew stronger. One teacher reported how she tried to spend as much time as possible at recess—not to supervise the children but to observe and learn from them. "The thing that struck me most strongly," she said, "was how many misconceptions and fragments of knowledge the children have that are waiting to be expanded and connected through follow-up classroom work."

Teachers commented that the children's reactions to the Yard were useful to them in their attempts to influence the students' perceptions and values through classroom activity. Carryover in the other direction also occurred, where classroom learning was exhibited in children's play and games.

A group of girls perform a dance in the meadow. "We are copying a Japanese lady who came to teach us," they explain.

Several children create a "garden" on Chaparral Hill—reliving, reviewing, and reinforcing their learning, transforming it, using whatever is at hand. They are part of a classroom group that works in the enclosed garden. "We're cleaning the dirt out from between the rocks. We call it 'soil' but really it's dirt. Soil is lighter and darker. You can make soil by mixing in sand and compost," they say. "We found some potato bugs that we're putting in and we're going to plant some stuff and add a scarecrow. We've been working on it for a week."

•

With a sufficient diversity of resources, there is no limit to children's learning when working with imaginative educators in a natural school environment. Deep themes can be addressed, such as domestic animal husbandry, the rituals of life and death, indigenous relationships with nature, the medicinal uses of plants, self-sufficient lifestyles, and so on. A far broader scope of experience and cultural development can be addressed in a hands-on style that is impossible on a regular, abiotic school site.

REFERENCES

1. Lewington, A. (1990). *Plants for People*. London: Natural History Museum.

2. Bremness, L. (1994). *Herbs: A Visual Guide to More Than 700 Herb Species from Around the World*. Eyewitness Handbooks. London: Dorling Kindersley.

3. Clarke, C. (1977). *Edible and Useful Plants of California*. Berkeley, Calif.: University of California Press.

CHAPTER 14

Animation!

Animation extends the spirit of free play into a specified cultural frame of reference. It is a culture-building process in which animators work *alongside* children, to suggest ideas, introduce resources, provide tools, ensure safety, and defuse social conflicts.

Animation can happen in any community setting or institution.

Animators guide cooperative decision-making, help children participate in the design of their physical surroundings, and assume play to be one of the raw materials of education—helping children to express, apply, and assimilate experience in personal and community life. They contribute special expertise that activates movement, vigor, and creative action while encouraging full and equal participation from all involved.

"Animation" suggests breath, soul, movement. Appropriately, it is the name of a nonformal method of working with children that brings out the vitality and motivation inherent in group activity, whether involving a small number of children or an entire community. The practitioners of animation, known as "animators," work alongside children suggesting ideas, introducing resources, providing tools, ensuring safety, defusing social conflicts, guiding group decision-making, and engaging participants to the fullest extent possible with each other and their physical surroundings. Other terms for this role include "playleader," "playworker," and "social pedagogue." This adult teaching-learning-playing role is common in a number of European, African, Asian, and Latin American countries. In developing regions, animation methods have been applied extensively in fields such as health education and community development, especially in rural areas where the formal education systems are still tradition-bound.

The primary goals behind animation are to broaden the range of learning opportunities for children with different learning styles and abilities, and to address topics that are difficult to cover in formal education. The effectiveness of animation rests on the power of participation that is not limited by age, income, gender, or ability. Animation is based on the assumption that each individual contributes to the learning environment—it de-emphasizes authoritarian roles in favor of more egalitarian approaches. Animators recognize the physical setting as a learning resource and work with all appropriate social and cultural characteristics within the locale.

The animator, believing that children hold the keys to their own learning, works as a curriculum organizer and playleader to facilitate a collective effort. The casual visitor should immediately sense an unusual level of engagement between people and place and the cementing of a common cultural bond. Animation is thus a culture-building process—not in the elite sense, but as something localized, something different in the neighborhood, something special on the block.

We want now to present further applications to show how learning processes in the extensive spaces of the Yard compared to the usual classroom instructional methods. Classrooms, of course, functioned as the primary educational base. From there, however, the learning process extended outdoors during school hours, as well as before and after school, on weekends, during summer breaks, and even overnight. Typically, these animated educational events and programs were led by nonclassroom animation staff who came to the Yard through a variety of channels.

In the Yard, people and place interacted constantly. Sometimes animated events were guided by the Yard philosophy, but to an equal extent the Yard philosophy was drawn forward, developed, and clarified by new ideas proposed by animators and participants. Most Yard animators contributed their special expertise for a limited period of time to a particular project, program, or event. They came from all walks of life, backgrounds, and ages. Some volunteered, while others were part of the extended teaching staff.

A retired college teacher, for example, brought his menagerie of snakes, rabbits, ducks, lizards, hamsters, and a wild cat to the Yard to share with the children. As several students had never handled a snake or lizard before, it was a significant event—an opportunity to overcome phobias and to learn to appreciate these fascinating creatures. This type of experience always required a knowledgeable adult.

Mimi Anderson, an intern from Evergreen State College in Washington, worked in the Yard for six months and "really helped us build the garden," one of the children explained.

"She helped teach the kids what nature was really like and what things to eat to stay healthy. We made news about the garden. She usually bought the seed, but we did the planting. We made maps of where to grow different things. It was different from regular school working with her, 'cause we did it outside and could work with her after school, too. And we could take stuff home. It was fun!"

When cotton was being grown in the garden, a mother brought a spinning wheel and colored yarns to school. She passed sheep's wool around for children to smell and feel, showed them how to card it, and then spun it as they looked on. The following week a child brought some raw cotton she had picked on her grandfather's farm in the Central Valley. This was carded and spun on a special spinning wheel from India. The cotton and wool threads were then compared to linen thread, which the children used to make yarn pictures.

Two volunteer university students, Ellen Skotheim and Ruth Kreshka, ran the barnyard. They had flexible schedules and extra time to work with children, who were so engrossed with caring for animals and inspired by the leaders that they happily stayed after school. For working parents, the barnyard was an alternative form of childcare, with their children productively engaged outside in the fresh air, instead of being cooped up in the school basement. When parents arrived to pick up their children, they often joined in for a few moments, joking about the pigs and petting the rabbits.

MANNEQUIN MAPS

There were many ways of defining animation—as events, settings, themes, and artifacts. Examples of the latter were the life-size dolls constructed by the children as a way of mapping their own bodies. Students lay on the floor as partners drew around them on large sheets of brown paper. Two outlines were cut out, stapled together, and stuffed with newsprint to produce puffy, full-size mannequins. By creating alter egos, students were able to observe and talk about each other with a new perspective. They could measure their own body parts and compare the size of one part with another. What better way to learn that a map is "something that represents something else," as one student explained.

The mannequin activity began indoors. The students sat the mannequins down at the tables and moved them to various locations in the room. They discussed how different furniture configurations affected the way they worked together. They observed the effect that doors, windows, sunlight, artificial lights, desks, shelves, and chalkboards could have on social interaction among themselves and with the teacher. It was interesting to see how the mannequins helped the students understand the relationship with space more clearly. With the teacher acting as "design facilitator," the students moved the furniture around to see if they could find a more satisfactory arrangement. They adjusted the Venetian blinds

Animation enriches children's lives by providing experiences that expand the basic curriculum and allow room for the affective domain of child development. They include handling a snake (top), exploring dramatic themes outdoors with mannequins (middle), and using real tools to build a clubhouse (bottom).

and discovered that by reducing the glare, they could see each other more clearly.

In a follow-up activity, the children took the mannequins outside to different locations in the Yard, so they could compare indoor and outdoor learning spaces. Children saw surrogates of themselves sitting among the redwoods, playing in the sand, running through the meadow, hiding on Chaparral Hill, sliding on the play structure, and climbing the monkey bars. Such poses helped children see themselves as part of their environment and provided a crucial step in understanding the many differences in size, scale, and character relative to inside and outside environments.

AFTERSCHOOL ACTIVITIES

Washington's first permanent afterschool program began in 1975. It was led by Penny Tees, a city recreation leader hired as a result of a joint agreement between the city and the school district—a major breakthrough.

Each afternoon, Penny explored the possibilities of the Yard with an enthusiastic group of children: investigating sunlight, playing New Games, organizing sandcastle competitions, building clubhouses out of natural materials, working in the garden, making dolls with found objects, producing puppet shows. Then there were costume parades, kite-flying competitions, storytime in the redwoods, cook-outs, boat sailings, and water fights. Every idea suggested a dozen more as the program matured along with the Yard environment—until Penny's position was cut by the 1979 tax initiative, Proposition 13.

Overnight, the children lost their afterschool program and were abandoned to their own inventiveness and the attractions of the streets. A year passed. Then Francesca Borgatta arrived (with support from the California Arts Council) to serve as artist-in-residence. She set up shop in "Kids HQ" (a storage area and administrative office built at the juncture of the Main Yard and the Natural Resource Area) and organized a group of parents to run a weekly puppetry workshop after school. Children mostly worked on the fifteen-inch-high (38 cm) stage, which not only provided an excellent work area, but also a place to perform the children's productions. One week, papier-mâché dragon masks were made for the annual Chinese New Year parade; another week a strange orchestra performed with instruments assembled from recycled objects; another week a shadow theater was concocted by stretching cloth over the mouth of the Mokelumne aqueduct tunnel, backlit by the low afternoon sun.

"We made Indonesian puppets out of cardboard for the shadow plays," says Dana. "You can tape sticks onto part of the puppet and move the hands and feet. They were really pretty. I did a play with my friends called 'The Bad Rabbit.' One of the characters in it was my friend's little sister, and she was the Bad Rabbit."

"I was left more or less by myself to get on with it," Francesca explained. "The children learned enough to work by themselves on more sustained projects. We did not bother with establishing 'themes,' but just took what we had and went from there. 'Oh, that looks good, how about this, you do it, try that,' just encouraging them to explore with what they already knew. It was a different method; harder, but the results were more permanent and came much more from them than from me. I tried to support them, give them confidence and a belief that they could produce something worthwhile." Francesca gave a very clear description of the light-handed facilitation role.

Animators often used the Yard as a performance space, as a setting or props for dramatic action. Performances temporarily modified the Yard, but their main purpose was for the animator to use dramatic form and content to help build a group performance around a dramatized theme, issue, or situation.

When Francesca arrived, the full potential of the Yard as a community performance space began to be realized. She swept in with a magnificent agenda of multicultural performances using low-cost or free recycled materials. There were parades; puppet shows; a "Halloween funhouse"; a Japanese fan dance; a Mayday festival with maypole dances and medieval games; parent-child dance sessions; a *Cinco de Mayo* celebration; workshops in Native American basketry; Chinese calligraphy; African instrument making; doll making; and Indonesian batik, music, and shadow puppetry.

Part of the program was held after school and many of the events were repeated at the Yardfest or were

Through animation, children celebrated Chinese New Year with a parade (top), performed circus acts (middle), and baked pots from clay extracted from the Yard (bottom).

specially produced performances at the Yardfest, which in effect became an annual school and community arts festival (see next chapter).

"We made a parade for Chinese New Year," a child says. "We got big cardboard boxes for the heads, covered them with papier-mâché, colored paper, and paint, and had a long piece of cloth for the tail. We made musical instruments, too. I made a sandpaper block. Other kids made thumb pianos, banjos, drums, and basses. Francesca banged a huge drum as we paraded all around the Yard."

The way the child emphasized "all" gave a sense of the varied configuration of meandering routes that could be taken in between the structures, along the edges of the Main Yard, and around the serpentine "green streets" of the Natural Resource Area. The vegetation on either side provided a more serene and captivating experience—in contrast to the harsher, though still worthwhile, parade-ground feeling of the Main Yard.

Parades celebrating Chinese New Year, Halloween, and Christmas had been a Washington tradition for many years, and became even more substantial as the Yard developed. Like nothing else, the parades demonstrated the difference between moving through an intrinsically interesting space and a boring, uninviting one. Sometimes, the parades took to the neighborhood sidewalks or marched up the street to perform on the lawn in front of City Hall.

THE CAMERA'S EYE

Photography and video had obvious potential, because of animation's emphasis on communication. These activities did not require much production time, and besides, they were fun! Cameras helped children to see, encouraging them to be selective and to discriminate among choices. Cameras also introduced a common medium for recording experiences and provided a visual stimulus for developing verbal skills in narration and scripting.

The main problem with using photography and video in education was the high cost. Various low-cost options were tried over the years, including "instamatic" cameras used when money for film was available. A community volunteer taught the fundamentals of loading, shooting, developing, and printing. Photography was difficult to teach during class hours, but it made a terrific afterschool project. Prints were produced by laying negatives on light-sensitive blueprint paper used by architects and engineers. Polaroid cameras produced the most efficient and satisfying results.

From an educational point of view, inexpensive shoebox pinhole cameras constructed by the students were the most relevant recording devices. There was no shortage of still-life subjects in the Yard. "Blackline" paper (similar to blueprint paper, but positive instead of negative) was used in the cameras and developed easily outdoors in a shady corner. The students obtained some wonderful results and picked up the basic principles of photography.

The Yard also made a great movie set. Over the years, classes produced wonderful child-scripted versions of *Treasure Island, Pinocchio,* and the Indian epic forest drama *Ramayana.* A short skit grew into a movie called *Fire Act,* with a cast of five boys from a special-education class. Francesca explained the development of this project:

"It was very elemental. I was interested in things that could evoke an image of fire . . . things like fireballs and fire sticks. I had a pair of fire sticks that I gave the students to play with and was intrigued by the way they used them. So fire became a theme I wanted to pursue: a burning house, somebody's trapped, how do they escape, how do the firemen get to the house, how do they take care of the flames? A very simple scenario.

"We made the play structure into the burning house, with people trapped on the upper floor. The kids had to figure out how to take care of the flames and rescue the people. They just went wild; they couldn't believe they were going to make a movie. You should have seen the wonderful expressions on their faces as they drove the fire truck [Big Toy], leaning out as they raced around corners, shouting 'Whoa!', just like in 'real' movies. They all made fire helmets and tied long strips of red paper to the play structure to represent flames. It was very realistic. The students who were trapped were yelling, 'Help! Help!' and jumped off into the blue play net. The firemen with the hose—an old one we got from the city fire department—climbed up the ladder onto the structure to put out the fire. Such a simple idea, but with such dramatic scope."

Francesca vividly described the reactions of the emotionally disturbed students to the project.

"It was an escape from the classroom. Most of them counted the minutes they had to be stuck inside where everything was measured and quantified . . . how many pages completed, how many good or bad points scored. The classroom structure was so confining that out on the Yard the kids just exploded with energy, fell to pieces, went to hide, reveled in the freedom. Getting from this point of sheer emotional release to a point of grounding, working their fragmented images into a coherent whole was tough but ultimately rewarding. The Yard offered a therapeutic environment that allowed them to go through many more transformations. It seemed to provide a genuine healing situation for these students who had such severe mental afflictions.

"My work generated a dual reaction. Some people got furious. Others pulled me aside and said, 'Hey, I think what's going on with these students is terrific.' Special education is normally conducted so rigidly, I sometimes wonder if the 'behavior modification' methods they use are as successful as people claim. It requires such a conservative educational environment that even forward-looking teachers find it hard to break out.

"The special day class teacher was always afraid the students would go out of control—which they did for a while, of course—so he would only let me take three at a time. But when he saw the movie, it was as if he was looking at the potential of the Yard. He remarked that it looked like a huge forest in which his kids were capable of many things."

The 8 mm sound-on-film, live-action format was much easier to edit than video, which required expensive studio equipment. However, video also fulfilled other important functions, particularly where group interaction and prompt replay were essential. For example, Francesca made a "Family Portrait" video of the students and their backgrounds showing off special objects, prized costumes, and traditional songs and dances. The composite tape was later screened so all could appreciate each other's cultural heritage.

SUMMERTIME

The more adventurous, creative children used the Yard constantly, summer included. But many did not. For one thing, most parents felt that supervision was essential. What if someone got hurt? Who would watch out for undesirable characters? Besides, some children had a hard time entertaining themselves. Beyond a certain point, adult animation was required to activate antidotes to boredom, lethargy, and antisocial behavior.

The summer months represented a major opportunity to exploit the Yard. In 1973, a visiting architecture student from Sweden ran the first "Summer on the Yard" program with the help of parent volunteers. Innovative

Students play a gamelan in the redwood grove.

PROJECT PLAE
1982 Summer Program

Fame: Children produced their own television shows, as directors, scriptwriters, reporters, and "advertisers." The workshop culminated with a television special for family and friends written and produced by the children.

Adventure Village: Using natural and scrap materials, children constructed and decorated a child-size village according to their own ideas and group rules for government. A village newspaper and artifacts were produced, including pottery, aqueducts, flags, signal devices, and cooking utensils.

Forest Drama: Using stories, song and dance from *Ramayana,* a forest epic from southern India, children invented puppets, masks, and "creatures" to create their own forest drama. Video was used by children to record their productions.

Magical Masks: Children explored masks from around the world. They created masks out of paper, papier-mâché, and textiles and learned about hinge joints that allow mask parts to move.

Sound Waves: Children learned to play the gamelan, a group of Indonesian musical instruments. They wrote songs, constructed instruments, made puppet musicians, and used their own voices to create music.

Pageants in the Sky: Children constructed and played with banners, flags, kites, windsocks, sails, paper airplanes, parachutes, windmills, wind chimes, solar hot air balloons, and sky sculptures. Teamwork was emphasized.

Living on the Frontier: Children experienced the daily life of frontier Californians. Activities included growing vegetables, grinding grain, baking bread, making jams and jellies, drying fruits, making soaps and candles, dyeing, quilting, weaving, cooking outdoors, making ice cream, foraging for food, storytelling, building bird feeders, making cornhusk dolls, and creating jewelry and leather products.

Mission Possible: Children were challenged to push their

bodies and spirits to new limits. The outside environment was used as a gymnasium to develop balance and coordination, body awareness and conditioning, problem solving, and risk taking.

The Spider's Web: Children created sky-high weavings and other fantasy yarn creations using the Yard as the "loom." Weaving techniques such as plaiting, paper weaving, basketry, knotting, and interlacing were explored.

Whimsical Monuments: Children imagined, invented, and constructed monumental "nothings" from scrap materials. Teamwork was emphasized as they built sandcastles, walls, and variations on Cristo-style environmental sculptures.

From Pulp to Paper: Working directly with pulp, children made sheets of paper, multicolored "pulp paintings," cast paper reliefs, and experimental papers with embedded objects and embossing.

Play Fair: Using theatrical techniques in combination with game playing, children developed new ways of expressing themselves and building self-confidence.

Tail of the Dragon: Children combined creative body movement with theater arts to develop performance skills. The movement work included warm-up exercises, body part isolation, awareness activities, and moving in relation to another person. They learned group problem solving and cooperation through nonverbal communication. The activities covered basic techniques in pantomime, improvisation,

character development, and spontaneous dialogue.

Circus Circus: Circus arts were explored including clowning, tumbling, costumes, juggling, storytelling, make-up, and tightrope walking. Children created a circus atmosphere and gave a performance that was videotaped.

Creature Feature: Children invent a land where giant creatures roam, using sculpture, puppetry, and life-size dolls. They hold a monster mash bash at the end of the workshop.

children built and created their own environments using ideas introduced from Swedish playparks. It was a good beginning, followed by several years of city support for the program developed by Penny Tees.

With Penny's departure, we realized that something more flexible, less centralized, and more cost effective was needed in response to the radically changed fiscal circumstances of the 1980s. Quality recreation programs for children were no longer on the agendas of the city or the school district. And yet working parents urgently called for such programs.

PROJECT PLAE

The summertime Yard became a community-run setting for animators with creative energy to share their talents working with children. This idea came to fruition in 1981 with the founding of Project PLAE (Playing and Learning in Adaptable Environments). The program was initiated by a group of parents who had difficulty enrolling their children with disabilities in city-run recreational programs. The parents worked with a local group of design and recreation professionals (including one of the authors) to develop the program and organization.

The purpose of PLAE was to break down barriers of prejudice and misunderstanding and to provide a learning environment where individuals, regardless of ability or disability, could develop through play and reach their maximum potential. For five straight days, the program offered half-day arts and environment workshops for integrated groups of children. Up to one third of the children in each workshop had some form of impairment (no child was ever turned away because of a disability). Professional artists and environmental educators ran the workshops. They were willing to work for a low fee because they enjoyed working with children in such a stimulating environment. The program ran for several years in the Yard and at other sites in the city.[1] "Adventure Village," one of the most popular workshops, illustrated how well the Yard worked for this type of program:

A parachute is suspended above the stage decorated with colored streamers. It is a pretend ship on a voyage across an ocean of asphalt. Debussy's *La Mer* plays in the background. Charlie, a twelve-year-old with Down's syndrome, volunteers to be the captain and pretends to steer with a hula-hoop "ship's wheel" in his hands.

One of the youngest children using a wheelchair begins to cry, overwhelmed by the action. A high school intern moves her to the meadow, where she quickly calms down.

The storm passage in the music crescendos.

"Help, the waves are getting higher!" shouts one of the animators. "Look at those big rocks over there . . . quick, steer the ship the other way!" Charlie laughs excitedly and turns the hula hoop faster and faster, trying to steer *towards* where he imagines the rocks to be.

"We're going to crash," continues the animator. "Help, we're going to crash! I see land ahead. Abandon ship!" Everyone climbs or wheels off the ship. The music becomes softer. Unsure of what is happening, the children file through the gate into the Natural Resource Area.

"Oh, we've landed on an island. What a nice island. How lucky we are. We could've all been drowned. Let's explore. I wonder how big the island is. Anyone got an idea?" The children look a bit bewildered, still adjusting to the new circumstances of their life for the next week.

"Let's split up and see what we can find." Groups of children wander off in different directions to explore.

"Johnny, give Sasha a push, please," one of the leaders instructs matter-of-factly about one of the wheelchair castaways. "Can you manage okay? Good." Johnny looks a little uncertain about his first encounter with a disabled child, but her welcoming smile soon puts him at ease. Johnny knows the Yard intimately; Sasha has only been here once before on a brief visit. He starts telling her everything he knows, pointing out features, taking her to his favorite spots, talking about all the things that he and his friends do there. Although Sasha has difficulty talking and Johnny has equal difficulty understanding what she says, this does not seem to hamper communication that much. He babbles on. She listens intently, interested in everything he has to say about their castaway island. Johnny learns an important lesson about people with disabilities—that just because someone talks and acts strangely does not mean they cannot be friends. He quickly realizes that Sasha's affliction is just physical. Later he finds out she has cerebral palsy.

The exploration parties reassemble at the Gazebo. "What needs to be done to make life on the island more comfortable?" the leader asks. "Make houses," someone suggests. A pile of scrap material had been stockpiled in preparation for this moment: lengths of bamboo, sheets of triple-ply cardboard, rolls of tape, pieces of wood, fabric remnants. The leader suggests that each group choose a site for their house. A trio of girls head for the grove of Monterey pines, another pair investigates the redwoods, a gang of boys survey Chaparral Hill. The leaders try to divert the children's tendency to segregate into boy and girl groups, but the desire to do so is too strong. Instead, the leaders concentrate on making sure that the children with disabilities are included in the activity. A couple of the boys decide they need to make a plan and sit at the picnic tables to design their shelter. One of the high school interns works with Sasha on a beautiful clubhouse model made from lengths of cattail woven with string and pieces of patterned fabric.

Construction gets underway, with playleaders in the background. Every now and then, the playleaders interject suggestions, occasionally helping groups with physical tasks and instructing them in the correct use of the two tools provided: small hammers and hacksaw blades bound with tape at one end.

For Sasha's shelter, made with other girls, interns help lash a ridge pole between two Monterey pines to support a wall of golden bamboo woven together with string. In the meadow, two boys erect a tepee of palm fronds salvaged from neighborhood prunings. A cardboard house takes shape deep in the redwood forest. The sheets of cardboard are supported by the tree trunks, taped where necessary. Another shelter is tucked along the edge of Chaparral Hill overlooking the meadow. It is made from a single sheet of cardboard bent over like an inverted "L" to form a back and a roof. The front edge of the roof is supported by cardboard tubes taped at each corner. The back has been painted with abstract designs; a sign taped to a stick wedged in the ground says "Shoshanna's House." Shoshanna is almost blind with cerebral palsy–like impairments, the result of oxygen starvation at birth. She is transferred out of her chair to the ground to play with village neighbors who come to visit at her house.

The village is named New Berkeley. As the shelters are completed and the village functions are located, they are added to a large village map hanging on the fence of the enclosed garden (renamed New Berkeley Farms).

In subsequent days, elaboration of the shelters continues as a focus of activity. A gorgeous tie-dyed entrance screen is made for the Monterey pine house, which boasts scraps of carpet laid on the floor and furniture constructed out of foam-plastic packing cases.

Besides building shelters, other village activities are introduced as opportunities arise. A town hall is set up in the Gazebo. A village bank opens in one of the corrals, issuing pretend money made by two girls. They also run a pet store in the same space when the bank is closed. Street signs are posted.

On the second morning, a village meeting is held at the town hall to elect a mayor and to determine village laws. After much discussion, the villagers vote in the following laws: No littering. No stealing each other's houses. Respect one another. No driving cars in the village. Save the trees. No bad words. No fighting. No screaming.

The villagers appoint a judge, sheriff, grocer, vet, zoo keeper, bandleader, banker, doctor, schoolteacher, cook, artist, gardener, sports director, scientist, editor of the *New Berkeley Bugle*—and a village cat!

Creating the village stimulates all kinds of interaction between the children. Some work together on specific tasks, others enjoy observing the activity from the sidelines. The environment is such that children feel comfortable just hanging out with each other, just gossiping.

On the third day, production of musical instruments for the village band draws the children's attention: bamboo flutes, a xylophone made from water-filled bottles, and an assortment of percussion instruments. Thousands of dollars are cranked out by the bank. Production of the *Bugle* is underway.

Children drafted a master plan for the village, surveyed the land, designed shelters, and produced a newspaper.

At the far end of the meadow, where the base dirt of the Yard is adobe-like, a "clay mine" begins operation. Excited cries accompany the digging operations.

"Look at this piece," shouts Thyjsen, uncovering a lump of smooth pliable clay. A couple of villagers construct a cart-like "dray" from a cardboard box to drag the "good stuff" from the mine to the "factory" where the clay is washed, kneaded, and shaped into small bowls and platters. Some villagers like this sensuous activity; others hate getting their hands dirty and choose another activity. The pots are left to dry in the sun. On the last day, they are fired in a charcoal barbecue pit. In one and a half hours, the gray clay burns to a dull red color mottled with black. Some pieces have the true "ring" of fired earthenware. Everyone, including the leaders, is impressed. They realize just how authentic the village has become as a result of the level of "adaptation" that has been achieved.

The "water pipeline" is another adaptive adventure. The village decides it needs its own water supply (although freely available from faucets nearby). Spliced together with tape, scrap cardboard tubes are laid from the upper pond to the village center in the meadow. To survey the pipeline's alignment, a theodolite (leveling device) and tripod are fashioned from pieces of bamboo. The front end of the pipe is balanced on the rocks; jutting into the waterfall, it scoops the falling water.

Now for the big test. Charlie picks up the delivery end of the water, squints into it, and shouts, "Hey water, where are you?" He puts the end back on the ground. As the water slowly trickles out, he dances with glee. "Water, water!" he yells, radiating delight from one end of his body to the other. This is a truly magical moment—engineered with such simple means.

The *Bugle* is published on the fifth day. The issue contains the pipeline story, the village map, and additional illustrations of village life. Also featured is the mayor's speech promising a village clean-up.

At the end of the final day, villagers take their parents on a tour of New Berkeley. Everyone gathers in the village center for a cook-out and sing-along, using the musical instruments made during the week. There are touching farewells as children talk about future workshops when they can meet up again.

FOR ALL CHILDREN

The primary goal of PLAE was to integrate children of all abilities into the community by using creative animation. The child-to-child approach worked well. For those of us new to these types of experiences, it was extraordinary to observe how quickly children accepted each other's differences. By playing together in a structured but nonformal educational environment, the children received a tremendous amount of stimulus from each other—especially those with disabilities from the able-bodied. Everyone learned about each other's abilities. It was instructive for the so-called able-bodied to discover that the so-called disabled had just as many abilities as they did—perhaps different, but just as many.

The broader goal of PLAE was to engage all the children in high-quality, creative play experiences. To achieve this, animators with all types of backgrounds participated. A local expert in hot-air balloons and kites ran a workshop called "Pageants in the Sky." Dressed as "birdpeople," children took advantage of the west wind blowing across the Yard to support hours of flying time for eighty-six-cent Tivek kites, decorated with all sorts of charmed signs to help win kite fights. Paper airplane competitions were popular. So were soap bubbles made by dipping soft-wire circles in a bucket of bubble mix, drifting upward on a golden afternoon. Children's heads tilted backwards, tracking the rainbow-tinted gossamer globes, testing acuity, until the bubbles either burst or melted into the perfectly blue, infinite sky.

The Main Yard sand area was the arena for "Circus, Circus," run by a professional circus artist. Tightropes were suspended between the play structures. A pride of children dressed as ferocious lions were caged in the play structure tunnel. Others practiced "clown walking" (pretending to trip but without falling) and wrote a skit called "Phantom of the Circus," inspired by watching *Phantom of the Opera* on television. One end of an open barrel was covered with paper with the word "Circus" painted across it. Charlie burst through it, arms outstretched, to start the performance.

Many other workshops were conducted, covering a great variety of themes:

"Whimsical Monuments" used the sand area to construct Egyptian pyramids and the Great Wall of China.

"Visitors from Outer Space" used the Gazebo as a spaceship that had crashed in the Yard. Alien beings emerged (professional animators) who had to be taught "Earthtalk" by the children (a wonderful language arts activity).

"Living on the Frontier," based in the garden, focused on survival skills using native plants and other natural resources of the Yard. Blackberry waffles and stir-fried vegetables cooked on an open fire were big hits.

"Sound Waves," a more specialized musical workshop, evolved around learning to play the gamelan (a communal instrument adapted from the original model from Java).

"On the Air" revolved around a radio station set up and programmed by the children. They conducted a telephone survey to gauge the community response to the idea of a children's radio

Animation encouraged children to be whatever they wanted to be: bank tellers, tigers, or just to enjoy the sheer love of life!

Group interaction was stimulated by simple artifacts like a Tyvek balloon, a cardboard shark in the reenactment of "Treasure Island," and a giant parachute and ball.

station, prepared stories, recorded music, and presented the final "mix" to parents on the last day.

The repertoire of workshops was built up over the years by a core group of animators, community artists, gardeners, and recreational specialists willing to use their creative talents to work with children on their own terms.

"I think it's a real privilege," says one parent at the conclusion of Adventure Village, "for my children to be involved in a program with special children. My daughter spent the afternoon with a little girl who couldn't speak, but she explained how they communicated by giving one squeeze of the hand for 'no' and two for 'yes.' She wheeled the girl down to the creek to wet her feet because it was a really hot day, and wheeled her through the leaves. It was a very rewarding experience which our children would normally never be exposed to. I know it's going to benefit them as a memorable experience for the rest of their lives."

"I agree," interjects the mother of a disabled child. "All children grow up and live in the same world. When I was a kid I had no contact with disability and as a result grew up feeling uncomfortable about it. Now there's a generation learning that we're all different, that all kids have abilities and disabilities."

"The children don't see each other as different," says the first parent. "It's adults who have strange ideas about disability. It was quite a while after my daughter began talking about your daughter that I realized how severe her disability was. My daughter could have been talking about any kid. Disability simply wasn't part of our conversation."

"Yes, kids tend to be curious at the beginning. They express their curiosity openly, ask questions, get them answered, then be done with it. They get on playing. That's their business."

More than anything, children with disabilities needed access to other children, everyday events, and ordinary places—to put their hands in the dirt, to smell the flowers, and to hang out with each other. This was in total contrast to their normal round of special places, special education programs, other special children, special teachers, special adaptations, everything in a "special" world far removed from everyday life and interaction with other children. PLAE provided an "unspecial" alternative, open to all children, based on working relationships with parents to let them guide us in meeting their children's special requirements. Our only requirement—to promote integration—was to keep the ratio of able-bodied to disabled children to less than two to one.

It is interesting to note how little the Yard had to be physically adapted to meet the accessibility needs of children with mobility and sensory impairments. The distant location of the school bathroom was the primary problem, something that could not be changed. Some parts of the Yard would always remain inaccessible to some children. On the other hand, there were so many other accessible options that it simply did not matter that not all spaces were fully accessible. The essential consideration was to challenge children to push themselves to higher levels of development. Diversity and choice of play opportunities were the keys to meeting this need. In this regard, the Yard excelled as a model of what is known as universal design (to create places that are usable by the greatest number of people regardless of ability or disability).

PLACE AS MEDIUM

The Yard was a stage, a place where the drama of its own creation unfolded, where all types of play and learning events could be animated and become building blocks of Yard culture. Artifacts produced by these events and programs were sometimes installed as semipermanent features, such as the murals, banners, figureheads, sculptures, and the products of the PLAE workshops.

Speaking as a community artist, Francesca gave voice to the dynamics of this culture-building process using the unique characteristics of the Yard:

"It gives a sense of reality which is not achievable indoors. On the Yard, it's so much easier for children to visualize the dramatic setting and get into their own character. Here, you're working with the energies of nature instead of working against the restrictions and negative associations of classrooms. It's just extraordinary, the scenery is all here. There are houses with two stories, all kinds of walls, barriers, caves, and forests, and even waterfalls, rivers, and lakes. The water is critical. The two ponds are so different. One is sunlit and open. The other dark and secret. The stream connecting them, all the rocks in the stream, make it visually rich and strong.

"Children have no trouble at all getting into character out there; whereas in the classroom, it takes tremendous effort to achieve the same result. A classroom can virtually never match the energy that comes from natural surroundings. The Yard is very intense in the way it is laid out. So many different kinds of spaces. All the different kinds of experiences of nature. There's always new places to discover. If you ask students to find their favorite place, each will find a different spot. The Yard has the character of individuality which really helps to establish the private connection with art. The fact that the Yard is an anomaly, that it doesn't happen at other schools, or normally in the middle of a town, is also part of its attraction.

"Out on the Main Yard in the sand area the children respond very differently. It allows for the maximum number of children. It's easy to watch them. It's much more like a school environment. It's

Animation in the Yard was an evolving drama—with each activity adding to the continuous interaction between personal emotions and group dynamics. Examples included classic drama from South India (top), visitors from outer space (middle), and circus performances (bottom).

more controlled. But it's still very evocative. I found that the play structure could as easily be turned into a beautiful palace, or a burning building! The barrels and wheel on the Big Toy made a perfect fire engine. In the *Pinocchio* movie, the rocks by the swings became the Blue Fairy's House and the blue net was the ocean where the Terrible Dogfish lived.

"The Yard is a dream come true as a place for a community artist to work and try out new ideas; to play around with the possibilities for sequential action, for instance, having the audience move from place to place according to a mapped script—children and parents together, sharing the action. I feel I'm only just scratching the surface of possibilities."

●

Animation can be a powerful strategy for social development, especially in a diverse natural setting. Our experiences in the Yard reinforced the notion that the principles of accessibility, adaptation, and integration were significant factors in the development of all children—not just those with disabilities, but children from different cultural and ethnic backgrounds, girls and boys, and a much broader range of ages than in a standard classroom.

Animation encourages mutual acceptance among children, helps them gain skills of organization and cooperation, and stimulates confidence in the use of tools and materials. Parents' testimony about the positive impacts of these experiences on their children supported the hypothesis that animated, naturalized spaces foster the development of the whole child and the whole community of children, regardless of their individual differences.

REFERENCES

1. Goltsman, S., S. McIntyre, and D. Driskell (1994). PLAE Scores: Thematic Play and Learning Programs for Children of All Abilities. *Circus City. Frontier Village. Treasure Quest.* Berkeley, Calif.: MIG Communications.

Community Commons

An essential component of village life is the village green, plaza, or compound, where residents of all ages can gather freely to exchange news, barter goods, celebrate festivals, or simply hang out and play. The Yard was one such place, built by the residents themselves to invite community life back into the naturalized "Washington Village."

As the Yard developed, it became the site of many neighborhood programs and events, not only during school hours but also on weekends and during the summer. We constantly searched for ways to extend the function of the Yard as a community space by programming educational and recreational events outside official school hours.

CAMP-OUT

One of the most significant out-of-school events involving parents—probably never to occur again, given current constraints—was a camp-out held during the early phase of Yard development. It took place during the Gas Crisis of 1974, when field trips were limited and teachers and students felt obligated to help conserve gas for more essential purposes. Yet springtime camping trips were an unshakable tradition, eagerly anticipated and meticulously planned weeks ahead.

The solution was obvious. Why not camp out in the developing Natural Resource Area or, as the children called it, the "dirt area"? At that time, it was still a rough-graded, meadowlike area of weeds, patches of grass, and bare dirt.

For the children to construct natural overnight shelters, truckloads of leafy tree prunings from the UC Berkeley campus were delivered to the Yard by a university landscape maintenance crew. Other materials such as sheets of cardboard and scraps of sawn lumber were also provided. Groups of children, parents, and teachers began staking out territories and assembling materials. They tackled the classic architectural problem of how to "make the most with the least" as they worked on an assortment of improvised shelters, each one reflecting the builders' varied levels of ingenuity.

Naturally, eating was an important part of the camp-out. The group organized a barbecue, which enabled people to participate even if they did not intend to brave the rigors of sleeping out. Grills set up in the Main Yard offered a special delicacy: rabbit shish-kebabs made from animals raised and slaughtered in Tom Javit's urban farming class (and marinated overnight in a special formula prepared by one of the teachers). Added to this was an assortment of ethnic foods brought by parents.

It was a particularly warm evening, tempting those who were not camping to linger beyond the time when Pacific breezes would have normally cooled the gossip. It was a good time for parents to get a close-up view of the Yard (which, until then, many had only seen from a moving car). They could prowl around with their children and share firsthand the things that interested them.

As the scattered primitive shelters caught the last rays of the sinking sun, our minds could drift back in history to catch a fleeting sense of life around the Bay before the European settlers arrived. Maybe this very spot had been the home of a group of Ohlone, living in a village far more elegantly constructed.

The early evening was like a recess period of infinite duration, allowing the children to do things that were not possible in a normal half-hour lunch period. "I never slept over with my whole class before!" someone said. A strange, liberating feeling came from camping in the schoolyard. Perhaps it was the opportunity to experience the dusk-to-dawn period of Earth's twenty-four-hour cycle on our own fragment of the planet.

A half-dozen children had organized a puppet show. A mobile proscenium was constructed from pieces of cardboard decorated with paint and crepe paper. A collection of hand puppets made from scrap material became the characters in a playlet that dramatized life in the Yard. It told a story about insects living in minute habitats, in clumps of grass, and under logs, about survival in rainstorms and under huge human feet. The production was a stunning example of an interdisciplinary playing-and-learning project that combined construction, logistics, arts, math, language skills, and the use of recycled materials. Above all, it was completely initiated and implemented by children.

Dusk fell. As the sky began to darken, a couple of incandescent camping lanterns were turned on. Suddenly the Yard boundaries receded to infinity as the visible landscape became reduced to two intense pools of light. The distinctive aroma of sun-baked dirt and vegetation carried on the cool night air. The characteristic fragrance of the rural Californian foothills was juxtaposed with the mechanical swishing of Friday night traffic on MLK Way—a perfect distillation of urban and rural contrasts. Here we were in the middle of the city, camping on a re-exposed half acre of dirt, as a first step towards reconnecting ourselves to the natural ecology and timeframe of the region.

"Let's tell ghost stories," one child suggested. Everyone gathered around one of the lanterns atop the yet-to-be Chaparral Hill, swapping the most grotesque inventions of childhood minds.

Meanwhile the full moon had risen—stimulating one teacher to start a discussion about the meaning of "lunatic" and lunar words like "moonstruck" and "moonshine." She and a small group of interested children talked about all kinds of lunar phenomena: sea tides caused by the moon's gravitational pull; fiddler crabs that change color from bright yellow at high tide to dark green at low tide; superstitious farmers who plant above-ground crops by the light of the full moon and below-ground crops by the dark of the new moon; examples of animal behavior dominated by the twenty-eight-day lunar cycle, including the human female; and the apparent coincidence between the lunar cycle and births and calls to the police about family disturbances. It was a unique opportunity for "moontalk," which had never been available in such a real way during daylight hours!

Finally the children made their way to bed, searching out their sleeping bags in the various burrows constructed earlier. Chatter and giggles died away, relinquishing the land to a nocturne of late-night vehicles, their occupants unaware that they were driving past, as far as we knew, Berkeley's first-ever schoolyard camp-out.

By five the next morning, it was turning light. Those awake were greeted by a brief period of stillness before early morning drivers began laying rubber tracks on MLK Way. The first notes of the dawn chorus started up, drifting from neighborhood backyards on one side of the Yard, in opposition to the increasing traffic noise on the other. We thought that perhaps the right habitat conditions could be created to attract more birds to the Yard as a melodic counterpoint to the dominant urban drone.

While most campers were hidden from view in their shelters, some slept out in the open. Perhaps they had not been organized enough to build something more

Building natural shelters (top), telling ghost stories (middle), and participating in a sing-a-long (bottom) were all part of the Great Yard Camp-out.

substantial or they had decided against unnecessary luxuries. They were the true primitives, protecting themselves against the damp dew with the minimum technology of cardboard sheets laid over their sleeping bags.

The Saturday morning traffic soon woke everyone. For a while we lay enjoying the dawn, gazing up at the paling stars, feeling the earth below. Ground-level glances through close-up weed patches gave filtered views of the school building in the background, its classroom tables, chairs, exercise books, and chalkboards far from our thoughts.

The camp-out celebrated the rite of passage of the Natural Resource Area from asphalt, to dirt, to weedy meadow, and eventually to an ecologically viable community landscape.

The event also prompted a change in consciousness: a realization that school activities such as camping trips could be transposed to the school site, with increased educational benefits and certainly reduced costs. Camping trips are never easy for urban schools. Anyone who has tried to organize such excursions knows how easily they can turn into logistical nightmares. Most of the effort is expended on getting people, food, and equipment to and from the campgrounds in an orderly manner, rather than on developing creative activities for everyone once they arrive at the site. Insurance requirements and administrative restrictions have made carpool trips impossible, and budget cuts have placed severe limits on bus trips.

Beyond these practical difficulties is the larger "hidden curriculum" issue of whether children should be taught that worthwhile outdoor educational opportunities can only be found outside their own neighborhoods.

"Usually I don't have the time to join in these trips," one parent said, "but as we live just down the street, here I am enjoying the fun with other families from the neighborhood. It's really wonderful. The children are friends at school, their parents are also friends and it really makes for a nice sense of community, which I guess the whole thing is about. Not just improving the physical environment, but connecting the people too, the human environment."

DO YOUR OWN THING

Not every activity in the Yard was part of a planned program. The Yard "curriculum" was the sum of every-thing people did there, whether as child, teacher, playleader, gardener, artist-animator, parent, local resident, or visitor from afar. People responded in their own particular ways. They engaged in photography, sketching, and bird-watching; they flew model airplanes; they looked for coins with electronic probes in the sand; they practiced tennis shots against the ball wall; and they conducted tai chi classes at the quiet west end in the early mornings. Some evenings the lilting notes of a solo flute partnered the birdsong in a free concert.

One Sunday afternoon two young men ran an extension cord from their apartment, in the building next to the Yard, through the fence to a television set sitting on the log by the upper pond. They lay back in the sun on a couple of easy chairs, wearing sunglasses, caps, and running shorts, and watched the ballgame!

A local writer remarked how nice it was to be able to bring along her son, who, while she worked on one of the picnic tables, could amuse himself and become acquainted with the school he would be attending the fol-lowing year. "We live in a small apartment down the street," she said, "where it's difficult to work. Here we're out in the sun and fresh air and there's so much for him to play with; he never distracts me like he does at home."

The Yard was a popular site for birthday parties. The Natural Resource Area was perfect for treasure hunts and hide-and-go-seek, with party treats laid out on a shady picnic table—a much more attractive alternative to an overheated apartment full of screaming children. Yard parties were also enjoyable for the parents; their children were eager to show them their favorite climbing tree, a secret hideaway, the best place to see the fish, a patch of pretty flowers, and so on.

The Yard was a place for family reunions, picnics, and potlucks, a place to relax, lie back, take in the sun, and open up a basket of goodies. "Me and my friend and my mom came over here one weekend to have a picnic," a boy reported with a broad grin. "Boy, did we have a good time!"

HANGING OUT

"A couple of days ago I noticed a high school student eating lunch and reading by the pond. After he left I checked and, sure enough, he'd left his trash on the ground. I ran after him and explained that he had left his trash and asked him please not to drop trash in the Yard. He was pleasant and said he'd forgotten. He said he really liked the Yard, and I said it was always open to everyone and I was glad he appreciated it. He was here again this morning studying at one of the picnic tables since he had a free period."

—Yard teacher's journal

The Yard provided a relaxed, recreational environment for all ages both during and after school: for parents and children to eat lunch (top), for children to ride their bicycles or go on a fishing expedition (middle), and for adolescents to just "hang out."

NATURAL LEARNING

Weekends enabled neighborhood children—both current and former Washington students—to spend more time playing with the natural resources. Children turned over the rocks in the meadow, searching for worms to take on fishing trips. A Washington graduate came by to check the pond for biological samples for his junior high science class.

"We pick the blackberries with our parents," a child confided, "and take them home and make muffins. Ooh, they're good." Another described how she picked some flowers and took them home for Mother's Day. "I picked some cattails, too," she added. "They're in a vase mixed with everlasting flowers in our front room."

BIKES

As soon as the dirt area had been graded, older children appeared on dirt bikes and began setting up jumps and racing circuits. We quickly realized that bike riding needed to be incorporated into the plans for the Yard from the beginning.

"We bike over here on weekends," Amy explains, "usually in the nature area because of the soft ground. It's a real dirt-tracking place. You can ride over bridges, through the mud and in and out of trees. On the Main Yard there's more space. You can do skids in the sand and set up jumps." Peddling furiously on a Big Wheel, Amy and her brother race around the central play area, yelping "Coming through!" as they swoop through the pepper trees on the path behind the swings.

"Sometimes we play Evel Knievel," Kevin and Eric boast. They pretend their bicycles are motorcycles.

"Careful, we might skid right into the pond."

"Are the daredevils ready?"

"It's gonna be a cool ride."

HANGING OUT

When looking for playmates, children would first check the Yard. Even if no one they wanted to play with was there, they could spend time on the swings, fishing, or riding bicycle circuits. Sometimes it took an hour or more for a group of friends to gather. Distractions and amusements were always available to avoid boredom.

The ponds ranked highly.

"We go right into them when it's really hot, don't we, yeah, yeah, yeah," Ben enthuses. "His mother gets mad when he goes in," referring to his friend George. "He gets real dirty y'know, real dirty . . . with mud squished up an' stuff. My ma used to get mad too, but she

doesn't anymore, 'cause it's getting too hot. She was worried about me catching a cold, but now it's hot, it's okay." The two boys wade in, sit on the fountain, and spray water in all directions.

A half-dozen children float and paddle on wooden cable spool sides, fighting for supremacy of the water. One weekend children haul over a plastic boat—large enough for a single child—and take turns rowing on what they call a "real lake."

Weekends allowed time for much more elaborate games than were possible during the short breaks in the school day.

"We're playing 'got lost,'" a group of girls explain one Sunday afternoon. "We've had a shipwreck and our folks died and we're trapped on the deserted island. We never find our way home so we just live out here. We salvage stuff and survive on lots of little foods, like coconuts and licorice."

"Today we've been collecting spices [leaves of different plants]," says another. "We're going to crush them and sprinkle them on the pretend fish we're going to eat. We're using some of the 'dishes' [plastic lunch trays] that we salvaged from the wreck."

It was interesting to observe how children demonstrated a natural sense of recycling and reuse of materials and objects in their informal play.

"She broke her ankle," says another girl, pointing to her friend who has a "splint" of wood loosely bound to her leg with lengths of cattails. "But it's not really broken!"

"Sometimes we pretend we're ranch girls and play living in the country . . . deep in the country. We don't have electricity so we have to chop firewood and make fires. We do it all at weekends or in the summer, 'cause there's never enough time at school."

Some high school students moved from the street corners and coffee shops to the Yard to "kick back" after school. One teenager said he liked to relax "where it's shady and quiet, especially under the trees around the pond—you can trip off there. It's cool."

Another said the Yard was her favorite place to write. "I find it inspiring . . . I want to go into journalism. It's where I come when I fight at home with my brother. It's just a nice, peaceful place to be."

FAMILY AFFAIRS

Late one afternoon, near the waterfall, a couple was leaning against a fence railing, arms around each other, talking intimately, while their two children played across the other side of the pond. It was not possible to walk up to them and begin asking questions without feeling like we were invading their privacy. We often had to rely on informal observations and a small collection of anecdotes to assess the feelings of neighborhood residents, who used the Yard as a private refuge or a special place for a stroll.

A mother and son sit in the clubhouse discussing whether trees have feelings.

Another mother sits with her two young children as they play in the pool below the waterfall, the running water serving as a medium for their intimacy.

Shrieks of laughter come from a family playing on the swing rope hanging from the tree on Willow Island. "Push me! Push me again!" the child cries. The father carries his daughter to the rope. Her hands reach out. She holds on tight as she swings out over the water.

The Yard was a perfect place to bring visitors on a summer evening or Sunday afternoon. Sometimes comments like "It's a really neat place . . . we discovered it last year" were overheard. People would express their feelings about being close to nature, about how rare it was to find a "wild" open space like this in the middle of the city.

"I come here to renew my spirit," a neighbor says. "With a place like this, I don't have to go up in the hills to escape . . . It's good for my soul."

One Sunday afternoon, two men enter, each with a boy high on their shoulders. A third boy tags behind.

"Here it is, here it is," one of the children shouts. "Want us to show you where the pond is?" Apparently neither adult has visited the Yard before.

They stop at the play structure, climb it together for a few minutes, then the men sit on a bench while the children continue playing. After a while they walk past the mural where a group of older children are standing on a picnic table picking blackberries from the overhanging branches.

"Gee, I didn't know you could eat blackberries," one of the men distinctly says. (Blackberries grew all over the Flatlands, in odd corners and vacant lots, and were considered a local delicacy.)

"Let's run round the lake," one of the children shouts. "Daddy, look, you can see clear down in the water. There's all kinds of animals in there." They squat beside the lower pond under the alders, gesturing, discussing the vegetation. The children run on ahead. "Can we cross here?" they ask at the stepping stones in the corner.

"Let's walk in the 'rain forest,'" one of them says as they approach the redwoods. The words "a nice place for them" are just discernible from one of the men as they emerge from the redwoods, following the path around the creek.

"Sure is a big lake, Dad," one of the children says. They wander around the backside of the upper pond, through the bamboo thicket, back past the railroad ties, and into the meadow.

A DARKER SIDE

Informal nighttime use of the Yard was the least documented. Clear traces, however, were certainly visible: beer cans, cigarette butts, and the like. A group of adolescents or homeless people were occasionally seen talking in the Gazebo or on the log by the pond.

During the summer, there were times when it was clear that people had slept out among the trees; firsthand observations of this activity were occasionally made. Fortunately, it involved just one or two people on an irregular basis and rarely with negative consequences requiring intervention. Anymore than that, however, would have made the lack of toilet facilities intolerable. And because a discussion on providing public facilities would have raised too many questions about the overnight camping, the activity could only exist *sub rosa*.

The Yard, of course, could have been locked at night. But we felt that the Yard should never become so precious that it had to be locked up by one group to protect it from another. As time passed, we became firmly convinced that the open-door policy was the only way to ensure its use by the community, and that the presence of people would protect the Yard from willful vandalism.

YARDFEST

The first Yardfest in 1972 was a groundbreaking— or rather, asphaltbreaking—celebration of the Yard's beginning. Formal invitations were sent out to the many people in the community and local government who had assisted in the Yard's development. Each subsequent year, the festival marked the Yard's birthday and its role as a stage for what Harvey Cox has called "Homo Festivus . . . by nature a creature who not only works and thinks but who sings, dances, prays, tell stories, and celebrates."[1]

Cultural diversity was the message of the Yardfest, a fitting extension to bountiful nature, a sign of the fertility of the creative human spirit in its many forms of expression.

YARDFEST

"The element of festivity can never be 'organized,' arranged, and induced ... Thus, when a festival goes as it should ... something [is received] that it is not in human power to give. This is by now the almost forgotten reason for the age-old custom of ... wishing one another well on great festival days ... the real thing we are wishing is the 'success' of the festive celebration itself, not just its outer forms and enrichments ... but the gift that is ... the true fruit of the festival: renewal, transformation, rebirth."

— Josef Pieper[2]

FILIPINO LUMPIA

ingredients:
lumpia wrappers (or egg roll wrappers)
ground beef (1 lb.)
1 Pkg. mixed frozen vegetables *
1 chopped onion (optional)
salt
garlic salt
soy sauce.
* fresh vegetables, chopped and boil

The Yardfest was an annual event to encourage interaction between everyone involved in creating the Yard. Decorations included handmade "super banners" suspended from the school roof (top). The event offered opportunities for young musicians and entrepreneurs to participate in a multicultural exchange.

Participants enjoyed live music of all sorts, especially jazz (part of a long tradition at the school), a highly appropriate accompaniment with its accent on improvisation in various genres. There was dancing from many lands: a parent-run East Mediterranean dance troupe, classical dances from India, a dance-drama from Java, *Cinco de Mayo* folk dances, Chinese New Year's dragon dances, fan dances from Japan, aikido and tai chi demonstrations, and Brazilian capoeira martial arts dances.

And there was a gourmet's delight of food. Tantalizing aromas represented the many ethnic groups and nationalities of the school: Japanese sukiyaki; American favorites like popcorn, hot dogs, barbecued chicken, and spareribs; Chinese Yangchow rice and won tons; Mexican tacos and hot links; Filipino lumpia; Mediterranean stuffed grape leaves, spaghetti, and pizza; German sauerkraut and sausages; and numerous "natural food" delicacies.

Lines of booths brought even more diversity: parent-run workshops on Japanese origami (paper folding) and Chinese calligraphy; a bike repair and spare parts exchange shop; a pet corner giving away kittens, puppies, and other surplus pets; and flea market booths with all kinds of used reading material, clothes, recorded music, toys, and other bric-a-brac for bargain seekers young and old.

Beautifully arranged tables displayed child-made goods prepared to raise money for special trips: vases crafted from recycled glass jars layered with paper maché and colored tissue, puppets of endangered species, and potted plants grown from seeds. The children used many basic skills to price the "market," to record sales, and to decide how to spend the profits. All of these activities derived from a "scrap economy" that helped reinforce conservation efforts in the community.

Child-to-child workshops offered mask making, face painting, African doll making, ceramics, kite making, musical instrument building, and basket weaving using pine needles, willow shoots, cattails, and bamboo from the Yard. The easy access to free materials enabled the children to run these activities with only minimum adult support.

The Great Snail Race was a wonderful example of the wacky, inventive games and shows created by children for children. Using brown snails seconded from their Yard habitat, the students devised an amusing game of chance to raise money for classroom supplies. Gastropods were named and placed in the center of a circular cardboard racetrack. Children then placed nickel-sized wagers on the snail they thought would travel to the edge of the disk in the shortest time—or in some cases, the longest time. Therefore, depending on the race, the first or last snail won the purse.

"Slow down, Champion! You're going too fast. Slow down!"

"Hey, Bigfoot, put up your radar before I lose my money."

"Go, go, Aces!" shouted supporters at this parody of real-world sports. Everyone thronged around the track, whooping up their favorite candidates as the snails followed tortuously circuitous paths. At the end of the afternoon, the snails were returned to their home in the undergrowth. It was a powerful example of the possibilities of an open learning environment, where imagination, physical resources, and environmental ethics could be nonformally combined.

The Yardfest was always a time to involve the local media and to encourage friends and organizations from other communities to participate. In 1972, a school group from neighboring Vallejo (twenty-five miles [16 km] north of Berkeley) attended the Yardfest as ambassadors of goodwill and presented a special flag to the Yard. The gesture was spawned by the enthusiasm and interest of the school's principal who had attended one of the Yard planning sessions earlier in the year. The presence of the Vallejo contingent suggested a carryover of ideas and tactics to their own school environment—which eventually happened.

Literal and metaphoric messages were transmitted each year in the making and display of signs and banners, providing opportunities to integrate elements of the Yard in multimedia productions.

A competition for children's designs for a Washington Environmental Yard t-shirt resulted in a composite design from several entries with the slogan "Our Great WEY." The design was silkscreened onto shirts and blouses. A professional calligrapher set up a stall where

The Yardfest was a true testimony to "building a sense of community." Everyone participated! Students, teachers, parents, neighbors, and friends from the surrounding Berkeley area came to be a part of the fun: the Great Snail Race (top), folkloric dance performances on stage (middle), and raffling off the "garden quilt" made by one class to raise money for a class trip (bottom).

NATURAL LEARNING

children could have their name inscribed on an "I'm a Friend of the Yard" placard.

The set of giant appliqué canvas banners (described in Chapter 7) were hung on facades of the building for the 1975 Yardfest, their bright colors adding to the festive feeling.

Environmental messages were reinforced each year by Bay Area groups, such as Save the Whales, the Ecology Center, and the Lawrence Hall of Science, who set up informational booths during the Yardfest. They were sometimes joined by the Berkeley Fire Department's dramatic bell clanging entrance, with firemen swarming up ladders to the school roof to demonstrate yet another essential aspect of environmental protection. The New Games Foundation brought its huge seven-foot (2.1 m) "Earthball" for people to play with and learn noncompetitive games, driving home a message about the need for cooperative, nonviolent group behavior.

•

Something important happens when community members realize that their collective efforts in natural-izing the environment can enhance their quality of life. At this level, the Yardfest was more than a prosaic fun-event. It became a statement of values, a manifesto of everyday life, combining aspects of recreation and education in a diversity of diversities. It provided a pipeline to personal action on the environment, helping people get unstuck from the feeling that the status quo could not be changed.

Yet the Yardfest was also a metaphor for truly democratic actions, not wholly planned and not totally anarchistic. The flexibility and openness of the project made the Yard an effective vehicle for school-community development.

The annual Yardfests brought the cast of the continuing ecodrama together on the stage—the Yard itself—to see each other as the "production company" and to celebrate the results of its combined efforts. The events renewed and extended the meaning of the Yard as an experience, as a memory, adaptable to other communities and other situations. Out-of-school use reminded the community of childhood values, lest anyone forgot what it is like and what it should be to be a child.

REFERENCES

1. Cox, H. G. (1969). *The Feast of Fools: A Theological Essay on Festivity and Fantasy.* Cambridge: Harvard University Press, 10.

2. Pieper, J. (1965). *In Tune with the World: A Theory of Festivity.* New York: Harcourt, Brace, and World (translated from the German, published originally 1963), 30–31.

Part III:
In the Interests of Children

CHAPTER 16

Speaking of Quality

Without Dynamic Quality the organism cannot grow. Without static quality the organism cannot last. Both are needed.

—Robert Pirsig, *Lila*

The academic performance of the Washington children, as measured by standardized tests, was highly competitive with that of students from other schools. To what degree was this due to the excellent teachers and their innovative programs? And to what degree was this due to the environmental and community focus of the school? We knew that all of these factors reinforced one another. As a research question, though, it was difficult to answer because no standard evaluation measures were available to assess this type of impact. After many years of observing Yard activity, however, one thing was absolutely clear: the repertoire of children's behavior broadened enormously with the increase in physical diversity of the school site. From this we concluded that opportunities for learning and development also increased.

In trying to elaborate this conclusion—essentially to determine the impact of the asphalt removal and the development of the Yard on the educational experience—we realized we had a group of true experts to consult: the children themselves, particularly the 1977 graduating class of fourth graders. These thirty-seven children were especially qualified to help us since most of them had entered kindergarten just prior to the groundbreaking in February 1972. They had experienced the heyday of Yard development, a period so successful that parents petitioned the school board to add a fourth-grade class so that their children could reap an extra year's benefit from the program.

This fortunate group of students rode the wave of innovation at Washington that had been gathering momentum in the years before, which, as the Yard took shape, buoyed the whole school forward. This expert group understood the value of Washington's extended learning environment. They had helped to create it and had experienced it for five years.

Through interviews, the group of students offered recollections and insights on the following topics: what the Yard used to look like, how they would describe the Yard to a friend, what they had learned in the Yard, what difference the Yard had made in their lives, and what would happen if the Yard were taken away and returned to asphalt. (Six members of this group were interviewed again in 1982, at age fourteen, ten years after the founding of the Yard, to tap once more their strongest memories. In 1995, two of them, then in their late twenties, were interviewed a third time.) We hoped that by listening to their stories, we would learn something about the benefits of the Yard's naturalized settings and the impact of the educational program.

DIVERSITY

Diversity was clearly the Yard's largest key to success. After years of observations and listening to children's comments, we concluded that high-quality, diversified settings have high developmental value.

"I've learned that you can do a million things here, like collect fossils. There's just so much to do all over the place. It has two ponds and a river. It has dirt and trees and plants and bushes. You can eat in there. You can watch frogs and fish and tadpoles . . . it's neat. There's swings and a slide and the sand and the bars and there's so much stuff to play on—it's just real fun."

"It's good to have swings and slides and structures. Maybe you hardly ever use them, but it is good to know they're there, so when you're not playing something else you can use them."

"There's a regular play yard and there's this whole other nature yard, with things living in it that children can discover. On the cement, boys feel like playing kickball . . . in the nature area it seems like you're in the woods. If you fall, it won't hurt you as much in the nature part. People don't get hurt because everyone is careful with everyone else. There's running water and picnic benches in the shade in a little enclosed area with birch trees and pussy willows. The ground is covered with plants, flowers, leaves, and soil. There's woodchips all over. It's just perfect. There's a little pasture surrounded by pine trees with needles and wooden fences to bounce on. There's a lake with a little creek that goes over a waterfall, under two bridges made of stone and wood. One pond has a fountain in it. The other is crowded with fish and is almost overgrown with cattails and rushes.

"And there's a sort of island with a weeping willow in the middle. There's lots of big trees and tiny animals like snails, potato bugs, leaf hoppers, pill bugs, bees, beetles, ants, ladybugs . . . I remember seeing a grasshopper being eaten by a spider once."

"There's a kind of a structure where kids play 'house' and have club meetings and eat lunch, or it can be a fort. And there's other little buildings with crooked branches around where kids meet. There's lots of color, mostly green with bluebirds. There's a big mound with a bunch of bushes all over it and another part with redwood trees we call Sherwood Forest. There's a garden place, too.

"The other part of the Yard is a big place that's covered with asphalt and surrounded by gardens and flowers. There's structures and stuff to climb, a big wide metal slide, a big net, a fireman's pole, swings, and a tunnel that's all the same structure. There's a big sandbox with a tall fence around it and a structure made of giant spools, and a compass with North, South, East, and West painted on the ground."

"People play much more now, lots of different kinds of games. There's more room to play. It's not so crowded. When people are spread out, they have the room they need. They can run a lot more."

Of course the Yard had not expanded physically during development. It had just become better utilized, and activity had indeed "spread out." It was no longer concentrated around a few pieces of equipment, and occupied a much wider range of settings in many different locations.

CHANGE

The group of expert children were well aware of the physical changes that had happened in the Yard, and also expressed a sense of how their feelings and behavior had changed as a result.

"It used to be a big, empty place with nothing to do. Now there's a whole bunch of trees and all this stuff. It's neat. It's a very good place. It's not like any other school I've seen. The Yard used to be just like other yards. Now it's more like a forest than a playground. It's one of a kind.

"Other schools just have huge blocks of cement—five miles of boring cement. This one has cement and nice, pretty places, where animals and butterflies live. At other schools I would never want to go out, I wouldn't even want to go to school. But here I just love coming to school everyday."

SENSE OF BELONGING

"How would you describe the Yard to a friend?" we asked, trying to get at the children's most persistent images. Their descriptions often reinforced one another.

"It kinda gives me something to brag about. Other kids have to play on cement every day. Same old thing, cement, cement. When I see another school I think, too bad, they've just got a cement yard and we've got trees and a river and ponds with fishes, frogs, tadpoles, snakes, and a turtle. It makes me feel good to tell other people about our school and what we have. It used to be a normal school. I played on the cement like everybody else. Now it's different. It's got a wildlife area with lots of birds. It's a place to go when you want to be quiet under a tree or something so the sun doesn't hurt you."

It is important that children feel good about the places where they have to spend so much of their time. Without this sense of belonging they feel alienated and unhappy—a state that would obviously affect the quality of their schoolwork. Schools especially need to be attractive

With loose parts of natural objects and materials to play with, it is almost impossible for a child to feel bored. There is always something new to try, to learn about. In this type of setting, a child can be alone if he or she wishes, without feeling left out.

in every aspect—not only with cosmetic planting along their public "fronts" but with private "backs" made so exciting that the children are eager to return each day.

Many of the children's comments indicated a strong sense of closeness to other species of animals and the natural habitat that we all depend on. Together, the animals, vegetation, and children provided a friendly, animated ambiance.

"I came from my country [Vietnam] last year. When I first came to school I thought the Yard looked friendly. It made me feel at home. There's a little stump under the willow tree beside the pond where I can eat lunch and talk with my friends. In the trees you can be alone. You can wander along little pathways and find lots of different places where you can feel private. It's a good place to come if you want to be by yourself."

The Yard was an antidote to the sadness of children who sometimes had no one to play with.

"It was lonely before we had the sandbox. Being alone doesn't bother me now. I can always wander around looking at stuff and watch people play."

Feeling welcome and at ease, having the option of being private or sociable—these are attributes of a good home environment. Home is a friendly companion, a place of contemplation full of reminders of happy times, of friends and family, of exciting trips: a treasure trove of nonverbal communication. The Yard functioned in similar ways.

"When I first came to Washington School I thought the nature part was somebody's yard. Ooo, I thought, I'm going to tell on you guys. Then I started going there and saw lots of kids and the Yard teachers, and so I asked my cousin, 'What's that great beautiful yard?' 'That's what we call the Environmental Yard,' he said. It looked beautiful, just beautiful, like blossoms in the spring. There's so many things, I can't say them all. It's my favorite part of the school. I'm going to miss it when I leave."

"It seems like one big family playing out there. You go on trips. Sometimes we pick flowers and take them home to our mothers. Yeah, you go on trips and see the sunlight through the trees just like a forest. I think the Yard gives me all the sunshine I need. I love the back path through the redwoods. The pond reminds me of a swamp that we went to when I was four or five. Sometimes when I look at the sky when I'm somewhere else, it reminds me of the Yard. And when I look at the clouds it reminds me of the ponds. When I look at the birds it reminds me of the kids."

"I make little horses out of pieces of wood by the stream and sit under the willow tree with one of my friends. It feels good there. Really quiet. Lots of kids just like to sit there and talk."

ENVIRONMENTAL LEARNING

"What have you learned from the Yard?" we asked, curious to know how conscious the children were about their own learning. They spoke extensively about learning from the natural environment.

"The Yard has gotten the whole school to think environmentally. We do all sorts of stuff with nature. I used to not care about the environment or know about plants and animals before I came. Now I've learned a lot . . . how caterpillars turn into butterflies . . . about redwings and swallowtails . . . about marshes and wet places. We've learned a lot about trees. If I hadn't been to the school I would never have thought about different environments. Now I think of my own backyard as an environment and I've noticed that some private schools have planted areas."

"I know how it feels to have ponds . . . I've studied them a lot. I know what lives there . . . water bugs, frogs, and fish. They multiply fast, almost as fast as rabbits. I've seen the way the ponds change. I've tried to sail pieces of wood across them."

"I've learned that plants are very special. I've learned to recognize them. What's good to eat, taste, and smell. I like to walk around looking at them. There's lots of insects and spider's nests in the trees. I know how plants grow, what makes them survive, which seeds to plant, which ones grow faster . . . Plants make the city look pretty."

The high learning potential of natural resources compared to that of asphalt was obvious to some children.

"You would never say, 'Let's go outside and learn about cement.' There's only one thing to know about a cement yard . . . It's a cement yard, period. I don't think I learned anything there. It was all open. There was never a moment without noise. You couldn't relax, there was always someone bothering you."

Animals were often the focus of attention.

"The wilderness area is a great place to think, to work, to make poems, to listen to the birds, or just to rest. It's a great breeding place for insects, especially ones that eat plants. We learned that different animals need different habitats. There's always something new to find out. Now we're studying wildlife habitats all over the world."

There was a strong awareness of the aesthetic appeal of nature, of how it affected feelings and behavior.

"It's much prettier to look at when you're trying to think. Cement is part of your environment, but it's nice to be surrounded by trees and flowers, to watch the fountain and play around in the bushes. You don't get hurt in the dirt."

A dissident voice was occasionally heard.

"The nature part of the Yard is so dirty, so many creatures living there—except ladybugs, they're okay. Gardening is boring. I like things to climb on and to jump over."

A child's sense of belonging in the natural world comes from absorbing its sensory richness.

Most children, however, were decidedly pro-nature. They were aware of its positive effects on their behavior and the importance of daily contact.

"I've learned to live closer to nature every day instead of three times a year on a camping trip. It's like having the countryside right in your neighborhood. I could study up and read about plants and animals, but it is nice to go out there and see and feel things and learn with real examples."

The possibility of direct interaction with living things made children think about cause and effect.

"I used to rip leaves off branches and didn't think about what would happen. But now I think about it. The nature area gives you something to think about in the future . . . something to come back to and visit after you leave school."

FRIENDLY PEOPLE

Much of the positive atmosphere of the Yard was due to the open-minded, child-oriented teaching staff. Students viewed them as helpful friends.

"The Yard has the people you need to help you learn. We learned new games. We went on top of the school building and made maps, measured the wind, wrote stories and poems. Another time we worked around the big compass and learned about the sun and planets and stuff."

"We worked on the garden and the compost, and learned how to recycle. We got waste from the cafeteria, mixed it up with dirt and weeds, and made compost. We planted sanamino [cinnamon] and frijoles that smelled so good. We learned that nature must be loved."

"It was really fun working with the garden teacher, especially making the map to show where all the plants were going to be. And I learned that you really have to take care of things if you want them to stay the way you like."

"I remember walking around the Yard with one of the teachers looking at all the things we knew, looking for ten different colors and trying to get their names. We spent a lot of time just walking around exploring, pointing out little coves I liked. She was like a friend and always listened to your problems."

WHAT IF THE YARD WERE REMOVED?

As a way to gauge the value of the Yard, we asked the ultimate question: "How would you feel if the Yard were removed and replaced with asphalt?"

"Kids would feel terrible . . . really horrible . . . awful . . . unhappy . . . just very sad."

These shocked reactions were expressed over and over again.

"What would happen? How would you justify keeping it?" we asked, overdramatizing the situation in the hope of getting direct answers about the meaning of the Yard—we did! Some mentioned the loss of life.

"The fish would die . . . They would lose their freedom. Lots of plants and flowers would die. Some birds have nests in the trees and I know there's a snake or two in the swamp."

Others focused on the loss of play and learning opportunities.

"Kids wouldn't be able to play anymore. Well, they'd still be able to play kickball, but that's not everything people like to do, it's not much at all. Lots of kids would rather look at fish, race boats, and climb trees."

"You couldn't play hide-and-seek games anymore. Kids can't play in an empty place. We eat in there. Hide from our friends. Have grass fights. Have fun. You can't do that with cement all around. Even if there's a lot of structures you can still do more if there's natural stuff. We love to use nature. Kickball would take over again."

There were comments about the loss of sensory stimulation.

"It would just be hot and gray. There wouldn't be any color left. Kids would just sit around doing nothing. People like to look at things. Without the Yard you would just sit there with all the ground around you but nothing in it."

Some children, with clear insight, dwelt on the antisocial consequences of removing the Yard.

"We'd fight, we'd get up to mischief and act mean. More fights would give more crimes later. Instead of talking, people would steal stuff from the school to get their revenge."

"All the kids who play in the bushes and peek on people and play with toy guns and stuff would feel really bad. They'd be really upset and restless. Nobody likes a blacked-over yard. Kids wouldn't behave so well with each other. Now, if they have a fight, they can go in the trees and be friends again."

Many discussed the actions they would take to save the Yard from destruction.

"All the kids would turn against the principal and try to get the Yard back the way it was. We'd get all our friends to help and we'd say, 'Please give us back the Yard the way it was because it was so beautiful. We liked it the way it was. Everyone enjoyed it. If there were no little paths, no shady places, we'd all have to sit on the hot cement!'"

"We'd write to the newspapers and we'd go to the school board, and tell them they should support nature and be nice to animals. It's very boring with just blacktop. Children like the forest. They want animals, ponds, streams, things growing. We got the blacktop off so children could plant trees and bushes and all the things that nature has made up."

"We'd say put everything back or we'll strike the school. Kids would be bored all the time. They'd act real mad and bad, then be sad 'cause all the stuff was taken away. We'd forget what school we were at 'cause it would look like everywhere else."

"It would be a pretty stupid thing to do. 'Put it back,' we'd say. 'You should look at Washington as something special, a new thing for the world. Other schools need the same influence. To tear down the Yard is just to put yourself down. Us kids love the Yard. We do special things there. It's the only place like it. If you tear it down there'd be a riot. We're gonna hate you for life and it's the truth.'"

One fourth grader offered this extraordinary insight:

"Schools like Washington are good for the economy. Having a dirt area is really good for the economy 'cause kids learn lots of extra things there."

And this ultimate point, referring to children's rights:

"What right do you have to take it away?"

PERSISTENT NATURE

Five years later, a half-dozen members of the 1977 graduating class were reinterviewed about their strongest memories, now distilled by the passage of time—ten years in one case. The most common recollection was the "greening" process.

"To think it was plain cement all through, then as the years went by, it became all green. Now you can get lost in there. It's just incredible. When it first started, I remember walking around looking at all the construction and the plants beginning to sprout."

As in the earlier interviews, memories of plants, animals, and ponds were recalled repeatedly, along with other special things that helped explain the Yard's lasting impact. Specific places—where some form of social interaction or interaction with the environment took place—figured strongly.

"It was a good place for clubs because of all the little clearings that felt really private even though there was a path right next door."

"The bridge over the stream. We used to just lean over and watch the water flowing underneath. [photograph, p. 41]"

"The tunnel, bouncing balls around inside to see how far they could go up, and laying on our stomachs on top looking down at the people inside. [photograph, p. 66]"

"The stepping stones in the overgrown corner of the pond by the bamboo, jumping across from stone to stone."

"All the bushes. There were incredible games of tag throughout the whole Yard. They were almost like war or something. I

TWENTY YEARS LATER

The theme of peace and quality of life were reinforced twenty years later in follow-up interviews with two of the former students from the original interview group. It was fascinating to hear their vivid memories of the Yard as five- and six-year-olds. Here is a summary of their comments:

"I remember thinking, how could they possibly get rid of all that asphalt and return it to dirt?"

"I took it for granted. It was such a huge part of my childhood. It really was my childhood as we were there every day. I watched it grow. It feels as if we spent most of our time there, after school, playing there at weekends, independently. It felt as if we spent the whole summer there. It was just as much a community park as it was a playground. It was a good place for families from the neighborhood. It always felt safe there. I never felt scared. There were paths, but you never felt you had to stay on them. It was not like a regular garden with regimented rows of plants. You didn't have to worry about stepping on the grass. I remember picking blackberries. What I liked was that you could try out stuff there without getting into trouble. There were endless possibilities of things to do and places to play, not like going to the same structure day after day. It was continuously changing. It was really exciting to be confronted with a different environment every day. There was such a diversity of areas, you were never bored. It was a place where you could make leaf

stew or do whatever you wanted. I don't remember any adults being around at all in the nature part. I remember them on the asphalt yelling at you."

"I learned how to climb a tree, how to prune a tree."

"The natural part contrasted with the asphalt part, not only the material, but the character, the feeling of it. It was a place full of birds and greenery. You could lose yourself there. The hiding aspect was very important. There were so many possibilities in the natural area. You could feel like an animal. Sometimes you could hide just to be by yourself in your own micro-environment, your own little cell by yourself. It was a place where you could get away, even though it was right there at the school. I never remember hearing cars, even though the Yard was right beside the main road. It was a nice place to study in. Tranquil."

"People thought it was a neat place to play in, to hang out. It was like a nest, a comfortable place, like a big, overgrown backyard. It was different from any other place I have ever seen since. It was just a good place. It felt like compact countryside, not too wild, not neatly mown, an authentic landscape with its own special style."

"The water was sort of magical. The pump was very mysterious. Where did the water come from? Where did it go? It felt as if there was a big difference between the two ponds, much more than in reality. The water seemed very precious as there was a drought in California at the

time. We felt privileged to have ponds. I remember observing the fish a lot, watching the water skaters. They were fascinating to us children because they looked like they were ice skating. Small insects were everywhere, under rocks and logs; there was quite a hum there sometimes. The animal and plant life were really an important part of the children's play. I don't kill bugs, not even spiders. I know that has a direct correlation to the Yard, because we learned how to respect all the life there. As an adult, I would call myself ecologically concerned. I'm sure that Washington School influenced me as we were exposed to environmental issues very early in life."

"We used to have an aquarium on our table in the classroom—it was like the Yard coming inside with us. We really observed plant and animal life on a daily basis. We took care of everything and

wrote about it in our journals, and made up stories.

"It was an easy way to explain to children about the environment, having it there right in front of everyone. You could explain how things work, how babies grow."

"The Yard was really an inspiring place to write poetry. You could talk about your surroundings and you automatically had a poem! I was really motivated. Without the Yard it would have been a lot harder, maybe impossible."

"I don't remember any kids fighting. It was not an aggressive type of environment. It was very peaceful, but you know, exciting at the same time for a child.

"Kids respected it. I never saw anyone defacing it."

"It just doesn't compare to most playgrounds. When you see them you ask yourself, who could design something so harsh and minimal?"

remember we'd always wear green clothes for camouflage. There were always nice places to duck into, go under, or over, or around."

"The curvy wall next to the school building. It had a little tunnel and a bench you could sit on and have lunch there. I used to call it a 'train' and try to balance along it—yeah, I walked a lot on fences. I remember one time trying to get from one side of the Yard to another without touching the ground."

"The big rock where all the paths met."

"The big cactus [century plant] on the hill. I can remember the big thorns we used to pick off and throw at each other."

"We loved picking the blackberries and eating them. I remember being surprised to find out about all the edible plants around. And I remember all the different smells of plants and just the musty smell of nature. One time we had to go out blindfolded with a friend and guess what different things were by touch and smell. The yard of the school I go to now smells terrible, oily, and artificial, and covered with bubble gum."

Memories of animal life remained vivid—small everyday insects and birdlife as well as the special animal events.

"There was a cool spot back in the far corner where you could turn logs over and find salamanders, slugs, and snails. We always liked catching salamanders. We'd play with them for a little while and then let them go. We just watched the snails. Sometimes we liked to look for cocoons and hunt ladybugs in the long grass."

"I remember watching the pigs and feeding the goats when the garden was a farm. The mother goat used to run all over the Yard."

"We spent a lot of time with animals. Once we found a pigeon whose foot was hurt and when it got better we let it go."

"I used the wildlife as background when I made up stories about the Yard."

The one place everyone remembered was the Gazebo, "with a pointed roof and four posts keeping it up. There was a ladder at the back where you could climb up to a loft to talk and have lunch or read in a private place. It was high up so you could see into the trees." Its unusual shape ("a funny loft thing like a half pyramid laying on its side") gave it a strong visual identity against the background of meadow and trees.

Another fascinating spot was "the pair of carriage wheels up on a hill that looked like old pioneers used to be there or something. I used to imagine big groups of people traveling in carriages like a wagon train." Another student remembered it as a "most magical place. I used to sit there and daydream. I pretended I was riding in the carriage and was a duke or prince, something fancy like that. One time I was dreaming so much, I didn't hear the bell ring, and I was five minutes late for class."

To most adults, except to the most discriminating and understanding, the carriage wheels looked like a piece of junk or a relic, certainly not a plaything (or "learnthing"). Yet students remembered it as one of the most potent, memorable spots in the landscape. Its unusual character helped create a place where a child's mind could roam free in an infinite landscape of imagination.

Special events were well remembered—again, especially where there was a strong interaction with the setting.

"I remember an experiment we did by throwing dry ice into the pond. It made it look like the water was boiling and gushing steam. It was weird."

"One of the best things I remember was making little huts from pieces of tree, which we slept over in, when we had rabbit barbecue."

The feelings most strongly remembered about the Yard were those of independence and caring—an interesting combination that boosted self-esteem.

"I really felt free and peaceful where it was all watery and wild. It made me feel all grown up and that I could take care of myself in the woods. I liked to feel the independence of just wandering through the trees and crawling under bushes. I got scratched up and fell into streams. But I liked being able to know what to do with a scratch instead of waiting for someone to come and pick me up. You could either wash it off right there in the stream or walk all the way over to the school to see the nurse."

"We felt it was our responsibility to take care of the Yard, to make it stay well. Everyone thought it was important to have a place where you could do a lot of things. It brought the whole school together. It was like a focal point. It felt like just ours. Everyone could point to something and say, 'I helped do that.' I still do when I go there now."

These former Washington students had reached an age where they were able to articulate and reflect on their special educational experiences with the Yard.

"It never seemed like regular school. You felt that you were learning lots of things besides just reading, writing, and arithmetic. We practiced them in Yard projects, but we didn't just learn one thing. It was a more balanced education that taught me a lot more about the environment, something that is still very important to me. I learned a certain respect for trees, grass, water, and wild animals. When kids were trying to throw rocks at the turtle, I remember I got

As adults, the children remembered places that were designed to be all "watery and wild."

NATURAL LEARNING

The Yard was a place to be together, to learn about the environment, and to have fun!

real mad, and me and a friend tried to force them out of the Yard. Now I don't litter. I'm very careful about where I put my garbage. And every time I see an animal run over or a kid smashing plants I feel awful inside. Every time I see animals I see them in a different way. I don't say, 'Ah, look at that cute animal.' I say, 'Those are part of a food chain. They're not here for our amusement. They're here because they have to be.'"

"With the Yard it wasn't just a one-sided education. It had a balance that many schools lack. If every school had a yard like that there would be a lot less problems with pollution and a lot more awareness of the environment. I can't really tell what the long-term effects will be. But the short-term effect was a lot less fighting. There was only one, maybe two, fights I remember. It was an incredible change. At other schools there's fights all over the place."

"The other lucky thing was the enthusiastic teachers. If you get one who says, 'Environmental Yard: blu-u-u-uh!' it's failed right away. It's no good. But we had all these great teachers who liked going outdoors. I just loved it. It was unforgettable."

Daily access to diverse, outdoor environments allowed these children to have many long-lasting, meaningful learning experiences that were a critical part of their healthy development, in some cases influencing their whole philosophy of life.

The absolutely fundamental point expressed in various ways by all the children was the motivational impact of the "hidden curriculum" or the message that Washington communicated through its physical environment, especially to the "at-risk" population. The positive impact of a humane environment on the learning process was tremendous.

"At Washington I never felt I was being kept at school. I felt lucky to be there. It was a place to be creative. Whatever you wanted to do, you could find some way to make it happen. It gave me a totally different view of school. It changed everything. It opened up a different part of the world I didn't know existed. It made me want to learn. I learned a lot."

PLAYFUL, EDUCATIVE FUN

Children use the word "fun" in many ways and in many contexts. In talking about the Yard, they seemed to use it as a synonym for playful—describing a particular quality of experience. The result of fun was that children felt good about themselves, their friends, and their school; in other words, a positive affect.

The absence of playing and learning is boredom. It extracts high costs in missed opportunities, with children growing up without fulfilling their potential. Boredom is not generally considered a significant social disease, yet some of its crippling symptoms, like high drop-out rates, drugs, and antisocial behavior, are issues of national concern. Boredom presents a great barrier to individual development, self-esteem, and social integration. Bland, hard surfaces breed boredom and animosity. They injure body and spirit.

Diversity of environment banishes boredom, supports each child's personality and skill, and provides essential opportunities for learning through playful exploration and manipulation of the environment. Diversity generates fun! As the Yard evolved, symptoms of boredom and alienation disappeared.

"The Yard is so much fun. We learn lots of things there. There are lots of things to play with. We catch fish and put 'em back. We pretend we're in a jungle. You can play tag, swing, and play house in the trees. It's really nice like a country place, a natural place, with ponds you can throw things into. It's fun to float things down the river and to bust dams."

Adults so often look at fun as somehow devaluing the learning process, as if education should be completely serious all the time. Yet it is happy times that people of all ages remember best. Happy, laughing faces are such a powerful general symbol of well-being, why not of education?

"It's like a gym, fun, playful, real active, groovy, out of sight, fantastic. I love it!" Picture this laughing child describing "jumping across streams . . . playing rock games [hopping from one rock to another without falling off] . . . spying on people we hate, people that tease . . . playing tag where there's lots of bushes to hide behind."

Having fun from the child's point of view was not necessarily being extrovert. It could also mean quiet, pensive, slow, wandering activity.

"It's really fun to explore the little paths. We used to go on trips and look at things . . . hunt bugs . . . collect rocks . . . discover places we didn't know about . . . It was like a maze."

Fun is often shared with others, with best friends or with the whole community.

"I like it when we have festivals and everyone comes to have a good time. We set up stalls and sell stuff we've made at school and invent games for people to play. We sell plants from the garden."

Having fun invariably focused on interaction with the environment. Often some form of manipulable "play

ENVIRONMENTAL AWARENESS

The children who spent their time in the Natural Resource Area expressed greater environmental awareness. They attended to natural events happening around them—animal life, seasonal changes, and the impact of weather, for example. They were more innovative in their play and less likely to allow themselves to be governed by rules or conventional dictates of the physical environment. They indulged in more fantasy play using objects that were readily available in the environment.

The most enthusiastic children interacted extensively with the natural environment outside of school. Some had lived in the country or went on camping trips with their families. Some liked vegetation and had a favorite tree at home, while some had gardens or parents who gardened. Others were fascinated with animals. For these children whose families valued the natural environment, the Yard provided opportunities for in-depth investigation that reinforced already well-developed environmental values. Environmental education was the connecting agent.

prop" was used. The most powerful were animals, small and large.

"The most fun thing that ever happened was the time we had pigs, goats, and chickens here."

PEACE

Peace is fundamental to the survival of the human species. The Washington students provided powerful testimony concerning the peaceful relationships brought about by the naturalized environment.

"We've learned so much more than we would have with just cement. It helps kids learn to get on with each other, makes them good with each other. "There was more fighting over things before, because there was not so much stuff. It was all bare. Just ball courts, bars, and cement. It was easy to slip and fall and hurt yourself. There's not so many knee injuries now because there's not so much asphalt. If you fall now it's not likely that you'll fall on something that really hurts . . . You won't get all scratched up."

"They would fight if they didn't have anything to play with. We've grown attached to it since we came to this school and watched the trees grow bigger and all the animals coming around."

"There used to be fights over the bars but the pressure's off now. There's not so many arguments and maybe only about ten big fights a year when somebody gets hurt. People get bored when there's nothing to do, and they get irritable and cranky. When some-

one asks you something, you're rude. You say, 'Get outta here!' And then a fight can start. It's dangerous to fight on asphalt; you can easily fall down and crack your skull. When you have dirt you don't fight so much 'cause you can do other things."

"Nature makes kids good with each other."

"Here kids learn you can't push other people around."

•

The comments of the Washington students about their naturalized schoolyard clearly indicate the long-term benefits to individual development, to social integration, and to the growth of deeply embedded environmental values. There is a sense here of a collective responsibility of children as future adults to care for each other as they care for planet Earth. This is illustrated by the comments of one the children who took part in the time capsule project in 1976.

"There's a time capsule we buried out there in the redwood grove, full of things we did this year. In the year 2000, whoever remembers is supposed to go there and get it. So on New Year's Day 2000, I'll be out there waiting to dig it up with other people from my class."

CHAPTER 17 # Call for Action!

In many parts of the world, urban children are facing unprecedented challenges to their quality of life. These challenges mirror dramatic new realities: urban poverty; parental unemployment; diminishing outdoor play opportunities; physically toxic environments; socially toxic environments (including child abuse and continuous exposure to violence through television, movies, and electronic toys); and diminished government funding in education, childcare, the arts, leisure, recreation, and basic social welfare.

Negative consequences of these trends are increasingly falling on the shoulders of our children. On their own, they are powerless to resist. However, the most important international treaty of the century is available to help: the *U.N. Convention on the Rights of the Child* (CRC).[1] Child advocates now have a powerful legal framework for protecting and enhancing children's standing in society and for improving their quality of life.

THE CHALLENGE OF POST-INDUSTRIAL CHILDHOOD

In our post-industrial developed world, the childhood scourges of communicable diseases and malnutrition have been conquered and education is universally accessible. Many developing countries are making impressive progress towards these ends, although in the least developed countries far too many children—especially girls—still lack the basic necessities of life, including access to education.[2]

The struggle for social and environmental justice has without doubt moved forward in the last several decades; however, the industrially developed world is now confronting new negative trends. Pockets of "Third World" conditions are reappearing in some countries. In addition, children in many parts of the world are being impacted by negative social trends, as documented by James Garbarino in his book, *Raising Children in a Socially Toxic Environment*.[3] The long-term social, cultural, and psychological consequences of these trends to society are as yet unclear. We know that young people are in trouble, but we pay little attention to their welfare. This is especially so in the United States, which at the time of writing stands arrogantly apart, under the moral gaze of the rest of the world, as the only major nation that has not ratified the CRC. The United States appears to be changing from a child-centered society to a child-controlling one.

The cumulative negative effect of long-standing social inequalities on the development of children in the United States, and the lack of effective policies to redress them, has been persuasively presented by Sylvia Ann Hewlett in *When the Bough Breaks: The Cost of Neglecting Our Children* and by the National Commission on Children in its final report, *Beyond Rhetoric: A New American Agenda of Children and Families*.[4] These reports, coupled with others such as David Elkind's *The Hurried Child: Growing Up Too Fast Too Soon*,[5] present an alarming diagnosis of the negative impact of childhood stresses resulting from rapidly changing lifestyles and technological change. In spite of the mounting evidence, we continue to cast aside the needs of our children.

Children born today have the same genetic inheritance as their ancestors did thousands of years ago. As it has always been, environmental quality makes an overwhelming difference in their developmental potential. Some children thrive and reach this potential, while others wither into dysfunctional individuals because their natural endowment never received appropriate stimulation, love, care, and attention during the critical early years.

Educators, planners, designers, and child advocates must join forces more closely than ever before to help reverse these trends. Following are proposed priorities to stimulate and guide action.

ACTIVATING CHILDREN'S ENVIRONMENTAL RIGHTS

We must use the CRC as a key moral weapon in the fight to improve the quality of children's environments. Brought into force in 1990, the CRC has received almost universal ratification by the world's nations. The forty-one articles of Part One include the rights to basic needs for survival such as nutrition, clean water, and shelter; the right to an identity (to have a name and nationality); and the rights to education, freedom of thought, and individual expression. Particularly relevant here are Article 29, which addresses the aims of education, and

Article 31, which addresses the right to play, leisure, culture, and the arts.

The Convention provides a comprehensive framework for action that can be interpreted generally as applying to the quality of the child's environment, including the right of children to participate in making decisions that affect their surroundings (Article 12). The comments of Washington School students in the previous chapter present a clear and substantial statement about the responsibility of child-related institutions—especially schools—to respond to the CRC, to ensure that children develop in a high-quality, natural environment.

RECONNECTING CHILDREN AND NATURE

To learn to protect the biosphere, children must have daily access to its basic elements (sun, soil, water, air, vegetation, and animals). Without continuous hands-on primary experience, it is impossible for children to acquire a deep intuitive understanding of the natural world that is the foundation of sustainable development. Many years ago, John Dewey identified this as hands-on learning in the natural environment:

> "No number of object-lessons, got up as object-lessons for the sake of giving information, can afford even the shadow of a substitute for acquaintance with the plants and animals of the farm and garden, acquired through actual living among them and caring for them." [6]

A critical aspect of the present-day crisis in education is that children are becoming separated from daily experience of the natural world, especially in larger cities. In *Childhood's Future,* Richard Louv notes the growing alienation of children from the natural world, a theme also addressed by Gary Nabhan and Stephen Trimble in *The Geography of Childhood: Why Children Need Wild Places* and by Robert Pyle in *The Thunder Tree.*[7] Reasons include the indoor appeal of television and electronic games, the destruction of nearby nature, traffic danger, and parental fear. Louv cites as a principal cause the "bogeyman syndrome" (the parental fear that children who play out of sight, outdoors, will be attacked or abducted)—a distorted urban myth perpetuated by the mass media and overzealous parent organizations.

CRC Article 29
Aims of education

States Parties agree that the education of the child shall be directed to:

(a) The development of the child's personality, talents and mental and physical abilities to their fullest potential;

(b) The development of respect for human rights and fundamental freedoms, and for the principles enshrined in the Charter of the United Nations;

(c) The development of respect for the child's parents, his or her own cultural identity, language and values, for the national values of the country in which the child is living, the country from which he or she may originate, and for civilizations different from his or her own;

(d) The preparation of the child for responsible life in a free society, in the spirit of understanding, peace, tolerance, equality of sexes, and friendship among all peoples, ethnic, national and religious groups and persons of indigenous origin;

(e) The development of respect for the natural environment.

Unofficial Summary: Education shall aim at developing the child's personality, talents and mental and physical abilities to the fullest extent. Education shall prepare the child for an active adult life in a free society and foster respect for the child's parents, his or her own cultural identity, language and values, and for the cultural background and values of others.

CRC article 31
Leisure, recreation and cultural activities

States Parties recognize the right of the child to rest and leisure, to engage in play and recreational activities appropriate to the age of the child and to participate freely in cultural life and the arts.

States Parties shall respect and promote the right of the child to participate fully in cultural and artistic life and shall encourage the provision of appropriate and equal opportunities for cultural, artistic, recreational and leisure activity.

Unofficial Summary: The child has the right to leisure, play and participation in cultural and artistic activities.

— *Extracts from the Convention on the Rights of the Child, adopted by the U.N. General Assembly November 20, 1989*

Rationally speaking, cars are a far more serious problem, claiming roughly twenty times more children's lives in the United States than abduction does.[8]

In response to these issues, Louv calls for the creation of child-friendly neighborhoods and cites the few examples in the United States and Europe, where "traffic calming," "design for pedestrians," and "urban greening" have been used to improve the experiential quality of the neighborhood environment for children.[9] A massive lobby is needed to speak on behalf of children to advocate their environmental rights with passion and conviction. Children themselves need to be involved in the political process. In many countries, this educational imperative is well underway.[10]

CREATING NEIGHBORHOODS FOR LEARNING

Most of the world's children live in close-knit communities in villages, towns, and small cities.[11] Children's quality of life is directly affected by the physical content and quality of the local environment.[12] In *Ready to Learn: A Mandate for the Nation*, Ernest Boyer, of the Carnegie Foundation for the Advancement of Teaching, advocates the re-creation of child-friendly neighborhoods, recognizing them as children's primary territory for learning and play.[13] He points to the many innovative play spaces and learning settings that have been developed in the last fifty years in Europe and the United States. There now exists a battery of nonformal education settings that have withstood the test of time (adventure playgrounds, city farms, ecological parks, children's museums, children's gardens, etc.) to make urban neighborhoods more child-centered and child-friendly.[14]

Improvement of school sites is a key strategy. These settings must be recognized as a potential educational resource during school hours, as well as a "safe haven" offering children a secure, engaging environment outside school hours. When formal classes are over, children need a nonformal curriculum of playful, creative activity, free play, and informal learning to enhance their development.

THE "MIDDLE WAY"

The exciting discovery we made was that the Yard provided for a new "middle way" of teaching and learning, integrating formal, informal, and nonformal domains of education. Many children, we discovered, learn best by combining these domains.

Informal education includes all learning, both good and bad, that results from children's daily interactions with the social and physical environment of family, home, neighborhood, playground, and experiences farther afield.

Children's free play is the mainstay of informal education. It provides a motivating force in the learning process. Springing from within, in response to freely discovered external stimuli, play is a natural, universal endowment of young humans as it is with many other species. Free play arouses children's innate curiosity, motivating them to actively learn. The problem is that many urban children do not have access to ecologically valid play spaces where interactions with the natural world are possible. The Yard provided an explorable, playful environment with enough complexity so that children continued to make discoveries there day after day. Discovery, by its very nature, is empowering. The child discovers and understands, feels competent, and acquires a sense of belonging. To play means to engage in harmonious discourse with one's surroundings, neither dominating them nor being dominated by them.

Good teachers recognize that playful environments can excite children and capture their interest. Play stimulates the desire to learn. The Yard allowed teachers to connect the motivational power of play to the formal curriculum, thus offering students a powerful vehicle for arousing their natural curiosity—their "sensory nature," as Johann Heinrich Pestalozzi called it.[15]

Formal education is what we usually associate with schools—lessons delivered to children, in classrooms, by teachers. The Yard was an attempt to broaden this narrow view. Like Dewey, we saw schools as institutions with a broad social mission. He conceived education as "a process of living," as "a continuing reconstruction of experience," and not just a preparation for the future.[16] He pleaded for a balanced pedagogy matching societal needs to produce useful, well-adjusted citizens while also respecting the interests and innate endowments of each individual.

Nonformal education provides the bridge between the informal and formal modes of education. At Washington School, the bridge's superstructure was the Yard. Nonformal education applies to learning that occurs in settings outside of formal classrooms. Examples are noted on the previous page and include many of the Yard's close relations.

Countries such as Sweden, Denmark, the Netherlands, Germany, and the United Kingdom have well-developed nonformal education centers. Staffed by professional playworkers, animators, or social pedagogues, the centers serve out-of-school children and youth. We attempted to replicate aspects of these models by establishing programs run by resource people from the community, including university students. These efforts extended use of the Yard beyond weekday school hours, to include weekends and the summer. Community events such as the annual Yardfest became an integral part of these offerings.

Nonformal activities linked school classrooms and the Yard curriculum with other nonformal educational spaces and educators in the community, including many parents with professional expertise. Activities included day trips to museums, ice cream factories, experimental gardens, farms, sewage facilities, and nature centers (see map, page 216). Overnight camping and hiking trips included socialization objectives that could not be accommodated by the time constraints of normal lesson plans.

Special pedagogical value lay in the wide range of learning processes the Yard offered, including field observation; discrimination of sensory attributes; collecting; sorting; classification; record keeping; enumeration; verbal description, library investigation, analysis, and evaluation; selection and presentation of information; and many more. The behavioral diversity supported by the Yard reflected the wide range of particular strengths, abilities, and special aptitudes of the students (who surely were no different from students at other schools, but unlike them, had more opportunities for free expression).

PROMOTING A BALANCED PEDAGOGY

By balanced pedagogy, we mean one that redresses the need of the state to produce useful members of society with the need of individuals to develop as whole persons. Dewey pleaded for this many years ago as a basis for educational reform. For him, children were the agents of cultural transmission, not adults. Childhood was a special culture. To retain its creative vitality, culture had to be carried forth by children through interactions with the physical world:

> "We live from birth to death in a world of persons and things which in large measure is what it is because of what has been done and transmitted from previous human activities. When this is ignored, experience is treated as if it were something which goes on exclusively inside an individual's body and mind . . .
>
> "A primary responsibility of educators is that they not only be aware of the general principle of shaping the actual experience by environing conditions, but that they also recognize . . . what surroundings are conducive to . . . experiences that lead to growth. Above all, they should know how to utilize the surroundings, physical and social, that exist so as to extract from them all that they have to contribute to building up experiences that are worthwhile."[17]

Dewey insisted, furthermore, that effective educational experiences should follow the principles of *continuity* and *interaction* with learning situations. He called these the "longitudinal" and "lateral" aspects of experience.[18] For him, interaction and situation were inseparable. Educational experience is always the result of transactions between children, adults, physical objects, and surroundings. All coact in the learning process that he called "dynamic quality, the developing force inherent in the child's present experience."[19] For Dewey, "everything depends on the quality of the experience" in this coaction.[20]

The principle of continuity recognizes that the child lives in a single, unified world, and that the learning gained from experience in one situation must be carried over and applied in the next (the "learning cycle" described in Chapter 18). The Yard provided such a unified, experiential world. Because the space was a continuous natural environment, it accommodated a high degree of interactive exploration and discovery that could be continuously reapplied at several levels of cognitive development.

The theoretical framework presented by Robin Hodgkin in *Playing and Exploring* suggests that when children use spaces with a rich, natural diversity, their "potential space" of creativity and imagination (Donald Winnicott's concept) will be enriched.[21] Teachers who have retained the capacity of visiting their own "potential space" are able to engage with children through play and facilitate their progress from intuitive to conscious learning, assisting them along the difficult road of acquiring competence and maturity.

When applied to natural learning resources, the theories of Dewey and Hodgkin suggest that teacher training in interdisciplinary environmental education is a primary need. This would add immense power to present-day educational missions—from basic competencies to sustainable development.

PATHWAYS TO EMPOWERMENT

Children need educational settings that immerse them in a feeling of ownership of their learning process. To be motivated to learn, children must feel that they are discovering their own path, with the teacher working with them to ensure the path has continuity and educational value (as Dewey insisted), as well as familiarity, mystery, and discovery of the unknown emphasized by Hodgkin.[22]

Children are individuals with particular strengths, abilities, styles of learning, types of intelligence, and special aptitudes. The notion that different types of children learn through different types of processes was made clear in the Yard as the range of learning settings and instructional strategies expanded. Many successes were reported of individual children whose learning styles were not well adapted to the indoor classroom. They were attracted to the Yard because of its hands-on orientation and its robust, complex environment. Body language that was inappropriate indoors was perfectly acceptable outdoors.

Lawrence Kohlberg's writings were also an important source of guidance, as they were rooted in a developmental philosophy that integrated the earlier thinking of Dewey and the discoveries of Jean Piaget, who both insisted that mature thought develops from interaction between child and environment. In his *Philosophy of Moral Education*, Kohlberg restates the experiential role, holding that "education should nourish children's natural interaction with society and environment . . . through a progression of . . . sequential stages . . . [with] the goal of eventual attainment of a higher level or stage of development in adulthood, not merely the healthy functioning of the child at a present level." For Kohlberg, this requires "an educational environment that actively stimulates development through the presentation of resolvable but genuine problems . . . The organizing and developing force in the child's experience is the child's active thinking, and thinking is stimulated by the problematic . . . ." Kohlberg sees the "acquisition of knowledge as an active *change in patterns of thinking* (authors' emphasis) brought about by experiential problem-solving situations."[23]

Kohlberg's ideas made a key contribution to the educational philosophy of the Yard, linking experience, thought, and ethics. His proposal that the "development of logical and critical thought . . . finds its larger meaning in a broad set of moral values" applied readily to the Yard. Because of its diversity of interactions, Kohlberg's stages of moral development were used to interpret child-Yard relations, ranging from "Stage 1, punishment and obedience" to "Stage 6, universal ethical principles."[24]

Like Kohlberg, we struggled to adapt and broaden the prevailing "cultural transmission" philosophy of education, not so much to circumvent its mandated objectives, but to adapt them to a new type of educational environment.

Inspired by Kohlberg, we recognized the impossibility of formally educating children for a future that cannot be predicted with certainty. We saw our educational task as providing children with the active knowledge to celebrate uncertainty and unpredictability, and to confront them with confidence and creativity. The children's varied response to the expanded range of learning settings and instructional strategies reinforced the notion of varied learning styles (described by Bernice McCarthy) and multiple intelligences (enumerated by Howard Gardner).[25, 26] Although the formative bases of learning style differences are not well understood, both genetic inheritance and environment are influential; in other words, learning styles are in part learned traits in the individual that can be modified or expanded through pedagogical action. The Yard was a flexible means for doing this. Activities could be carried out in parallel or assigned to groups of students, always with the possibility of modification to match changes in individual motivations. Because the Yard was not rigidly bounded, activity formats could be modified at will.

The Yard especially provided a vehicle for nurturing children's creativity and supported the personal attributes that Robert Sternberg and Todd Lubart consider crucial to creativity in children and adults. They include tolerance for ambiguity ("green," middle-mode learning), willingness to take risks (open environment with many choices for action, adapted to many types of children), intrinsic motivation (stimulated by informal play), and motivation to excel (supported again by diversity of choice). Sternberg and other students of creativity highlight the significance of experiential learning environments that stimulate innovation (doing something different) and that tolerate mistakes (unpredicted results).[27] In such environments, like the Yard, mistakes become learning opportunities for further exploration and discovery. This notion of creativity seems closely aligned to concepts of intrinsic motivation presented by Mihaly Csikszentmihalyi and the "natural intelligence" annunciated by Howard Gardner.[28,29]

The creativity of the Yard gave Washington School teachers many opportunities to help children become more flexible and creative, providing them with the wisdom to deal with the increasing variety of environments encountered in a lifetime. Even though individual children were better adapted to one style than to another, our observations indicated that children could learn to operate in more than one learning style according to the type of setting and to the task or problem before them. The Yard helped concrete thinkers to be more abstract, active thinkers to be more reflective, and so on. Yard observations indicated indeed that learning styles can be developed through pedagogical action.

CRC ARTICLE 12

The child's opinion

States Parties shall assure to the child who is capable of forming his or her own views the right to express those views freely in all matters affecting the child, the views of the child being given due weight in accordance with the age and maturity of the child.

For this purpose, the child shall in particular be provided the opportunity to be heard in any judicial and administrative proceedings affecting the child, either directly, or through a representative or an appropriate body, in a manner consistent with the procedural rules of national law.

Unofficial Summary: **The child has the right to express his or her opinion freely and to have that opinion taken into account in any matter or procedure affecting the child.**

Flexible outdoor spaces are empowering. In this domain, children have the feeling of collaborating with the extraordinary restorative power of nature. They have further opportunities to work cooperatively; for the more skilled to assist the less skilled and for children with different learning styles to work more closely together. Instead of wasting time and energy trying to control individual students' body language, teachers are able to devote their full attention to individualized instruction and the facilitation of child-to-child activity.

CHILD-TO-CHILD

One of the most rewarding aspects of the Yard was to see the ease with which child-to-child learning was accommodated. The child-to-child concept, developed originally in the United Kingdom during the 1970s, has been used as a major educational strategy in countries where teachers are in short supply. In the Yard, child-to-child strategies helped to stretch limited adult teacher resources as well as to provide qualitative educational advantages. By facilitating communication between students and contact with each other's experiences and discoveries, teachers were able to encourage the natural proclivity of children to cooperate, to help each other apply the results of their learning.

The flexible open environment of the Yard offered many play-stimulated opportunities for mutual assistance, with the more skilled assisting the less skilled. Children with different learning styles could work more closely together than was possible in physically constrained classroom settings. The wider range of group settings provided more opportunities for intense cooperative learning.

IMPROVING SCHOOL GROUNDS

Those involved in childhood education must focus attention on the environmental quality of the whole school site—indoors and outdoors. The first requirement of a living, resilient environment is diversity. In the construction of many schools, the natural diversity of the site is more often than not bulldozed away to create space for buildings and sports fields. Granted, this is a practical requirement of the educational program. The

problem is that the topsoil, streams, flora, and fauna are rarely restored because they are not considered to have educational or social value. As a result, the new school site is a barren, degraded environment, thinly grassed, devoid of trees, and surrounded by metal, prisonlike fencing and asphalt parking lots. To avoid this, the planning guidelines for school development must be expanded in scope to include environmental quality as a high priority. Such an instrument would help school administrators in their struggle to replace monocultures of asphalt, mown grass, and chainlink fencing with more adequate educational settings.

The institutional context of education is the controlling factor that ultimately aids or hinders success in developing on-site natural resources. Species selection, tree planting, and technical aspects of landscape establishment are easy to accomplish compared to the development of an interdisciplinary environmental curriculum—which is still outside the educational mandate of most states. This makes it difficult to expand the scope of responsibility beyond the professional commitment of teachers who are attracted because of their personal values and educational philosophy. Parents become motivated for the same reasons, reflecting personal values and a strong desire to improve the school environment for their children.

The tightening accountability in public education and the continuing search for viable solutions point towards the school site as a challenge worthy of our labors. It is perhaps a good time in communities seeking long-term educational reform to respond to the crisis in childhood and youth by creating habitable, empowering school environments. It is an appropriate place to start, since young people are legally required to spend so much of their lives there.

At the same time, there are barriers to overcome. Many school systems are rigidly controlled by central authorities overly sensitive to public pressure. Much faith has been placed, for example, on meeting standardized test score targets, no matter how much research shows that they are not valid.[30] Unshakable belief in these procedures continues to serve a top-down model of management and decision making. Heavy-handed administrative styles still get in the way of worthwhile innovation and make teachers feel insecure.

Intuitively, many teachers believe they must involve the "whole child" if not the "whole family" in the educational process, but they confront the prevalent "back-to-basics" focus whose proponents complain that the child's time is being wasted by "peripheral activities." Our challenge is to demonstrate that the "peripherals" of diverse outdoor learning spaces and interdisciplinary curricula are equally "basic." If they are included, back-to-basics strategies will become more effective for more children.

FINDING ALLIES

In pushing for a broadening of the curricular scope in public education, the results of educational research are bright lights on the horizon. An ambitious beginning was the *Eight Year Study: Adventure in American Education*, completed in 1940.[31] Although this study focused on secondary education, it offers several key indicators for progressive elementary education. These, and findings from other research, address critical issues such as cognitive ability, thinking styles, motivation, creativity, interdisciplinary education, cooperative learning strategies, humanistic psychology, and the importance of the "sense of place" in education (which the Yard demonstrated). There is much support for a progressive education action agenda focused on the environment and the arts, which over the years have progressively become marginalized in public education—in the United States at least.

In countries such as Sweden, France, Belgium, and the Netherlands, major national initiatives have been taken to improve the condition of schoolyards as educational resources. The United Kingdom has made major advances through the Learning Through Landscapes Trust. Similar initiatives are underway in Canada through the Evergreen Foundation, and in Sweden, through *Skolans Uterum* (Schoolyards Unlimited). In the United States, several states have launched school site rehabilitation programs. The City of Boston, Massachusetts, has a citywide schoolyard initiative. The Institute for Ecosystem Studies has developed sites in both North and South America. The National Wildlife Federation has started a schoolyard habitat development program. The momentum seems to be growing.[32]

However, the vast majority of these actions have been led by private individuals, committed school principals, private organizations, and environmental professionals, rather than the educational establishment. This means that the results are highly vulnerable once the organizers move on. To achieve long-term change and continuity, a more substantial institutional base of enablement and leadership must be created. The educational establishment must become committed to interdisciplinary environmental education through state and local partnerships with universities and community organizations. Above all, interdisciplinary environmental education must be integrated into the training of teachers, not as a separate subject but as an educational mission, as a way of teaching, and as a type of educational environment. Until this happens, progress will be limited to the achievements of a few dedicated teachers, working essentially outside the system.

CHILDREN'S PARTICIPATION IN CURRICULAR REFORM

The CRC states that children have a right to a voice in decisions that affect their lives. What better exercise of this right than participation by children in curricular reform. At first this may appear a silly idea, but in reviewing the participatory process through which the Yard-as-curriculum developed, it is not so far-fetched. As William Schubert notes, curricular development is a complex, conflictful process embedded in a context of political and social values, occurring formally and informally, involving both teachers and parents—but rarely with the participation of the subjects of reform themselves: the children.[33]

Because the Yard was a living, physical entity, it presented a magnificent opportunity for children to get involved in the reform process itself. The initial focus on positive, dramatic change eventually mimicked real life. The Yard merged dimensions of legitimate conflicts in nature and their proper resolution in a healthy educational environment. Through play, children became involved in this process and learned how to negotiate the impacts of conflicting forces. They experienced how laws are made, and how the focus of concern can move eventually from the individual to the collective interest. Taking advantage of these unplanned opportunities, teachers had to rethink their approach to curricular alignment (the difference between the stated intention and what is actually taught). They had to value as an *intention* the unpredictable results of intervention in a living environment.

This outcome reflected the work of noted leaders in education and psychology. Schubert, reinforcing earlier beliefs of Dewey, has articulated the notion that the influences of family, peers, and other out-of-school informal experiences are as influential in the development of the individual as those of formal education.[34] In this sense, the Yard provided a healthy environment where the merging of formal and informal experiences was made more possible for the child to manage than in traditional settings. By linking inside and outside environments, learning was facilitated among students who had difficulty excelling in the formal classroom. The outdoors stimulated positive development of their character.

Curricular reform must also accommodate the plural nature of contemporary childhood. In *Beyond IQ*, psychologist Robert Sternberg supports this notion by describing the processes of *adaptation, shaping*, and *selection* in relation to the child's environment.[35] For example, children in an extremely restricted or chaotic family situation are more likely to have difficulty adapting to the formal classroom. For their psychological health, these children inevitably attempt to shape their environment at school to compensate for experiential deprivation at home. Selecting a new environment is not a typical option for these children. The effects of their negative circumstances at home can be psychologically devastating unless they find a compensating environment at school.

In *Magical Child*, Joseph Chilton Pearce stresses the importance of imagination and play as critical survival strategies in helping children cope with growing up in stressful, dysfunctional environments.[36] James Garbarino refers to "socially toxic" environments as an increasing threat to childhood.[37] An interpretation of

Piaget's theory of the development of human intelligence suggests that children lose their capacity for coherent thought when overwhelmed by an emotional overload forced upon them by their external environment. For the economically deprived or culturally ignored child, this overload and inability to select, shape, or adapt to their environment increase. Encouraging play and creating a stimulating and interactive learning environment can provide children in these situations a greater opportunity to achieve academic success. The same strategy is relevant to children who are overly stressed by being pushed to achieve beyond their developmentally appropriate level in kindergarten or even in preschool. As Pearce notes, "Intelligence, like the body, can be injured or nurtured, stimulated or starved."[38]

A different issue relates to elementary-school students defined as "gifted and talented" who quickly learn how to feed information back to get high grades. There is some indication that when these students progress to middle school and are placed in novel situations requiring creative problem-solving skills, they often do not fare so well.[39] These children can also benefit from an open, diverse environment that they can select from and shape to stimulate the process of growth of their creative skills.

A healthy psyche is a predictor of later success. To be able to adapt, select, and shape environments the child must rely on creative capacities that draw on every facet of development: hands, head, heart, and interactions with peers. To teach only from the perspective of mental capacity can limit, rather than facilitate, academic growth.

ACCOMMODATING THE WHOLE CHILD

The indoors-only, 3-Rs view of the learning process is not education. It is a literacy/numeracy training program, teaching essential skills to those fortunate children whose learning styles are well adapted to narrowly defined, highly structured learning environments. But not all children fit this mold. Every class has its share of abused children, children from broken homes, children emotionally neglected from birth, as well as naturally high-spirited misfits sometimes erroneously labeled as "learning disabled." Respect and ingenuity are required to accommodate the varied learning styles of these children so that their development may also flourish.

Learning environments need to liberate rather than limit learning. Accessibility for children with physical disabilities is an obvious example of this issue. If a child using a wheelchair cannot physically enter a school because there is no accessible route, we do not blame the child. Instead, we upgrade the environment. The physical environment is the handicapping agent, not the child. This concept it is now taken for granted (helped enormously by the force of law) in the design of educational programs. The same conceptual blockbusting must now be applied to removing other, more subtle barriers to the learning process. Not all children learn effectively within the four walls of a classroom. Some feel just as powerless as the wheelchair user if the environment is structured in a way that denies them hands-on access to the content of learning. Alternatives are needed, especially outdoors.

Washington School reinforced the development of the "whole child" with an experiential philosophy incorporating nontraditional delivery systems. Classrooms functioned as unusually rich learning centers—their activities extending into the outdoors, where a broad variety of learning styles could be accommodated, where positive socialization was supported, and where children from a multi-ethnic community could freely interact and appreciate each other.

BUILDING ON BIOPHILIA

Children have a natural affinity towards nature. Dirt, water, plants, and small animals attract and hold children's attention for hours, days, even a lifetime—so eloquently portrayed by Robert Pyle.[40] This conclusion, drawn from observations of children over many years, supports the "biophilia hypothesis" of biologist E. O. Wilson, which suggests that humans are genetically programmed to be drawn to nature—not surprising, since we are an integral part of the natural system.[41]

Ask any group of adults to recall their most powerful memories of places where they played as children. Most often they will talk of basic natural elements: dirt, water, vegetation, and animals, rather than equipment made of invariant synthetic materials. Edward Reed makes a pow-

erful case for reasserting the necessity of primary experience in education (devalued by 300 years of Western epistemological tradition).[42] Louise Chawla's study of nature, poetry, and childhood memory suggests that the primary experiences most deeply embedded in the human psyche are things of nature—things that smell, that sound, that are sensitive to the touch, that have color, that move, that each day are different, and that constantly invite exploration and opportunities for discovery.[43]

Children are born curious. It is part of their genetic endowment, their pathway to learning. Investigation of the world always springs from this intrinsic motivation. You cannot tell children what to learn. They must discover it, driven by their own desire. This is the first step in progressive education. Adults can extend the scope by helping children move from intuitive knowledge to higher orders of thinking where knowledge is transposed into ideas, concepts, causes and effects—transferred eventually to other realms of future problem solving.

Science and the humanities must work hand in hand. Science is not everything. Without humanity it is a soul-less path. The greatest problems facing the human species at this point in history are not scientific or technological but moral. To survive, we must learn to work together, to achieve solidarity on a global scale. We are one species, living in a single biosphere: an incredibly resilient home, able to resist abuse and recover from damage. But not infinitely. Now the biosphere is failing to sustain itself—if we do not change our ways as a species we will suffer greatly. We must decide now, collectively, whether to steal resources from generations unborn or to create a sustainable future.

WORKING TOGETHER

The only way to address the issue of childhood environmental quality is through education—at all levels and in all forms. It is the only hope for a more healthy future for our children. We urge educators to grasp the firebrand of childhood environmental quality, holding it proudly aloft. Winning this marathon will require cunning and courageous creativity to circumvent inevitable roadblocks. Collaboration with equally motivated, risk-taking architects and landscape designers is also required.

The eventual professional prize is a rich learning opportunity—a rare gem in education that occurs only in isolated pockets. Like-minded individuals must voyage together looking for others in positions of power and moral influence who will lend support. In government, educators must look beyond the pervasive atmosphere of intimidation and anxiety to search out valuable "insider" allies who can resist "don't rock the boat" attitudes. Other allies can be found in both the environmental and experiential education movements, especially where the scope has been broadened to fully embrace the urban environment.

Our mission is to show the adult world that the future of the planet depends on a revolution in the way we educate our children—informally, formally, and non-formally. If we fail in this mission, now embodied in Agenda 21 from the 1992 United Nations Rio Conference on Environment and Development,[44] we fail Earth and rob future generations of their right to enjoy its generous bounty. We must counter opposing arguments not with tears but with moral reason. To hone our psychological stamina, we must develop a sense of solidarity with all those working for a sustainable future, especially youth.[45]

Success in education demands a pioneering, dauntless spirit, eventually rewarded by psychic fulfillment. In life, such a journey is hard to find. The key to success is to cultivate an inner-directedness towards the true purpose of childhood education. Overcoming bureaucratic inertia, political roadblocks, and the superficial diversions of other educational issues requires rigor, resourcefulness, persistence, and—most important of all—imagination. But here also is a warning. In the continuing struggle, we must be careful not to lose our humanity. We must be personally vigilant for insidious holier-than-thou attitudes, or feelings of self-pity and persecution that can easily stop others from listening to what we have to say.

•

Education holds the promise of escape from hedonistic, egocentric, present-centered lifestyles. Learning to love planet Earth must be part of the solution. Humans know what love is; of woman and man, of children, of favorite pet, of country. Now we must focus our love on our shared home in the universe that binds us together both in the present and in the future eons of generations to come. We must assume responsibility through a new social-environmental ethic, a new culture of care. All must learn to love, to dance, to write poetry, to imagine, to take risks, to create gardens, to plant trees, to make peace . . . to restore Earth.

REFERENCES

1. United Nations. (1989). *The Convention on the Rights of the Child.* New York: UNICEF.

2. UNICEF. (1996). *The State of the World's Children.* Oxford: Oxford University Press.

3. Garbarino, J. (1995). *Raising Children in a Socially Toxic Environment.* San Francisco: Jossey-Bass.

4. Hewlett, S. A. (1991). *When the Bough Breaks: The Cost of Neglecting Our Children.* New York: Basic Books.

   National Commission on Children (chaired by U.S. Senator John D. Rockefeller). (1991). *Beyond Rhetoric: A New American Agenda of Children and Families.* Washington, D.C.: U.S. Government Printing Office.

5. Elkind, D. (1981). *The Hurried Child: Growing Up Too Fast Too Soon.* Menlo Park, Calif.: Addison-Wesley.

6. Dewey, J. (1959). *Dewey on Education.* New York: Teachers College Press, 37.

7. Louv, R. (1990). *Childhood's Future.* Boston: Houghton Mifflin.

   Nabhan, G. P. and S. Trimble (1994). *The Geography of Childhood: Why Children Need Wild Places.* Boston: Beacon Press.

   Pyle, R. M. (1993). *The Thunder Tree: Lessons from an Urban Wildland.* New York: Houghton Mifflin.

8. Jambor, T. and R. C. Moore (1996). "Confronting the Bogeyman: Myths and Realities of the Risk to Children in Outdoor Play." In Guddemi, M., T. Jambor, and A. Skrupskelis, eds. *Play: An Intergenerational Experience.* Proceedings of the IPA/USA Conference. University of Alabama at Birmingham. August 24–27, 1995. Little Rock, Ark.: Southern Early Childhood Association.

9. Louv. *op. cit.*

10. Hart, R. (1997). *Children's Participation: The Theory and Practice of Involving Young Citizens in Community Development and Environmental Care.* London: Earthscan.

11. The best sources of information concerning the complex dynamics and state of global urbanization are the publications of the

International Institute of Environment and Development (IIED, 3 Endsleigh Street, London WCIH ODD, UK). See for example:

Environment and Urbanization, special issue on Future Cities and Habitat II, 8(1), April 1996.

Hardoy, J. and D. Satterhwaite. (1989). *Squatter Citizen: Life in the Urban Third World*. London: Earthscan.

12. Moore, R. C. (1987). *Childhood's Domain: Play and Place in Child Development*. Berkeley, Calif.: MIG Communications.

13. Boyer, E. L. (1991). *Ready to Learn: A Mandate for the Nation*. Princeton, N.J.: Princeton University Press.

14. Brett, A., R. C. Moore, and E. Provenzo. (1993). *The Complete Playground Book*. Syracuse, N.Y.: Syracuse University Press; Chapter 4: "Innovative Playgrounds—An International Survey."

    Westland, C. and J. Knight. (1982). *Playing, Living, Learning: A Worldwide Perspective on Children's Opportunity to Play*. State College, Pa.: Venture Publishing.

15. Gutek, G. L. (1991). *Education in the United States*. Needham Heights, Mass.: Allyn and Bacon, 72.

16. Dewey, J. (1959). *op. cit.*, 22, 27.

17. Dewey, J. (1963, first published 1938). *Experience and Education*. The Kappa Delta Pi Lecture Series. Collier Books edition. New York: Macmillan, 39–40.

18. Ibid., 44–45.

19. Dewey, J. (1959). *op. cit.*, 101.

20. Dewey, J. (1963). *op. cit.*, 27.

21. Hodgkin. R. A. (1985). *Playing and Exploring*. New York: Methuen, 23–27.

    Winnicott, D. W. (1971). *Playing and Reality*. New York: Basic Books, 102–3; Chapter 4: "The Place Where We Live."

22. Hodgkin. *op. cit.*

23. Kohlberg, L. (1981). *The Philosophy of Moral Education*. San Francisco: Harper and Row, 54.

24. Ibid., 17–18.

25. McCarthy, B. (1987). *The 4MAT System: Teaching to Learning Styles with Right/Left Mode Techniques*. Barnington, Ill.: Excel, Inc.

26. Gardner, H. (1993). *Multiple Intelligences: The Theory in Practice*. New York: Basic Books.

27. Sternberg, R. J. and T. I. Lubart (1995). *Defying The Crowd*. New York: Free Press, 205–31.

28. Csikszentmihalyi, M. (1975). *Beyond Boredom and Anxiety: The Experience of Play in Work and Games*. San Francisco: Jossey-Bass.

29. Interview with Howard Gardner. (1995). *Dimensions of Early Childhood*, 3(4), 5–7.

30. Gardner (1993). *op cit.*, 69–70.

31. Aikin, W. (1942). *The Story of the Eight Year Study*. New York: Harper and Bros.

    Yeomans, E. (1967). "Adventure in American Education: The Eight-Year Study, Then and Now." *The Independent School Bulletin*. February 1967, 12–20.

    See also comments in: Schubert, W. H. (1986). *Curriculum: Perspectives, Paradigm, and Possibility*. New York: Macmillan, 263–65.

32. See Appendix B for addresses.

33. Schubert, *op. cit.*, 160.

34. Ibid.

35. Sternberg, R. J. (1985). *Beyond IQ: A Triachic Theory of Human Intelligence*. Cambridge: Cambridge University Press, 49–52.

36. Pearce, J. C. (1977). *Magical Child: Rediscovering Nature's Plan for Our Children*. New York: E. P. Dutton; Chapter 15.

37. Garbarino. *op. cit.*

38. Pearce. *op. cit.*, 4.

39. Davis, M. and R. C. Moore (1993). *Education Through Design: The Middle School*. Raleigh, N.C.: North Carolina State University School of Design.

40. Pyle. *op. cit.*

41. Wilson, E. O. (1984). *Biophilia*. Cambridge: Harvard University Press.

    Kellert, S. R. and E. O. Wilson (1993). *The Biophilia Hypothesis*. Washington, D.C.: Island Press.

42. Reed, E. S. (1996). *The Necessity of Experience*. New Haven, Conn.: Yale University Press.

43. Chawla, L. (1994). *In the First Country of Places: Nature, Poetry, and Childhood Memory*. Albany, N.Y.: State University of New York Press.

44. United Nations. (1992). *Earth Summit: Agenda 21: The United Nations Programme of Action from Rio*. The final texts of agreements negotiated by governments at the United Nations Conference on Environment and Development (UNCED). Rio de Janeiro, Brazil. June 3–14, 1992. New York: U.N. Department of Public Information. Sales No. E.93.1.11.

45. Children's Task Force on Agenda 21. (1994). *Rescue Mission Planet Earth: A Children's Edition of Agenda 21*. London: Kingfisher Books. New York: Larousse Kingfisher Chambers.

Part IV:
Guidelines for Action

Beyond Classroom Walls

Interdisciplinary Environmental Education means using all senses, all subject areas, and all environments near and far (but especially those on the school grounds and in the neighborhood) as a central feature of the educational mission; that is, learning *through* the environment as well as learning *about* the environment—especially the places used by children in their daily lives.

At Washington, the curriculum evolved with the Yard. It embraced the physical resources of the school community: space, objects, materials, and tools. The Yard was the critical new ingredient, tailored to the needs of the school community, which had participated in its design. It allowed a diversity of people—children, teachers, parents, community members, and volunteers—to take part in the school's educational program. The teachers, of course, were the key actors in identifying the resources, developing the activities, and delivering the program. The Yard, a diversified environment rich in natural resources, it supported the experiential philosophy of the educational program. As a result, a broader, new interdisciplinary environmental education curriculum grew out of the existing base. The main focus was on learning both *through* the environment and *about* the environment.

Many teachers were interested in environmental education but lacked the necessary instructional tools. The first step was to convince them that the interdisciplinary learning process could be strengthened by extending it outdoors. Once they agreed, they became motivated to search for activity ideas.

The children led the way. In the first few days of Yard redevelopment, students were observed testing their strength and construction ingenuity. Children lifted heavy clods of dirt to build a fort; learned about animal behavior by watching ants haul bread crumbs back to their nest; improvised their own "appropriate technology" by using sharp sticks to dig holes in the ground; adapted milk cartons to transport water; used rocks, bottle caps, seed pods, and small toys to make miniature landscapes interwoven with dramatic tales; and so on.

These spontaneous activities challenged teachers to integrate them into the formal curriculum. Some teachers immediately recognized the vitality of the children's own informal curriculum; others took longer, but came around after peer discussions. Everyone then began to experiment with ways to extend the children's high level of motivation into instructional activities.

CURRICULUM SWITCHBOARD

In recognizing the realities of teaching practice and the restrictions of mandated curricula, the Curriculum Switchboard (Figure 1) was developed to help teachers expand their range of learning activity options. The switchboard was structured using five critical instructional concepts: the Learning Cycle, Ecological concepts, Interdisciplinary Learning, Teaching-Learning Modes, and Developmental Skills. Each concept carries a number of principles, each of which can be "switched" on or off to help define or profile specific activities. Combinations of the twenty-five "switches" provide a broad range of activity profiles.

The switchboard established a framework to stimulate ideas for developing lesson plans. Equally, and perhaps more importantly, it provided creative teachers a method of describing, evaluating, and accounting for their classroom activity in a way that could respond to the tight accountability required in public schools. More broadly still, the switchboard provided a common framework that embraced children's play as part of the learning process, as well as guiding the design and management of the playing-and-learning environment.

The switchboard presents education as a fundamentally ecological process, addressing human society and biosphere in a dynamic state of evolution. In the broadest sense, it focuses on the development of cultural values in relation to the physical environment and therefore with the moral education of children—about their relationships with each other, their surroundings, and society at large.

The Learning Cycle

Child development and environmentally based learning starts with hands-on experience with real objects, places, and people.[1] From this fundamental pedagogical stage, the learning process progresses from action to intuition, from concrete to abstract, and from fact to theory. Creative play follows a similar pattern.

Starting with free exploration, children select particular spaces, objects, and materials to work and play with to create specific ideas, expressions, constructions, and games. The learned patterns of experience are later reapplied to new surroundings, spaces, objects, and playmates. In this way, children build their own culture of games, rituals, and myths, influenced by and adapted to the many cultural and commercial forces of our time. This concept of the learning process takes the form of multiple cycles, spiraling continuously through variously extended time intervals. Piaget's principle of assimilation and accommodation is very much part of this process, with the accommodative processes more likely to occur in the later stages of the cycle.

Hodgkin's modified version of Jerome Bruner's four modes of learning—interpersonal, enactive, iconic, and semiotic—are also embedded in the learning cycle model.[2] The interpersonal mode (learning through interaction with others) and the enactive mode (learning through autonomous actions) apply to the process of exploration and discovery through play. The iconic mode (learning through visual imagery and models) is especially relevant to the processes of recording and expressing discoveries. The semiotic mode (learning through language), because of its greater flexibility and ability to transform ideas, becomes more relevant in the application and transfer stages of the learning cycle.

This method of defining modes of learning and instruction is especially powerful because it acknowledges that children are at the center of their own learning processes. They must first discover and learn for themselves before the intervention of adults (parents, caregivers, playworkers, teachers) can help them transform their discoveries into understanding and useful knowledge—to be assimilated, accommodated, and used to make further discoveries.

These notions of child-centered pedagogy and the need for learning to be based on personal interaction with the environment are not new. Indeed, John Dewey began to articulate them almost a century ago![3] He stressed the importance of the interlinked concepts of *situation, continuity,* and *interaction* in the learning process.[4] We found these criteria particularly helpful in understanding the curricular effectiveness of the Yard. We realized that it offered children and teachers a myriad of learning settings or situations to be engaged in, to interact with, in a holistic environment that offered continuity of experience in both space and time. This is why it had such a powerful influence on the children.

Our version of this multifaceted, progressive theory of learning and instruction was simplified for in-service training into six stages:

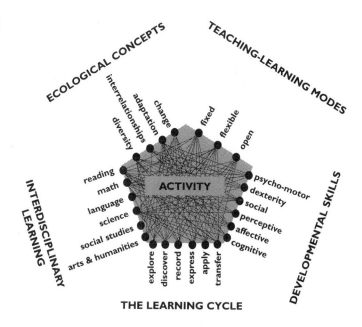

THE LEARNING CYCLE

1. CURRICULUM SWITCHBOARD

The Curriculum Switchboard combines five critical instructional concepts. The concept switches can be activated to define activities in each switchboard "cell" according to the type of activity required. Conversely, the switchboard can be used *ex post facto* as a common framework for describing, evaluating, and clarifying activities. It gives teachers a common frame of reference.

Exploring. Stimulated by their multisensory surroundings, children move around selected territories, observing, manipulating, investigating, and experimenting. By playing freely in the interpersonal and enactive modes of informal education, by acting on the world, and by assimilating information, each child builds an intuitive understanding of how the world works.

Discovering. Differentiated items in the environment capture the attention of children. In an educational context, this stage can be enhanced by using measuring instruments such as thermometers, scales, and counting devices; by making observations with magnifying glasses, microscopes, and binoculars; by sampling the environment through transects and mapped locations; and by employing basic scientific methods such as classification and ordering. Through whatever means, the discovery must have enough significance to motivate the students to continue to the next stage. The discovery could be something searched for to fulfill a plan, something related to an earlier discovery, or something related to a later stage of another cycle.

Exploring and discovering encompass the everyday life of the child. They provide the repository of experiences up to the present moment and can be used to initiate new learning activities.

For example, a teacher might ask children studying the hydrologic cycle to describe their favorite memories of water. They could put on rain clothes and enjoy the experience of a heavy rain, observe what happens when the water flows across the ground, the noise, the reflections, the patterns and textures of movement. They could observe the different ways that water flows from a faucet. They could look at examples of water surfaces: pond, stream, bottle of soda, toilet—the possibilities are many. The teacher should always ask the question: "What did you discover?"

Recording. Observations must be recorded using a chosen medium (paper, audiotape, film, video, etc.) and organized using words, numbers, and images. Alternative media can be used to expand the sensory range of material. Recording formats must be chosen. Categories must be developed to discriminate observations and different levels and types of information. Student teamwork here comes to the fore to decide categories. Learning is consolidated through the compilation and interpretation of observational data. Activities are developed to introduce new concepts to reinforce, consolidate, or contradict previous perceptions and theories.

Expressing. Here the focus shifts to the iconic mode of learning, to communicate explorations and recorded discoveries in expressive forms: graphs, charts, stories, role-playing, demonstrations, model making, dramatics, etc. Teachers must help students translate learning from the affective domain of memorable events into retention aids.

Applying. In this stage, students become involved with a variety of examples that can be connected by a common theme. Student reports about composting suggested that learning occurred on several levels. These reanged from understanding that decomposition made compost hot to seeing a connection between rabbits, composting, nutrition, and health. In another class, the theme of habitats was first explored with examples of animals living in the Yard and ended with children making designs for their own habitats (bedrooms) at home—a fascinating activity for many of the students. This evaluation stage can emphasize interdisciplinary connections, where teachers can help students recycle previous learnings into new situations.

Transferring. This final stage takes place out of school, at home, in the community, where the results of education become part of the broader context of life.

One teacher, having investigated the sun and attributes of sunlight, wanted to give children a historical perspective on the location of our planet in the universe. She took Galileo, the seventeenth-century astronomer who, in the face of the Inquisition, upheld Copernicus's assertion that the Earth was not the center of the universe, but one of several bodies orbiting the sun.

The dramatic story of Galileo's life, his belief in seeking and publicizing the truth, and his diplomatic, nonbelligerent attitude towards authority held much appeal to the children. This was reinforced by a study of the fascinating Leaning Tower of Pisa, on which Galileo supposedly conducted the experiments to derive his celebrated principle concerning falling objects. This and other scenes from Galileo's life were illustrated and written about by the children. And there was also Galileo's boot-shaped country to study. Children paraded green, white, and red Italian flags around the school.

Galileo's life prompted many stimulating lesson plans: the concept of "authority," for instance. What is authority? Is it useful? Should those in authority always be obeyed? Who were the authorities in the children's own lives—parents, teachers, storekeepers? Were they always obeyed without question? What did the children do when they thought authority figures were wrong? Are there still people in the world who are persecuted because of their beliefs? All of these questions stemmed from an exploration of sunlight.

Ecological Concepts

Diversity, Interdependence, Adaptation, and Change (DIAC) are the basic ecological concepts underlying nature and society. They apply to all living systems and provide powerful design and curricular concepts for educational settings.

Diversity. A diverse environment can stimulate and support the diverse behaviors and needs of students. Unrestricted in their interactions with the environment, users can explore an endless variety of relationships between themselves and their surroundings. Diversity gives children a chance to observe, sample, compare, classify, and organize their perceptions of the vastness and complexity of their environment. Over the course of time, diversity enables the discovery of new relationships that lead to new adaptations between users and their environment and the growth of intuitive environmental values based on experience. Diversity helps children become informed decision makers.

Patterns, similarities, and differences are basic characteristics of diversity. Leaves provide a simple example. A diversity of trees and bushes immediately enables children to explore many textures, colors, shapes, sizes, and seasonal changes. It also allows teachers to develop lesson plans that take advantage of this curricular resource.

Interrelationships. Children need opportunities to experience the interdependent linkages of life. They need to understand how everything is interconnected and how disturbing one element affects the entire system. Examples include food webs, families, social clubs, string quartets, and composting efforts.

Adaptation. Adaptation describes how organisms adjust to environmental conditions. It speaks to the way children learn to cope with themselves, others, and the larger "society" of school, home, and community. Adaptation is an everyday affair, describing the impact of the environment on the individual and vice versa. As children conceptualize diversity and interdependence, their understanding of adaptation becomes more developed.

Change. Children need to experience the incredible array of changes occurring in and about themselves. They need to understand how attitudinal and behavioral changes by both children and adults accompany new experiences. Children need to experience the variables of dynamic processes and understand how people constantly intervene in their environment and affect its quality, consciously or unconsciously.

After a weekend workday, Washington students could tour the Yard, record the changes—a tree planted, grass cut, fences removed, brambles cut back—and discuss the consequences. In this way, the children began to understand that successional changes are basic to life's structure.

To learn, students must be able to act on their environment, manipulate it, make changes, experiment, and monitor the results. Above all, they must be able to understand the difference between actions that can lead to either improved or degraded ecological quality. Discussion can cover examples of intervention that are conscious or unconscious, with intended or unintended results, sometimes predicted on the basis of past experience and sometimes not.

Interdisciplinary Learning

Diverse play environments generate rich, complex patterns of behavior that can stimulate language, numeration, scientific testing, creative dramatization, and humorous productions. Observant teachers will be able to expand these play episodes into other interdisciplinary instructional activities to support and nurture each of the primary subject areas: reading, math, language

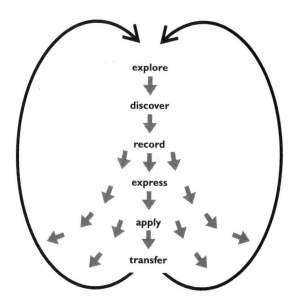

2. THE LEARNING CYCLE

The learning cycle provides a universal means for describing the educational process initiated through playful exploration and discovery. By recording and expressing discoveries, the child learns problem-solving skills that can be applied to new problems in the future.

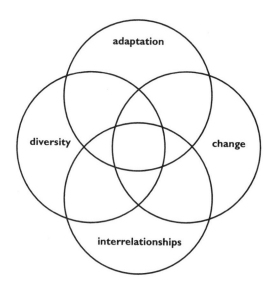

3. ECOLOGICAL CONCEPTS

Ecological concepts are key ideas that bind people and the environment together in an educational mission. The concepts apply just as well to social and cultural development as they do to natural ecology—in this case the co-evolution of social and natural systems through education. To be resilient, people and environments must be diverse in order to adapt to change (which is inevitable). To learn, we must interact and relate to each other and our surroundings.

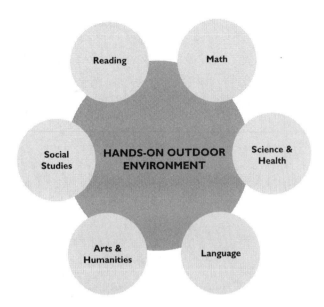

4. INTERDISCIPLINARY LEARNING

The hands-on environment motivates the child to learn in a way that naturally builds connections among subjects or fields of study. Participatory outdoor learning situations make it easy to integrate arts and science, language and math, and so on. This approach is more likely to help a child acquire a sense of the wholeness of life and knowledge. It avoids the present-day issue of overspecialization and fragmentation of information that misses the central elements required for more in-depth knowledge to occur.

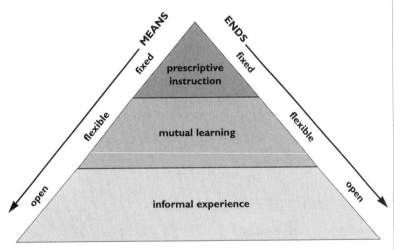

5. TEACHING-LEARNING MODES

Children learn in a variety of ways, and teachers have different methods and approaches to educational practice. The learning process therefore is inherently and uniquely diverse in terms of its defining characteristics and requires teaching strategies that are flexible in meeting the challenges of students' preferred learning styles. Hands-on experiences outdoors introduce a balance between teaching and learning and are able to accommodate learning styles that are mismatched with traditional methods of teaching.

arts, science and health, social studies, and the arts and the humanities.

Teaching-Learning Modes

There is no single correct pedagogy. Different teaching-learning styles are needed to address the varied needs of children, who come from different social backgrounds and who have individual natural gifts to be nurtured. This concept acknowledges that not all children are college bound or learn effectively through traditional methods. Creativity, the ability to interact with others, and imagination are sought-after skills in the job market and can be developed more effectively in diverse settings both within and beyond classroom walls.

Teachers, too, vary in their approaches to education and classroom style. Some take more risks than others; some rely more heavily on personal experience (examples abound of individuals originally inspired by a schoolteacher's passion for a particular topic). Other teachers seek assistance from auxiliary volunteers. Different subjects can be taught in a variety of ways. Even specific aspects of the same subject can be taught using diverse methods.

In managing classroom instruction, progressive teachers recognize that there are several learning theories to select from and apply in any given situation. Educationally designed outdoor environments can accommodate this diversity of choice by providing a structure that allows for investigation and discovery by children with different learning styles. In less rigid, naturalistic instructional environments, each child can become fully engaged in his or her own way. This also removes stress from the teacher, who can move away from being an "expert" in everything to being a person with expertise in some areas, able to rely on children to initiate their own learning processes.

Teaching modes recognize that both the ends and means of education can be fixed, flexible, or open. A variety of approaches gives children a wide range of experience and teachers a host of options relative to "tight" or "loose" instructional formats.

Fixed curricular modes represent the rational, verbal, linear, sequential, standardized patterns of learning that emphasize predictable performance and quantifiable results. The effectiveness of this mode can be measured with standardized tests; effectiveness, however, is often mistakenly equated with accountability. In our opinion, the linear, logical curriculum sequence is overemphasized in Western culture. Our language and behavioral patterns mirror this dominant, time-ordered ethic, which differs greatly from children's natural language and behavioral patterns. In our present-day climate of exponential change, development of a flexible personality is good preparation for the work environment where employers are increasingly seeking staff who can easily adapt to rapidly changing conditions and ambiguity in the workplace.

Fixed modes treat learning as work. Jerome Bruner calls it "right-handed knowing." Others regard it as "compensatory education," to fill up or make up the "achievement gap." Many children require assistance to work in this way, to be taught discipline and rigor—valuable personal traits in all walks of life. But educators must be careful not to produce mental *rigor mortis* by overemphasizing the right hand.

In the most extreme fixed mode, both the ends and means are structured (as in conventional classroom science, where an apparatus is set up in a prescribed way to get a completely predictable result). In this model, individual initiative and imagination are not rewarded.

At the opposite extreme, the open mode celebrates intuitive learning patterns. Nothing is fixed; the ends and means are undefined. For example, a teacher could instruct the class to "take this pile of stuff and do something creative with it." There is open acceptance and fulfillment in exploring unmapped roads and rejoicing in meeting fresh settings and new challenges. Fantasy and dreams feed this risk-taking perspective.

In this mode, Bob Samples suggests, children glutted with standardized replays of a dull, mandated repertory will be liberated. They will invent new solutions rather than rehearse old ones.[5] Instead of work, the open mode is a muse that integrates learning and play. Play behavior in early childhood is characterized by the exploratory drive of curiosity, which produces a tremendous motivation to learn.

Open education, however, has a high risk of failure. Take the open-education movement of the 1960s for example. One of the movement's biggest mistakes was its insistence that the whole system be open, bypassing the stages in organizational development necessary to support a high degree of innovation. Change happened so fast that the school subculture could not adapt quickly enough. The organization collapsed and the new educational ideas lost credibility. In some cases, the school never recovered (the "adaptation" switch was ignored, ironically by education leaders who were often supporters of environmental education).

Most people find too much freedom difficult to handle, especially if presented without prior warning. If

suddenly neither ends nor means are defined, we become lost or paralyzed in a sea of infinite choice. Most of us need some definition of ends or means to help us chart a course of action.

The flexible mode takes a middle-road approach, providing a balance between excessive and insufficient structure. Play settings can be described in these terms. For example, fixed settings such as traditional play equipment and flexible, free-play natural settings are both necessary for a healthy, developmentally stimulating environment.

The flexible mode accommodates a wider range of teaching and learning styles. At Washington, most of the Yard activity and environmental curricula were framed in this way. "Blue" (fixed), "green" (flexible), and "yellow" (open) became useful shorthand terms of reference for different learning activities, types of educational settings, varied learning styles, and even aspects of different teachers' approaches to instruction.

Developmental Skills

The switchboard is designed to help teachers develop activities that relate to all areas of child development: psycho-motor, dexterous, social, perceptive, affective, and cognitive. By focusing on developmental skills, we acknowledge that a child is a whole, living, feeling, thinking personality—not a set of stimulus-responses or a cognitive information processor.

We do not know of any way to stimulate the developmental skills of every child with one type of environment. We do know that all skills are addressed naturally through children's play, certainly more so than through formal education. Educators should engage children in holistic learning programs and settings to stir their emotions, to stretch the limits of their senses, to engage them in fruitful, positive social relations, to stimulate their imaginations in dramatic play and scripting, to exercise their large and small motoric systems—to unleash their fullest potential.

Educational programs must give equal attention to all of the developmental systems. The challenge now is to develop learning activities that fall within the less common domains of the switchboard and that focus on the developmental areas.

STARTERS AND INPUTS

"How can I get going? Where do I start?" are often a teacher's first thoughts. We hope that the switchboard has begun to broaden the range of possible learning activities that can be developed. In this section we offer

PERCEPTION

To understand something via the senses.

What the child can see, hear, and feel is combined into a totality which is worked on and interpreted from previous experience and which enables the child to understand.

The continuous development of images or perceptual maps of the child's reality.

Perception is dynamic!

—Ylva Ellneby[6]

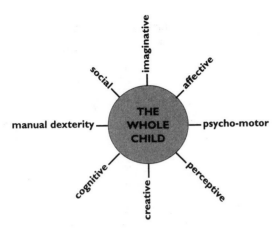

The Whole Child: imaginative, affective, psycho-motor, perceptive, creative, cognitive, manual dexterity, social

6. DEVELOPMENTAL SKILLS

Active learning in outdoor settings stimulates all aspects of child development more readily than indoor learning environments—especially in the areas of social-emotional and gross motor development. Outdoor experiences also offer opportunities for creative and imaginative play, and expression—especially for children who have difficulty responding and adapting to more traditional classroom environments.

a further framework of suggestions for activities to use in conjunction with the switchboard.

The ideal primary school curriculum offers a balance of structure and openness. Thus the confident teacher can choose from many options; conversely, the less experienced teacher has clear guidelines and specifics to rely upon. Intermediate curricula can draw on a great variety of initiating stimuli, some more predictable than others. For example, the seasonal cycle can offer a series of relatively predictable possibilities. In contrast, depending on the climatic zone, day-to-day changes in the weather can offer unpredictable learning opportunities each day.

Curriculum Guides/Packages

Packaged guides and materials are useful if you can afford them. If not, many universities maintain these resources within their departments of education. While this information may not focus specifically on urban neighborhoods or school grounds, it can be adapted for this purpose. When selecting guides, look for those that include critical components such as teaching strategies, motivational devices, and modes of evaluation. They should also offer curricular dimensions such as scope, sequence, interpretation, and a balance of subject matter approaches. Guides are useful as well in organizing the necessary support systems for quality instruction. By freeing the teacher to concentrate on the inner development of the child, these resources can be particularly beneficial for beginning teachers.

The Yard's curriculum included the use of several published guides available during the project's implementation. The focus on science drew particularly on material from SCIS (Science Curriculum Improvement Study). Because of its Piagetian orientation, SCIS provided a useful framework for developing activities that reinforced the Yard's curricular concepts. To broaden the interdisciplinary scope and expand the format into other subject areas, we used the Curriculum Switchboard.

When using packaged resources keep in mind that the format tends to reduce the number of opportunities for open-ended exploration. Critical to this process are the spontaneous feedback children naturally provide while learning and the teacher's ability to build upon their "discoveries." Teaching strategies such as the Curriculum Switchboard can be effective in encouraging happenstance events.

New approaches reflective of the Yard's focus include Project Learning Tree and the OBIS guides (based in San Francisco and at UC Berkeley respectively). We benefited greatly from these resources, which were in the first stages of development as the Yard's curriculum took shape. The guides have since been joined by Project Wild and Project Wet, which, together with the California State Environmental Education Guide, provide excellent sources for instructional use (see Appendices B and C).

Based on our experience however, we recommend developing your own curricular approach. For use with the Yard, a set of activity cards was created that demonstrated the practical use of the Curriculum Switchboard. These were later published by the UC Berkeley School of Education as the *Seed Packet*.

Physical Resources

Much of this book has documented activities stimulated by particular, mostly natural, resources. We hope these examples give a sense of the limitless possibilities of interdisciplinary learning activities embodied in diverse living environments.

Resource People

A resource person is someone outside the regular school staff with special skills, knowledge, and experience in working with children. Many types of individuals are available in every community. The main hurdle to overcome is the initial effort required to locate them, establish a commitment, and secure financial support (if required) for their work.

Institutions involved in public or community education should be the first place to look. For the Yard educational program, local environmental organizations provided resource people for activities on whales, rabbits, composting, snakes, gardening, and recycling. University students animated many types of activities ranging from food webs to ecodrama puppet productions. Student interns based at the school implemented substantial programs. Regional park rangers led children on "one-hundred-inch" hikes. Audubon Nature Trainers worked with the students in the vegetable garden, showed them how to make balloon-and-pasta models of the reproduction system of plants, and taught bird recognition through beak-and-claw games.

Other resource people were hired professionals; several were supported by public funds to work at the school. An outdoor science specialist and Yard manager were supported by an employment-assistance, federal training program. Two community artists worked in the Yard with support from the California Arts Council; one was a poet and the other an interdisciplinary artist specializing in dance, theater, and the visual arts.

Activity-Focused Learning

Hands-on learning activities are the principal medium of interdisciplinary environmental education. General categories include field trips, camping, harvesting, climbing, and "hunting."

"Today on our field trip we did a research report on organisms," one child wrote. "We had to find a plant or animal that was more than one and put the number on the paper and then draw a picture of it and put the name of it at the top of the page and try to get a piece of it. I did dandelions."

Seasonal Activities

Seasonal activities are suggested by the predictable cycles of climate, related social behavior, and cultural consequences. Seasons provide the most potent sequence of predictable intervention in the natural environment. The Yard was a remarkable example of the possibilities, considering its small size. Seasonal topics included mushrooms, metamorphosis, blooming flowers, weather studies, pruning, animal life, death and decay, plant changes, insect behavior, aquatic studies, bird watching, and bird behavior. Any small natural area can offer similar possibilities—if managed to support this purpose. That is to say, it must not be manicured and tidied up like a traditional park but rather maintained as a "wild garden," as discussed in Chapter 20.

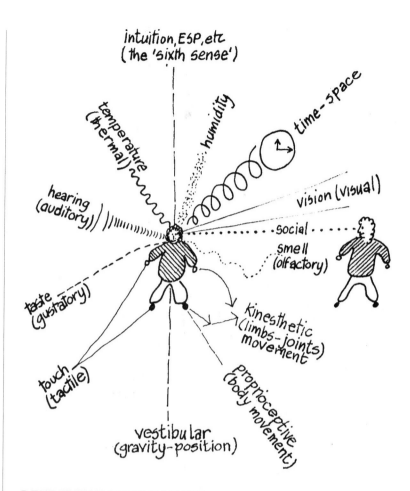

7. THE HUMAN SENSE MACHINE

Learning begins with experience, which comes via our senses. The external world is, in fact, our sensory memory; hence, each of us has a different world. The number of physiologically identifiable sense-mechanisms that actually exist is an ongoing debate; whatever the number, there certainly appear to be more than the proverbial five. For the dual sense of time and space no mechanism has been discovered. We need to use this marvelous machine more fully. A trio of interrelated senses provide an overall feeling of body-in-space:

Kinesthetic: Sense of movement and steady positions of joints and limbs (e.g., touching nose with eyes closed; knowing when foot is pointed or fist is clenched).

Proprioceptive: Sense of body movement and position. Spatial orientation without visual clues. Knowing where your joints are in space without movement (e.g., knowing where foot and floor meet).

Vestibular: Also called "equilibrium sense." Sense of gravity and position of body in space (e.g., acceleration/deceleration and seasickness). Very important and stimulating for children. Explains attraction of swings and slides!

— *Encyclopedic Dictionary of Psychology,* 3rd ed., 1986.

— *Longman Dictionary of Psychology and Psychiatry,* 1984.

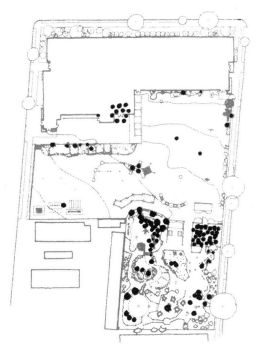

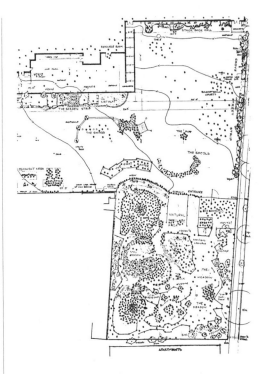

8. LOCATION OF SIGNIFICANT CURRICULAR EVENTS

PEET teachers recorded the locations of the most significant curricular events in the Yard during the 1975–76 project year. In rank order they were:

- **Whole Yard**
- **Litter parades**
- **Enclosed garden**
- **Ponds/wetland/stream**
- **Orchard Wayside**
- **Natural Resource Area**
- **Redwoods**
- **Edges**
- **Basement greenhouse**
- **Chaparral Hill**
- **Railroad ties**
- **Gazebo**

Comparison with the perception map (top right) shows a strong correlation between curricular significance and dominant perception of the natural environment.

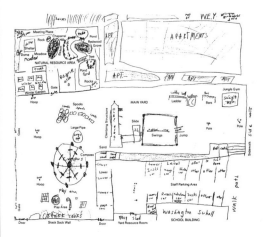

9. THE POWER OF NATURE

The perception map (top) was based on a compilation of hundreds of individual drawings prepared by each child in the school (bottom). Each dot represents a physical element mentioned in the drawings. The compiled "mental maps" demonstrate that the Natural Resource Area and aquatic settings were the most memorable for the children and offered the strongest learning potential. The garden, climbing structures, and swings were also significant, as were the edges of the Main Yard (which acted as private refuges and exploratory routes). Traditional play equipment and climbing structures also had a strong perceptual impact. The asphalt, on the other hand, was hardly mentioned; perceptually, it was a nonentity.

Change-Oriented

Think of change as an ecological concept, particularly in relation to activities that produce change such as gardening, planting, shelter building, weather observations, art productions, and creative activities. Also think of change in relation to perceptions, behavior, and values that change as the environment changes or as students move from one setting to another. The Yard, for example, presented many such lessons as students moved back and forth between the Natural Resource Area and Main Yard.

Special Events

Festivals, carnivals, street theater, and similar events offer huge learning potentials both in the preparation of activities and in the event itself. The annual Yardfest was the most substantial event at Washington (see Chapter 15). Others included the Chinese New Year's parade, the *Cinco de Mayo* festival, Halloween, spring and winter solstices, and plant-in days. Each provided springboards for classroom involvement and became the hubs of additional spin-off learning activities. Many of the examples were existing cultural traditions, easily transferred to the school environment with the assistance of appropriate resource people.

Environmental Issues

Topics such as traffic, pollution, nutrition, energy, water conservation, global warming, and land use provide useful foci for the development of learning activities. They belong to later stages of the learning cycle. Many environmental education programs, in our opinion, make the mistake of focusing too quickly on environmental problems. This type of pedagogical short circuit is not effective as it goes straight to the "problem" without involving the child in a prior understanding or feeling for the ecological-social-political context (which is the real problem).

The general thrust of interdisciplinary environmental education should be to help children appreciate the irresistible beauty of the world and their place within it, not to immediately start confronting global environmental problems and the negative feelings that accompany them. The best approach is to address these problems (neighborhood traffic, for instance) as an integral part of other learning activities.

Child-Initiated

Suggestions for learning activities can often arise from children's play activities. The variety and intensity of children's play in a diverse outdoor environment will constantly demonstrate this potential, as shown in the earlier chapters.

Personal possessions such as toys and pets often provide a stimulus. One day, a boy's toy soldier collection arrayed in battle formation in a corner of the meadow made a connection to the American Revolutionary War. Another time, a pet duck was brought to school to try out the ponds and stimulated a sequence of duck-related activities (see Chapter 13).

These types of events open direct links to students' homes, communities, and cultures and can be encouraged and legitimized by the teacher through carefully presented probes and invitations. It is one thing for a teacher to see a toy as a distraction but quite another to see it as a way to elicit children's natural interest as a part of a class assignment. The toy as a favorite play object represents the children's personality or some other aspect of their private life. The potential for learning—linking home and school—can become a fascinating enrichment of classroom life.

Family-Initiated

Family life can act as an activity stimulus: the birth of a baby sister or brother, weekend trips to the seashore, and so forth. If students are encouraged to talk about their out-of-school activities in class, these experiences can be linked into the learning cycle and developed in appropriate ways.

Community Resource Sites

Many of the resource people who worked in the Yard were affiliated with community institutions pursuing educational goals similar to those at Washington. These included several units of UC Berkeley (the Oxford Tract Experimental Garden, the Botanical Garden, and the Lawrence Hall of Science); Wagner Ranch, a natural resource area on the other side of the East Bay Hills; the Audubon Nature Training Center at Berkeley's Aquatic Park; the Oakland Museum; and the Tilden Regional Park Nature Area.

Field trips to these types of places are a primary way to extend the learning cycle beyond the school site (Figure 10), with the added advantage of being able to work with resource people at their home base. Additional concepts are learned, brought back, and integrated into the on-site program.

Many curricular activities can be initiated by visits to community facilities and organizations in the area: a fire station, city hall, businesses, college campuses, manu-

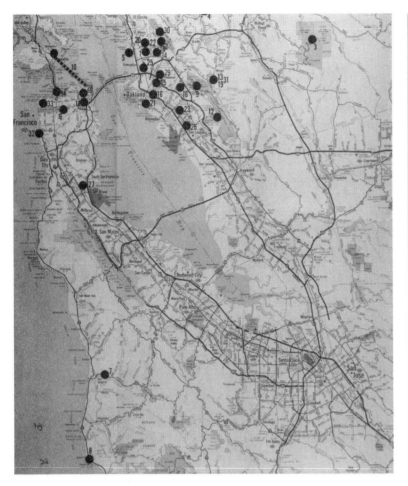

10. EXTENSIONS OF THE SCHOOL SITE

Day and overnight trips to community resource sites provided a valuable extension of the Yard-based learning process and introduced children to another level of educational opportunity. The map shows twenty-eight trips organized by parent-teacher groups during one school year.

facturing plants—the possibilities are endless. Washington students made memorable visits to a bakery, an ice cream factory (a big hit!), a newspaper, Chinatown, a zoo, a sheep farm, a pumpkin patch, and others. Such trips had enormous educational stimulus.

Resource sites need not be located far away; they can include nearby parks and vacant lots. In the neighborhood around Washington, for example, two residents opened their innovative backyards to a visiting group of students. The children got an up-close look at exotic flowers, wildlife, rabbits, and chickens—all within a ten-minute walk.

Overnight Trips

Camping trips and other overnight events fall into a special category of "peak" experiences. Such trips take time and energy to organize, but the educational benefits are substantial—as they satisfy the social area of child development that is difficult to address in the finely divided time of day-to-day classroom settings. Such trips, which bring both children and adults together for several days in a natural environment, promote solidarity and social development. This in turn makes cooperation and group activity easier to accomplish. Students bring back to school memorable discoveries that serve as affective learning experiences to extend the learning cycle.

The San Francisco Bay Area offered an extraordinary array of overnight camping opportunities, though in many cases they had to be searched out and the site staff persuaded to take on a group of schoolchildren. In other communities, the opportunities may be fewer in number but nevertheless exist and wait to be identified and exploited. Their educational value suggests the need for local educational leaders to establish agreements with the owners or administrators of potential educational sites to make them available for school use.

Generic Themes

Learning can be initiated by several broad classes of phenomena, including topics such as differences, populations, lifestyles, habitats, cycles, and food webs (as found in many packaged environmental curricula); intervention strategies such as transects, mapping, poetry, and photography; and landscape characteristics such as holes, hills, edges, patterns, territories, topography, entrances, paths, tunnels, sound, color, and light. All need a diverse natural environment to work well. Less experienced teachers may find them more challenging to implement, but for others they offer a fertile place to start interdisciplinary connections. Remember Food Webs in Chapter 5, Nooks and Crannies in Chapter 6, Fungi Fun in Chapter 7, and Transects and Mapping in Chapter 12. These are all examples of generic themes.

Happenstance

The more natural a learning environment, the more likely unintentional, fortuitous, or serendipitous learning opportunities will occur. For example, mud and grass in the Yard provided materials for cliff swallows to build their gourd-shaped nests under the eaves of the school roof. The spot the birds selected for their new homes was only a few feet from the windows of the main staircase. As a result, children were able to observe the entire nest-building process. Teachers

CURRICULUM GUIDES/PACKAGES	PHYSICAL RESOURCES	RESOURCE PEOPLE	ACTIVITY-FOCUSED LEARNING
C Useful place to start, if you can afford the price. Indoor-oriented but can be adapted to the outdoors. D Design school site settings so that materials can be used outdoors.	C Activities suggested by a specific resource (e.g., ponds, animals, climbing structure). D Create these resources on site.	C People from outside the school with special skills, knowledge, and experience to share with children. D Designers as educators can fulfill this role. Design site to attract resource people.	C Action and experience are the medium (e.g., field trips, camping, harvesting, climbing). D Focus design on user needs. Create a diversity of opportunities.
SEASONAL ACTIVITIES	CHANGE-ORIENTED	SPECIAL EVENTS	ENVIRONMENTAL ISSUES
C Predictable cycles of climate and related social behavior. D Accent design on seasonal change.	C Applies to changeable elements (e.g., gardens and planting, shelter building, and arts activities to change perceptions, behavior, and values). D Design changeable settings.	C Traditional community events and special events: festivals, carnivals, street theater. D Design support settings such as amphitheaters and booth areas.	C Selected local issues and curriculum developed around them. D Develop settings that children can use to understand the issue (e.g., wetlands for local water quality issues).
CHILD-INITIATED	FAMILY-INITIATED	COMMUNITY RESOURCE SITES	OVERNIGHT TRIPS
C Suggestions from children or stimulation from personal possessions such as toys and pets. D Focus on children as clients.	C Something stimulated by family at home or elsewhere that carries over to school. D Design school environment to welcome family members and make them feel at home.	C Visits to community facilities and organizations (e.g., fire station, city hall, neighborhood trips, and related resource people). Create curricular connections to school site. D Community as a planning/design resource.	C Focus on social development and curricular connections to classroom and school site. D Ensure school site natural settings reflect regional ecosystems.
GENERIC THEMES	HAPPENSTANCE Unintentional	Serendipitous	Fortuitous
C Focus on populations, habitats, food webs, transects, holes, hills, edges, patterns, territories, entrances, paths, tunnels, etc. D Design these elements into the curriculum.	C Be on the lookout for spin-offs from pre-established activity. D Ensure sufficient diversity so that the unforeseen extensions of previous actions can be supported.	C/D A quality residing inside the teacher/designer; the faculty of making desirable but unsought-for discoveries. The result of trained senses and awareness.	Fortuitism: The doctrine or belief that adaptations in nature come about by chance and not by design. C/D Make the most of happy accidents.
	ENVIRONMENTAL LEARNING STATIONS		
	C Develop a range of ELS's, both permanent and temporary. D Predict curricular needs and build them in.		

11. STARTERS AND INPUTS

Curriculum development can be initiated and guided from many sources. Once the school grounds are brought into the concept of the learning process, a variety of possibilities become available. "C" in the diagram above indicates the curricular opportunity associated with the theme of a particular cell. "D" indicates the design or management actions required to guide this process. Many of the suggestions require a degree of flexibility and openness on the part of the teacher to take advantage of the many curricular opportunities. The designer's awareness of educational issues is a crucial variable that can help or hinder curriculum development.

helped the children figure out the connection between the nest building and the natural resources on the school site.

The ability to take advantage of happenstance learning opportunities is a teaching skill that requires trained senses and curricular awareness. Washington teachers with this aptitude, for example, would always switch gears to exploit unexpected changes in the environment caused by heavy weather. On the day following a storm, they would invariably take their class out into the Yard, where the students were sure to make some interesting discoveries.

Other examples of happenstance events were social in nature, like the time Jessie's brother Scott, who attended another school, spent the day working with Jessie as a member of a tree-planting crew. Jessie's teacher, on the lookout for spin-offs from pre-established activity, described how Scott helped fill the tree wells with screened soil, cut the tree cans, joined in the tree-planting ceremonies, and assisted with the watering. "He was really interested in the Yard," the teacher said, "and constantly quizzed the other kids in the planting crew, forcing them to find answers in a way that they would not normally have to do. It was a neat relationship which made the day."

One day, a student crew cleaning the pump filter found it overflowing with water snails. They placed the snails in a tin can and discussed with the teacher what to do. The students recalled that one of the classrooms had a chicken—and that chickens ate snails. So they brought the snails over and explained their discovery. After giving some of the snails to the hen, the students watched intently to see if she would eat them. But being used to terrestrial snails and dry food, the hen was not enthusiastic. As a result, the group put the snails back in the pond and returned to their own class to talk about their impromptu experiment.

Environmental Learning Stations

Learning stations are a standard part of contemporary classroom management and instruction. Classroom space can be used more effectively by rearranging the furniture and subdividing the room into smaller, task-oriented learning stations, each stocked with the materials and tools required to conduct the activities on a particular topic, theme, or subject. Most importantly, this strategy divides the classroom population into flexible activity groups to facilitate independent work. Learning stations function as semipermanent but flexible instructional settings. They are excellent for meeting the Dewey

criteria of situation, continuity, and interaction in the learning process. Normally they cannot be changed more than once per school term, although temporary stations housing time-dependent themes are also useful.

An environmental learning station (ELS) follows the same concept but with an emphasis on physical resources (Figure 12). Yard ELS's were developed around resources and types of activity with high potentials for continuity and interaction. Station themes reflected the main systems of the Yard as instructional and curricular components. They included climate and weather; gardening and nutrition; vegetation; the water cycle; animals; and human land use.

The Yard ELS's satisfied the need for an intermediate environmental education frame of reference between the indoor classroom and the community. Each provided materials for the direction, management, and assessment of learning within a system of indoor and outdoor space, varying in size and complexity, and endowed with both natural and people-made resources.

Each station had its own strong identity and purpose, although common strands of instructional methods connected them together. Different parts of the Yard had inherent capacities for different kinds of instructional activity. Some activities, such as observing, measuring, and sampling, could take place almost anywhere. Others were adapted to the characteristics of specific locations (e.g., the potential of the waterfall for multisensory observations), specific settings (e.g., the potential of the redwood grove, meadow, pond, and stream for comparing animal populations and microclimates), or more general zones (e.g., the school roof as a weather station, the surrounding neighborhood as a land-use station).

ELS's enabled teachers to "green" their instructional mode, allowing them to act as facilitators, gatekeepers, and suppliers of equipment, tools, and resources. They could move around and help children discover and record their findings. They coordinated the activities of resource people such as university interns and community volunteers, building on their ideas but at the same time making sure that key curricular concepts were not watered down.

The Yard ELS's provided a core stability to the environmental curriculum yet also allowed for great instructional flexibility, ranging from projects planned ahead of time to spontaneous free-form activity. As children moved back and forth between different stations inside and outside, engaged in a variety of learning processes, they discovered opportunities that were adapted to their

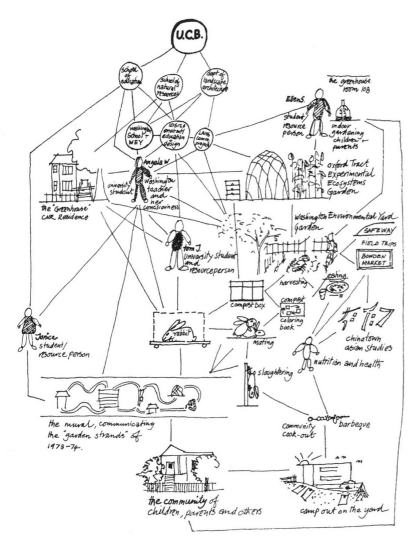

12. ANIMAL ENVIRONMENTAL LEARNING STATION

The diagram shows a webbing connection to the community (resource people and sites) of the animal learning station. This was typical of the expanded concept of thematic stations structured for curriculum development. Many connections among people and places both on and off the school site were a vital part of the process. The animal learning station was created using a web of relationships including the university, its students, the neighborhood, an experimental garden, Audubon Nature Training, and many other community resources.

learning style. The animal ELS (see Chapter 5) was a good example of this principle.

Opportunities for children to display their work was an important ELS function. The full cycle of learning could be exhibited at a single location. One of the teachers and her students set up an attractive display about gardening and nutrition under a colorful silk parachute hung from the classroom ceiling. Displayed on a placard was a beautiful poem about the garden scarecrow. An animal station group made a display about metamorphosis in the Yard using the anise swallowtail butterfly as an example.

TEACHER INVOLVEMENT

In the initial phase of curriculum development using natural resources, we found that it was important to allow as much openness as possible so that teachers and children could explore many learning-by-doing options. The curriculum must be allowed to evolve from the character-

istics of the individuals involved, the resources available, and their growth and change through time. In the Yard project, activities were not mandated from above but grew out of the teaching-learning experiences of participants. The teachers initiated action and were able to measure their success as a peer group with a clear understanding of each other's educational intentions.

Failure is impossible with this type of educational philosophy because every action is a test of latent educational possibilities. Increments of success occur, both large and small. Each can be built into subsequent actions to broaden and deepen the long-term educational impact. Gardening, for instance, was a constant curricular success in the Yard. From its modest beginnings, it continued to evolve both physically and educationally over the years (see Chapter 3).

Many of the teachers found the idea of extending the curriculum beyond classroom walls as something new and challenging; others had to overcome personal and

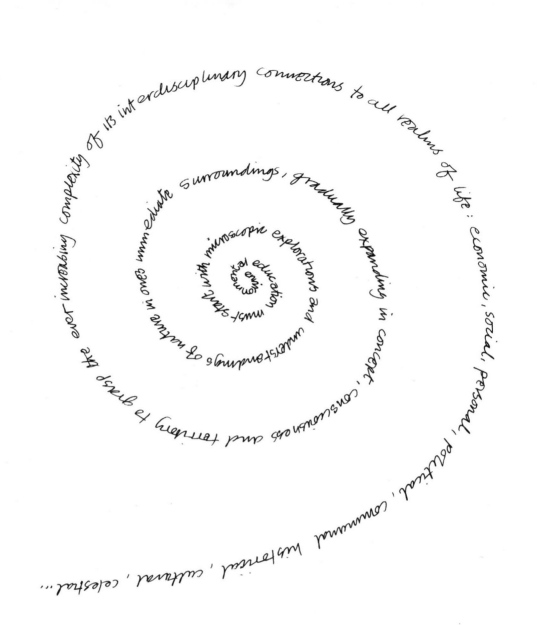

...environmental education must start with microscopic explorations and understanding of nature in one's immediate surroundings, gradually expanding in concept, consciousness and terrain to grasp the ever increasing complexity of its interdisciplinary connections to all realms of life: economic, social, personal, political, communal, historical, cultural, celestial...

professional barriers before fully taking part. A key to success was to encourage them to document the results of their learning activities and to share them with the rest of the staff. The Yard teachers met weekly to share progress and to develop new activities. They created and constantly updated an activities manual, which described what they and their students had done and what they were learning through the evolving curriculum. The document contained lesson plans, photographs, and examples of students' work using the language and terminology of the curricular framework presented in this chapter.

ADMINISTRATOR AS FACILITATOR

In the early days of the Yard project, the rate of progress often became a question of whether or not administrative "permission" was required for teachers to carry out certain actions; and if so, who needed to seek permission from whom, and in what manner was it to be granted.

"Permission" in a school context implies a typical organizational structure: a stable institution, established lines of authority, and commonly agreed upon procedures for making decisions. But new initiatives like the Yard start with none of these characteristics. To try to impose them prematurely usually bogs down the initiative and spells failure. Administrators who like to run a tight ship on a predictable course probably should not take on initiatives such as these.

In order to learn, teachers must initiate activity without necessarily knowing the outcome ahead of time. More than anything else, this ability is a matter of individual personality and experience. Some teachers are risk takers; others find it challenging to try out new ideas. At Washington, we found it difficult to "train" curricular risk taking. We tried, but perhaps traded off considerable time and energy that could have been used to greater advantage. Some of the most professional teachers in fact had the hardest time coping with the curricular challenge of the Yard. It simply had no place in their highly developed professional scheme; and besides, their way of doing things had always been successful, so why change?

If nothing else, administrators must encourage teachers to act! Some of the most imaginative and worthwhile curricular activities in the Yard's early days were initiated by teachers who did not wait to be sanctioned. They took responsibility into their own hands and got on with the job, often in response to unexpected learning opportunities—which they had been trained to take advantage of.

Actions, however, were not always successful. Minor setbacks occurred from ideas that had not been carefully thought through or that produced unpredictable, negative consequences. The open style of curriculum development was an invigorating administrative challenge, but the educational benefits far outweighed the costs of the additional administrative effort required. The critical administrative role was to encourage peer support and collaboration, to help teachers accept and learn from partial successes.

Initially, the open approach required a certain amount of "muddling through"—an organization strategy that Geoffrey Vickers, a pioneer in organizational development, considered respectable and appropriate when applied to innovative programs.[7] Muddling through is stressful, confusing, and hard to defend, but it must sometimes be used as a short-term strategy to get results. If everything needed in the initial phases of the Yard had been decided in a formal committee, and mapped out according to a carefully prepared logistical plan, the enterprise would never have got off the ground.

In the longer term, an enabling administrative environment must evolve out of the "muddle," which will continue to motivate teachers to work as a peer group, supporting each other to continue to take risks, to keep the curriculum alive, constantly evolving, responsive to its ever-changing educational context—the children, the school community, and planet Earth.

REFERENCES

1. Moore, R. C. (1990). *Childhood's Domain: Play and Place in Child Development*. Berkeley, Calif.: MIG Communications (published originally by Croom Helm, London, 1987), 10–12.

2. Hodgkin, R. (1976). *Born Curious. New Perspectives in Educational Theory*. New York: John Wiley, Chapter 11: "The Four Modes of Instruction."

3. Dewey, J. (1959). *Dewey on Education*. Selections, Introduction and Notes by Martin S. Dworkin. New York: Teachers College Press. All the material selected for this volume is relevant to the philosophy of the Environmental Yard. Refer particularly to *My Pedagogic Creed* (originally published 1897).

4. Dewey, J. (1938). *Experience and Education*. New York: Macmillan.

5. Samples, B. (1987). *Openmind/Wholemind: Parenting and Teaching Tomorrow's Children Today*. Rolling Hills Estates, Calif.: Jalmar Press.

6. Ellneby, Y. (1991) *Children's Rights to Develop: A Handbook on Children's Motor, Perceptual, and Language Development*. Stockholm: Swedish Educational Broadcasting Company, 128.

7. Vickers, G. (1972). *Freedom in a Rocking Boat: Changing Values in an Unstable Society*. Harmsworth, Middlesex: Penguin Books.

CHAPTER 19

Taking Part

CONVERSATION

Two children were sitting in the Gazebo one day talking.

"I just love the Environmental Yard."

"Me too. I wish my back yard at home was like this."

"I think the Environmental Yard is the best part of the school."

"Yes. At least I know that one part of the world has been saved."

Planning theorist John Friedmann once defined planning as "intelligence applied to the future."[1] In planning the Yard, we closely followed this philosophy. But a key question persisted: whose intelligence should we apply? Our goal was to tap as much intelligence of the community as possible and thus free ourselves from the "myth of the expert" (exclusive reliance on our own technically proficient, but limited and inevitably biased, professional expertise). Our own and others' expertise was only useful and valid within the broader context of community participation.

Education and participatory planning share the same goal: the identification, development, and transmission of values. Both try to reconcile the tension between "what is" and "what ought to be." The task of education is to help people understand the underlying values of the choices being made. The task of planning is to develop a means for implementing them.

PARTICIPATORY PLANNING

The participatory, experiential philosophy of the Yard differed greatly from the planning processes normally conducted by public institutions. It focused on the needs of children as the primary users, along with the related needs of teachers, parents, and residents. The assumption was that these groups knew best what they wanted, but procedures and techniques were needed to help them express their needs and feed them into the master plan.

Collectively, the community had knowledge that no outside expert could ever acquire independently. The best thing to do was to collaborate with the community in the development process. The ultimate aim of this process was educational, to help people learn how to control their own environment and design it to suit their own purposes.

Community planning threw everybody's varied needs together in the same pot—namely, the site. From this complex brew of conflicting needs and values, we had to develop a master plan through which resource allocations and adjustments could eventually be determined. The master plan was a holding pattern of projected actions for step-by-step implementation.

ESSENTIAL MASTER PLAN

The master plan was an essential medium of communication. It presented user needs on paper so they would be taken seriously. It recorded planning and design decisions as they were made, as well as further modifications from user feedback. The plan also guided implementation on the ground; as construction took place, it was adjusted in detail.

The master plan began as an embodiment of the desired relationships between the site and its users. Eventually, it became a description of the *fait accompli*, a permanent record of what actually got built (Figure 13). Early on, it served as a critical fundraising tool. The eagerness of potential donors could be measured in direct proportion to the sense of reality presented by a good-looking, convincing master plan.

THE ROLE OF LEADERSHIP

Leadership was an essential catalyst in the orchestration of community involvement. It was a role assumed by the authors, by Herb as principal of the school and by Robin as coordinator of planning, design, construction, and community participation. We were not elected in any formal democratic sense (we were still years away from the establishment of an independent community organization). For many months we tried to avoid the leadership role and deny its importance. The task, however, was thrust upon us by others in the heart of the action. The sheer force of events obligated it. We tried, then, to develop a facilitating style, stimulate ideas, help articulate goals, and guide progress towards meeting them.

Although the conventional organizational method was to form a committee, the development of the Yard never quite worked that way, at least not in the first years. At that time, there was a communitywide mistrust of established, bureaucratic procedures. It was a period when direct-action politics and mass demonstrations were the more standard approaches to dealing with issues in the public domain. The beginning of the Yard reflected this style. Many community participants felt that progress could easily get bogged down in endless committee procrastination. Since there was no source of

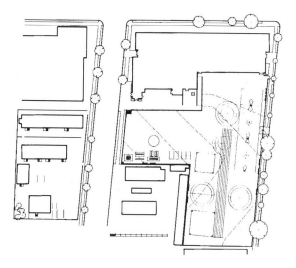

The existing site before development.

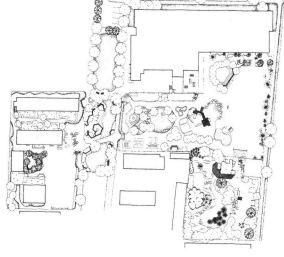

The Yard master plan.

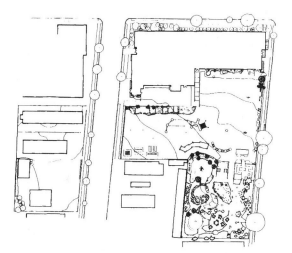

The Yard after five years.

13. SITE EVOLUTION

The existing site before development (top left) was dominated by asphalt and the surrounding chainlink fences. If
institutional support had been greater, the redeveloped
Yard might have reflected the design illustrated at the
top right—an educational/community park incorporating
a portion of the adjacent street and an extended school
site on the other side. Nevertheless, many elements of
the master plan became a reality. After five years of
development (bottom left), the Yard showcased the
Natural Resource Area at the south end, plantations
around the edges, and play structures in the center. After
ten years (bottom right), the Yard was a truly diverse
landscape that served all users.

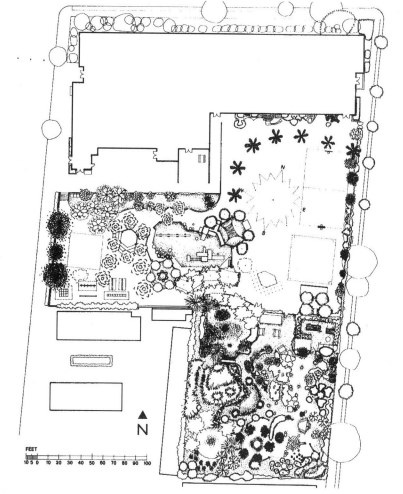

The Yard after ten years.

14. COMMUNITY CONNECTIONS

Redevelopment of the Yard led to connections with many other institutions and groups that contributed to the success of the project.

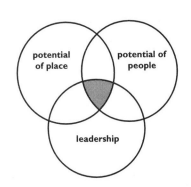

15. ROLE OF LEADERSHIP

Long-term, committed leadership is an essential ingredient for success. Leadership must help create and support a new vision of people and place as a vehicle for progressive education (shaded area).

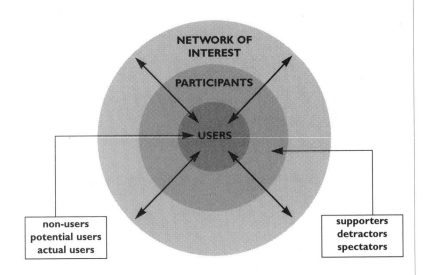

16. CONCENTRIC COMMUNITY

At the core of the Yard community were the user groups: students, parents, teachers, administrative staff, afterschool users, and neighborhood residents. Community participation was a dynamic process that linked users, participants, and the broader network of interest to the evolution of the Yard.

authority to impose a structure from the outside, the organizational structure developed from within. A small coordinating core group was established, along with several short-term action groups, proceeding on the basis of consensus as much as possible.

As site administrator, Herb had to be clear about the constraints of his position regarding actions proposed by the group. If action was held back too much, momentum faded and people lost interest. If things happened too quickly, people followed blindly, hasty decisions were made, and the community failed to fully support the proposals. The risk then was that the results on the ground would not be highly valued, fully used, or defended if threatened by official action. People had to participate in constructing the master plan in order to believe in it and take ownership of it. The process took time and, beyond a certain point, had to be supported by action on the ground.

COMMUNITY PARTICIPATION

There were three concentric circles of community associated with the Yard (Figure 16). First, there was the core of actual or potential *user groups*. In the early days, almost everyone was a potential user, except the students who were required by law to use the site. As the master plan was implemented and more people began using the site, potential users became actual users. They became actively involved and able to comment on the proposed revisions to the master plan. Second, there was the *participant* group of individuals and organizations who either viewed the Yard positively (hopefully to become users), were neutral fencesitters, or were detractors, visible only when calling to complain. The participatory strategy encouraged involvement from spectators and detractors. Third, there was the *network of interest*—activists, educators, and researchers in the local region and beyond working on similar projects and interested in sharing experience.

The toughest struggle in the first couple of years was to shatter the stereotypes about schoolyards and to help people visualize what the Yard could really become. People had to recognize that the schoolyard was public property paid with taxes; therefore the community, including the children, had a right to determine how the site should be used, especially outside of school hours. Through face-to-face group interaction, attitudes gradually changed and coalesced into consensus on the master plan. Strong community solidarity was essential before seeking adoption of the plan by public authorities.

MEETINGS

Meetings were the mainstay of participation. They ranged from informal day-to-day encounters to occasional "summit" meetings of representatives from the city, school district, public agencies, university, and community.

In the early phase of planning, before an organizational structure had evolved, small-group meetings were frequent. Although we pondered how to avoid so many, we concluded that they were necessary to pierce the shield of inertia that insulated the schoolyard from innovative thinking and change. As others have found, it took extensive discussion to build up momentum towards a shared image of a new reality among the wide circle of participants.

Techniques of meeting facilitation were used to speed up decision making and to help people gain more personal satisfaction from their participation. A neutral facilitator was appointed to ensure all voices were heard. Discussions were recorded on large sheets of newsprint taped to the wall to create a "group memory" so that everyone, especially latecomers, could review the record of earlier decisions. Facilitation helped improve timely reporting of decisions and follow-through with action.

A group of teachers and the authors formed the core group that addressed curriculum development and physical implementation of the project. University students, auxiliary staff, parents, and advisors also participated periodically. Weekly meetings kept us moving during the tumultuous first two years of action. Members of the group took turns publishing minutes in a weekly newsletter, which became an essential way to keep everyone apprised of the many disjointed events of the planning process.

Ad hoc meetings occurred on a daily basis, resulting from actions precipitated by external events that needed immediate response: grant application deadlines, insurance inspections, unexpected offers of assistance, maintenance problems, presentations to city agencies.

As time passed and different Yard projects became established, meetings became more specialized, more decentralized, and more directly related to particular action agendas (e.g., curriculum development, tree planting, fundraising, publicity, insurance negotiations). Small-group meetings worked best. When agendas were short and clearly defined, the groups achieved positive outcomes such as coordinating action, assigning responsibility, and endorsing decisions.

WORKSHOPS

Small-group meetings, however, were not always appropriate in the early days. Controversial issues required a more open meeting structure and more time (one and a half to two hours rather than forty-five to sixty minutes). Planning sessions on topics such as site development, activity programming, fundraising, and community involvement were treated as workshops because these complex issues required ample discussion and clarification before decisions could be made. Small-group techniques were still essential, though, because large gatherings were often subdivided into smaller task groups to formulate plans of action.

Brainstorm sessions were a common feature of workshops. The aim was to generate a list of ideas in a creative free-for-all, without worrying whether they were feasible or not. Later, participants carefully sifted through the list and decided which ideas were short-term or long-term, cheap or expensive, labor-intensive or required heavy equipment, were politically opportune or not, and so on.

As a warm-up exercise for the first brainstorm session, a group of UC Berkeley architecture students recalled their most vivid memories of their own childhood environments. These memories were used to generate a list of proposals for the Yard: "fungus farms," "compost pile," "rock collections," "fire," "mud flats," "sundial," "butterflies," "scarecrows," "waterfall," "tree houses," "barnyard," "maze," "sculpture garden," "kite flight," "caves," "weedfield," "islands," "death and decay," "ducks," "frogs." At the time, many of these ideas seemed wild and impossible. In retrospect, it is amazing to realize how many of them eventually came to fruition one way or another.

Workshops also served as in-service teacher training sessions. An early workshop dealt with the teachers' own childhood experiences. Entangled with the memories of joyful childhood discovery were also distressing recollections. For example, a teacher born in mainland China recalled people dying in the streets as her family fled the revolution—a powerful story that reminded us not to romanticize childhood as universally carefree and idyllic. We realized that some people grow up affected by childhood traumas and stressful family situations, making it difficult for them to interact naturally with their social and physical surroundings.

Other workshops addressed practical matters of curriculum development. A local ecology group conducted a composting workshop where everyone learned how to

During the planning and development phases, many meetings and workshops were required: with teachers (top), community members (middle), and city officials (bottom).

Ecology Action, a local nonprofit organization, leads a composting workshop for the teachers.

make jam-jar compost piles. Local utility district staff conducted a workshop on water conservation. Workshops on teaching techniques, curriculum packages, and classroom management were also held. Evening workshops on subjects such as houseplant care ("After-Dinner Gardening") were offered to parents as a way to connect them more closely to their children's daytime gardening activity.

Occasional workshops were based on walking surveys, a particularly effective method of site evaluation. Participants followed a predesignated route around the site, stopping at stations to record their observations and opinions about what they saw. Back indoors at a debriefing session, participants compared notes and set priorities for change.

IN-SERVICE TRAINING

To deepen and extend the participatory process, the Yard eventually became a training site. Weekend environmental education workshops were offered through the UC Berkeley Extension Program. One workshop, entitled "It's a Small World," attracted teachers and educational workers from as far away as Nevada and Oregon. These activists became part of the network of interest and took the participatory approach back to their local communities.

Training and dissemination workshops were also held at state, national, and international professional conferences, including a conference in Gothenberg, Sweden, held in 1979, during the International Year of the Child. The conference was part of a national campaign to improve Swedish schoolyards. (This initiative has recently been reactivated in a program called *Barnens Landskap*—see Appendix B.)

BEHAVIOR MAPPING

To document existing use of the schoolyard prior to the changes, a team of UC Berkeley student researchers kept a weeklong record of everything that happened in the Yard from eight in the morning until eight in the evening.

Before school. The site was practically devoid of activity, except for Berkeley High School students cutting across to reach their campus on the opposite side of MLK Way.

During school. Few classes used the site except for physical education. During recess there were two dominant centers of activity: ballgames on the asphalt—mostly basketball, kickball, and strike out—and play on the traditional equipment, which sometimes became severely

overcrowded. Hopscotch and four-square were also common. Many children were observed walking around, socializing, sometimes eating lunch. A variety of games with small plastic toys, hula hoops, and jump ropes (also used to play "horses") was observed, along with the traditional "girls-chase-the-boys" and "monsters."

The most prevalent observation was the antisocial atmosphere. Squabbling and fighting among the children were common. During the five days of observation, two serious fights occurred, in which one or both of the boys were bloodied. In each case, a crowd of children watched, egging the combatants on.

The teachers' primary connection with the outdoor environment was "playground duty," a universally disliked chore in which they exchanged the comforts of the staff lounge for police duties—breaking up fights, listening to complaints, and standing around observing routine activity.

After school and weekends. During the nine days of observation outside school hours, ballplay continued to be the dominant activity, with older boys and adult males from the neighborhood joining in. Bike riders, roller skaters, and joggers occasionally passed through. Several people practiced tennis shots against the ball wall. Three brief baseball games took place, each time with less than six players, even though the baseball "field" occupied the entire southern section of the site. Basketball occurred more often.

After school and during weekends, the majority of population counts showed between zero and a dozen users, with occasional peaks over twenty when organized basketball games were in progress. At other times, the site was devoid of activity. Clearly the space was drastically underused, even though it was the only sizeable recreational area in the neighborhood (apart from the Berkeley High athletics field on the other side of MLK Way). These observations provided ample evidence to recommend redevelopment.

SCHOOL-COMMUNITY SURVEYS

Survey research provided additional input into the master plan and served as a way to systematically document the need for change. Each major user group—students, parents, teachers, administrative staff, after-school users, and neighborhood residents—was surveyed using a variety of easily administered questionnaires. These low-cost surveys provided solid input from the entire community, in addition to the opinions of workshop participants.

DEVELOPMENT PHASES

Looking back at the development of the Yard we identified seven overlapping chronological phases:

Formulation. A small group of leaders conceived the idea and began to seek official support and financing. Media productions provided a major means of getting the concept across to local movers and shakers.

Planning and design. Community input and participation were actively sought; needs identified; goals and objectives defined; priorities established; other sites and facilities visited; surveys and workshops conducted; site constraints assessed; and resource capabilities investigated and specified. A preliminary master plan was drafted with initial suggestions for physical change.

Initiation. The first physical changes were made, some permanent and some temporary. The community of users became physically involved. This was a short-lived, euphoric phase, when many small-scale, nonpermanent changes were implemented.

Establishment. People responded to the initial physical changes and influenced the planning and design of future changes. "Big fixes" were finally decided upon and implemented. Asphalt was removed. From this point on, there was no turning back.

Feedback-feedforward cycles were set in motion by each subsequent change that guided development and modified the site master plan.

Media productions provided channels of communication to inform, promote, and raise funds for the project.

This was the phase of greatest struggle, of endless crises, of huge gaps between goals and achievement, and of vast distances between financial need and financial support. Failure constantly seemed imminent.

Consolidation. Eventually, gaps in credibility were reduced. The likelihood of failure diminished, although funding, insurance liability, and bureaucratic crises still flared up. Physical development progressed more smoothly.

Order began to emerge from the incremental additions of many small parts. Inexorably, the gap between the way things used to be and the way they were supposed to be (according to the plan) gradually decreased.

The Yard began to be used regularly as an environmental education site.

Maturity. Crises disappeared. Major physical development was completed. The site took on a strong visual identity. The master plan was almost entirely a description of development on the ground, with the exception of three or four major items that now received attention.

Children, teachers, parents, residents, and visitors began to enjoy a shared sense of place. Major media pieces were produced to help transfer the model to other communities.

Institutionalization. The developmental cycle came full circle, now at a much higher level of people-environment quality. The Yard was recognized and accepted by the city and the school district, consummated in an official partnership with the neighborhood group—Friends of the Yard. The potential of the Yard as a site for Project PLAE and other community programs was maximized. The master plan, now in its fifth iteration, had become a carefully rendered descriptive document of the Yard "as is."

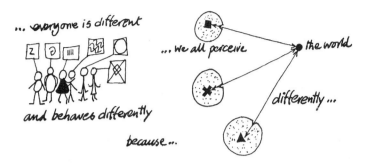

... everyone is different and behaves differently

... we all perceive the world differently ...

because ...

... but similarities in values creates homogeneous communities

... one thing ties us all together, our dependency on the environment — hence the need for shared environmental values.

...some people like the mix of values in heterogeneous communities

environmental education is concerned with the growth and development of such values.

17. WHY VALUES?

Interdisciplinary environmental education must find a way to connect the individuality of each learner to a sense of value for the planet we all share.

−2−	PARENTS

13. Do your children ever play on the yard at weekends?
seldom

14. What do you think the school yard should be used for?
A relaxed place for playing. A community Park after-hours. Attraction for small animals

15. What changes would you like to see made to the school yard? (Imagine that money is no object!)
Make "secluded" quiet areas TREES bare EARTH and WATER ... A garden area ... ropes to climb. Things built by the kids. Grass and FLOWERS. picnic tables. HUMAN SPACE!

16. Please use this space to say anything else you want about the Washington School Grounds.
This old style concrete, institutionalized space limits educational experience. Should be designed by the kids and everyone else. Could improve neighborhood greatly.

Please return this questionnaire to school, to your child's teacher. Thank you very much for your cooperation.

I would help work on construction

18. PARENT SURVEY

The many requests from parents for radical change were a critical reason why the Yard became such an ambitious project. Parents wanted to see a massive upgrading of the quality of their children's environment.

The banner project was a wonderful, participatory way of giving visibility to the Yard.

Students. Students filled out questionnaires administered in the classroom. They were asked what they liked about the existing schoolyard, what they did not like about it, and what they would like to see added or changed. Even five-year-olds could put a few words down or at least dictate them to their teacher. For older children, the survey was treated as a language arts assignment.

The results showed students liked the games they played on the asphalt, like running around, skipping, hot potato, and hopscotch. The boys liked ballgames. However, there were many complaints about the asphalt: it was hurtful, it was too hot, it was too cold, it was too windy, and it was boring (the most frequent comment).

The girls especially liked the bars, while both boys and girls mentioned the benches as a favorite spot— even though they consisted of uncomfortable, narrow planks cramped against the chainlink fences. Clearly, more and better seating was needed. Many children wanted additional equipment like sundecks, play structures, playhouses, slides, seesaws, swings, and "Tarzan ropes." There was also a strong desire for aquatic features (ponds, lakes, and streams), animals, and vegetation (grass, trees, flowers, bushes, and gardens). One student requested "flowers everywhere."

Some students, satisfied with the status quo, liked everything and disliked nothing. It was a classic example of the "planner's dilemma." Since some users found little fault with the schoolyard, we could have naïvely concluded that the situation was not critical and that only modest improvements were needed. Instead, we assumed that some students lacked personal experience on which to base their assessments. To counter this, we tried to educate the children and stimulate discussion by showing films and slides of "best practice" play environments from around the world. Individual classes extended this approach by taking field trips to playgrounds and conducting design workshops.

Students also drew pictures of both the existing site and what they thought the site should look like in the future. They accompanied the drawings with stories about what could happen in the redeveloped schoolyard. For this age group, imaginative ideas were more easily expressed in pictures than in words.

Teachers. Several teachers visualized the Yard as a living laboratory for environmental education, children's play, and neighborhood recreation. Many emphasized the importance of gross motor activity. Some teachers, however, did not comment on the educational potential of the site. This was a clear message that in-service training was needed to help generate more creative approaches to outdoor education.

Administrative staff. The clerical and maintenance staff recommended many useful changes that would make the site a better place from a management perspective. For example, they requested that enough trash cans be provided, as well as outdoor faucets so garden hoses could be used.

Parents. Parents strongly agreed with their children about the need for natural resources. This result, more than any other, was taken as a mandate to proceed with removing asphalt to create the Natural Resource Area. Without this forthright consensus, it is doubtful that we would have taken such a radical approach. Some parents suggested even more sweeping changes than their children. Others also expressed strong support for the traditional virtues of asphalt as a place to let off steam and engage in team games and sports.

Afterschool and weekend users. For seven days, interviews were conducted with every fourth person entering the site. By the end of this period, we had interviewed fifty people. A third of the participants were Washington students, a mix of girls and boys who came to hang out on the bars or play ball. More than a third were older children from the neighborhood (mostly Washington graduates) who came to play ball. The remaining interviewees consisted of adult male basketball players, largely college students from nearby apartments and a scatter of older residents.

Ballplayers of all ages were generally happy with the site. Their sole interest was the sports facilities, for which they suggested minor improvements.

Younger children also liked what was already there, but expressed desire for "sand," "slides," "cargo net," "rope ladder," "fort," and "swings." Some girls complained that there was too much "boys' stuff."

The heaviest demand was for asphalt to be replaced with "soft ground." Some said they wanted to see it "contoured." The second most frequent request was for water. Several people mentioned the need for night lighting.

The survey familiarized people in the neighborhood with the project and gave them an opportunity to participate in the planning process. More than ten percent of those surveyed offered to help: a band to play at Yard events, help with gardening and construction work, use of a truck, film, photography, typing, and offers to do "anything."

Neighbors. What about the surrounding residential community? We had to trawl the views of neighbors who did not currently use the Yard, but might do so if the space were redeveloped to meet their needs. Although only a small number attended the meetings and workshops, we did not assume they were uninterested. First, it was difficult to get information to them (we mostly relied on announcements stapled to utility poles in the neighborhood). Second, prospective participants had other priorities such as job and family, as well as many other local issues that placed demands on their time.

A door-to-door sample survey of neighborhood residents living within five blocks of the school was conducted eight months after the groundbreaking. We wanted to gauge their response to changes already made and to determine what kinds of facilities they wanted to see added or expanded during further phases of development.

Responses varied from extremely critical to highly positive. The owner of a new multifamily apartment building, for example, felt that property values would decrease as a result of disruption caused by construction work in the Yard. "People won't move in here," he complained. "The school's a real mess and they won't want to send their kids there." On the other hand, one of his tenants, a divorced mother with a five-year-old son, said she moved there because of its proximity to the school. She also offered help with the gardening, noting that she had her own garden before moving (her present apartment had no outdoor space).

An overwhelming number of residents asked for grass, trees, flowers, and natural landscape forms. They also expressed desire for water features such as "places for water play" and fish ponds. Other requests included conventional play equipment, ball courts, and farmyard animals. Many residents envisioned the Yard as an outdoor learning environment and a leisure facility complete with picnic tables and grills.

DESIGN WORKSHOPS

Once initial survey results and technical data about the site had been collected, the different community groups came together for the first design workshop to discuss priorities for the design program (the codified set of required spaces and facilities).

The workshop was held as part of a school open house, thus ensuring a good attendance. Several hundred people stopped by during the course of the evening. They viewed slides, studied survey results, and examined possibilities for layout of the site. They added further to a pyramid of ideas that had been accumulating from the survey results by drawing or writing comments on an enlarged site plan. Small groups met with core group members to discuss program details. In this

way, the workshop communicated a philosophy of openness in the planning and design process. People could see that plans were not being made behind closed doors and that their comments were being taken seriously. Subsequently, the evolving master plan (showing the spatial form of the design program) was displayed and discussed as "just a piece of paper" that could be changed anytime until implemented on the ground.

Individual classes held their own design workshops and produced detailed designs of special features. One class conducted a sophisticated "demand study" based on an initial brainstorm of the things the students wanted to see in the Yard (Figure 19).

Another student design workshop focused on the closure and redevelopment of a section of residential street that separated the two main sections of the school site. Three UC Berkeley architecture students worked with small groups of children to generate design ideas. First, they measured the width of the street by lying across it head to toe. A couple of students pretended to be dogs and identified spots that felt best: lamp posts, trees, entrances, and fire hydrants! Using scrap material, paint, and glue, the children added their proposed changes to a large-scale base model, with the university students serving as design facilitators. It was amazing to see how rapidly and creatively the students responded.

"Hey, let's have a fountain for people to play in."

"We need benches to sit on. Arrange them in a circle so people can see each other."

"We need trees for shade . . . and birds."

"What about a lawn for little kids to play on . . . and a basketball hoop."

One morning a boy gleefully arrived with an item he had found at home: a shoe box with the brand name "Easy Street" printed in large letters on the top. "Let's call it Easy Street," he exclaimed and positioned the box on one side of the model to represent a building. Elaborating on the idea, two students spent the rest of the morning making an arch over the street entrance with "Welcome" inscribed on it (see photographs at right).

Subsequent groups moved, added, and removed elements. The facilitators recorded each configuration. The observations were used to help represent the students' views in the final design of the street, along with input from other community groups.

SPECIAL EVENTS

Back to School Night, Open House, and the Yardfest provided important opportunities for people to participate in the Yard's evolution and review the progress.

Children were intimately involved in the design process. They worked with university students who engaged them in many creative, educational adventures, such as the redesign of the street separating the two halves of the school site.

19. DEMAND CHART

Children in one classroom decided by consensus on the twenty most important items they wanted developed on the site (swings, climbing structures, trees, sandboxes, mazes, ropes, gardens, etc.). Each child then had five votes to cast. The item shooting off the chart is water! This again lent support for developing an aquatic component.

Each event served as a vehicle for updating people on recent developments, attracting their interest, and obtaining their commitment to get involved.

Annual plant-ins, when every child in the school planted something in the Yard, instilled a sense of community, with every student and teacher participating in the collective effort.

Once development on the ground started, periodic workdays offered a more personal level of involvement in the evolution of the Yard. It gave families a chance to participate in neighborhood improvement through the fruits of their own labor. For parents with desk jobs, there were the health benefits of heavy manual work. Workdays were also social gatherings for people to meet their neighbors, socialize, and eat together on the "community commons."

ENVIRONMENTAL SIMULATION

Before removing the asphalt, we needed to be able to visualize the Yard after development. To construct this initial vision, we collected photographs of child-oriented open spaces in other neighborhoods, including some from other countries (amazingly, we did not find a single good example of an urban public school site). These photographs were interwoven with a set of renderings by a UC Berkeley architecture student showing how the Yard might look in the future. The primary purpose of this display was to sell the project to the community and to city agencies. Ten minutes on meeting agendas meant that presentations had to be tightly packaged. The technology was simple, inexpensive, and effective.

Documentation was another essential activity. A tremendous variety of material was collected: meeting minutes, survey results, drawings, models, and journalized notes. At that time, photography was the most important medium. To construct the initial simulation, we used slides. Later, we recorded live-action in the Yard, such as the groundbreaking, the first Yardfest, and user responses. New slides were periodically inserted into the presentation, replacing older material. Thus the original simulation of the Yard "as it might have been" gradually turned into a description of the Yard as it currently was.

PUBLICITY

With the Yard serving as a demonstration project, getting the word out to local, national, and international audiences was a key goal. We used several media. Photographs displayed at the Yardfest gave everyone, especially newcomers to the community, a historical perspective on the project. Former Washington students loved to see themselves in the pictures. "Hey, look, that's me!" a thirteen-year-old exclaimed at the 1981 Yardfest, when he spotted himself in a photograph. He pointed to a little boy sitting under the young weeping willow by the pond, taken five years previously almost to the day.

Help Change This Yard!, a "time-lapse," 16 mm movie, was made during the first few months of physical change on the site. The original idea was to produce a rigorous research document shot from the school roof, showing how behavior changed as the environment changed. However, it quickly became obvious that the result of hours of static stop action film would be too boring to hold anyone's attention. So we started to zoom in on episodes of particularly amusing, revealing, or interesting behavior, and eventually took the camera down from the roof to get really close to the action. The result was a completely willful but dramatic portrayal of the children's imaginative use of the Yard's new resources. This powerful and amusing film demonstrated how the physical environment could directly influence child behavior and development.

Audio documentation received increasing attention as the Yard developed and people had more to say about it. The recorded comments of children were an especially rich and revealing source of insight and expression.

"Hey, he's got a recorder on us," one of the boys joked. "Let's say something . . . let's give him some news about the Environmental Yard."

In 1977, we combined live recordings with slides to produce a film-strip package. This rather daunting exercise reduced the project to a few feet of film and a twenty-five minute narration divided into three segments.

The "Green Book" (so-named because of its bright green cover) was our most important early publication. The brochure contained descriptions of the site and surrounding community, the philosophy behind the Yard development, survey and workshop results, the master plan, and an artist's renderings of the future Yard.

20. GARDEN EXTENSIONS MURAL

Murals can turn gray concrete retaining walls into attractive assets. Children painted a record of garden-related learning experiences.

ENVIRONMENTAL
YARDREPORT
Friends of the Yard, Inc., September 1981

TEN YEARS ALONG . . . AND INTO THE FUTURE

A decade has passed since the early months of 1972 when the pie crust of asphalt was bulldozed from the south end of what was then a completely black-topped Washington School yard. Over the years, literally hundreds of people of all ages have been involved in creating the diversity of the Environmental Yard: trees, swings, bushes, ball playing areas, gardens, clubhouses, wildlife, benches, ponds, play equipment, meadows, sand boxes, quiet nooks, busy corners, shady spots, a stream, a stage..and the

years, we decided to create a legal organization for stability and longevity beyond the particular individuals. Hence Friends of the Yard came into being and was eventually incorporated in 1979.

The Yard has matured. Physical development is almost complete. Our attention has shifted to caring for the resources that have been created and promoting their use by the school and community.

In the past two years Friends of the Yard has also matured. We have a

21. YARD NEWSLETTER

Communication is key to community involvement. The *Yardreport* newsletter was published by Friends of the Yard with participation from children and parents. It contained information about the expanded program of activities and events, and disseminated a progress report to the broader community.

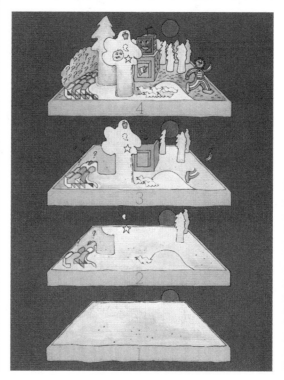

22. THE "GREEN BOOK"

Communication tied everything together. It helped people extend the meaning of the Yard beyond the purely functional level, creating a shared process where everyone took responsibility for change. The "Green Book," sponsored by an international corporation, was an effective promotional tool.

A federal government official visits the Yard.

Copies were distributed worldwide at conferences, by mail, to visitors, and at special events and workshops. The brochure was a great example of organizational partnership—designed as part of a master's thesis in visual design and sponsored by a major corporation.

Publicity efforts were designed to satisfy the basic information needs of a broad audience, both near and far. Initially we focused on local publicity, especially newspapers and magazines, to keep the local network of interest informed. Luckily, we attracted the interest of Bay Area newswriters who were willing to help disseminate information.

Newsletters were the basic medium for stimulating a sense of collective participation. Published at frequent intervals by several classes, they showcased work by the children. "Friends of the Yard," a nonprofit organization set up by the community, also sent out a newsletter periodically.

Environmental art pieces, such as the "Dream Wall," banners, garden murals, and decorated entrance boards added colorful reinforcement to the users' images of the Yard. We tried to think of each Yard surface as a place for communication, including the ground—like the whale drawings described in Chapter 5.

The most distant orbits of disseminated information were research papers published in journals and academic texts that slowly circulated through professional networks in child development, recreation, education, community development, landscape architecture, horticulture, and environmental design.

VISITORS

The most direct way of participating in the Yard, aside from working in it, was to visit the site. We encouraged critics of the project to take this crucial step, especially those who based their negative opinions on hearsay or a quick glance from their car. Once critics spent a few minutes taking a closer look, they invariably changed their minds.

Most individuals visited the Yard because they had seen publicity about the project or had heard about it from a colleague. They came from all over the world—teachers, community activists, child development experts, landscape architects, naturalists, parents, writers, recreational specialists, child-environment builders, researchers, and community development staff. Visitors returning to their own communities with positive information about the Yard project were the best public relations network we could ever hope for.

RECOGNITION

Awards were a formalized means by which other institutions participated in the achievements of the Yard. One class received the President of the United States Environmental Citation for their environmental education program. The "Urban Garden Ecosystems" program (which included the barnyard project and the Yard animal census) and the "Learning from Our Winter Environment" program both received the Alameda County Environmental Merit Award. The design of a statewide conservation poster earned first- and second-place awards. The Yard was selected as one of nineteen exemplary demonstration projects in environmental design research by the U.S. National Endowment for the Arts. Each of these "third-person qualifiers" brought valuable prestige to the project. The greatest benefit was that they encouraged people to take the Yard seriously and perhaps take a second look to reconsider their initial hasty judgment.

ASSESSMENT OF BEHAVIORAL IMPACT

In 1977, five years after work on the site began, we conducted a series of surveys of user groups to assess the Yard's impact and to determine what was missing or should be modified. The surveys included most of the original questions, as well as in-depth interviews of the "before-and-after" cohort of children discussed in Chapter 16.

At this time, a major behavior-mapping investigation was conducted to analyze how children used the Yard during lunchtime recess. For example, the behavior maps showed that some sections of asphalt were underused; as a result, they were taken for tree planting and construction of a community play area.[2]

We could not assume, however, that areas of the Yard not heavily used were not valued by the children. To investigate this issue further, we conducted a perception survey to find out which parts of the Yard were most vividly or persistently remembered (Figure 9, page 214). For example, the ponds, particularly the waterfall and fountain, were repeatedly mentioned, out of proportion to their actual amount of use. Conversely, the asphalt, parts of which were used heavily for ballgames, rarely appeared in the children's images.

SUCCESS BREEDS SUCCESS

Getting people involved, connecting them into the network of communication and decision making, and tapping their intelligence created a vortex of energetic participation. More and more users embraced the philosophy of community environmental education symbolized by the site.

The process began with pushing people into taking part and eventually evolved to a point where the redeveloped Yard began pulling people in, inviting them to celebrate its life. The founding of Project PLAE, the program that integrated children with disabilities (see Chapter 14), marked this point of genuine community "placeness." The site, children, educators, community artists, playleaders, and the programs that bound them together became the indivisible parts of a vital and renewed culture. Gradually, the Yard became a self-fulfilling prophesy, first guided by—and then exemplifying—the participatory, ecological approach embodied in its founding.

As the physical environment became increasingly developed, the options for programmed activity grew infinitely more rich. By now, teachers no longer felt the need to seek permission to implement study programs since a framework for action was well established. The Yard had become an institution with a stable organizational core.

RESOLUTION 44795

"How can we get the city to buy into this crazy idea?" we thought at the beginning of the project. It seemed too radical and we had no convincing evidence to prove that it was a practical or worthwhile idea. "What we need is a 'whereas statement,'" Mary Jefferds, our political advisor, suggested, "for the city council, commissions, and the school board to buy into—something they can't refuse without denying basic community values." Resolution 44795 turned out to be the most important political step we ever took.

It took months to carry the statement around the city commissions and school board to get it endorsed. In effect, we acquired an explicit symbol of involvement: an undeniable agreement with city authorities on the primary goals of the project. We still harbored the feeling of "so what?" until we ran into conflict with those same authorities about the slow progress of construction. At that point we pulled out Resolution 44795 and said, "Give us a chance. It's not easy. Rome wasn't built in a day. We're doing the best we can to implement the goals the city already endorsed." It was a strong defense, and surely kept the project from being shut down and reasphalted.

The final line in the story came several years later, when Friends of the Yard was firmly established and the political climate was a lot more positive. Resolution 44795 was pulled out again and used as the basis of a "Resolution of Cooperation between Berkeley Unified School District, City of Berkeley, and Friends of the Yard, Incorporated," subsequently endorsed by the school district and the Berkeley City Council. The partnership became official.

REFERENCES

1. Lecture, Massachusetts Institute of Technology, 1965.

2. Moore, R. (1986). "The Power of Nature: Orientations of Girls and Boys Toward Biotic and Abiotic Environments." *Children's Environments Quarterly* 3(3), 52–69.

Site Development Strategies

The technical process of planning the Yard was conducted alongside the participatory process, with frequent crossover between the two. Planning began with the identification of resources: community members and organizations, natural resources and phenomena, objects and materials, tools, money, time, and space. Development was driven by the availability of resources—there was no point in planning for what we did not have or could not get. From the beginning we tried to view everything as a resource. We wanted to put all idle resources to work, especially the resources with the greatest potential: the site and the people of the community.

SITE ASSESSMENT

The first step in making the master plan realistic was to thoroughly understand the capacities, potentials, and problems of the site. We viewed the acre and a half of asphalt as a great potential, provided the resources could be found to develop it.

Service area. The site was a public open space. What special characteristics could attract community use? What were the potentials of its location in the jigsaw of neighborhood geography?

Along the east side ran MLK Way, a major arterial abruptly edging the neighborhood. From other directions, the site was accessible by pedestrians from a forty-block area. However, research on the use of neighborhood parks in Berkeley indicated that the rate of use dropped off sharply for people living more than two to four blocks away.[1] As a result, we defined a smaller thirty-five-block area as the primary service zone (Figure 23). The zone was home to nearly three thousand residents, 260 of whom, according to the census, were between the ages of five and fourteen. The much larger 110-block "school attendance zone" housed over three hundred Washington student families. This population was regarded as the prime target. Although most would probably not use the Yard informally as neighborhood residents, we hoped they would turn out for special events and programs.

Boundary conditions. The chainlink fence along MLK Way made the site visible to thousands of drivers every day—and vice versa. Street traffic was a major source of acoustic and visual intrusion that needed buffering (Figure 25). We thought of creating hanging or vertical gardens on the fence, believing it could be used as a highly visible display setting. These eventually developed into "edge habitats," discussed below.

The friendlier western boundary fence bordered a quiet residential street, facing away from downtown towards the heart of the Flatlands.

The remaining boundaries were overlooked by buildings. Three-story apartment buildings faced the west and south boundaries. To the north was the school building, from which hundreds of students streamed out at each recess (Figure 24).

Access and circulation. Accessibility was good. The school was situated along a major bus route, with a bus stop located at the site. Service was frequent. Pedestrian entrances were available from each street, connecting to heavily traveled pedestrian neighborhood routes that were incorporated into the master plan. A double-gated vehicle entrance connected to MLK Way. An additional pedestrian entrance was needed so that people could enter midway along the boundary fence. The location of access points was a key factor in the site-planning process (Figure 24). Functional requirements included wheelchair access, solid waste pick-up, supply deliveries, and emergency vehicle access.

Size, shape, and volume. The total area (one and one half acres) and squat "T" shape of the site directly influenced what could or could not be developed. The Natural Resource Area for instance, was located at the far end where it was protected on three sides by boundary fences and was farthest away from the crowds of students exiting the building. Consideration of the vertical dimension highlighted the educational potential of the roof of the school building.

Fixed features. The undeveloped site was practically featureless. Detailed observation of behavior, however, revealed highly valued features such as the drinking fountain, traditional play equipment, and ballplay areas. These features needed to be incorporated into the master plan.

Vegetation. Vegetation, although sparse, attracted much attention from the children. Blackberry vines climbing the western boundary fence (behind the apartments) bore ample fruit, which many children picked and ate. A great thatch of Plumbago (*P. auriculata*) hung down the fence behind the bars. An aggressive colonizer of chainlink fences, this plant provided untold numbers of delicate gray-blue flowers for many generations of Washington children to pick, take home, present to teachers, stick in each other's hair, or decorate their bodies. Branches of peach and flowering plum trees thrust through the southern boundary fence and provided a touch of spring color.

All existing vegetation was located either on or behind the fence. Not a single blade of grass grew on the site itself.

Topography. The existing ground surface was a flat asphalt sheet, sloping gently away from the school building, engineered to deliver precipitation as quickly as possible to the nearest drain. The drain locations were a critical consideration in proposing major changes to the topography of the site.

Microclimate. Microclimatic zones included a protected sunny edge adjacent to the school building (extremely hot in summer); a cool southern end shaded by adjacent apartment buildings; and a constant, cool westerly breeze across the Main Yard. Traffic noise, considered an acoustic dimension of microclimate, was extremely intrusive, especially along the eastern boundary (Figure 25).

Ancillary Spaces. The need for the following indoor spaces adjacent to the site was identified:

- a small office with a desk, telephone, and filing cabinet for paperwork, research materials, and documentary archives;

- a space for meetings, workshops, and children's activities; and

- a lockable storeroom for tools, equipment, and materials.

These needs were met mostly with small, dimly lit, rather inaccessible rooms in the school basement. The solution was not ideal, but acceptable—and certainly a lot better than nothing.

Outdoor storage was needed early on for storing construction materials and gardening tools. Later, a small fieldhouse ("Kids HQ") was constructed between the Main Yard and Natural Resource Area, housing a telephone, program supplies, and equipment.

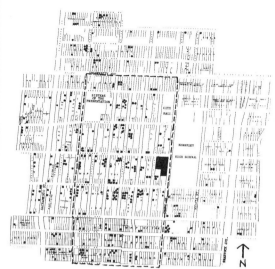

23. SERVICE AREA MAP

This map shows the 110-block service area of the school. The broken line defines the thirty-five-block area within four or five blocks of the school—assumed to be the primary walking distance for weekend users from the neighborhood. Each dot represents the location of a student's home.

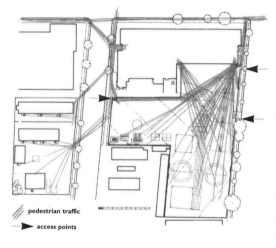

pedestrian traffic

access points

24. PRE-DEVELOPMENT ACCESS POINTS AND CIRCULATION

The pattern shows how the site was used as a mid-block pedestrian route. Also shown is the rush of children out of the exit doors at recess time, heading for the few settings suitable for play (mostly ballgames). Arrows show access points.

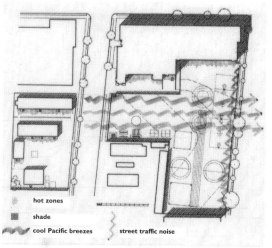

hot zones

shade

cool Pacific breezes   street traffic noise

25. PRE-DEVELOPMENT MICROCLIMATIC ZONES

The site had a distinctive microclimate: cool, westerly Pacific breezes; distinct hot and cool zones created by buildings that either shaded or reflected the sun's rays; and the traffic noise from adjacent MLK Way—an intrusive dimension of the acoustic environment.

A college student improves soil conditions by mixing in truckloads of leaves.

TIME

Time conservation was one of the original justifications for developing the Yard. As every teacher knows, time is a dominant constraint on what can or cannot be included in the daily curriculum. The development of outdoor learning environments on the school site conserved time by reducing the need for field trips away from school. In fact, it enabled most teachers to use the outdoors on a daily basis, instead of relegating outdoor educational activities to occasional field trips or special events.

Time was also scarce in the participatory planning process. It took months to get people involved and reach consensus on decisions, even though special techniques were used to manage the process as efficiently as possible, as described in the previous chapter.

The ecological systems developed in the Yard were time-dependent, too, with diurnal, monthly, and seasonal cycles of decomposition and rebirth punctuating the larger scale of the Yard's evolution through time.

Careful design consideration was given to the temporal cycles of nature: ponds as the spawning ground of terrestrial life; coast redwoods (*Sequoia sempervirons*) as one of the longest-living and tallest species; horsetail (*Equisetum funstoni*) as an ancient species. Shadow patterns were designed to draw attention to the passage of the Earth around the sun. Flowering shrubs and trees accentuating fall color marked the passing seasons. The daily "fog cycle" of Bay Area weather could be observed from the school roof.

FUNDRAISING

We sought three types of financial support: funds for supplies and equipment (benches, trees, hammers, and other items on a "want list"); funds for people (student assistants, community artists, ancillary staff, and consultants); and funds for site development work (asphalt removal, grading, drainage, vegetation, fencing, and play structures). Over several years, most funding came from federal, state, and local grants administered through the school district.

The biggest challenge was dealing with annual budget cycles that caused us to seesaw between periods of affluence (when it was difficult to make decisions fast enough to spend allocated funds) and periods of poverty (when there was insufficient funding to implement decisions already made). To balance out the cash flow, we had to cooperate closely with school district administrators willing to bend the rules to make the best use of limited finances.

CONSTRUCTION MATERIALS

We collected a vast array of construction materials for Yard redevelopment, including utility poles, sewer pipe sections, soil amendment, tree trunks, and fencing materials. Many items were donated by local companies and city departments.

NATURAL RESOURCES

Because of their self-regenerative, self-sustaining characteristics, natural resources offered a high benefit-cost ratio; for example, the forty redwood saplings donated by the California Redwood Association became the redwood grove. The cost was minute compared to the enormous benefit offered to the children each day, once the trees grew a few feet high. We also could argue that the costs of asphalt removal and ground preparation in the whole Natural Resource Area compared favorably with the long-term benefits for hundreds of children.

Volunteer, indigenous plants and animals invaded the site, free of charge. Likewise, sunlight, moonlight, wind, precipitation, clouds, fog, gravity, fire, vegetation decay, and the formation of fertile ground were dimensions of the biosphere that, because of the Yard, we were able to integrate into the curriculum.

TOOLS

We defined a tool as anything that increased the effectiveness of another resource. Basic tools included hammers, saws, wrenches, power drills, a portable circular saw, a small gas-powered chain saw, garden tools, a wheelbarrow, and a stepladder. Larger tools such as a jack hammer or cultivator were borrowed or rented as needed.

Curriculum tools such as clipboards, yardsticks, hand lenses, and thermometers were simple yet crucial items. These tools increased the students' scope and intensity of interaction with the environment, enabling them to "read" it more clearly and more closely. Some tools were constructed by the students, such as the wind vanes erected on the school roof.

STAFF

Our greatest need was for skilled, committed people to crew the ship—to plan, design, and manage the site; to conduct research; to develop curricular activities; to organize the community; to raise funds; to coordinate feedback into the development program; to write copy; to draft grant applications; and to deal with insurance. The need was massive and never fully satisfied.

There was the school staff, of course, but the need far exceeded their capacity. University students filled many gaps, but often lacked the professional experience necessary for high-profile, "front-end" tasks. Their strength was project work with the children. They were hired as grants came in. We relied primarily on parents with professional skills and campus colleagues willing to lend a hand. Occasionally, grants were used to support professional services.

We kept a sharp lookout for "self-starter" types, people with fertile ideas, willing to plunge in and try things out. At the same time, they needed to be tuned in to the Yard's philosophical wavelength, or initiatives could result in undesirable consequences.

The teaching staff was an exceptional in-house professional community with a number of strengths not found in the average elementary school. The teachers showcased strong multicultural interests and fluency in several languages and dialects, including Japanese, Spanish, and Chinese (Mandarin and Cantonese). Interest and involvement in the arts was widespread. A faculty jazz combo performed regularly at school functions. With pianos in the classrooms, teachers incorporated song and dance into the daily curriculum. Other teachers shared their enthusiasm for visual arts and crafts with their students.

FLEXIBILITY

In the initial phases of development, tight organization and communications were needed to hold the project together. Personnel had to be skilled and flexible enough to assume a variety of tasks. One reliable full-time person was far more effective than several part-time staff members. Early on, before routine administrative procedures had been formulated, we worked in an environment of constant change and unpredictability. We had to rely almost entirely on daily, face-to-face contact and coordination to achieve progress. In later phases, as the project became consolidated, tasks became more specialized and organization could be more dispersed.

People with the least amount of time to spare were the students' parents. They had young children to raise, careers to establish, houses to clean, gardens to weed, and cars to maintain, leaving little time for community work. For this reason, we expanded the boundaries of the "support community" to include others with less constrained schedules, such as university students and several wonderful, energetic retirees.

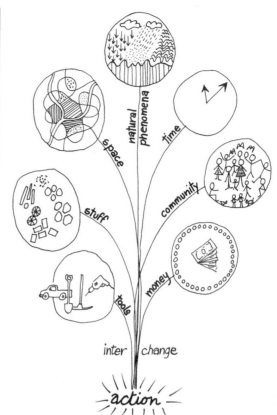

26. A BOUQUET OF RESOURCES

All resources (tools, materials, space, natural phenomena, time, community, money) coact to produce results on the ground. All must be identified and involved in the process.

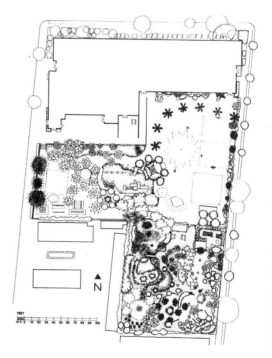

27. MICROCLIMATIC IMPROVEMENT

This drawing shows the dramatic diversification of the Yard microclimate. A major problem with most urban school sites is the lack of shade, a critical issue given the negative effects of excessive sunlight on skin.

In seven years, the quality of the Yard was dramatically improved by tree growth, which provided a broad range of microclimatic choice. As trees got larger, however, some groundcovers were shaded out, thus reducing overall plant diversity.

BIG FIXES

We tried to keep the master plan as flexible as possible during the initial phase of development. Still, a number of critical site development decisions had to be made before physical development could proceed. Some "big fixes" were inevitable and reflected physically dominant elements of the site: its size and shape, major circulation routes, microclimatic patterns, vehicular access, as well as the location of existing facilities such as play equipment and utility lines.

Other big fixes were forced upon us by the "lumpy" character of the front-end elements of the project (i.e., large changes that could not be subdivided into phases). These included the sizeable Natural Resource Area, the large central community area, the play structure, and retained asphalt areas for ballgames.

Six or seven fixes that were defined as "big" influenced the layout of the entire site. Since they were the first major decisions to be made, they became the major structural elements of the master plan and at the same time, once implemented, the first set of physical constraints that limited future action.

The vegetation plan was a more flexible big fix that had to be carefully thought through. Planting opportunities were not distributed evenly over the site. "Edge habitats" were created by planting the protected zones along site boundaries (MLK Way buffer, giant planter, stack-sack wall, and Orchard Wayside). The Natural Resource Area was laid out as an integrated ecosystem of plant communities and habitats. Within a few years, rapid tree growth throughout the Yard improved the microclimate and physical comfort of the users dramatically (Figure 27).

BEHAVIOR-ENVIRONMENT ECOSYSTEMS

As Yard development progressed, we tried to maintain maximum openness in the planning process. But the need to make decisions—to act, to implement development on the ground—meant that the level of flexibility and the range of remaining choice narrowed constantly.

The master plan was like a set of nested Chinese boxes. There was the biggest box of the Yard, which itself contained three primary-zone boxes: the Natural Resource Area, Main Yard Systems, and Asphalt. Inside each of these three boxes were sets of boxes arranged according to the structure of each zone. As development took place and design decisions were changed, boxes were revised and their nesting structure reshuffled.

Fifty-eight Activity Places (smaller boxes within the three primary-zone boxes) were eventually identified behaviorally and physically as discrete places by the way they were used (Figure 28), named, or visually perceived and graphically represented in children's drawings (Figure 9, p. 214).

Each Activity Place was also part of a Behavior-Environment Ecosystem (BEE). The Gazebo, for example, was one of ten structures that made up the "meeting/working" ecosystems of the Natural Resource Area (which contained four additional ecosystems). The Yard comprised a total of ten behavior-environment ecosystems (Figures 29 and 30).[2]

Each place contained an assortment of fine-grain elements that contributed functional diversity, such as fence posts, trees, shrubs, rocks, painted game lines, benches, trash cans, and water spigots (Figure 31). The Gazebo, for instance, was built from five wooden columns as the main structure, plus a plywood roof, upper platform, access ladder, and four benches spanning between the columns at ground level.

THE ECOLOGY OF PLANNING, DESIGNING, AND BUILDING

In the beginning of the design process, the boxes lay on the drafting board like the pieces of a Rubik's Cube waiting to be fitted together. Their size, contents, and nesting relationships were influenced by community inputs and site assessments, by the finite space available, and by the availability and aesthetics of the compositional elements. A diversity of settings was designed and constructed, changed as users responded (Figure 32), gradually meshing and evolving into a set of Behavior-Environment Ecosystems, and eventually into the whole Yard ecosystem.

Some initial choices felt arbitrary because of the lack of physical constraints. As further decisions were made, the flexible ecosystem structure began to guide development in a more definite direction. Eventually, as boxes were filled with content and fitted together, design options became increasingly constrained until there was only one way to go—we were literally "boxed in." From then on, modifications caused a wave of additional modifications and refinements to flow through the rest of the system.

•

Long before construction of the Yard was complete, we realized that the planning, design, and construction process was itself an ecological process. We also realized that the outcome was much more

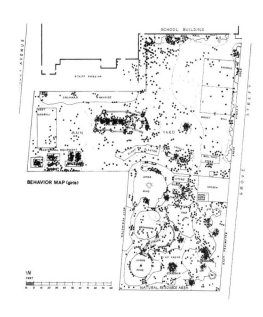

BEHAVIOR MAP (girls)

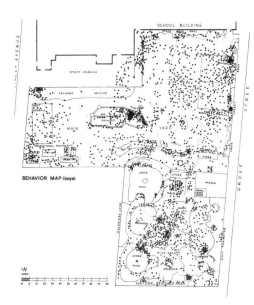

BEHAVIOR MAP (boys)

28. BEHAVIOR MAPS

These maps show the locations of girls and boys during lunchtime recess. Girls used the traditional equipment more than boys and spent more time sitting and talking, especially in the Natural Resource Area.

Boys moved around more and spent much more time on the asphalt playing ballgames. In the Natural Resource Area, they played with the water more than the girls.

ENVIRONMENTAL YARD

3 Primary Zones

NATURAL RESOURCE AREA   MAIN YARD   ASPHALT

10 Behavior-Environment Ecosystems

Meeting/work areas · Aquatic places · Pathways · Trees/bushes · Meadows · Play structures · Edges · Traditional equipment · Ballplay areas · Circulation/game areas

58 Activity Places											Total
Number of Activity Places	11	8	5	6	2	4	12	1	4	5	58
Percent Use	11	9	6	6	6	14	12	7	17	12	100
Percent Space	4	6	5	6	5	7	13	8	26	20	100
Use/Space Ratio (USR)	2.0	1.7	1.1	0.7	0.7	2.2	0.8	1.9	0.7	0.6	1.0

29. USE/SPACE RATIO

Each Behavior-Environment Ecosystem (BEE) includes a set of related Activity Places.

Use/space ratio (USR), shown on the bottom line, gives a measure of how well each BEE was used in relation to its area. Values above and below 1.00 indicate above- and below-average use efficiency. For example, play structures (2.2) were the most effective use of space; asphalt was the least (0.7/0.6). Other well-used BEEs included the meeting/work places (2.0), the traditional equipment (1.9), and the aquatic places (1.7).

30. BEES MAP

Natural Resource Area
- **Meeting/work areas**
- **Aquatic places**
- **Pathways**
- **Trees/bushes**
- **Meadows**

Main Yard Systems
- **Play structures**
- **Edges**
- **Traditional equipment**

Asphalt
- **Ballplay areas**
- **Circulation/game areas**

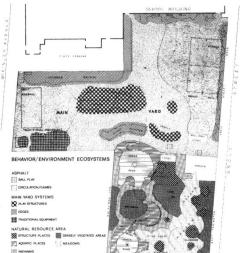

BEHAVIOR/ENVIRONMENT ECOSYSTEMS

ASPHALT
- BALL PLAY
- CIRCULATION/GAMES

MAIN YARD SYSTEMS
- PLAY STRUCTURES
- EDGES
- TRADITIONAL EQUIPMENT

NATURAL RESOURCE AREA
- STRUCTURE PLACES
- AQUATIC PLACES
- PATHWAYS
- DENSELY VEGETATED AREAS
- MEADOWS

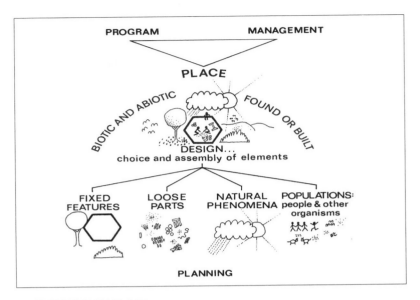

31. ELEMENTS OF PLACE

Each place is designed to combine (or naturally acquires) a mix of different types of elements: biotic, abiotic, found, and constructed. The design process is concerned with the choice and assembly of these elements: fixed features, loose parts, natural phenomena, and populations (people and other living things—plant and animal).

It is an ongoing, dynamic process that in an educational context must be managed to meet a program of learning objectives and child development goals. And here is the difficult part of the process, as these goals and objectives are a direct reflection of local educational philosophies and political commitment; if they are not aligned with the purposes of hands-on, outdoor learning, the mission will eventually fail.

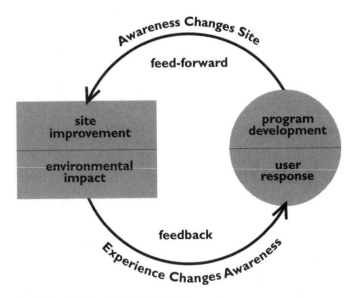

32. EVOLUTIONARY DESIGN PROCESS

As the planning process advances, as the master plan is developed, as the educational program evolves, and as resources are applied and physical development becomes a reality, users test the evolving environment and change their behavior and perceptions. This user response "feeds back" to modify the flexible master plan, which in turn "feeds forward" to modify the physical site, and so on. The whole process is subject to a high level of uncertainty at the beginning, which lessens as the site is "built out." New projects must be constantly introduced to maintain the creative interest of children and teachers.

STAGE		TIME

I
Initiation
	Preliminary site survey
	Community survey and interaction
	Discussion and review of existing
	  developments
	Curricular explorations of existing
	  conditions
	Project endorsement by local, state,
	  and national authorities
	Search for money
	Preliminary master plan
		**1–2
		years**

II
*Small
Changes*
	On-site, temporary changes, impor-
	  tation of materials
	Documentation
	Evolution of small-scale permanent
	  elements
	Community feedback and incorpora-
	  tion into master plan
	Search for money
	Development of master plan
		**2–3
		years**

III *Big Changes*	Big decisions, big-scale changes Incremental development of zones Firm master plan Search for money	**3 years**
IV	Possible conflicts with insurance, administration, etc. Legitimization Regional significance Service and training activities Discussion of new personnel roles H.Q. enclosed space needed	**2–5 years**
V	Regional training site	**3–5 years**
VI *Evolution*	Institutionalization and maturity Transfer to other sites	**5–10 years**

VII
Renewal
	Renewal, new initiatives, responses
	  to new conditions or danger of
	  collapse
		**10–20
		years**

33. LIFE HISTORY PROFILE

The chart above profiles the life history to expect with a school grounds development project like the Environmental Yard. Think in terms of at least five years to become firmly established. Consider how to keep the project constantly evolving and renewing.

diverse than would have happened had the Yard been constructed in a definite construction phase, a task that would have taken as little as six months. Instead, it took ten years. During that time, many modifications were made to the landscape—some were major, most were positive and deliberate, and a few were negative and forced upon us. The process of change, adjustment, and renewal was continuous, and, most importantly, was embedded in the school-community educational process.

In looking back at this process and comparing the "instant" landscape approach with the "evolutionary" one, we find that the instant approach cannot achieve the same depth of involvement and co-evolution of values and environmental experience. The evolutionary model leads continuously towards higher levels of dynamic quality, in both human development and landscape development. There is no end result. Because the context is educational, it always offers new opportunities for discovery, for adventure, and for learning about oneself, the community, and the biosphere—and their interrelationships.

The history of the adventure, the place, and the people co-evolve as well, always open to new twists and turns. In instant landscapes, there is no possibility of creating history-through-action, as the action is short-lived, preordained, and pre-empted by the closed design process.

We are not suggesting that all public urban landscapes should follow this co-evolution process, or even that all educational landscapes should. This approach obviously would not work with athletic fields (although it could still happen around their periphery). However, we are convinced that this philosophy should be applied to at least part of each school site if the desire is to create an authentic outdoor learning environment.

Only one requirement is absolutely essential for success: official institutional commitment. Outdoor, natural learning environments must be placed at the same level of priority as updated textbooks, computers, desks, and a roof on the school building. Without this weight of value, no matter how strong the commitment of individuals in the school community, the effort will eventually wither away, just as the Yard became a shadow of its former self (see Epilogue). Along with institutional commitment there must be committed leadership with a passion for keeping the dynamic quality alive. Local commitment is a microcosm of commitment to the whole planet. The two are one.

REFERENCES

1. Mason, G., et al. (1975). *Berkeley Park Use Study.* University of California, Berkeley.

2. For full details of this research, see Moore, R. C. (1986). "The Power of Nature: Orientations of Girls and Boys Toward Biotic and Abiotic Environments." *Children's Environments Quarterly* 3(3), 52–69.

Child-Centered Outdoor Educational Settings

Children's environments, especially those used as educational resources, should contain a diversity of settings. The more diverse the environment, the broader the range of curricular options available to the teacher and the more likely that all the cells in the Curriculum Switchboard (page 207) can be covered. Increased diversity, of course, also provides increased play options—enabling playing and learning to be more closely linked. The following list of seventeen types of settings provides a general guide for teachers, designers, and community groups as they begin planning a new environment or upgrading an existing one. More detailed design guidance is available elsewhere.[1]

OUTDOOR PLAY AND LEARNING SETTINGS

1. **Entrances**
2. **Pathways**
3. **Signage and displays**
4. **Fences and enclosures**
5. **Manufactured equipment and play structures**
6. **Multipurpose game settings**
7. **Groundcovers and safety surfaces**
8. **Landforms and topography**
9. **Trees and vegetation**
10. **Garden settings**
11. **Animal habitats**
12. **Aquatic settings**
13. **Sand and dirt settings**
14. **Play props**
15. **Gathering, meeting, and working settings**
16. **Performance settings**
17. **Field stations and storage settings**

1. ENTRANCES

Entrances should welcome visitors to the site and reinforce the sense of arrival and departure. They should express or symbolize the educational, social, and cultural mission of the site. Entrances should be designed as gathering places and information points, with ample space for socializing. They should also serve as the transition space between arrival and play areas. As places where children are picked up or dropped off, they must be fully accessible to people of all abilities.

A variety of sensory cues can be provided to help orient and guide visitors. Cues can be visual (e.g., bollards, paving patterns, landmark towers, flagpoles, screen walls), tactile (e.g., paving surfaces, tactile maps, signs), and acoustic (e.g., wind chimes, the sound of children playing, songbirds).

2. PATHWAYS

From the entrance area, primary pathways should provide direct, accessible pedestrian routes to centers of activity, important landmarks, and facilities such as toilets, drinking fountains, telephones, and meeting rooms. As part of this network, signage must provide clear directions and related information that can be easily read and understood by people of all ages and abilities.

Secondary pathways should provide less direct routes and become part of the play setting itself, such as for hiding and chasing games. These paths can take many forms as places where users can interact with the natural landscape and explore. They can serve as environmental education trails where children can make discoveries at their own pace.

Some pathways can provide hard surfaces where children can ride wheeled toys, tricycles, or pull carts—a common activity in preschools.

3. SIGNAGE AND DISPLAYS

In conjunction with pathways, signage must clearly communicate directions and other important information. Signs must provide a comprehensive system that meets strict functional requirements for accessibility and wayfinding. Signs can also enhance the atmosphere of play and exploration. The design, typographic style, and materials used should blend harmoniously with the surroundings, while meeting functional requirements.

In outdoor play and educational environments, there are several types of information that need to be displayed through signage systems:

Directional signs should be located at all entry and decision points. They should present information indicating direction to a space or facility, a change in route, or confirmation of a correct route.

Informational signs should be placed at all entry points. They should present general information about permanent features of the site, and the locations of circulation routes and main facilities.

Identification signs should present information in both words and pictographs about specific features or facilities.

Regulatory signs should notify users about rules, requirements, warnings, and restrictions. They should be used for traffic delineation and control.

Bulletin boards should be used to display day-to-day information about educational programs and community events. Too often, bulletin boards are not designed large enough and are insufficient in number.

Expressive displays should use vertical and ground surfaces, structures, overhead spaces, utility poles, skywires, and roof lines to suspend artwork generated by the educational program or special events. The infrastructure to support these possibilities should be designed into the site from the beginning.

4. FENCES AND ENCLOSURES

Fences and enclosures help delineate pathways, enclose activity areas, and define social settings. They also protect vegetation and other fragile environments by directing the flow of pedestrian movement. In urban areas, particularly those with high volumes of vehicular traffic, fences and enclosures help ensure safety and security for children at play.

Fences and enclosures should reflect the physical structure of the site and the patterns of activity within. Fences can be designed to double back on themselves to provide small outdoor classroom settings. Low walls can help define different activity zones of a play area, as well as become part of the play setting for children and provide informal seating for adults. Vegetation can also serve as an effective enclosure, defining the boundaries of settings and screening them from adjacent areas.

Fences and enclosures also play an important role at the interface of natural habitats and more structured play settings. Visual access to natural areas should be maintained, but fragile environments must be protected from unwanted intrusions. Fence designs should protect natural areas without compromising their visual quality.

5. MANUFACTURED EQUIPMENT AND PLAY STRUCTURES

The primary function of manufactured play equipment is to support gross motor development. Carefully selected structures can also help foster creativity and cooperation among children. Even in the most diversified play environments, equipment settings attract a high density of use. Typical pieces of equipment include balance beams, climbers, multilevel structures, net structures, overhead runways, rocking equipment, slides, spinning equipment, swings, and upper-body structures.

Play structures attract children because they offer physical challenges and opportunities for risk taking. Well-designed play structures provide these challenges without posing undue safety hazards. Children should be able to climb to a reasonable height without exposing themselves to a dangerous fall. In the United States, safety guidelines for play equipment and surfacing have been established by both the Consumer Product Safety Commission (CPSC) and the American Society for Testing and Materials (ASTM). Standards have also been set by organizations and government agencies in Canada,

the United Kingdom, Australia, New Zealand, and Germany. A European standard is under consideration.

Play equipment should be selected and sited as part of a comprehensive master plan. By selecting equipment that promotes different types of play activity for different age groups, designers can create a diverse gross-motor play setting that allows children to choose the activities they enjoy and to seek appropriate challenges. Most manufactured equipment is available in modular formats that offer many configurations to support a wide range of play activities for various age groups. All types of play activity that can be accommodated by fixed structures must be considered, such as large-group play, active play, solitary play, quiet play, and dramatic play.

In today's society, children increasingly lack opportunities to shape their environment. Such activities are critical for children's mental health and self-esteem. They are especially critical for children from very restricted or chaotic home situations where they have no control over their environment.

Open-ended structures provide an excellent way for children to shape their environment. By positioning wooden posts at the corners of a raised platform, children can add materials to create forts, houses, and other structures. When not being used for structure building, the posts and platform can function as a miniature stage or as a meeting place for small groups.

A variety of items can be added to extend a structure's role as a stimulus for play activities. Manufacturers now offer items such as compasses, clocks, tic-tac-toe boards, telescopes, and binoculars. Such elements can boost children's interest in the play structure, stimulating a wider range of dramatic play and increasing the programming potential of the setting. Combining manufactured equipment with natural settings or with opportunities for sand and water play can also enrich the play setting.

In addition to providing physical challenges, manufactured play equipment should promote opportunities for dramatic play and social interaction. A crucial function of children's play is socialization, which involves processes such as communication, negotiation, and cooperation. Play environments should include semi-private spaces where children can socialize without interruption or distraction from nearby activities. Several manufacturers offer modular elements that can be added to play structures to stimulate this type of play.

Permanent structures are needed in play areas to support dramatic play. As much as possible, these structures should exhibit a strong visual identity and sufficient complexity to maintain children's interest for long

In the Natural Resource Area, waist-high, single- and double-rail fences (shown above as dark lines) were used to define new pathways and planted areas.

PRINCIPLES FOR DESIGNING PLAYFUL PLACES

- Identify design opportunities.
- Employ sensitive site assessment.
- Include participation by all groups.
- Emphasize child development objectives and needs by age.
- Articulate curricular strategies.
- Give priority to circulation.
- Apply playing and learning settings concept.
- Emphasize play value of settings.
- Pay attention to microclimate.
- Discuss visibility and supervision.
- Use evolutionary approaches.
- Consider play leadership and animation.
- Give first priority to quality in children's environments.
- Integrate natural environments.

**CRITERIA FOR
SITE DESIGN**

- **Accessibility
  (universal design).**
- **Safety.**
- **Graded challenge.**
- **Diversity and clarity.**
- **Flexibility.**
- **Defensible space.**
- **Supervision.**
- **Permanence.**
- **Change.**
- **Open-endedness.**
- **Manipulability.**
- **Multisensory
  stimulation.**
- **Ambient microclimate/
  year-round use.**
- **Shelter.**
- **Social interaction.**
- **Design for all ages.**
- **Variety of social spaces.**
- **Variety of spatial
  experiences.**
- **Refuges.**
- **Completion points.**
- **Spatial orientation.**
- **Landmarks.**
- **Multisensory cues.**
- **Scale, size, shape,
  enclosure, continuity.**
- **Play above ground.**
- **Differentiated settings.**
- **Edge effects.**
- **Undefined places.**
- **People-plant
  interaction.**
- **Wildlife habitats.**
- **Domestic animals.**
- **Mix of people-made
  and natural elements.**
- **Indoor-outdoor
  relationships.**
- **Ease and economy
  of construction.**

periods of time. In some cases, diversity can be increased by combining play structures with indigenous materials and artifacts.

A long-standing debate has focused on the value of thematic structures compared to more abstract designs. Critics argue that thematic structures limit children's imagination. In reality, though, this does not appear to happen, especially for younger children, as long as the thematic structure is complex enough to stimulate a wide range of dramatic play scenarios.

Play equipment can also be created on-site using simple materials and imagination, though safety guidelines must still be followed.

6. MULTIPURPOSE GAME SETTINGS

Multipurpose game settings support informal games and ballplay activity. They may be hard surfaced or lawns. Because they are large, flat spaces, trade-offs between these settings and other types of space-demanding settings have to be made at the master planning stage.

To save space, ballplay and game settings can be designed as purely informal settings. In this form, they take less space and can be more flexibly programmed. Observations of such settings reveal children's capacity for adapting traditional games to the characteristics of the setting (e.g., three-dimensional ball tag on a play structure). Size constraints oblige children to exercise ingenuity and creativity. From this point of view, such spaces may even be preferable.

7. GROUNDCOVERS AND SAFETY SURFACES

The surfacing of each part of the play environment must respond to the needs of the intended activities and user groups. Considerations include durability, toxicity, allergenicity, slip-resistance, all-weather use, climatic zone, habitat value, maintenance, aesthetics, erosion control, accessibility, play value, and required shock absorbency. Both soft and hard play surfaces are needed to support different types of educational play activity.

A primary consideration is the safety surfacing located under and around play equipment and elevated structures. Since the majority of outdoor play injuries are caused by falls from equipment, much attention has focused recently on the development of synthetic safety surfaces. Although expensive and often antiseptic in appearance, they are a sure way of meeting safety standards. With a little ingenuity, synthetic safety surfacing can be designed to enhance safety without detracting from the play area's aesthetic and play value. Checkered

patterns, for example, will stimulate skipping, hopping, balancing, and jumping games.

If synthetic surfaces are economically infeasible, sand may be used to provide fall absorbency (although additional maintenance and accessibility issues must be addressed). Or if a more naturalistic appearance is desired, woodchips and processed wood fiber products are a possible alternative.

In non-equipment areas, natural groundcovers are recommended because they provide habitats for small animals and microorganisms, and place children in close contact with them. Options include unmown, rough areas of wild grasses and plants, naturalized dirt areas interspersed with informal plantings of indigenous species, and carefully managed, high-quality lawns suitable for group activities.

Meadow habitats provide an excellent medium for exploration, play, and education if allowed to grow wild as part of a natural ecosystem. Children of all ages enjoy walking, exploring, and sitting in tall grasses observing the variety of wildlife. Meadow habitats must be carefully managed to maintain species diversity and to minimize human impact.

Groundcovers are also required for erosion control. Where possible, species with play value as well as erosion mitigation properties should be selected.

8. LANDFORMS AND TOPOGRAPHY

Natural and people-made landforms add interesting three-dimensionality and encourage a variety of play activities, such as rolling, crawling, sliding, balancing, and jumping—activities that support motor development. Topographic variety stimulates fantasy play, orientation skills, and hide-and-go-seek games. It provides opportunities for getting up high and looking out over the surroundings, which all children enjoy doing. With ingenuity, low mounds can be made accessible to all children.

Landforms are a fundamental dimension of the terrestrial environment. They can therefore be designed to stimulate learning about the interrelationships between land, sunlight, vegetation, and water—including erosion and soil conservation. Landforms increase diversity and add potential for interdisciplinary studies of language, math, social studies, and the arts.

Landforms such as gently graded berms supporting accessible routes can be combined with manufactured and site-built play equipment to improve accessibility. Integration of landforms and fixed structures can enhance play value and protect the site against erosion, for example by using retaining walls, recycled tires, rocks, and plant materials on steep slopes.

Older children need challenging, exciting places to ride their bicycles. Most neighborhood streets are no longer available for bike riding because of traffic hazards. Modest topography in woodland settings is an ideal setting because of the low environmental impact and flexibility of use. Woodland zones, a common feature in Swedish playparks, also allow children to engage in other types of adventure activities, including camp building, exploration, and ranging games.

9. TREES AND VEGETATION

Plants are intrinsically interesting to children. Individually, collectively, or in combination with built features, plants can greatly extend the range of play activity.[2] Together with soil, sand, and water, plants provide manipulative settings that offer a welcome contrast to the static character of fixed play structures. Climbable trees are especially important. Plants are a major source of play props, including leaves, flowers, fruit, nuts, seeds, and small sticks.

Renewed interest in the therapeutic and medicinal properties of plants lends further weight to the importance of their integration into children's environments.

Plants stimulate the senses and add a positive ambiance to play settings through their mix of shade, color, fragrance, texture, and enclosure. Plant-enclosed "refuges" can become favorite places to escape, relax, and socialize in small groups. Shrubs can be used to create intimate spaces where children can interact with the natural environment and with one another.

Vegetation stimulates exploration and discovery, fantasy and imagination, and provides an ideal setting for dramatic play, hide-and-go-seek games, and orienteering activities. Specimen plants can provide important orienting elements. In short, vegetation is the ultimate interactive playing and learning environment—and is virtually cost-free once established.

Trees and vegetation give greater spatial and textural variation to educational settings. Indoor-outdoor transitions can be softened with vegetation—especially for people whose eyes adjust slowly to changing light levels. Plantings placed along paths create a sequence of texture, smell, light, shade, and color. Trees add a positive ambiance to play settings through light modification, color, texture, fragrance, and softness of enclosure—sensory stimuli that both adults and children appreciate.

Tree climbing is universally popular among children. It stimulates and reinforces a sense of connection to the natural world and the history of human culture. Unfortunately, many children living in cities do not have access to trees that are suitable for climbing. However, all climatic zones have tree species that can support climbing, either in their natural state or as the result of pruning. Low-slung, thick branches are critical to a tree's climbability. Branches need to be only a few feet (1 m) off the ground to provide a challenge for many young children, while higher branches offer challenge for older and more adventuresome children. A climbable tree should have suitable safety surfacing around its base to protect children from injury if they fall.

Plants have substantial interdisciplinary educational value because of their multisensory qualities and because they provide wildlife habitat. Vegetation marks the passing of the seasons and provides a sense of time in the child's environment. Vegetated settings can serve as outdoor classrooms for the study of botany, biology, natural history, geology, chemistry, physics, meteorology, and numerous other subjects. Because children eagerly participate in activities related to the natural environment, these settings can also be used to support activities across the curriculum, including language arts and mathematics.

Planting designs should emphasize the integration of plants into educational settings, rather than creating segregated "nature areas." Children do not structure the environment in this artificial way and are more stimulated by a mix of natural and synthetic elements.

Plants are important for erosion control on play sites. Broad-leaved deciduous trees can reduce the direct impact of heavy rain and extend the run-off period. Surface root systems bind the soil and help it resist erosion.

Regrettably, plants are a highly underused resource in educational settings. Vegetation is still considered a low priority in the design or redesign of educational environments. Sites for new schools are often bulldozed, removing the topsoil along with everything else. Re-establishing a natural habitat can be extremely difficult and expensive. Hopefully, the earlier chapters have provided convincing evidence of the importance of plants in educational settings.

10. GARDEN SETTINGS

Gardening is one of the easiest and most popular interdisciplinary environmental education activities. A basic vegetable and flower garden for schools and nonformal community education programs should contain several components: beds at different heights to accommodate

UNIVERSAL DESIGN

Universal design is an approach to environmental design that broadens the scope of usability to include the most users, regardless of their level of ability. It is achieved by thoughtful planning at all stages of the project.

— Ron Mace

children of different ages and abilities; low-rise beds for small children who like to kneel or work in a prone position; waist-high beds for older children and children who use wheelchairs.

Beds can be made from treated lumber or masonry. A wide ledge around the raised bed is useful for resting tools and other gardening paraphernalia. A worktable near the planting beds is essential for demonstrating gardening techniques and for preparatory work.

Normally, it is a good idea to surround the garden with a high fence to protect against informal use. Low-rise beds can be placed against the fence to create opportunities for climbing plants (beans, tomatoes, etc.). Circulation space should be generous to accommodate classroom groups and provide sufficient space for wheelchair users. Surfacing can consist of straw or woodchips.

Some form of potting shed or greenhouse space is needed to store tools and to grow seedlings for transplanting. Any small, lockable structure with a sunny window can serve this purpose (a translucent roof is unnecessary and often difficult to maintain).

A composting facility is an essential garden feature, reinforcing the basic principles of recycling and regeneration. A variety of designs are possible.

The final ingredient for success is a staff. Teachers, playleaders, or other professionals are essential to ensure proper management and to maximize learning opportunities. Gardens stimulate social interaction, fine motor skill development, and the honing of sensory awareness.

Gardens and gardening activity offer immediate educational potential, especially for teachers who feel unprepared to use more elaborate settings requiring more background knowledge for instructional purposes. Gardens enable children to interact with nature and learn about the ecological cycle. By cooperating with each other, peers achieve almost immediately visible results from their hard work.

11. ANIMAL HABITATS

Animals are an endless source of wonder for children, fostering a caring attitude and a sense of responsibility towards living things. Children interact naturally with animals, talk to them, and invest in them emotionally. Animals can also have a powerful therapeutic effect on individual children, and offer many opportunities for interdisciplinary learning.

Animals are a powerful socialization medium. They provide companionship in nonthreatening ways and almost always come back for more contact. This can be critical for children with limited self-esteem. Caring for animals can produce a strong sense of personal competence and pride.

Through careful selection of plant species (especially those with flowers producing nectar or bearing fruits, nuts, and seeds), many types of animals can be drawn into a play environment. Vegetation and natural features such as ponds provide essential food and shelter. Particular plant species can be selected to attract birds and butterflies. In educational environments, consideration should be given to several categories of animals:

Nonharmful insects and insect-like organisms. Many of us think of wildlife as consisting of large, exotic creatures. Smaller, more prolific animals, however, are just as wild and are much easier to design for in a play setting. They stimulate children's exploration of nature and provide many opportunities for interdisciplinary environmental education. Insects will move into any vegetated setting. They add a critical element of life to the playing and learning environment, and require very little maintenance. The vast majority of insects are beneficial to the human race and do not bite, eat valuable plant materials, or spread disease. Indigenous species provide fascinating, close-up nature lessons. Caterpillars, butterflies, moths, ladybugs, beetles, pillbugs, spiders, millipedes, and snails are particularly attractive.

Specific types of plants can be used to attract butterflies. Each butterfly species in larval form generally lives on specific types of plants or even on one or two specific species; for example, the caterpillar of the beautiful anise swallowtail (*Papilio zelicaon*) lives primarily on sweet fennel anise plants (*Foeniculum vulgare*), although it can also be found on other members of the parsley family and on citrus plants. In adult form, most butterflies have equally specific preferences for nectar plants.

Birdlife. It is difficult for children to make close contact with birds (unless caged); nonetheless, birds add sensory dimensions of movement, color, and sound to play settings. Specific habitat requirements include high places for nesting, sources of nesting materials, and food-producing plants. To be able to observe birds more closely, bird-watching hides can be designed if space allows.

Small animals, amphibians, and reptiles. Salamanders, tortoises, squirrels, toads, mice, moles, snakes, and lizards are typical species. Each is adapted to specific conditions that may be replicated through design. Gerbils are a popular caged animal for classroom use.

Pond life. Fish and frogs and other pond organisms are very attractive to children (see Aquatic Settings).

Domesticated and farmyard animals. Farmyard animals can be incorporated into play environments if there are trained playworkers responsible for their care (although children and student volunteers can do most of the work). Possible animals include donkeys, ponies, sheep, pigs, goats, rabbits, chickens, geese, ducks, guinea pigs, and hamsters. European urban farms and adventure playgrounds accommodate these types of animals. Rabbits are a fantastic educational resource and extremely popular with children. Rabbit hutches are an easy and relatively inexpensive way to introduce animals into children's play settings.

12. AQUATIC SETTINGS

Aquatic systems are critical to the health of humans and our habitat. For that reason alone, they have a substantial educational potential. Aquatic settings range from dew-covered leaves to ponds, streams, and marshes. They support a variety of terrestrial and aquatic life that fascinate children. They have a strong perceptual impact and are vividly remembered in adult years. In other words, educational activities with water have a high level of retention by the student. Water both excites and relaxes.

Water settings are highly valued by children for their rich and varied sounds, textures, reflections, changes in state, and feelings of wetness. Like vegetation, water is highly interactive; it can be splashed, poured, dammed, and used to float objects. By mixing water with sand, dirt, and vegetation, children have a broad palette of materials for creating their own imaginary world. Water adds a substantial aesthetic dimension to any educational or recreational setting.

Water settings are a primary attraction, promoting social interaction and cooperative play. They can be designed to require children to work together to maximize their play value.

Some of the most successful water settings replicate natural environments. Designers of these settings use soil, rocks, and vegetation—in addition to concrete and other building materials—to create streams, cascades, wetlands, and ponds. Children will spend hours in these settings, drawing on the available natural materials and experimenting with the water's movement.

13. SAND AND DIRT SETTINGS

The younger the children are, the more likely they are to play in dirt wherever they find it. Using "props" such as twigs, small plastic toys, or a couple of stones, children can create an imaginary world in the dirt—such as around the roots of a tree. When playing with dirt, children are literally interacting with the surface of the planet. Like water, dirt (soil by another name) is critical to planetary and human life, and therefore commands high educational significance. Educationally, students can make hands-on comparisons between good quality, fertile soil, various qualities of dirt, and sand.

Sand is a refined and sanitized version of dirt and works best if the setting is designed with intimate, small group spaces; play surfaces; and access to water and small play props. Sand is an excellent educational medium for stimulating creative play and social interaction. It is easy to move and mold. It can be dug, sifted, sculpted, poured, and drawn upon. In large sand areas, children can engage in expansive sand play and create imaginary landscapes using all manner of loose parts.

Sand, because of its softness and malleability, is one of the most popular play materials. When combined with water, it provides even more opportunities for creative and imaginative play. When properly installed and maintained, sand is also an acceptable safety surface under play equipment.

Think of the sand area of a playground as a beach—deep, wide, and near water. For hygienic reasons, the sand should be at least four feet (1.2 m) deep with good drainage; rain, air, and sunshine will help keep it clean. If the sand area is exposed to falling leaves or to cats and dogs during the night, a fine-mesh or canvas cover can be used as temporary protection.

Besides providing convenient access to water, faucets can be playful design elements. Hoses and buckets can also be used to draw water from a nearby source. More elaborate designs such as recirculating streams or hand pumps can incorporate water and sand play into the larger landscape.

To ensure accessibility, the sand area should be located near a path and should have a ramped approach so that children and caregivers using wheelchairs can enter easily and safely. A transfer bar or raised sand surface can help people transfer out of their wheelchairs and into the sand. Access can also be provided by placing rubber mats on the sand. Multilevel sand areas have been designed that facilitate transfer and include features such as "sand shelves" to provide access for individuals unable to transfer from their wheelchairs.

14. PLAY PROPS

Play props help children manipulate the environment and transform it into their own imaginary world. They

ADVANTAGES OF NATURAL SETTINGS FOR PLAYING AND LEARNING

- Stimulate all aspects and stages of child development.
- Offer multisensory experiences.
- Stimulate informal play, experiential learning, and natural learning cycles.
- Stimulate imagination and creativity in a special, boundless way.
- Integrate children by age, ability, and ethnicity.
- Help children feel good about themselves. Enhance self-esteem.
- Offer children a peaceful feeling.
- Center children in the environment where they live.
- Help children understand realities of natural systems.
- Demonstrate the principle of cycles and processes.
- Support interdisciplinary, environmental education curricula.
- Provide flexible and forgiving settings.
- Are aesthetically appealing to all people.

provide a low-cost strategy for enhancing any play environment. There are several categories of play props.

The most common are small found objects, which may be natural or synthetic, including insects, bottle caps, popsicle sticks, leaves, twigs, rocks, dirt, and sand.

Plant parts are also part of this category. They are widely available and highly valuable play props. Children can transform virtually any natural object into a prop. Plant materials can also be powerful props for enhancing educational programs and teaching practical concepts and skills through craftwork and the cultural arts. All natural educational settings should be designed to be manipulated in this way so that play and learning values can be maximized.

The range of props can be extended by adding objects such as logs, rocks, pieces of lumber, lengths of textile, sections of plastic pipe, pieces of rope, sheets of heavy cardboard, as well as manufactured modular blocks and similar construction material. Dramatic play can be enhanced with dress-up clothes. By using these larger-scale props, spaces can be transformed into temporary educational settings for special programs. Closest to this concept is the adventure playground—the nonformal educational setting that was founded in Copenhagen in 1943 and has spread to several other countries over the years.[3]

15. GATHERING, MEETING, AND WORKING SETTINGS

Social interaction is a basic component of playing and learning. Well-designed seating and gathering areas provide settings in which children can broaden and strengthen their social relationships with each other and the adults around them. On educational sites, small, comfortable gathering places are required where students and teachers can meet and work together. Forms include benches, decks, patios, verandas, gazebos, and sitting circles.

Gathering settings should be provided to accommodate groups of different sizes. Intimate settings invite children to sit and socialize in small groups while larger settings enable children to work on group projects.

Through careful design and location, gathering areas can provide sheltered or enclosed places where children can play quietly or withdraw from the noise and distractions of more boisterous activities. They can also provide an area for parents to watch their children at play or a transition space between indoor and outdoor areas.

The design of seating and gathering areas can add playfulness to an educational site, creating an inviting, whimsical atmosphere. Unusual forms can invite people of all ages to sit, talk, and linger. When used as educational activity stations, they must have a strong identity and be located near display settings where children's work can be exhibited.

16. PERFORMANCE SETTINGS

Performance settings attract presentations by classroom groups that would not otherwise occur. They stimulate presentation of self, encourage teamwork, and foster a sense of community. They are places where local culture is created. Forms include campfire circles, stages, arenas, and small amphitheaters. When not used for performance, they can be used as gathering, meeting, and working settings where students can implement large group projects.

17. FIELD STATIONS AND STORAGE SETTINGS

When educational programs move out of the classroom to the school grounds, some type of field station is needed as a program and communications base. It must also serve as an emergency or first-aid post, storage, and toilet location. The relatively high cost of field stations makes them difficult to justify, although in Europe they are a traditional element in playparks and adventure playgrounds. In new or redeveloped school buildings, field facilities should be provided to serve these purposes.

Storage is frequently underprovided in the design of educational settings, yet it makes a large difference to the viability of hands-on educational programs that use moveable equipment and props. Provisioning of sufficient storage space helps to reduce clutter that can limit educational activity. Accessible storage areas that are clearly defined, labeled, and properly placed will also encourage children to clean up after themselves.

REFERENCES

1. For more technical details of the seventeen types of settings, see Moore, R. C., S. M. Goltsman, and D. S. Iacofano, eds. (1992). *Play For All Guidelines: Planning, Design, and Management of Outdoor Play Settings for All Children,* 2nd ed. Berkeley, Calif.: MIG Communications. Although not oriented specifically towards the design of educational environments, much of the material is directly applicable to school site development.

   Also of interest is the *Play For All* CD-ROM by Robin Moore and Susan Goltsman, containing almost one hundred images and text of best-practice examples of play settings from around the world. Available from MIG Communications.

2. Brett, A., R. C. Moore, and E. Provenzo (1993). *The Complete Playground Book.* Syracuse, N.Y.: Syracuse University Press.

3. Ibid.

Epilogue

Visitors to Washington School today will not find the Environmental Yard described in *Natural Learning*. When the school was renovated in 1995–96 to meet new earthquake standards, the community play area, Orchard Wayside, stage, outdoor storage, Kids HQ, and more than thirty shade trees were removed and replaced with a rectangle of grass and basketball courts. Although neighborhood residents protested energetically, they were not strong enough to counter the will of the school district. Needless to say, the students and neighborhood residents did not have a genuine voice in these decisions to radically change their environment.

The rationale for returning back to the monoculture of the old schoolyard, according to the school authorities, was to increase open space for ballplay of older students (primarily boys) in the reconfigured school. This was achieved at the cost of the diversity of experience and comforting microclimate for all children. This same issue of ballplay versus diversity of choice was resolved in favor of diversity when the Yard was first created.

Now that much of the diversity has been removed, an interpretation of the children's testimony presented in Chapter 16 strongly suggests that some of the present generation at the school must again be frustrated and bored, making interpersonal conflict more likely. We also predict that vandalism will increase because of the negative messages of the new "hidden curriculum" (that adult authorities can make massive changes to the quality of life of children without involving the children in these decisions).

Remaining elements of the Natural Resource Area still offer support for more holistic child development, but the scope is greatly limited compared to the earlier era of the Yard. Commercial play equipment has been installed in place of the lower pond. The waterfall and "river" no longer function. The upper pond has been enclosed behind a ten-foot (3.5 m) chainlink fence and locked gate—a "protected" study area accessible only for formal learning activities.

It is interesting to note that the garden has been the only setting used continuously throughout the life of the Yard and to this day survives intact. For many years it has been managed by children working with a group of students and faculty from UC Berkeley.

As the Yard's life history comes almost full circle, one message is clear. The creation of high-quality outdoor school environments will require a change in both values and governance in K–12 education.

Until children are regarded as young citizens with rights and responsibilities, until they are treated with respect and dignity, it will not be possible to initiate the community processes necessary to create environments with high social and physical ecological quality.

For these processes to be sustainable, new forms of governance must be established to support co-working relations between school and community—so clearly exemplified by the earlier years of the Yard. To guarantee success, a higher level of district and state governance, policy support, and leadership is required to achieve long-term school-community partnership.

Although the Yard no longer exists as a physical space, it lives on through the several hundred Washington students who benefited from growing up with the experiential richness of nature each school day. As adults, they are now applying the results of their natural learning in social skills, creativity, collaboration, scientific understanding, and love of nature in their families, work environments, and communities.

Fortunately, there is a revival in recognizing the power of nature to help children develop in healthy ways. Many initiatives are underway in the United States and other countries, applying the principles of natural learning to reconstruct curricular settings and programs that integrate children experientially into biological processes and values.

This final coda of hope is offered to those engaged with young people to move the human evolutionary process into the next millennium, to create neighborhoods and schools where playing and learning in natural settings can help sustain society and planet.

List of Yard Species

PLANTS

Acacia
  Bailey Acacia *A. baileyana*
  Black Acacia *A. melanoxylon*
  Sydney Golden Wattle (multi-trunked)
    A. longifolia
African Daisy *Osteospermum spp.*
Alder *Alnus*
  Red Alder *A. oregonia (A. rubra)*
  White Alder *A. rhombifolia*
Alfalfa *Medicago sativa*
Algerian Ivy *Hedera canariensis*
Almond 'Nonparail' and Pollenizer
Alyssum *spp.*
American Grape *Vitus labrusca*
American Sweet Gum *Liquidambar styraciflua*
  'Burgundy' and 'Palo Alto'
Anise (Sweet) or Fennel *Foeniculum vulgare*
Annual Yellow Sweetclover *Medicago indicus*
Arrowhead *Sagittaria*
Arum *spp.*
Avocado *spp.*
Bamboo *Bambusa spp.* (clumping varieties)
Bear's Breech *Acanthus mollis*
Belladonna Lily (Naked Lady)
  Amaryllis belladonna
Big Leaf Maple *Acer macrophyllum*
Bird-of-paradise *Strelitzia reginae*
Blood-red Trumpet Vine *Distictis buccinatoria*
  (Bignonia cherere, Phaedranthus
    buccinatorius)
Blue-eyed Grass *Sisyrinchium bellum*
Blue Flax *Linum lewisi*
Blue Marguerite Felicia amelloides
Borage *Borago officinalis*
Bottlebrush (Callistemon) *Callistemon citrinus*
  (Lemon Bottlebrush)
Bradford Pear *Pyrus calleryana* 'Bradford'
Brass Buttons *Cotula coronopifolia*
Bristly Ox Tongue *Picris echioides*
Brodiaea
  B. tubergenii
  B. laxa

Bull Mallow *Malva nicaeensis*
Bur Clover *Medicago polymorpha*
Calendula (Pot Marigold) *Calendula officinalis*
California Bay Laurel *Umbellularia californica*
California Black Walnut *Juglans hindisii*
California Buckeye *Aesculus californica*
California Fuchsia (Hummingbird Flower)
  Zauschneria
California Pepper Tree *Schinus molle*
California Poppy *Eschscholtzia californica*
Calla Lily *Zantedeschia aethiopica*
Candytuft *Iberis spp.*
Ceanothus *Ceanothus*
  C. G. Louis Edmunds
  C. griseus horizontalis 'Yankee Point'
  C. 'Sierra blue'
Century Plant *Agave americana*
Chaparral Broom (Coyote Brush) *Baccharis*
  pilularis
Chicory *Cichorium intybus*
Chinese Elm *Ulmus parvifolia*
Coast Redwood *Sequoia sempervirens*
Coast Silktassel *Garrya elliptica*
Comfrey *Symphytum officinale*
Common Cattail *Typha latifolia*
Common Chickweed *Stellaria media*
Common Field-speedwell *Veronica persica*
Common Fig *Ficus carica*
Common Horsetail *Equisetum arvense*
Common Knotweed *Polygonum aviculare*
Common Sunflower *Helianthus anuus*
Common Tule (Tule Cattail) *Scirpus acutus*
Common Valerian (Cat's Valerian) *Valeriana*
  officinalis
Cotoneaster *Cotoneaster spp.*
Cow Parsley (Queen Anne's Lace) *Anthriscus*
  sylvestris
Coyote Brush (Dwarf Chaparral Broom)
  Baccharis pilularis
Crabapple *Malus spp.*
Crocus *Iridaceae spp.*
Curled Dock *Rumex crispus*

Daffodil *Narcissus spp.*
Dandelion *Taraxacum officinale*
Date Palm *Phoenix loureiri*
Deodar Cedar *Cedrus deodara*
Duckweed
    Greater Duckweed *Lemna polyrhiza*
    Lesser Duckweed *Lemna minor*
Dwarf Pomegranate *Punica granatum* 'Nana'
English Ivy *Hedera helix*
English Lavender *Lavandular angustifolia*
Eucalyptus *Eucalyptus*
    E. ficifolia Red-Flowering Gum
    E. globulus Blue Gum
    E. globulus 'Compacta' Dwarf Blue Gum
    E. polyanthemos Silver Dollar Gum
European Olive *Olea europaea* (multi-stemmed)
European White Birch *Betula alba*
    (multi-stemmed)
Fanwort *Cabomba caroliniana*
Fennel (Sweet Anise) *Foeniculum vulgare*
Fiddleneck *Amsinckia douglasiana*
Field Bindweed *Convolvulus arvensis*
Field Forget-me-not *Myosotis arvensis*
Field Mustard *Brassica campestris*
Firethorn *Pyracantha coccinea*
    'Lalandei Monrovia'
Flax-leaved Fleabane *Conyza bonariensis*
Flowering Plum *Prunus cerasifera*
    'Atropurpurea' (Purple-leaf Plum)
Foxglove *Digitalis purpurea*
Fuchsia *Fuchsia spp.*
Fuchsia-flowered Gooseberry *Ribes speciosum*
Fungi
    Agarics
    Puffballs
    Shelf Fungi
Garden Vegetables
    Beets
    Cabbage
    Carrots
    Chard
    Eggplant
    Fava Beans
    Green Peppers
    Lettuce
    Pea
    Pumpkins

    Scarlet Runner Beans
    Snap Beans
    Sweet Basil
    Tomatoes
    Zucchini Squash
Geranium *Pelargonium*
    Common Geranium *P. hortorum*
    Martha Washington Geranium *P. domesticum*
German Ivy *Senecio mikanioides*
Grape Hyacinth *Muscari spp.*
Grasses
    Annual Bluegrass *Poa annua*
    Annual Ryegrass *Lolium multiflorum*
    Bermuda Grass *Cynodon dactylon*
    Foxtail Barley *Hordeum jubatum*
    Foxtail Brome *Bromus rubens*
    Foxtail Fescue *Festuca megalura*
    Kikuya Grass *Pennisetum clandestinum*
    Knot Grass *Paspalum spp.*
    Low Amaranth *Amaranthus deflexus*
    Perennial Ryegrass *Lolium perenne*
    Rabbit's Foot Grass *Polypogon monspeliensis*
    Smilo Grass *Oryzopsis miliacea*
    Wild Oat *Avena fatua*
Greater Plantain *Plantago major*
Greenbriar *Smilax californica*
Groundsel *Senecio vulgaris*
Hebe spp.
Hens and Chicks *Echeveria imbricata*
Himalayan Blackberry *Rubus procerus*
Hollyhock *Althaea rosea*
Honeysuckle *Lonicera*
    Giant Burmese Honeysuckle
        L. hildebrandiana
    Japanese Honeysuckle *L. japonica*
Hornwort *Ceratophyllum demersum*
Horseweed *Conyza canadensis*
Ice Plant *Drosanthemum spp.*
Iris *Iris douglasiana* (Sky Blue Iris)
Italian Buckthorn *Rhamnus alternus*
Jacaranda *Jacaranda acutifolia*
Japanese Acuba *Acuba japonica*
Japanese Camellia *Camellia japonica*
Jasmine *Jasminum*
    Italian Jasmine *J. humile*
    J. polyanthum
Jerusalem Artichoke *Helianthus tuberosis*

Johnny-jump-up or Wild Pansy
Viola pedunculata
Lamb's Quarters (Pigweed, Goosefoot)
Chenopodium album
Lesser Periwinkle *Vinca minor*
Lily-of-the-Nile *Agapanthus africanus,*
A. 'Peter Pan'
Lippia *Phyla nodiflora* (Lippia repens)
Liquidambar *L. styraciflua* American Sweet Gum
'Burgundy' and 'Palo Alto'
Liverwort *Marchantia*
Loquat *Eriobotrya japonica*
Maidenhair Tree *Gingko biloba* 'Fairmount'
Mallow (Cheeseweed) *Malva parviflora*
Manzanita *Arcostaphylos desiflora* Vine Hill
Manzanita
Marigold *Tagetes spp.*
Marsh Pennywort *Hydrocotyle vulgaris*
Matilija Poppy *Romneya coulteri*
Mayweed *Anthemis cotula*
Milk Thistle *Silybum marianum*
Milkweed *Asclepias fasciculans*
Miners Lettuce *Claytonia perfoliata*
Mint *Mentha*
Golden Apple Mint *M. gentilis*
Orange Mint *M. citrata*
Peppermint *M. piperita*
Spearmint *M. spicata*
Monkey Flower *Mimulus cardinalis*
(Scarlet Monkey Flower)
Mugwort *Artemisia ludoviciana*
Mulberry *Morus alba* (fruitless form)
Mullein *Verbascum thapsus*
Narrow-leaved Plantain *Plantago lanceolata*
Nasturtium *Tropaeolum majus*
Nut Grass (Chufa) *Cyperus esculentus*
Oak *Quercus*
Coast Live Oak *Q. agrifolia*
Valley Oak *Q. lobata*
Olive *Olea europea*
Orchard Morning Glory *Convolvulus arvensis*
Oregano *Origanum vulgare*
Pacific Wax Myrtle *Myrica californica*
Pampus Grass *Cortaderia selloana*
Parrot's Feather *Myriophyllum aquatica*
Passion Vine *Passiflora alatocaerulea*
Peach *spp.*

Photinia *fraseri*
Pigweed (Lamb's Quarters, Goosefoot)
Chenopodium album
Pine *Pinus*
Aleppo Pine *P. halepensis*
Italian Stone Pine *P. pinea*
Monterey Pine *P. radiata*
Pineapple Weed *Matricaria matricarioides*
Pittasporum crassifolium
Plumbago *P. auriculata* (Cape Plumbago)
Poplar *Populus nigra*
Prickly Lettuce *Lactuca serriola*
Prickly Sow Thistle *Sonchus asper*
Primrose *Primula spp.*
Purslane *Portulaca oleracea*
Pyracantha *Pyracantha coccinea*
'Lalandei Monrovia'
Queen Anne's Lace (Cow Parsley)
Anthriscus sylvestris
Red Clover *Trifolium pratense*
Red Elderberry *Sambucus callicarpa*
Red Flowering Currant *Ribes sanguineum*
Red Hot Pocker *Kniphofia uvaria*
Red-stemmed Filaree (Storksbill, Clocks,
Pin Grass) *Erodium cicutarium*
Redwood Sorrel (Violet-flowered Oxalis)
Oxalis oregana
Rock Rose *Helianthemum scoparium*
Rose *Rosa banksiae* Lady Banks' Rose
'Alba plena'
Rosemary *Rosmarinus officinalis*
Rushes *Juncus*
Baltic Rush *J. balticus*
Common Rush *J. effusus*
Sage *Salvia*
Garden Sage *S. officinalis*
Gentian Sage *S. patens*
St. John's-wort *Hypericum perforatum*
Scarlet Flax *Linum grandiflorum rubrum*
Scarlet Pimpernel *Anagallis arvensis*
Scotch Broom *Cytisus scoparius*
(low-growing form)
Sedges *Carex spp.*
Sedum (Stonecrop) *S. spectabile* and others
Shasta Daisy *Chrysanthemum maximum*
Sheep Sorrel (Sour Dock) *Rumex acetosella*

Shepherd's Purse (Mother's Heart) *Capsella bursa-pastoris*

Silk Tree (Mimosa in Eastern United States) *Albizia julibrissin 'Rosea'*

Silkworm Mulberry *Morus alba* (fruitless variety)

Sneezeweed *Helenium puberulum*

Snowberry *Symphoricarpos albus*

Soap Root (Soap Plant, Amole) *Chlorogalum pomeridianum*

Sour Grass (Yellow Oxalis) *Oxalis corniculata*

Southern Magnolia *Magnolia grandiflora*

Sow Thistle *Sonchus oleraceus*

Star (Fringed) Water Plantain *Machaerocarpus californicus*

Strawberry Bush *Arbutus unedo*

Sweet Anise (Fennel) *Foeniculum vulgare*

Sweet Bay *Laurus nobilis*

Sycamore (Plane) *Platinus acerifola*

Teasel *Dipsacus fullonum* Fuller's Teasel

Thyme (Garden Thyme) *Thymus vulgaris*

Toyon (Christmas Berry, California Holly) *Heteromeles arbutifolia*

Tree of Heaven *Ailanthus altissima*

Tuberous *Begonia spp.*

Watercress *Nasturtium officinale*

Water Fern (Fairy Moss) *Azolla filiculoides*

Water Lilies *Nymphaea spp.*

Watermeals *Wolffia spp.*

Water Plantain *Alisma plantagoaquatica*

Western Hazelnut (Filbert) *Corylus cornuta californica*

Western Redbud *Cercis occidentalis*

White Alder *Alnus rhombifolia*

White Clover *Trifolium repens*

Wild Cucumber *Marah fabaceus*

Wild Onion *Allium spp.*

Wild Peppergrass *Lepidium virginicum*

Wild Radish *Raphanus sativus*

Wild Sweet Pea *Lathyrus vestitus*

Willow *Salix*
    Corkscrew Willow *S. matsudana 'Tortuosa'*
    Pussy Willow *S. discolor*
    Red Willow *S. laevigata*
    Weeping Willow *S. babylonica*
    Yellow Tree Willow *S. lasiandra*

Wisteria *W. sinensis* Chinese Wisteria

Yarrow *Achillea millefolium*

Yellow-eyed Grass *Sisyrinchium californicum*

Yellow Oxalis (Sour Grass) *Oxalis corniculata*

Yerba Buena *Satureja douglasii*

ANIMALS AND INSECTS

Wingless Insects (Apterygota)

Bristletails (Order Thysanura)
    Common Silverfish *Lepisma saccharina*

Winged Insects (Pterygota)

Mayflies (Order Ephemeroptera)
    Mayflies—various species and nymphs (naiads)

Dragonflies and Damselflies (Order Odonata)
    Dragonflies (Big Red Skimmers, Green Darners, Blue Darners)—various species and nymphs (naiads)
    Damselflies (Bluets, Dancers)—various species and nymphs (naiads)

Cockroaches (Order Blattodea)
    American Cockroach *Periplaneta americana*

Crickets, Grasshoppers, Katydids (Order Orthoptera)
    Grasshoppers, various species
    Fork-tailed Bush Katydid *Scudderia mexicana*
    California Camel Cricket *Ceuthophilus californianus*
    Jerusalem Cricket (Potato Bug) *Stenopelmatus fuscus*
    Field Crickets *Gryllus spp.*

Earwigs (Order Dermaptera)
    European Earwig *Forficula auricularia*

True Bugs, Hoppers, Aphids, Scales (Order Hemiptera)
    Common Milkweed Bug *Lygaeus kalmii*
    Common Water Strider (Water Skater) *Gerris remigis*
    Kirby's Backswimmer *Noton ecta kirbyi*
    Common Water Boatman *Corisella*
    Common Water Scorpion *Ranatra brevicollis*
    Spittlebugs, various species
    Leafhoppers, various genera and species
    Aphids, various genera and species
    European Elm Scale *Gossyparia spuria*

Nerve-winged Insects (Order Neuroptera)
    Common Green Lacewing *Chrysopa carnea*

Pacific Brown Lacewing *Hemerobius pacificus*
Common Antlion *Brachynemurus*
Flies, Gnats, and Midges (Order Diptera)
  Crane Flies and larvae, various genera and
    species
  Gnats, various genera and species
  Gall Midges, various genera and species
  Mosquitoes and larvae, various species
  Common Hover Flies, various species
  Housefly *Musca domestica*
  Green Bottle Fly *Phaenicia sericata*
  Common Blow Fly *Eucalliphora lilaea*
  Caterpillar Destroyer (Tachinid Fly) *Lespesia
    archippivora*
  Fruitflies, various genera and species
Caddisflies (Order Trichoptera)
  Caddisflies and larvae, various species
Moths and Butterflies (Order Lepidoptera)
  Western Lawn Moth *Crambus bonifatellus*
  Omnivorous Looper (Inchworm larva)
    Sabulodes aegrotata
  Acrea Moth *Estigmene acrea*
  Common Checkered Skipper *Pyrgus
    communis*
  Fiery Skipper *Hylephila phyleus*
  Common Hairstreak *Strymon melinus*
  Purplish Copper *Epidernia helloides*
  Gulf Fritillary *Agraulis vanillae*
  Monarch *Danaus plexippus*
  Mourning Cloak *Nymphalis antiopa*
  West Coast Lady *Vanessa annabella*
  Painted Lady *Vanessa cardui*
  Buckeye *Junonia coenia*
  Cabbage Butterfly *Pieris rapae*
  Orange Sulfur Butterfly (Alfalfa Sulfur) *Colias
    eurytheme*
  Western Tiger Swallowtail *Papilio rutulus*
  Anise Swallowtail *P. zelicaon*
  Caterpillars (larvae of moths and butterflies)
Beetles (Order Coleoptera)
  Predacious Water (Diving) Beetles
    (Dytiscidae)
  Common Whirligig Beetles *Gyrinus spp.*
  Black Calosoma *C. semilaeve*
  Darkling Ground Beetles
  California Ladybird Beetle *Coccinella
    californica*

Convergent Ladybird *Hippodamia convergens*
Western Spotted Cucumber Beetle *Diabrotica
  undecimpunctata*
Leaf Beetles, various species
Nymphs (larval forms)
Ants, Wasps, Bees (Order Hymenoptera)
  Argentine Ant *Iridomyrmex humilis*
  Pennsylvania Yellow Jacket *Vespula
    pensylvanica*
  Golden Paper Wasp *Polistes fuscatus*
  Yellow and Black Mud Dauber *Sceliphron
    caementarium*
  Bumble Bee *Bombus spp.*
  Honey Bee *Apis mellifera*

Mollusks (Mollusca)

Gastropods (Class Gastropoda)

Gray Slug *Derocerus reticulatum*
Banana Slugs *Ariolimax spp.*
European Brown Snail *Helix aspersa*
Pond Snails *Lymnaea spp.*
Ramshorn Snails *Planorbis spp.*

Annelids (Class Oligochaeta)
Earthworms *Lumbricus spp. Eisnia spp.*

(Class Oligochaeta)
Mudworms

(Class Hirudinea)
Leeches

Platyhelminthes (Class Turbellaria)
Flatworms

Arthropods (Class Crustacea)
Pillbugs *Armadillidium vulgare*
Sowbugs *Porcellio spp.*

(Class Cladocera)
Water Fleas

(Class Amphipoda)
Scuds

(Class Copepoda)
Copepods

(Class Isopoda)
Isopods

Myrlapods (Class Chilopoda)
Centipedes, various species

(Class Diplopoda)
Millipedes, various species

Spiders (Class Arachnida)
Harvestman *Leiobunum bimaculatum*
Black Widow Spider *Latrodectus mactans*
Banded Garden Spider *Argiope trifasciata*
Wolf Spiders *Lycosa spp.*
Crab Spiders, various species
Water Mites, various species

Amphibians (Amphibia)
Arboreal Salamander *Aneides lugubris*
Western Toad *Bufo boreas*
California Slender Salamanders *Batrachoseps attenuatus*
Bullfrog *Rana catesbeiana*
Tadpoles

Reptiles (Reptilia)
Western Fence Lizard *Sceloporus occidentalis*
Western Pond Turtle *Clemmys marimorata*
Garter Snakes *Thamnophis spp.*

Mammals (Mammalia)
House Mouse *Mus musculus*
Broad-footed Mole *Soapanus latimanus*
California Ground Squirrel *Spermophilus beecheyi*
Domestic Cats

Fish (Pisces)
Mosquito Fish *Gambusia offinis*

BIRDS

Allen's Hummingbird *Selasphorus sasin*
American Goldfinch *Carduelis tristis*
American Robin *Turdus migratorius*
Anna's Hummingbird *Calypte anna*

Barn Swallow *Hirundo rustica*
Bewick's Wren *Thryomanes bewickii*
Black Phoebe *Sayornis nigricans*
Brewer's Blackbird *Euphagus cyanocephalus*
Brown Towhee *Pipilo fuscus*
Bush-tit *Psaltiparus minimus*
California Gull *Larus californicus*
Cedar Waxwing *Bombycilla cedorum*
Chestnut-backed Chickadee *Parus rufescens*
Clapper Rail *Rallus longirostris*
Cliff Swallow *Hirundo pyrrhonota*
Dark-eyed Junco *Junco hyemalis*
Downy Woodpecker *Picoides villosus*
English Sparrow *Passer domesticus*
Herring Gull *Larus argentatus*
House Finch *Carpodacus mexicanus*
Hutton's Vireo *Vireo huttoni*
Lesser Goldfinch *Carduelis psaltria*
Mourning Dove *Zenaida macroura*
Olive-sided Flycatcher *Contopus borealis*
Pine Siskin *Carduelis pinus*
Plain Titmouse *Parus inornatus*
Red-breasted Nuthatch *Sitta canadensis*
Red-shafted Flicker *Colaptes auratus*
Red-tailed Hawk *Buteo jamaicensis*
Red-winged Blackbird *Agelaius phoeniceus*
Ring-billed Gull *Larus delawarensis*
Rock Dove (Domestic Pigeon) *Columba livia*
Ruby-crowned Kinglet *Regulus calendula*
Rufous-sided Towhee *Pipilo erythrophthalmus*
Scrub Jay *Aphelocoma coerulescens*
Song Sparrow *Melospiza melodia*
Starling (European Starling) *Sturnus vulgaris*
Western Flycatcher *Empidonax difficilis*
Western Mockingbird *Mimus polyglottos*
White-crowned Sparrow *Zonotrichia leucophrys*
Wilson's Warbler *Wilsonia pusilla*
Wren-tit *Chamaea fasciata*
Yellow-Rumped Warbler *Dendroica coronata*

Useful Organizations

Boston Schoolyards Initiative
Private-public partnership to revitalize Boston's schoolyards into active centers for learning and community use.

    The Boston Foundation
    One Boston Place, 24th Floor
    Boston, MA 02108
    United States
    (617) 723-7415
    fax (617) 589-3616
    kmeyer@tiac.net

Evergreen Foundation
Dedicated to establishing natural urban areas through education and action programs.

    355 Adelaide Street West, Suite 5A
    Toronto, ON M5V 1S2
    Canada
    (416) 596-1495
    fax (416) 596-1443
    info@evergreen.ca
    http://www.evergreen.ca

The Green Brick Road
Specializes in resources and information for students and teachers of global and environmental education.

    c/o 8 Dumas Court
    Don Mills, ON M3A 2N2
    Canada
    (416) 465-1597
    http://gbr.org

Learning Through Landscapes Trust
National campaign, training program, and materials development for school grounds development in the United Kingdom. Active internationally.

    3rd Floor, Southside Offices
    The Law Courts
    Winchester, Hampshire, SO23 9DL
    United Kingdom
    44 (0) 1962 846258
    fax 44 (0) 1962 869099
    charity@tcp.co.uk

Project Learning Tree
Pre-kindergarten through twelfth-grade environmental education curriculum and training program related to trees, forests, and their environment.

    1111 19th Street N.W.
    Suite 780
    Washington, DC 20036
    United States
    (202) 463-2462
    fax (202) 463-2461

Project Wet
Kindergarten through twelfth-grade environmental education curriculum and training program related to wetlands and related aquatic systems.

    The Watercourse
    201 Culbertson Hall
    Montana State University
    Bozeman, MT 59717-0057
    United States

Project Wild
Kindergarten through twelfth-grade curriculum and training program related to wildlife in the United States.

    5430 Grosvenor Lane
    Bethesda, MD 20814
    United States
    (301) 493-5447
    fax (301) 493-5627
    natpwild@igc.apc.org

School Nature Area Project (SNAP)
Grants and partnerships with schools in Minnesota for schoolyard improvement. Produces publications.

    St. Olaf College
    1520 St. Olaf Avenue
    Northfield, MN 55057
    United States
    (507) 646-3599
    fax (507) 646-3930
    snap@stolaf.edu
    http://www.stolaf.edu/other/snap

Schoolyard Ecology for Elementary School Teachers (SYFEST)

Strategies and training program for teaching/learning ecology using school grounds in North and South America.

> Institute for Ecosystem Studies
> P.O. Box R
> Millbrook, NY 12545
> United States
> (914) 677-5358
> fax (914) 677-6455
> 74301.1575@compuserve.com

Schoolyard Habitats

National school certification program.

> National Wildlife Federation
> 8925 Leesburg Pike
> Vienna, VA 22184
> United States
> (703) 790-4582
> fax (703) 790-4468
> griffen@nwf.org
> http://www.nwf.org/prog/habitats

Skolans Uterum (Schoolyards Unlimited)

Swedish national project working with school-grounds and with opening up of the traditional classroom to the outdoors.

> Bollhusgrand 3A
> 11131 Stockholm, Sweden
> 46 8 210811
> fax 46 8 210812
> skolans@uterum.se
> http://www.uterum.se

Using the Outdoors to Teach Experiential Science (UTOTES)

Program to establish natural habitats on North Carolina school grounds as a vehicle for teaching science. Twenty-four schools at any one time, each committed to a two-year training program with an assigned staff naturalist.

> North Carolina Museum of Natural Sciences
> 102 North Salisbury Street
> Raleigh, NC 27603
> United States
> (919) 733-7450
> fax (919) 733-1573

Volunteer Investigations in Neighborhood Ecology (VINE)

Volunteer-led, urban environmental educational program for eight- to eleven-year-olds. Volunteer high school students, parents, and other adults receive training and lead small groups to explore neighborhood ecology.

> North American Association for
> Environmental Education (NAAEE)
> P.O. Box 400
> Troy, OH 45373
> United States
> voice and fax (513) 676-3514

Bibliography and Suppliers

Agyeman, J. (1995). *People, Plants, and Places.* Crediton, Devon, United Kingdom: Southgate Publishers.

Ajilvsgi, G. (1990). *Butterfly Gardening for the South.* Dallas: Taylor Publishing Company.

Allison, L. (1975). *The Reasons for Seasons.* Boston: Little, Brown and Company.

Althea (1990). *Insects and Other Small Creatures.* Mahwah, N.J.: Troll Associates.

Appelhof, M. (1982). *Worms Eat My Garbage.* Kalamazoo, Mich.: Flower Press.

Ardley, N. (1991). *The Science Book of Things that Grow.* London: Dorling Kindersley Limited.

―――― (1992). *The Science Book of Weather.* London: Dorling Kindersley Limited.

Art, H. W. (1988). *Creating a Wildflower Meadow.* Pownal, Vt.: Storey Communications.

Barker, C. M. (1985). *A Flower Fairy Alphabet.* London: Blackie and Son, Ltd.

―――― (1985). *Flower Fairies of the Garden.* London: Blackie and Son, Ltd.

―――― (1985). *Flower Fairies of the Spring.* London: Blackie and Son, Ltd.

―――― (1985). *Flower Fairies of the Wayside.* London: Blackie and Son, Ltd.

Billimore, B., J. Brooke, R. Boothe, and K. Funnell (1990). *The Outdoor Classroom.* London: HMSO.

Booth, P. R. (1990). *Ecology in the National Curriculum.* Winchester, Hampshire, United Kingdom: Learning Through Landscapes Trust.

Bremness, L. (1994). *Herbs: A Visual Guide to More Than 700 Herb Species from Around the World.* Eyewitness Books. London: Dorling Kindersley.

Brett, A., R. C. Moore, and E. F. Provenzo (1993). *The Complete Playground Book.* Syracuse, N.Y.: Syracuse University Press.

Brown, V. and D. Hoover (1967). *California Wildlife Map Book.* Healdsburg, Calif.: Naturegraph Publishers.

Buller, D. (1980). *Obis Pond Guide.* Hudson, N.H.: Delta Education.

Caduto, M. (1985). *Pond and Brook.* Hanover, N.H.: University Press of New England.

Caduto, M. and J. Bruchac (1996). *Native American Gardening.* Golden, Colo.: Fulcrum Publishing.

Callegari, J. and K. Durand (1977). *Wild Edible and Medicinal Plants of California.* El Cerrito, Calif.: Jeff Callegari and Keith Durand.

Carr, A. (1979). *Color Handbook of Garden Insects.* Emmaus, Pa.: Rodale Press.

Carson, R. L. (1956). *The Sense of Wonder.* New York: Harper and Row, Publishers.

Cawdell, P. (1987). *Starting a Butterfly Garden.* Spalding, Lincolnshire, United Kingdom: School Garden Company.

Chestnut, V. K. (1974). *Plants Used by the Indians of Mendocino County, California.* Mendocino County, Calif.: Mendocino County Historical Society.

Clark, R. and P. Walters (1992). *Trees in the School Grounds.* Crediton, Devon, United Kingdom: Southgate Publishers.

Clarke, C. B. (1977). *Edible and Useful Plants of California.* Berkeley, Calif.: University of California Press.

Cleave, A. (1994). *Field Guide to Trees of Britain, Europe, and North America.* Ramsbury, United Kingdom: The Crowood Press.

Clegg, J. (1956). *Pond Life.* London: Penguin Books.

Cobb, E. (1993). *The Ecology of Imagination in Childhood.* Dallas: Spring Publications.

Conradson, D. R. (1966). *Exploring Our Baylands.* Palo Alto, Calif.: Palo Alto Chamber of Commerce.

Coombes, A. (1992). *Trees.* London: Dorling Kindersley Limited.

Cox, D., I. McMaster, and J. Obuch (1990). *Grounds for Learning.* Surrey Hills, Victoria, Australia: Dellasta Pty Ltd.

Editors of Sunset Books (1974). *Attracting Birds to Your Garden.* Menlo Park, Calif.: Lane Publishing Co.

———— (1979). *New Western Garden Book.* Menlo Park, Calif.: Lane Publishing Co.

Ellneby, Y. (1991). *Children's Rights to Develop: A Handbook on Children's Motor, Perceptual, and Language Development.* Stockholm: Swedish Educational Broadcasting Company.

Environmental Concern, Inc. (1995). *Wonders of Wetlands: Educator's Guide.* P.O. Box P, St. Michaels, MD 21663-0480, USA, and The Watercourse, 201 Culbertson Hall, Montana State University, Bozeman, MT 59717-0057, USA.

Faber, P. and R. Holland (1988). *Common Riparian Plants of California.* Mill Valley, Calif.: Pickleweed Press.

Falk, J. (1980). *Obis Lawn Guide.* Hudson, N.H.: Delta Education, Inc.

Farrand, J. (1988). *Familiar Insects and Spiders.* New York: Alfred A. Knopf, Inc.

Feltwell, J. (1991). *Slugs, Snails, and Earthworms.* Crediton, Devon, United Kingdom: Southgate Publishers.

———— (n.d.). *Recycling.* Crediton, Devon, United Kingdom: Southgate Publishers.

Ferris, R. S. (1968). *Native Shrubs of the San Francisco Bay Region.* Berkeley, Calif.: University of California Press.

Flatt, G. (1989). *Pond Design Guide for Schools.* Devon, Exeter, United Kingdom: Wheaton Publishers.

Foster, S. and J. A. Duke (1990). *Eastern/Central Medicinal Plants.* New York: Houghton Mifflin Company.

Gale, D. (1987). *Starting a School Garden.* Spalding, Lincolnshire, United Kingdom: School Garden Company.

Gale, F. and C. Gale (1975). *Experiences with Plants for Young Children.* Palo Alto, Calif.: Pacific Books Publishers.

———— (1982). *Experiences with Animals for Young Children.* Ann Arbor, Mich.: West Hawk Industries Publishers.

———— (1984). *Experiences in the Natural Environment for Young Children.* Ann Arbor, Mich.: West Hawk Industries Publishers.

———— (1985). *Experiences in the Physical Environment for Young Children.* Ann Arbor, Mich.: West Hawk Industries Publishers.

George, J. C. (1982). *Acorn Pancakes, Dandelion Salad, and 38 Other Wild Recipes.* New York: HarperCollins Publishers.

Gilliam, H. (1962). *Weather of the San Francisco Bay Region.* Berkeley, Calif.: University of California Press.

Goltsman, S. M., S. McIntyre, and D. Driskell (1994). *PLAE Scores: Thematic Play and Learning Programs for Children of All Abilities. Circus City. Frontier Village. Treasure Quest.* Berkeley, Calif.: MIG Communications.

Green Teacher. *Special issue on transforming school grounds.* Issue 47. April–May 1996. See address under resource suppliers.

Grillos, S. J. (1966). *Fern and Fern Allies of California.* Berkeley, Calif.: University of California Press.

Hart, A. and P. Mantell (1996). *Kids Garden!* Charlotte, Vt.: Williamson Publishing Co.

Hart, R. M. (1991). *Using Beneficial Insects.* Pownal, Vt.: Storey Communications.

Henry, P. (1995). *Gardening to Attract Birds and Butterflies.* New York: Avon Books.

Hodgkin, R. A. (1976). *Born Curious.* London: John Wiley and Sons.

Howard, A. D. (1962). *Evolution of the Landscape of the San Francisco Bay Region.* Berkeley, Calif.: University of California Press.

Hunter, C. (1994). *Everyone's Nature.* Helena, Mont.: Falcon Press.

Johnston, J. (1990). *Nature Areas for City People.* London: London Ecology Unit.

Keaney, B. (1993). *English in the School Grounds.* Crediton, Devon, United Kingdom: Southgate Publishers.

Keaney, B. and B. Lucas (1992). *The Outdoor Classroom.* Leamington Spa, Warwickshire, United Kingdom: Scholastic Publications.

Kneidel, S. (1994). *Pet Bugs.* New York: John Wiley and Sons, Inc.

Lang, S. S. (1995). *Nature in Your Backyard: Simple Activities for Children.* Brookfield, Conn.: Millbrook Press.

Learning Through Landscapes Trust (1997). *Thinking About Seating in School Grounds.* CD-ROM. Partridge Green, United Kingdom: Learning Through Landscapes Trust.

Lewington, A. (1990). *Plants for People.* London: Natural History Museum.

Lewis, C. (1996). *Green Nature, Human Nature: The Meaning of Plants in Our Lives.* Chicago: University of Illinois Press.

Lippert, W. and D. Podlech (1993). *Wild Flowers of Britain and Europe.* London: HaperCollins Publishers.

Lovejoy, S. (1991). *Sunflower Houses.* Loveland, Colo.: Interweave Press, Inc.

Lucas, B. and A. Mountfield (1995). *A Guide to Fundraising for School Grounds.* Winchester, Hampshire, United Kingdom: Learning Through Landscapes Trust.

Margolin, M. (1985). *The Earth Manual.* Berkeley, Calif.: Heyday Books.

Manuel, R. (1991). *Pond Life.* Glasgow: HarperCollins Publishers.

Matthews, N. (1992). *Garden for Birds.* Spalding, Lincolnshire, United Kingdom: SGC Books.

Merrick, L. (1993). *Land and Water Invertebrates: Identification in the School Grounds.* Crediton, Devon, United Kingdom: Southgate Publishers.

Miller, C. (1995). *Tales from the Plant Kingdom.* Lima, Ohio: Pourquoi Press.

Moore, R. C. (1986). *"The Power of Nature: Orientations of Girls and Boys Toward Biotic and Abiotic Environments."* Children's Environments Quarterly 3(3), 52–69.

——— (1993). *Plants for Play.* Berkeley, Calif.: MIG Communications.

Moore, R. C. and S. M. Goltsman (1995). *Play For All CD-ROM: Images and Ideas for Outdoor Play Environments.* Berkeley, Calif.: MIG Communications.

Moore, R. C., Goltsman, S. M., and D. S. Iacofano, eds. (1992). *Play For All Guidelines: Planning, Design, and Management of Outdoor Settings for All Children, 2nd ed.* Berkeley, Calif.: MIG Communications.

Munz, P. A. (1961). *California Spring Wildflowers.* Berkeley, Calif.: University of California Press.

Nabhan, G. P. and S. Trimble (1994). *The Geography of Childhood: Why Children Need Wild Places.* Boston: Beacon Press.

National Wildlife Federation (1986). *Planting an Oasis for Wildlife.* Washington, D.C.: National Wildlife Federation.

Pearce, J. C. (1977). *Magical Child.* New York: E.P. Dutton.

Potter-Springer, W. (1990). *Grow a Butterfly Garden.* Pownal, Vt.: Storey Communications.

Powell, J. A. and C. L. Hogue (1979). *California Insects.* Berkeley, Calif.: University of California Press.

Rhydderch-Evans, Z. (1993). *Mathematics in the School Grounds.* Crediton, Devon, United Kingdom: Southgate Publishers.

Rivkin, M. S. (1995). *The Great Outdoors: Restoring Children's Right to Play Outside.* Washington, D.C.: National Association for the Education of Young Children.

Rowntree, L. (1980). *Hardy Californians.* Salt Lake City, Utah: Peregrine Smith.

The Royal Society for the Protection of Birds (1992). *Wildlife and the School Environment.* Sandy, Bedfordshire, United Kingdom: RSPB.

Rupp, R. (1995). *Everything You Never Learned about Birds.* Pownal, Vt.: Storey Communications, Inc.

Schools Council (1975). *Using the Environment 4 Ways and Means.* London: Macdonald Educational.

Schools Council Project Environment (1972). *Case Studies: Schools Council Environmental Studies Project.* London: Rupert Hart-Davis Educational Publications.

——— (1974). *Learning From Trails.* London: Longman.

——— (1974). *The School Outdoor Resource Area.* London: Longman.

Sharsmith, H. K. (1965). *Spring Wildflowers of the San Francisco Bay Region.* Berkeley, Calif.: University of California Press.

Sibley, P. (1989). *Starting a Wildlife Pond.* Spalding, Lincolnshire, United Kingdom: School Garden Company.

Sly, C., L. Comnes, and S. Brislain, eds. (1990). *Water Wisdom: A Curriculum for Grades Four Through Eight.* Hayward, Calif.: Alameda County Office of Education.

Sly, C., L. Comnes, and C. Cuomo, eds. (1988). *The California State Environmental Education Guide for Kindergarten Through Sixth Grade.* Hayward, Calif.: Alameda County Office of Education.

Starcher, A. (1995). *Good Bugs for Your Garden.* Chapel Hill, N.C.: Algonquin Books.

Stebbins, R. C. (1972). *California Amphibians and Reptiles.* Berkeley, Calif.: University of California Press.

Stidworthy, J. (1990). *Ponds and Streams.* Mahwah, N.J.: Troll Associates.

Stine, S. (1997). *Landscapes for Learning.* New York: John Wiley and Sons.

Stokes, D. and E. Williams. (1991). *The Butterfly Book.* New York: Little, Brown and Company.

Storey Gillis, J. (1967). *Puddle Jumpers.* Pownal, Vt.: Storey Communications, Inc.

Tekulsky, M. (1985). *The Butterfly Garden.* Boston: Harvard Common Press.

Thomas, G. (1992). *Science in the School Grounds.* Crediton, Devon, United Kingdom: Southgate Publishers.

Titman, W. (1992). *Play, Playtime and Playgrounds.* Crediton, Devon, United Kingdom: Southgate Publishers.

——— (1994). *Special Places; Special People: The Hidden Curriculum of School Grounds.* Godalming, Surrey, United Kingdom: World Wide Fund for Nature.

Tufts, C. and P. Loewer (1995). *Gardening for Wildlife.* Washington, D.C.: National Wildlife Federation.

Venning, F. (1984). *A Guide to Field Identification of Wildflowers of North America.* Racine, Wis.: Western Publishing Company, Inc.

Vessel, M. F. and H. H. Wong (1977). *Natural History of Vacant Lots.* Berkeley, Calif.: University of California Press.

Walsh, P. (1988). *Early Childhood Playgrounds.* Victoria, Australia: Robert Andersen and Associates.

Walters, J. (1992). *Gardening with Peter Rabbit.* London: Penguin Group.

Wentworth, D. F., J. K. Couchman, J. C. MacBean, and A. Stecher (1972). *Mapping Small Places.* Minneapolis: Winston Press.

Wilson, E. O. (1992). *The Diversity of Life.* New York: W. W. Norton and Company.

Winnicott, D. W. (1971). *Playing and Reality.* New York: Basic Books.

Wong, H. H. (1993). *The Backyard Detective: A Guide for Beginning Naturalists.* San Mateo, Calif.: Nature Vision.

Wyzga, M. (1994). *Homes for Wildlife.* Durham, N.H.: University of New Hampshire Cooperative Extension.

Young, K. (1990). *Learning Through Landscapes: Using School Grounds as an Eduational Resource.* Winchester, Hampshire, United Kingdom: Learning Through Landscapes Trust.

RESOURCE SUPPLIERS

Acorn Naturalists

Resources for exploring the natural world.
Annual catalog. Newsletters.

17300 East 17th Street, Suite J-236
Tustin, CA 92680
United States
(800) 422-8886, (714) 838-4888
fax: (800) 452-2802, (714) 838-5869
http://www.acorn-group.com

Gardens for Growing People

Resources for garden-based education.
Annual catalog.

P.O. Box 630
Point Reyes, CA 94956
United States
(415) 663-9433

Green Brick Road
Guide to environmental and global education resources.
  c/o 8 Dumas Court
  Don Mills, ON M3A 2N2
  Canada
  (416) 465-1597
  http://gbr.org

Green Teacher: Education for Planet Earth
Bimonthly magazine for educators and community activists.
  95 Robert Street
  Toronto, ON M5S 2K5
  Canada
  P.O. Box 1431
  Lewiston, NY 14092
  United States
  (416) 960-1244
  greentea@web.net
  http://www.web.ca/~greentea/

Growing Ideas
Teaching tools to help young minds grow. Annual catalog. Newsletters.
  National Gardening Association
  180 Flynn Avenue
  Burlington, VT 05401
  United States
  (800) 538-7476
  fax (800) 538-7476
  http://www.garden.org

Learning Through Landscapes
  3rd Floor, Southside Offices
  The Law Courts
  Winchester, Hampshire, SO23 9DL
  United Kingdom
  44 (0) 1962 846258
  fax 44 (0) 1962 869099
  charity@tcp.co.uk

Let's Get Growing
Environmental science and nature education supplies. Semiannual catalog.
  1900 Commercial Way
  Santa Cruz, CA 95065
  United States
  (800) 408-1868
  fax (408) 476-1427
  http://www.LetsGetGrowing.com

MIG Communications
Ideas, tools, and technologies for improving our communities.
  800 Hearst Avenue
  Berkeley, CA 94710
  United States
  (800) 790-8444, (510) 845-0953
  fax (510) 845-8750

Index

at original Washington School, 3
at weekends, 4
batterball, 96
bay laurel tree
see California bay laurel tree
beach, 68
bean house, 31
beans, 25
Beep-Beep the duck, 150
beehives
at Oxford Tract, 32
in neighborhood, 32
bees, 182
as play object, 120
beetles, 28, 51, 55, 63, 82, 84, 182
beets, 27, 31, 78
behavioral repertoire
as reflection of environmental
diversity, 181
behavior-environment ecosystems in
site development, 238–39
behavior maps
as assessment tool, 232
as site planning tool, 72, 226
boys, 239
girls, 239
Berkeley Fire Department
at Yardfest, 177
Bermuda grass, 23
berries
as ammunition, 104
best friends, 111
bicycle use, 173
"big fixes" in site development,
237–38
big rock, 68
as the moon, 107
memories of, 187
Big Toy, 75
as car, 119
as fire truck, 102
as police headquarters, 102
as ship, 102
as spaceship, 102
bindweed, 16
binoculars to observe birds, 54
biophilia hypothesis (E. O. Wilson),
202
bioregion
ecological pull on, 53
Yard as reflection of, 16
birch trees, 182
as heralds of spring, 84
birds
and gardens, 30
and sense of belonging, 182
as heralds of spring, 84
feeders, 54
houses, 54

in the Yard, 54
learning about, 62, 184
nests and nesting, 54, 84
observations of, 20, 53–54, 62–63,
183
birthday parties, 172
blackberries
as edible plant, 147
Himalayan, 16
memory of, 186
picking at weekends, 172
blackbirds, 30
blue flax, 23
boats
as afterschool activity, 157
made from sticks, 9
body language
comparison of old and new yard,
90
body measures
and scale, 132
bogeyman syndrome, 194
boredom
consequences of, 190
prior to Yard, 5
Borgatta, Francesca, 157
Boston, City, school grounds initiative,
200
Botanical Garden (UC Berkeley)
as community resource site, 216
boundary conditions
in site assessment, 234
Boyer, Ernest (Ready to Learn), 195
boys
fights prior to Yard, 5
segregated play, 4
Bradford pear trees, 72, 75
brainstorm sessions
in the planning process, 225
brass buttons, 40, 41
bread mold, 83
bridge, 182
as base, 91
memory of leaning over, 186
stone, 182
see also wooden bridge
brown mice, 52
Bruner, Jerome
four modes of learning, 207
buckeye butterfly, 59
buckeye trees
as heralds of spring, 84
as fruits of the fall, 85
flowers as "cooking" ingredient,
118
seeds as Native American food, 146
bullfrogs, 46, 52
breeding, 47
see also frogs

bulrushes
as play material, 118, 146
for building canoe, 40, 41, 146
see also tule rushes
butterflies, 51, 56
plant foods for, 22

C

cable spools, 69, 70, 73
as rocket observation post, 111
as submarine, 102
California Arts Council, 128, 157
California bay laurel tree
as edible/medicinal plant, 146
leaf play, 104
California buckeye, 31
California pepper trees, 20
California poppies, 18, 23
as heralds of spring, 84
California Redwood Association, 17
camp-out in the Yard, 169
memories of, 18
candytuft, 31
captioned drawings, 127
carex
seeds as "cooking" ingredient, 118
caring for the Yard
memories of, 188
carriage wheels, 67, 69
as "base," 67
as "evil wheels," 103
as magical place, 188
as swinging device, 67
memories of, 187
carrots, 25, 27, 31
Carson, Rachel (Silent Spring), 84
cartwheels, 97
cat burial, 151–52
caterpillars, 52, 56
cattails, 21, 40, 41, 182
as edible plant, 146
in winter, 81
ceanothus, 18
as "cooking" ingredient, 118
as medicinal plant, 146
cement yards
negative consequences of, 191
negative feelings about, 182, 184
see also asphalt, concrete
census, 60
centipedes, 29, 51
century plant, 72
memories of, 187
Cezanne, Paul, 101
Chadwick, Alan, 34
chainlink fence
as edge of garden, 25

old one on Yard, 54
dragonflies, 52, 56, 59
    lifecycle of, 59–60
Dream Wall, 10
Dutch Elm disease
    negative insecticide effects, 84
dynamic quality (Dewey), 196

E

"earthquake" day, 152
earthworm farm, 28
earthworms, 51
East Bay Regional Parks District, 39,
    147
    Josh Barkin, 147
    rock placement, 40
eclipse, solar, 78–79
ecodrama
    as analogy, 11–13
    as classroom activity, 12
    as language arts activity, 20
ecological concepts
    in learning process, 208–9
ecologically concerned adult
    as a result of Yard experience, 187
ecological parks
    as nonformal education sites, 196
Ecology Action, Berkeley, 26
Ecology Center, Berkeley
    at Yardfest, 177
ecology of planning, designing, and
    building, 238
Ecosystem Studies, Institute for, 200
ecotones, 57, 136
edge habitats in site development, 238
edible and medicinal wild plants
    listing, 146–47
eggs, 51
    snail, 57
    damselfly and dragonfly, 59
Eight Year Study, 200
Einstein, Albert, 101
elements of place, 240
Elkind, David (The Hurried Child),
    193
empowerment
    afforded by flexible outdoor
    spaces, 199
enclosure as design element, 243
entrance settings, 242
environmental alphabet, 127
environmental art, 232
environmental education
    interdisciplinary definition of, 206
    interdisciplinary integration in
    teacher training, 200
environmental geometry, 132

environmental issues
    role in the educational program,
    215
environmental learning, 184
Environmental Learning Stations
    definition of, 218
    role in the educational program,
    218
Environmental Protectors, 44
environmental quality
    influence on playing and learning,
    6
environmental simulation
    in the planning process, 230
Environmental Yard site designs
    223
Environmental Yard sign, 67, 75
estimate, 60
evening primrose, 23
Evergreen Foundation, Canada, 200
evolutionary design process, 240
eucalyptus trees, 16, 68–69
    as favorite hiding place, 93
    as firewood, 17
    as medicinal plant, 146
    fences, 22
    ficifolia, 72
    to play on, 97
European brown snail, 58
European community-based leisure
    programs, 89
existing site
    of the Environmental Yard, 223
expeditions
    as curricular activity, 57
experiential learning
    in Washington School classrooms,
    4
Exploratorium, San Francisco, 53
exploring
    as free play activity, 185
    in the learning process, 207
expressing
    in the learning process, 208
extended classroom, 153

F

facilitating style
    of leadership, 222
family-initiated activities
    role in the educational program,
    215
Family Portrait
    video project, 160
family use of Yard
    for ballgames, 96
    on weekends, 173–74

favorite part of the school
    Yard as, 183
fear
    of natural environment by adults,
    11
feeling at home in the Yard, 183
feeling good about school, 182,
    185–86, 188–91
feeling words
    most popular in the Yard, 127
fences as design element, 243
"fiddling around," 103
fieldhouse
    as educational setting, 248
    as lunch place, 73
    as place space, 73
field sorrel, 16
field stations as educational settings,
    248
field trips
    to get Yard ideas, 11
    as extensions of school site, 216
fights
    between boys in old schoolyard, 5
filaree
    as medicinal plant, 146
finches, 30
Fire Act, 159–60
fire pit, 152
fish
    and sense of belonging, 182
    learning about, 184
    memory of, 190
    play with, 43–46
    something to observe, 15, 136, 182
    see also mosquito fish
fish farm
    at Oxford Tract, 32
fishing
    as wildlife attraction, 45
    boys' obsession with, 45
    devices for, 44
    expeditions, 45
    skills, 43, 45–46
fixed-loose matrix, 69
fleabane, 16
flexibility in site development, 237–38
flies, 82
flowering plum trees, 72, 107
    as heralds of spring, 84
    Japanese fan dance for, 20
    leaves as "potion" ingredient, 105
flowers, 182
    aesthetic appeal of, 185
    as bouquet for teacher, 9
    as community request, 15
folk arts tradition
    using plants, 147
follow-the-leader, 96

food webs, 61
forest (Yard)
    children like, 185
Forest Drama, 159
formal education/curriculum
    definition, 195–96
    of the Yard, 195–96
formative bases of learning, 197–98
forts
    child-made, 10
    see also clubhouses, shelters
found objects, 65–67
fountain
    aesthetic appeal of, 185
4-H Club and barnyard, 148–49
Friedman, John (definition of
    planning), 222
friend
    Yard like a, 185
friendly people
    who helped us to learn, 185
frog and cat story, 55
frogs, 20, 44, 45
    and sense of belonging, 182
    learning about, 184
    play, 46
    something to observe, 182
    see also bullfrogs
fruits of the fall, 85
fundraising in site development, 236
Fuller, Buckminster, 78
Fuller's teasel, 19, 23
    as herald of spring, 84
    as fruits of the fall, 85
fun
    memories of Yard as, 189–91
fungi, 16, 69, 82–83
    as heralds of spring, 84
    see also mushrooms

G

Galileo
    math, 79
    studying about, 78
Garbarino, James (*Raising Children in
    a Socially Toxic Environment*), 193
garden extensions mural, 231
gardening, 25–34
    "Adventures of Gardenman," 31
    as afterschool activity, 157
    as Environmental Learning Station,
        218
    child's description, 185
    irrigation, 26
    language, 33
    mapping, 185
    math, 33

settings, 245
garden quilt
    Yardfest raffle, 176
gardens
    as ecosystems, 27
    at Washington School in early
        1900s, 4, 25
    garden ecosystem project, 27
    garden logs, 30
    garden journals, 128
    garden quilt, 176
    garden strip, 25–26
    herb healing garden, 32
    in classrooms, 25
    plate gardens, 28
    protecting, 26
    see also composting, greenhouse
garden slugs, 58
garlic, 30
Gardner, Howard (multiple
    intelligences), 197, 198
garter snake, 44, 46, 47, 52
gathering spaces, 70–72
    as educational settings, 248
Gazebo, 70–71, 73
    as base, 91, 119
    as space fortress, 107
    as structure place, 138
    description, 71
    memories of, 187
gender equity, 113–14
generic themes
    role in the educational program,
        216
geometry
    Yard environmental, 132
gerbils
    in classrooms, 4
ghost stories
    during Yard camp-out, 170
giant water bugs, 47
"gifted and talented" children
    special needs of, 201
gingko trees
    as indicators of fall, 85
    leaves as "cooking" ingredient, 118
girls
    segregated play, 4
global environment
    curricular connections to, 4
Goldberg, Rube, 44
Golden Gate Park
    as source of aquatic plants, 40
grape hyacinth, 31
grass
    as dollhouse (doll and donkey),
        108
    as headdress in play, 9
    as pioneer plants, 16

Bermuda, 23
    bouquet of, 98
    kikuya, 23
    memories of hunting ladybugs in,
        186
    seed heads as "potion" ingredient,
        105
    seed heads in imaginative play, 103
grasshopper, 182
Great Snail Race at Yardfest, 176
"Green Book," 231–32
greenhouse
    in classroom, 28
    in school basement, 31
groundcovers, 244
group memory
    importance of in meetings, 225
gulf fritillary, 59
guppies, 44

H

habitats, 136
    learning about, 184
    logs as, 51, 69
    rocks as, 51
    rotting logs as, 57, 61
    willow as, 59
    woodchips as, 63
Halloween
    as special event in the learning
        program, 215
    funhouse, 158
handicapping agent, 202
hand lenses, 47, 57, 61, 83
    to study pond life, 47
hands-on learning
    and higher orders of knowledge,
        194
hanging out
    after school and weekends, 173
happenstance events
    role in the educational program,
        216
happenstance science, 135
Happy Greenhouse, 28
hazelnut trees
    as heralds of spring, 84
healthy psyche, 201
Help Change This Yard! time-lapse
    movie, 231
hen
    fed with snails, 218
heralds of spring, 82, 84
Hewlett, Sylvia Ann (*When the Bough
    Breaks*), 193
hidden curriculum, 189
hide-and-go-seek, 16, 93

seasonal activities
    role in educational program, 213
sedentary lifestyles of contemporary
    childhood, 89
sedges, 40, 41
seed-eating birds, 31
Seed Packet (Environmental Yard
    Activity Cards), 212
seeds, 15
selection in relation to the child's
    environment (Robert Sternberg),
    201
self-esteem
    barriers to, 190
    Yard as a boost to, 188
self-starter staff types, 237
sense of belonging, 182
sense of place, 65, 68
    criteria for, 71
senses as curricular activities, 123–25
sensory cues in entrances, 242
sensory nature (Johann Heinrich
    Pestalozzi), 195
service area in site development, 235
shade
    comments about, 182
shadow theater, 78, 158
shaping in relation to the child's
    environment (Robert Sternberg),
    201
Shasta daisies, 23
    as "cooking" ingredient, 118
shelters
    child-made, 10
    for Yard camp-out, 169–70
    on Chaparral Hill, 19
    see also clubhouses, forts
Sherwood Forest, 17–18, 182
sidewalk surveys, 132
sign
    Environmental Yard, 67, 75
signage and display settings, 242
Silent Spring, 84
silk trees (mimosa), 67, 72
silkworms
    and Japanese kimonos, 59
    and Marco Polo, 59
    and mulberry trees, 59
    and Paris, 59
    projects, 59
site assessment, 10, 234
site design criteria, 244
Simon, John Oliver, Poet-in-the-Schools,
    128
Simon says, 91
site administrator
    role in the planning process, 224
situation (John Dewey)
    in the learning process, 207

skippers, 59
sky
    observations of, 79, 183
sky sculpture, 79
sliding, 95–96
slugs, 51, 82
    memories of, 186
smell as a curricular activity
    examples of plants and items used,
    125
snails, 51, 52, 56, 57, 59, 182
    as "garbage men," 58
    educational value, 58
    Great Snail Race, 175
    memories of, 186
    play with, 57–58
    water, fed to hen, 218
snakes
    and sense of belonging, 182
    as animated event, 156
    see also garter snake
snapdragons, 25
soap bubble play
    in summer, 164
soap plant, 17
social pedagogue, 155
    see animator
soil quality improvement, 26
soil study, 7, 16
soil test, 27
solar
    activities, 77–79
    afterschool activities, 157
    aspect of site, 77–79
    clock, 77
    eclipse, 78
    food dryer, 33
    see also sundials
sour grass, 17
    as herald of spring, 84
    see also oxalis
sow thistle, 16, 56
space wars, 107
sparrows, 30
special education children, 159
special events
    role in planning process, 229-30
    role in the educational program, 215
special needs children
    of economically deprived, culturally
    ignored or from dysfunctional family,
    201
spiders, 15, 29, 51, 53, 55, 182
spring solstice
    as special event in the learning
    program, 215
springtime eruption, 51
spools
    see cable spools

spying, 18
squash, 25, 27
squirrels, 15, 52
stack-sack wall, 60, 72, 74
    memories of, 187
staff role in site development, 236–37
stage, outdoor
    activities, 72
    as Spanish galleon, 165
    for puppetry workshop, 157
starters and inputs
    chart of, 217
    in learning process, 211–19
stereotypes about schoolyards
    problem of, 224
Sternberg, Robert, 198
    adaptation, 201
    Beyond IQ, 201
    shaping, 201
    selection, 201
steering wheel, 75
Stein, Gertrude, 4
Steinhart Aquarium, San Francisco, 53
Stephenson, George, 101
stepping stones, 96
    memory of, 186
Stevens, Wallace, 128
sticks
    as play objects, 9
storage settings, 248
storytime
    as afterschool activity, 157
stream
    feeling good, 183
    memory of, 186
    see also creek, river
strike-out, 96
students
    survey of, 228
*Suggestions for Garden Work in
    California Schools* (UC Berkeley
    College of Agriculture), 4
summertime programs, 160 foll.
sundials
    in classrooms, 78–79
sunflowers, 74
sun pictures, 78
super banners, 81
super compass, 77–78, 182
survey, community, 15
Swedish playparks
    as nonformal education sites, 89
    influence on summer program,
    161
swinging, 95–96
    bail-outs, 95
    parachutes, 95
swings, 75

walkabouts
    as curricular activity, 57
    in search of words, 80
war games, 118–20
    and adult values, 120
warblers, 30
Washington School community
    characteristics, 4
Washington School grounds
    pre-Yard conditions, 4
wasps, 51
water boatman, 47
water conservation workshop with
    teachers, 38, 226
watercress, 40, 41
water cycle, 44, 47
    as Environmental Learning Station,
    218
waterfall
    activation event, 41
    fantasy games, 42
water insects, 47
    feeding in classroom, 47
    learning about, 184
water lilies, 41
water plantain, 40
water play
    and self-esteem, 49
    as teacher's childhood memory, 11
water scorpions, 47
water settings, 37–49
    adult memories of, 49
    and conservation education, 37
    and language development, 48, 123
    and rocks for contemplation, 68
    children's fascination with, 41
    fights as afterschool activity, 157
    interactions with, 48
    maintenance/insurance issues,
    37–38
    memory of, 186
    preliminary puddles, 39
    stimulus for playing and learning,
    37 foll., 49
water skaters, 45, 52
water striders, 47
water words, 123
weather
    as Environmental Learning Station,
    218
    marked by the Yard, 80, 136, 142
    study of, 77–81
    terminology, 143

    with people that help you learn,
    185
    see also solar
weather station
    on school roof, 141–43
weekend users, survey of, 228
weeping willow trees, 80, 182
    as favorite hiding place, 93
    as play setting, 20
    Marco Polo game, 91
west coast ladies, 59
western tiger swallowtails, 59
WEY tree puzzle, 126
"What are Little Boys and Girls
    Made Of?," 55
what if the Yard were removed?
    actions, 185–86
    losses, 185–86
    negative feelings, 185–86
whirligig beetles, 47
wild cat
    as animated event, 156
wild currant
    as edible plant, 146
wildflower seed mixes, 23
"wild garden"
    management principles for
    children's outdoor learning
    environments, 214
wild iris, 18
Wildlife Federation, National, 200
wildlife safaris
    as curricular activity, 57
    see also expeditions, walkabouts
wild mustard
    as "cooking" ingredient, 118
    as edible/medicinal plant, 146
"wild" open space
    appreciation by neighborhood
    users, 174
willow, 17
    and sense of belonging, 183
    as butterfly habitat, 59
    as indicators of fall, 85
    as medicinal plant, 146
    cuttings, 40, 41
    feeling good, 184
    see also pussy willow
Willow Island, 40, 68, 72, 182
    and sense of belonging, 184
    as social space, 184
Wilson, Edward O., 51

wind chimes, 79
windmills, 79
windsocks, 79
Winnicott, Donald ("potential space"),
    44
winter in the Yard, 81–82
winter solstice
    activities, 81
    as special event in the learning
    program, 215
woodchips
    as decomposition example, 136
    as insect habitat, 63
    as loose parts, 112
wooden bridge, 182
    play, 42
    see also bridge
wooden pilings
    Japanese style pond edge, 41
woodlice, 29
wood sorrel, 16, 18
    see also oxalis
word mazes, 126
word power, 125
working settings, 248
workshops
    role in the planning process, 225
    see also design workshops
work-up, 96
worms, 28, 53
    collecting for fishing expedition,
    23
    see also earth worms
wrens, 30
writing stories, 30
    with people that help you learn, 185

Y

Yard
    as fun, 190–91
    good for the economy, 186
    memories of, 181 foll.
    newsletter, 231
    remembered as a maze, 190
    responsibility to care for, 189
    something special, 186
    see also Environmental Protectors
Yardfest, 81, 174–77
    as nonformal education event, 196
    memories of, 191